SOCIAL PSYCHOLOGY 98/99

Second Edition

Editor

Mark H. Davis
Eckerd College

Mark H. Davis received a doctorate in psychology from the University of Texas at Austin and is currently an associate professor at Eckerd College, in St. Petersburg, Florida. He is a member of the American Psychological Association and serves as a consulting editor for the *Journal of Personality and Social Psychology*. His primary research interest is the study of empathy. He is the author of a number of articles on this topic, as well as the book *Empathy: A Social Psychological Approach* (Westview Press, 1996).

A Library of Information from the Public Press
Dushkin/McGraw-Hill
Sluice Dock, Guilford, Connecticut 06437

Visit us on the Internet—http://www.dushkin.com/

The Annual Editions Series

ANNUAL EDITIONS, including GLOBAL STUDIES, consist of over 70 volumes designed to provide the reader with convenient, low-cost access to a wide range of current, carefully selected articles from some of the most important magazines, newspapers, and journals published today. ANNUAL EDITIONS are updated on an annual basis through a continuous monitoring of over 300 periodical sources. All ANNUAL EDITIONS have a number of features that are designed to make them particularly useful, including topic guides, annotated tables of contents, unit overviews, and indexes. For the teacher using ANNUAL EDITIONS in the classroom, an Instructor's Resource Guide with test questions is available for each volume. GLOBAL STUDIES titles provide comprehensive background information and selected world press articles on the regions and countries of the world.

VOLUMES AVAILABLE

ANNUAL EDITIONS
- Abnormal Psychology
- Accounting
- Adolescent Psychology
- Aging
- American Foreign Policy
- American Government
- American History, Pre-Civil War
- American History, Post-Civil War
- American Public Policy
- Anthropology
- Archaeology
- Astronomy
- Biopsychology
- Business Ethics
- Child Growth and Development
- Comparative Politics
- Computers in Education
- Computers in Society
- Criminal Justice
- Criminology
- Developing World
- Deviant Behavior
- Drugs, Society, and Behavior
- Dying, Death, and Bereavement
- Early Childhood Education
- Economics
- Educating Exceptional Children
- Education
- Educational Psychology
- Environment
- Geography
- Geology
- Global Issues
- Health
- Human Development
- Human Resources
- Human Sexuality
- International Business
- Macroeconomics
- Management
- Marketing
- Marriage and Family
- Mass Media
- Microeconomics
- Multicultural Education
- Nutrition
- Personal Growth and Behavior
- Physical Anthropology
- Psychology
- Public Administration
- Race and Ethnic Relations
- Social Problems
- Social Psychology
- Sociology
- State and Local Government
- Teaching English as a Second Language
- Urban Society
- Violence and Terrorism
- Western Civilization, Pre-Reformation
- Western Civilization, Post-Reformation
- Women's Health
- World History, Pre-Modern
- World History, Modern
- World Politics

GLOBAL STUDIES
- Africa
- China
- India and South Asia
- Japan and the Pacific Rim
- Latin America
- Middle East
- Russia, the Eurasian Republics, and Central/Eastern Europe
- Western Europe

Cataloging in Publication Data
Main entry under title: Annual Editions: Social psychology. 1998/99.
    1. Psychology—Periodicals. I. Davis, Mark, comp. II. Title: Social psychology.
302'.05   ISBN 0-07-292509-4   ISSN 0730-6962

© 1998 by Dushkin/McGraw-Hill, Guilford, CT 06437, A Division of The McGraw-Hill Companies.

Copyright law prohibits the reproduction, storage, or transmission in any form by any means of any portion of this publication without the express written permission of Dushkin/McGraw-Hill, and of the copyright holder (if different) of the part of the publication to be reproduced. The Guidelines for Classroom Copying endorsed by Congress explicitly state that unauthorized copying may not be used to create, to replace, or to substitute for anthologies, compilations, or collective works.

Annual Editions® is a Registered Trademark of Dushkin/McGraw-Hill, A Division of The McGraw-Hill Companies.

Second Edition

Cover image © 1998 PhotoDisc, Inc.

Printed in the United States of America   Printed on Recycled Paper

Editors/Advisory Board

Members of the Advisory Board are instrumental in the final selection of articles for each edition of ANNUAL EDITIONS. Their review of articles for content, level, currentness, and appropriateness provides critical direction to the editor and staff. We think that you will find their careful consideration well reflected in this volume.

EDITOR

Mark H. Davis
Eckerd College

ADVISORY BOARD

Anita P. Barbee
University of Louisville

Thomas Blass
University of Maryland
Baltimore County

Bernardo J. Carducci
Indiana University
Southeast

Susan E. Cross
Iowa State University

Stephen L. Franzoi
Marquette University

Karen L. Freiberg
University of Maryland
Baltimore County

Curtis Haugtvedt
Ohio State University

Martin Heesacker
University of Florida
Gainesville

Robert J. Pellegrini
San Jose State University

Ronald E. Riggio
Claremont McKenna College

Mark Schaller
University of British Columbia

Jonathan Springer
Kean University

Charles G. Stangor
University of Maryland
College Park

Michael R. Stevenson
Ball State University

Abraham Tesser
University of Georgia

Shelley A. Theno
University of Alaska
Anchorage

Fred W. Whitford
Montana State University

Staff

Ian A. Nielsen, Publisher

EDITORIAL STAFF

Roberta Monaco, Developmental Editor
Dorothy Fink, Associate Developmental Editor
Addie Raucci, Senior Administrative Editor
Cheryl Greenleaf, Permissions Editor
Deanna Herrschaft, Permissions Assistant
Diane Barker, Proofreader
Lisa Holmes-Doebrick, Program Coordinator

PRODUCTION STAFF

Brenda S. Filley, Production Manager
Charles Vitelli, Designer
Shawn Callahan, Graphics
Lara M. Johnson, Graphics
Laura Levine, Graphics
Mike Campbell, Graphics
Joseph Offredi, Graphics
Juliana Arbo, Typesetting Supervisor
Jane Jaegersen, Typesetter
Marie Lazauskas, Word Processor
Kathleen D'Amico, Word Processor
Larry Killian, Copier Coordinator

To the Reader

In publishing ANNUAL EDITIONS we recognize the enormous role played by the magazines, newspapers, and journals of the *public press* in providing current, first-rate educational information in a broad spectrum of interest areas. Many of these articles are appropriate for students, researchers, and professionals seeking accurate, current material to help bridge the gap between principles and theories and the real world. These articles, however, become more useful for study when those of lasting value are carefully *collected, organized, indexed,* and *reproduced* in a *low-cost format,* which provides easy and permanent access when the material is needed. That is the role played by ANNUAL EDITIONS. Under the direction of each volume's *academic editor,* who is an expert in the subject area, and with the guidance of an *Advisory Board,* each year we seek to provide in each ANNUAL EDITION a current, well-balanced, carefully selected collection of the best of the public press for your study and enjoyment. We think that you will find this volume useful, and we hope that you will take a moment to let us know what you think.

The field of contemporary social psychology is a little difficult to define. Historically, of course, it was easier. Initially, social psychology was the study of groups (or crowds, or mobs), and, in particular, the effect that groups had on individual behavior. As the years have gone by, however, social psychology has steadily expanded its focus to encompass phenomena that are less clearly "social" in nature. Social psychologists today now study a wide variety of topics, some of which necessarily involve groups (even if the group is only two people), but many of which deal with internal cognitive processes that can occur when a person is completely alone.

In fact, one way to define contemporary social psychology is this: It scientifically examines the thoughts, feelings, and actions of normal humans. As you may notice, this is an incredibly broad definition. While it eliminates persons with psychological disorders, it keeps for itself the study of virtually anything that the average person might think, feel, or do. The good news, for those about to read *Annual Editions: Social Psychology,* is that many of the most interesting kinds of human activity will be represented here.

The form in which social psychological research is usually summarized and communicated is the research article, written by scientists for scientists. The goal in such writing is precision and, although it is sometimes hard to believe, clarity. Unfortunately, such writing is often impossible for a nonprofessional audience to understand or enjoy. The purpose of this volume is to provide interesting, highly readable examples of some of the ideas and insights that social psychology can offer about the human experience. The selections come primarily from magazines and newspapers in the popular press, a medium that sacrifices some detail and precision in exchange for a much livelier style of writing. My hope is that by reading these articles in conjunction with your textbook, you can have greater appreciation for just how fascinating and important the topics of social psychology can be.

This volume is divided into 10 units, each of which deals with an issue of contemporary social psychology's areas of concern. Although social psychology textbooks differ somewhat in how they "carve up" these topics, you will probably find that each of the units in this volume corresponds, at least roughly, to one of the chapters in your text. The articles generally fall into one of two categories. Some of them describe, in an interesting and readable way, social psychological research in a particular topic area. Other selections take a different approach and explicitly try to apply social psychological findings to real-world problems and events. Some articles, of course, do both.

Although the units are organized to mirror the content usually found in social psychology textbook chapters, you might also find it useful to consult the *topic guide* that appears after the *table of contents.* This guide indicates how each article in the volume is related to a number of different topics that have traditionally been of concern to social psychology. Thus, no matter how your own textbook is organized, it should be possible to find articles in this volume that are relevant to any subject.

New to this edition of *Annual Editions: Social Psychology* are *World Wide Web sites* that can be used to further explore the topics. These sites are cross-referenced by number in the *topic guide.*

Finally, I hope that you will take the time to provide some feedback to guide the annual revision of this anthology. You can do this by completing and returning the article rating form in the back of the book; by doing so you will help us understand which articles are effective and which are not. Your help in this revision process would be very much appreciated. Thank you.

Mark H. Davis
Editor

Contents

UNIT 1

The Self

Six articles in this section examine the evolution of an individual's personality and sense of self.

To the Reader	iv
Topic Guide	2
Selected World Wide Web Sites	4
Overview	6

A. THE SENSE OF SELF

1. **Evolutionary Necessity or Glorious Accident? Biologists Ponder the Self,** Natalie Angier, *New York Times,* April 22, 1997. — 8

   One of the most striking features of humans, and perhaps some other primates, is our *self-awareness*—the ability to recognize that we ourselves exist, and to think about ourselves in the same way that we think about others. In this article, Natalie Angier presents some recent ideas from psychologists and *biologists* about the sources of this ability.

2. **The Tarzan Syndrome,** Karen Wright, *Discover,* November 1996. — 12

   Why would a sense of *self-awareness* ever develop in humans and other great apes? While some evolutionary theorists believe the primary factor has to do with the challenges of social life among early primates, this article reports on a very different explanation, also based on *evolutionary psychology,* offered by Daniel Povinelli.

B. SELF-CONCEPT

3. **First Born, Later Born,** Geoffrey Cowley, *Newsweek,* October 7, 1996. — 17

   Science historian Frank Sulloway has argued that one factor that powerfully shapes one's *personality* and *self-concept* is birth order: first-born *children* tend to be more dominant and conscientious, while later-borns are more sociable and open to change. This article describes Sulloway's massive efforts to test this theory, using historical data from the past 500 years.

4. **Race and the Schooling of Black Americans,** Claude M. Steele, from *Psychology Is Social: Readings and Conversations in Social Psychology,* HarperCollins, 1994. — 20

   Social psychologist Claude Steele argues that one reason for poor academic performance by black *children and adolescents* is that such performance is not often a part of their *self-concept,* and therefore does not much affect their *self-esteem.* In part because of negative racial *stereotypes,* black students' good performance is often overlooked, and, as a result, they frequently "disidentify" from school and *education.*

5. **Who Is Happy?** David G. Myers and Ed Diener, *Psychological Science,* January 1995. — 27

   After decades of emphasizing negative *emotions,* social psychologists have begun to explore the factors that contribute to human happiness, or *subjective well-being.* The authors review much of this research and uncover some surprises. Some of the variables that are examined are emotions, *personality, self-esteem,* and *social support.*

6. **Team Spirit Spills Over into Real Life for Fans,** Nathan Seppa, *APA Monitor,* July 1996. — 36

   For some people, a potent source of their *self-concept* comes from identification with a favorite sports team. In fact, both the *emotions* and *self-esteem* of such fans can fluctuate depending on the team's success. Nathan Seppa reviews some of the interesting research conducted on this topic.

The concepts in bold italics are developed in the article. For further expansion please refer to the Topic Guide and the Index.

UNIT 2

Social Cognition

Four articles in this section discuss how an individual gains a sense of reality and social understanding.

Overview   38

7. **Like Goes with Like: The Role of Representativeness in Erroneous and Pseudoscientific Beliefs,** Thomas Gilovich and Kenneth Savitsky, *Skeptical Inquirer,* March/April 1996.   40
   Given the overwhelming amount of information with which we are faced each day, it is not surprising that humans often use mental shortcuts known as *heuristics* to make decisions easier. This article by two social psychologists describes how one such shortcut—*representativeness*—may sometimes constitute a *cognitive bias* that leads us to accept erroneous and pseudoscientific beliefs.

8. **Creating False Memories,** Elizabeth F. Loftus, *Scientific American,* September 1997.   47
   Is it possible for false *memories* of *childhood* abuse to be artificially created in adults? The research described by Elizabeth Loftus suggests that this is entirely plausible. It appears that completely normal people can have false memories created through simple suggestion, imagination, and, perhaps, a bit of social pressure. Such a possibility has enormous implications for the role of "recovered memories" in the *legal system*.

9. **The Process of Explanation,** Douglas S. Krull and Craig A. Anderson, *Current Directions in Psychological Science,* February 1997.   51
   How do human beings explain the things that they observe? Douglas Krull and Craig Anderson present a general model describing how explanations are produced, with an emphasis on both the *automatic* and *controlled* processes that are part of this search for meaning.

10. **Influences from the Mind's Inner Layers,** Beth Azar, *APA Monitor,* February 1996.   56
    Recent research suggests that the mind can react virtually *automatically* to environmental stimuli of which we have no conscious awareness. *Stereotypes,* for example, can be activated unconsciously yet still exert an influence on our conscious thoughts and behaviors.

UNIT 3

Social Perception

Four selections in this section consider the process of how an individual develops social perception.

Overview   58

A. PERCEPTION PROCESSES

11. **Inferential Hopscotch: How People Draw Social Inferences from Behavior,** Douglas S. Krull and Darin J. Erickson, *Current Directions in Psychological Science,* April 1995.   60
    Social inference is the attempt to draw conclusions about people or situations based on observing social behavior. Research suggests that such inference is a multistage process, with observers typically making a quick dispositional *attribution* to an individual in an *automatic* fashion, followed by a more effortful, *controlled* revision of that initial judgment.

12. **Motivational Approaches to Expectancy Confirmation,** John T. Copeland, *Current Directions in Psychological Science,* August 1993.   64
    An interesting phenomenon in social psychology is the *self-fulfilling prophecy*—in which our expectations about people lead us to act toward them in such a way that they come to exhibit the behaviors we expect. John Copeland's work on *social inference* has focused on the ways in which the observer's *motivations* influence this process.

B. PERCEPTION AND ACCURACY

13. **The Truth about Lying: Has Lying Gotten a Bad Rap?** Allison Kornet, *Psychology Today,* May/June 1997.   69
    A major task in everyday *social inference* is to discern whether another person is engaging in *deception*. This article describes some recent research that examines the phenomenon of lying: how common it is, who engages in it, what kind of lies are most common, and how successful we are at detecting them.

The concepts in bold italics are developed in the article. For further expansion please refer to the Topic Guide and the Index.

UNIT 4

Attitudes

Three articles in this section discuss how an individual's attitude can be influenced by memory, other people's opinion of them, and propaganda.

14. **Spotting Lies: Can Humans Learn to Do Better?** Bella M. DePaulo, *Current Directions in Psychological Science,* June 1994. 72
Much research indicates that the ability of humans to distinguish lies from truthful statements is not impressive. Social psychologist Bella DePaulo argues, however, that *accuracy* might be improved through practice, particularly if ways can be found for people to access the implicit knowledge they seem to possess about *deception.*

Overview 76

15. **Mindless Propaganda, Thoughtful Persuasion,** Anthony Pratkanis and Elliot Aronson, from *Age of Propaganda: The Everyday Use and Abuse of Persuasion,* W. H. Freeman, 1992. 78
People respond to *persuasion* attempts in different ways, and one approach to understanding this is the *elaboration likelihood model.* One of the model's key propositions is that people are sometimes motivated to think carefully about persuasive messages but at other times to react in a less thoughtful manner. The implications of this for deliberate persuasive attempts such as *advertising* are considered.

16. **How to Sell a Pseudoscience,** Anthony R. Pratkanis, *Skeptical Inquirer,* July/August 1995. 81
In this article, social psychologist Anthony Pratkanis outlines a number of ways in which social psychological *persuasion* techniques are used to "sell" an audience on irrational beliefs. Included among these tactics are the *foot-in-the-door technique, credibility of the source,* and the use of *heuristics.*

17. **In Work on Intuition, Gut Feelings Are Tracked to Source: The Brain,** Sandra Blakeslee, *New York Times,* March 4, 1997. 88
Our *attitudes* toward people or objects are often the result of conscious, deliberate thought. However, the research described in this article illustrates how unconscious *emotional* reactions can also affect our behavior even without our awareness.

UNIT 5

Social Influence

Three selections in this section look at how social dyamics influence an individual.

Overview 90

18. **Making Sense of the Nonsensical: An Analysis of Jonestown,** Neal Osherow, from *Readings about the Social Animal,* W. H. Freeman, 1993. 92
The mass suicide at Jonestown in 1978 is almost unimaginable. Neal Osherow argues that several familiar social psychological principles contributed to the willingness of more than 900 people to follow their *leader* into death, including *conformity* pressures, powerful *persuasion* techniques, and rationalizations resulting from *cognitive dissonance.*

19. **Reciprocation: The Old Give and Take . . . and Take,** Robert B. Cialdini, from *Influence: Science and Practice,* New York: HarperCollins, 1993. 102
One of the most powerful tools for producing *compliance* in others is to invoke the *norm of reciprocity.* Social psychologist Robert Cialdini describes just how effectively this method of social influence has been employed by groups ranging from the Hare Krishnas to Amway distributors.

20. **Suspect Confessions,** Richard Jerome, *New York Times Magazine,* August 13, 1995. 108
Can police interrogation tactics lead people to confess to crimes they did not commit? Psychologist Richard Ofshe believes that interrogation tactics can be so strong that they produce exactly that kind of *compliance.* This article describes Ofshe's work and some of his experiences in trying to apply social psychological insights to the *legal system.*

The concepts in bold italics are developed in the article. For further expansion please refer to the Topic Guide and the Index.

UNIT 6

Social Relationships

Six articles in this section consider how social affiliation and love establish personal relationships.

Overview 112

A. SOLITUDE AND AFFILIATION

21. **Solitude Provides an Emotional Tune-Up,** Hugh McIntosh, *APA Monitor,* March 1996. 114
   Although humans are generally a pretty social species, having some time alone also seems to be important. This article describes the rejuvenating effect of occasional solitude on our *emotions* and *subjective well-being,* and also notes the fact that one's *personality* seems to affect how much solitude is needed.

22. **Social Ties Reduce Risk of a Cold,** Susan Gilbert, *New York Times,* June 25, 1997. 116
   Social support has long been thought to play a role in helping people better handle life stress. This article describes some findings from *health psychology* that illustrate an even more direct benefit of social relationships: having a greater variety of people in one's social network is associated with a greater resistance to colds.

B. EVOLUTIONARY PSYCHOLOGICAL PERSPECTIVES

23. **The Biology of Beauty,** Geoffrey Cowley, *Newsweek,* June 3, 1996. 118
   What makes someone *physically attractive* to another person? Although some standards of beauty vary from culture to culture, *evolutionary psychologists* argue that other physical features are seen as attractive in all cultures and, in fact, are used as indicators of biological and reproductive fitness.

24. **Infidelity and the Science of Cheating,** Sharon Begley, *Newsweek,* December 30, 1996/January 6, 1997. 123
   Research indicates that there are *gender* differences with regard to jealousy: men tend to be more upset by a partner's sexual infidelity and women by a partner's *emotional* infidelity. This article describes the way that this finding is explained by *evolutionary psychology* and provides some of the counterarguments to this view.

C. LOVE AND MARRIAGE

25. **The Lessons of Love,** Beth Livermore, *Psychology Today,* March/April 1993. 126
   Social psychological research on *love* has approached the topic from a number of different perspectives. This overview of research includes approaches that emphasize the role of *emotions, attachment, evolutionary forces, and cultural influences.*

26. **Rescuing Marriages before They Begin,** Hara Estroff Marano, *New York Times,* May 28, 1997. 132
   Conflict is inevitable in marital relationships, and learning how to handle conflict successfully is therefore an important skill. This article describes some programs developed by psychologists to help couples in *love* learn this skill before getting married.

UNIT 7

Prejudice, Discrimination, and Stereotyping

Seven articles in this section look at what influences an individual's sense of prejudice, discrimination, and stereotyping.

Overview 134

A. PREJUDICE

27. **Prejudice Is a Habit That Can Be Broken,** Beth Azar, *APA Monitor,* October 1995. 136
   Recent research strongly suggests that even people who consider themselves nonprejudiced are likely to "show subtle *bias* when interacting with certain ethnic groups." It thus appears that some components of *prejudice* can occur without conscious awareness; inhibiting these automatic reactions requires deliberate, *controlled* effort.

The concepts in bold italics are developed in the article. For further expansion please refer to the Topic Guide and the Index.

28. **Breaking the Prejudice Habit,** Patricia G. Devine, *Psychological Science Agenda,* January/February 1996. 138
Prejudice seems to consist of both *automatic and controlled processes* in the individual. Patricia Devine reviews some of her influential research in the area of automatic versus controlled processes in prejudice. Her work reveals that people who see themselves as not prejudiced frequently find themselves wrestling with conflicting impulses: their immediate, prejudiced reaction and their conscious rejection of that automatic response.

B. DISCRIMINATION

29. **Crimes against Humanity,** Ward Churchill, *Z Magazine,* March 1993. 140
How powerful is language in perpetuating racial and ethnic *prejudice* and *discrimination*? Ward Churchill argues that words are very powerful indeed, and he offers numerous examples of the ways in which Native Americans are routinely demeaned in contemporary U.S. society, especially in the area of sports symbolism and mascots.

30. **Study: Racism Is Health Risk to Black Americans,** Sue Landry, *St. Petersburg Times,* July 17, 1996. 145
What effect does racial *discrimination* have on the person who is discriminated against? The research described in this article suggests that racial confrontation not only increases negative *emotions,* but also produces *biological* changes such as dramatically increased heart rate and blood pressure. Racism may therefore constitute a threat to the actual *health* of minority individuals.

31. **Societal Values Dictate Job Paths for Women,** Tori DeAngelis, *APA Monitor,* August 1997. 146
Not all *discrimination* is blatant. In this article, recent research described by Tori DeAngelis suggests that one form of more subtle *gender* discrimination is for employers to "channel" women into particular types of jobs—jobs that match the employers' *stereotypes* regarding those women's values.

C. STEREOTYPING

32. **Minorities' Performance Is Hampered by Stereotypes,** Tori DeAngelis, *APA Monitor,* October 1996. 148
This article describes research by social psychologist Claude Steele on *"stereotype* threat"—that is, the damaging effect on an individual's performance that results from a negative stereotype about that individual's *gender* or racial group. It also describes some successful interventions that can help overcome stereotype threat.

33. **Who Is a Whiz Kid?** Ted Gup, *Newsweek,* April 21, 1997. 150
Even when *stereotypes* are positive rather than negative, they can still have damaging effects on the individual. Author Ted Gup writes about the burden of positive expectations placed on his adopted Korean son, especially with regard to *education.*

Overview 152

A. BIOLOGICAL FACTORS

34. **The Biology of Violence,** Robert Wright, *The New Yorker,* March 13, 1995. 154
Robert Wright discusses recent controversies concerning the effects of *biological* factors on the expression of *aggression*. Drawing upon *evolutionary psychology* and research on the connection between serotonin levels and violence, Wright suggests that environmental factors associated with low social status can influence serotonin levels, which may then influence subsequent aggression.

UNIT 8

Aggression

Six selections in this section consider how biology, early social experiences, and the mass media impact on the level of an individual's aggression.

The concepts in bold italics are developed in the article. For further expansion please refer to the Topic Guide and the Index.

35. **Damaged,** Malcolm Gladwell, *The New Yorker,* February 24–March 3, 1997. 161
A *biological* factor that may be important in explaining violent *aggression* is brain damage (in the aggressor) caused by physical trauma and abuse. Malcolm Gladwell describes the research of psychiatrist Dorothy Otnow Lewis and neurologist Jonathan Pincus that suggests that physiological changes in the brain resulting from trauma can produce violent aggressive behavior.

B. PSYCHOLOGICAL FACTORS

36. **Car Wars: Taming Drivers' Aggression,** Scott Sleek, *APA Monitor,* September 1996. 171
One setting within which *aggression* seems increasingly apparent is the nation's highways. This article summarizes some of the recent work on aggressive driving, including such possible causes as *stress,* territoriality, and feelings of anonymity.

37. **Gunslinging in America,** Fred Guterl, *Discover,* May 1996. 173
What is the link between gun ownership and *aggression*? This article considers the conflicting evidence for two competing arguments: that having a gun in the home leads to a greater likelihood of violence, and that having a gun in the home serves to deter violent crime.

C. MASS MEDIA EFFECTS

38. **Televised Violence and Kids: A Public Health Problem?** *ISR Newsletter,* University of Michigan, February 1994. 177
In a famous and influential study of the effect of television on *aggression,* Leonard Eron and L. Rowell Huesmann examined television viewing and *children's* aggressive behavior. Later they examined the same children as young adults. Results suggested that exposure to violent content in *mass media* (television) at young ages produces greater aggressiveness in later life.

39. **Menace to Society,** John Davidson, *Rolling Stone,* February 22, 1996. 180
In this selection, John Davidson examines the question of *mass media* effects on *aggression,* including the views of some critics who believe that such effects have not yet been convincingly demonstrated. He argues that the issue is more complicated than it may at first appear.

UNIT 9

Helping

Four articles in this section examine how an individual develops a sense of social support and personal commitment.

Overview 184

40. **The Roots of Good and Evil,** Geoffrey Cowley, *Newsweek,* February 26, 1996. 186
What are the *biological* roots of *helping* behavior? Geoffrey Cowley summarizes recent research on *cooperation* and *conflict* among our closest primate relatives and finds that chimpanzee communities, like human ones, develop norms that serve to protect the general good and to punish individual rule breakers.

41. **Volunteerism and Society's Response to the HIV Epidemic,** Mark Snyder and Allen M. Omoto, *Current Directions in Psychological Science,* August 1992. 188
Millions of Americans every year engage in an important form of *helping*: volunteer work. By focusing on AIDS caretakers, Mark Snyder and Allen Omoto examine the processes by which volunteering comes about. They consider the *motivations* that lead to volunteering and the experiences that promote continuation of this behavior.

The concepts in bold italics are developed in the article. For further expansion please refer to the Topic Guide and the Index.

UNIT 10

Group Processes

Four selections in this section discusses how an individual gains a sense of the social community.

42. **Cities with Heart,** Robert V. Levine, *American Demographics,* October 1993. 192
    In this fascinating article, social psychologist Robert Levine describes research carried out in 36 U.S. cities to discover if their citizens differed in their *helpfulness* to strangers. In general, the larger the city, the less helpful were its citizens. This finding may be due to the effects of urban crowding, *stress* levels in the population, or a diminished sense of *community.*

43. **Cause of Death: Uncertain(ty),** Robert B. Cialdini, from *Influence: Science and Practice,* New York: HarperCollins College Publishers, 1993. 197
    One of the most influential social psychological theories of *helping* has been the *bystander intervention model* developed by John Darley and Bibb Latané. In this selection, Robert Cialdini describes the model and what led to its initial formulation, and he offers some very specific advice on how someone who needs emergency help should go about getting it.

Overview 202

44. **Group Decision Fiascoes Continue: Space Shuttle *Challenger* and a Revised Groupthink Framework,** Gregory Moorhead, Richard Ference, and Chris P. Neck, from *Psychology Is Social: Readings and Conversations in Social Psychology,* HarperCollins, 1994. 204
    The *decision making* that occurs in groups can lead to disastrous consequences. I. L. Janis's theory of *groupthink* offers one account of how this happens. Using the space shuttle *Challenger* explosion as an example, this article traces the characteristic *cognitive biases* of groupthink in the discussions leading up to the decision to launch the spacecraft.

45. **What Messages Are behind Today's Cults?** Philip Zimbardo, *APA Monitor,* May 1997. 210
    Rather than explaining cult membership in terms of the *personality* of the individual members, social psychologist Philip Zimbardo argues that it is wiser to determine why cults attract members initially. According to the article, in addition to employing familiar psychological methods of *compliance,* cults also offer many individuals a very comforting feeling of *community* and belonging.

46. **The Heavy Burden of Black Conformity,** Bill Maxwell, *St. Petersburg Times,* May 12, 1996. 214
    One power that groups can have over their members is *conformity* pressure. In this selection, columnist Bill Maxwell describes the conformity pressure he feels from what he describes as the "Soul Patrol": fellow African Americans who discourage attempts to criticize their own ethnic group.

47. **Group Processes in the Resolution of International Conflicts: Experiences from the Israeli-Palestinian Case,** Herbert C. Kelman, *American Psychologist,* March 1997. 216
    Social psychologist Herbert Kelman has been working for years on a project designed to foster *conflict* resolution in the Middle East. Using social psychological principles, he has created interactive problem-solving workshops made up of Israelis and Palestinians, in an attempt to create greater *cooperation* between members of these often antagonistic groups.

Index 225
Article Review Form 228
Article Rating Form 229

The concepts in bold italics are developed in the article. For further expansion please refer to the Topic Guide and the Index.

Topic Guide

This topic guide suggests how the selections in this book relate to topics of traditional concern to psychology students and professionals. It is useful for locating articles that relate to each other for reading and research. The guide is arranged alphabetically according to topic. Articles may, of course, treat topics that do not appear in the topic guide. In turn, entries in the topic guide do not necessarily constitute a comprehensive listing of all the contents of each selection. In addition, relevant Web sites, which are annotated on pages 4 and 5, are noted in bold italics under the topic articles.

TOPIC AREA	TREATED IN	TOPIC AREA	TREATED IN
Accuracy	14. Spotting Lies *(9)*	Community	42. Cities with Heart 45. What Messages Are behind Today's Cults? *(14, 28, 29, 30, 38)*
Aggression	34. Biology of Violence 35. Damaged 36. Car Wars 37. Gunslinging in America 38. Televised Violence and Kids 39. Menace to Society *(28, 29, 30)*	Compliance	19. Reciprocation 20. Suspect Confessions 45. What Messages Are behind Today's Cults? *(8, 9, 14, 28, 38)*
Attachment	25. Lessons of Love *(16, 18, 19, 20, 22, 23)*	Conflict	26. Rescuing Marriages 40. Roots of Good and Evil 47. Group Processes in Resolution *(14, 15, 16, 18, 28)*
Attitudes	17. In Work on Intuition *(10, 11, 12)*	Conformity	18. Making Sense of the Nonsensical 46. Heavy Burden of Black Conformity *(8, 24, 25)*
Attribution	11. Inferential Hopscotch *(9)*		
Automatic and Controlled Processes	9. Process of Explanation 10. Influences from Mind's Inner Layers 11. Inferential Hopscotch 27. Prejudice Is a Habit That Can Be Broken 28. Breaking the Prejudice Habit *(9, 24, 25, 26, 27)*	Cooperation	40. Roots of Good and Evil 47. Group Processes in the Resolution of International Conflicts *(28, 29, 30, 38)*
		Credibility of the Source	16. How to Sell a Pseudoscience
Biology	1. Evolutionary Necessity 23. Biology of Beauty 30. Study: Racism Is Health Risk 34. Biology of Violence 35. Damaged 40. Roots of Good and Evil *(1, 2, 3, 4, 5, 6, 19)*	Deception	13. Truth about Lying 14. Spotting Lies *(9)*
		Decision Making	44. Group Decision Fiascoes Continue *(14, 38)*
Bystander Intervention Model	43. Cause of Death *(14, 36, 37, 38)*	Discrimination	29. Crimes against Humanity 30. Study: Racism Is Health Risk 31. Societal Values Dictate Job Paths *(24, 25, 26, 27)*
Childhood and Adolescence	3. First Born, Later Born 4. Race and the Schooling of Black Americans 8. Creating False Memories 38. Televised Violence and Kids *(6, 7, 8, 9)*	Education	4. Race and the Schooling of Black Americans 33. Who Is a Whiz Kid? *(24, 25)*
Cognitive Biases	7. Like Goes with Like 44. Group Decision Fiascoes Continue *(8, 14, 36, 37, 38)*	Elaboration Likelihood Model	15. Mindless Propaganda, Thoughtful Persuasion *(10, 11, 12)*
Cognitive Dissonance	18. Making Sense of the Nonsensical *(8)*	Emotions	5. Who Is Happy? 6. Team Spirit 17. In Work on Intuition 21. Solitude Provides an Emotional Tune-Up 24. Infidelity and the Science of Cheating

TOPIC AREA	TREATED IN	TOPIC AREA	TREATED IN
Emotions (cont.)	25. Lessons of Love 30. Study: Racism Is Health Risk (8, 16, 18, 24)	Personality (cont.)	45. What Messages Are behind Today's Cults? (1, 7, 13, 14, 38)
Evolutionary Psychology	2. Tarzan Syndrome 23. Biology of Beauty 24. Infidelity and the Science of Cheating 25. Lessons of Love 34. Biology of Violence (7, 13, 15, 16, 18, 28, 29)	Persuasion	15. Mindless Propaganda, Thoughtful Persuasion 16. How to Sell a Pseudoscience 18. Making Sense of the Nonsensical (10, 11, 12)
Foot-in-the-Door Technique	16. How to Sell a Pseudoscience	Physical Attractiveness	23. Biology of Beauty
Gender	24. Infidelity and the Science of Cheating 31. Societal Values Dictate Job Paths 32. Minorities' Performance Is Hampered (15, 18, 21, 22, 23)	Prejudice	27. Prejudice Is a Habit That Can Be Broken 28. Breaking the Prejudice Habit 29. Crimes against Humanity (14, 24, 25, 26, 27)
Groupthink	44. Group Decision Fiascoes Continue (14, 38)	Representativeness	7. Like Goes with Like (11, 12)
Health Psychology	22. Social Ties Reduce Risk of a Cold 30. Racism Is Health Risk (1, 16, 17, 24, 25)	Self-Awareness	1. Evolutionary Necessity 2. Tarzan Syndrome (6, 7)
Helping	40. Roots of Good and Evil 41. Volunteerism and Society's Response 42. Cities with Heart 43. Cause of Death (31, 32, 33, 34, 35)	Self-Concept	3. First Born, Later Born 4. Race and the Schooling of Black Americans 6. Team Spirit (1, 6, 7)
Heuristics	7. Like Goes with Like 16. How to Sell a Pseudoscience (6, 9, 11)	Self-Esteem	4. Race and the Schooling of Black Americans 5. Who Is Happy? 6. Team Spirit (1, 6, 7)
Leadership	18. Making Sense of the Nonsensical (13)	Self-Fulfilling Prophecy	12. Motivational Approaches (11, 12)
Legal System	8. Creating False Memories 20. Suspect Confessions (12)	Social Inference	11. Inferential Hopscotch 12. Motivational Approaches 13. Truth about Lying (9, 11)
Love	25. Lessons of Love 26. Rescuing Marriages (16, 17, 18)	Social Support	5. Who Is Happy? 22. Social Ties Reduce Risk of a Cold (6, 7, 8, 17)
Mass Media	38. Televised Violence and Kids 39. Menace to Society (11, 12)	Stereotyping	4. Race and the Schooling of Black Americans 10. Influences from the Mind's Inner Layers 27. Prejudice Is a Habit That Can Be Broken 31. Societal Values Dictate Job Paths 32. Minorities' Performance Is Hampered 33. Who Is a Whiz Kid? (9, 11, 24, 25, 26, 27)
Memory	8. Creating False Memories (7, 8)		
Motivations	12. Motivational Approaches 41. Volunteerism and Society's Response (11, 33, 34)	Stress	36. Car Wars 42. Cities with Heart (29, 32, 33, 34)
Norm of Reciprocity	19. Reciprocation (13, 14)		
Personality	3. First Born, Later Born 5. Who Is Happy? 21. Solitude Provides an Emotional Tune-Up	Subjective Well-Being	5. Who Is Happy? 21. Solitude Provides an Emotional Tune-Up (6)

Selected World Wide Web Sites for *Annual Editions: Social Psychology*

All of these Web sites are hot-linked through the *Annual Editions* home page:
http://www.dushkin.com/annualeditions (just click on a book). In addition, these sites are referenced by number and appear where relevant in the Topic Guide on the previous two pages.

Some Web sites are continually changing their structure and content, so the information listed may not always be available.

General Sources

1. Psychology Web Archive—*http://swix.ch/clan/ks/CPSP1.htm*—The links listed at this public noncommercial site mostly focus on social psychology issues. This archive is an excellent jumping-off place for students of social psychology.

2. Compendium of Social Psychology Web Resources—*http://pilot.msu.edu/user/amcconne/social.html*—This site, maintained by Allen R. McConnell, offers links to social psychology resources, programs, and research available on the Internet.

3. Journals Related to Social Psychology—*http://www.wesleyan.edu/spn/journals.htm*—Maintained by Weslyan University, this site is a link to journals related to the study of social psychology.

4. Yahoo–Social Psychology—*http://www.yahoo.com/Social_Science/Psychology/disciplines/social_psychology/*—This link takes you to Yahoo!'s social psychology Web sites.

5. Society of Experimental Social Psychology—*http://www.weslyan.edu/spn/sesp/*— SESP is a scientific organization dedicated to the advancement of social psychology.

6. Social Psychology Network—*http://weslyan.edu/spn/*—The Social Psychology Network bills itself as the most comprehensive source of social psychology information on the Internet.

The Self

7. FreudNet—*http://plaza.interport.net/nypsan/*—FreudNet is part of the Abraham A. Brill Library of the New York Psychoanalytic Institute. This site provides information on mental health, Sigmund Freud, psychoanalysis, and the Brill Library.

Social Cognition

8. Cognitive and Psychological Sciences on the Internet—*http://matia.stanford.edu/cogsci/*—This site, maintained by Ruediger Oehlmann, is a detailed listing of cognitive psychology Web sites. Information on programs, organizations, journals, and groups is at this site.

Social Perception

9. Nonverbal Behavior and Nonverbal Communication—*http://zen.sunderland.ac.uk/~hb5jma/1stbersn.htm*—This fascinating site has a detailed listing of nonverbal behavior and nonverbal communication sites on the Web, including the work of historical and current researchers.

Attitudes

10. The Psychology of Cyberspace—*http://www1.rider.edu/~suler/psycyber/psycyber.html*—The purpose of this site is to study, and better understand, the psychological dimensions of the environments created by computers and online networks.

11. Social Influence Website—*http://www.public.asu.edu/~kelton./*—This Web site is devoted to social influence—the modern scientific study of persuasion, compliance, and propaganda.

12. Propaganda and Psychological Warfare Research Resource—*http://www.lafayette.edu/mcglonem/prop.html*—Here is a Web site that provides links to sites that use propaganda to influence and change attitudes. At this site, you can link to contemporary fascist propaganda, political propaganda, religious propaganda, and Holocaust revisionist propaganda.

Social Influence

13. Center for Leadership Studies—*http://www.som.binghamton.edu:80/cls/HOME.HTM*—The Center for Leadership Studies (CLS) is a not-for-profit educational institution organized for the research and development of the full range of leadership in individuals, teams, organizations, and communities worldwide.

14. AFF Cult Group Information—*http://www.csj.org/*—AFF is a secular, not-for-profit research center and educational organization. It's mission is to study psychological manipulation and cult groups, to educate the public and professionals, and to assist those who have been adversely affected by a cult experience.

Social Relationships

15. American Men's Studies Association—*http://www.cybersales.net/amsa/*—The American Men's Studies Association is a not-for-profit professional organization of scholars, therapists, and others interested in the exploration of masculinity in modern society.

16. Coalition for Marriage, Family, and Couples Education—*http://www. smartmarriages.com/*—CMFCE is dedicated to bringing information about and directories of skill-based marriage education courses to the public. Nonpartisan and nonsectarian, it hopes to lower the rate of family breakdown through couple-empowering preventive education.

17. Family.com—*http://www.family.com/*—According to this site, Family.com is an online parenting service that offers comprehensive, high-quality information and a supportive community for raising children.

18. Marriage and Family Therapy on the Web—*http://www.nova.edu/ssss/FT/web.html*—This site is maintained by the School of Social and Systemic Studies at Nova University. It is a link to numerous marriage and family therapy resources on the Web.

19. The Society for the Scientific Study of Sexuality—*http://www.ssc.wisc.edu/ssss/*—The Society for the Scientific Study of Sexuality is an international organization dedicated to the advancement of knowledge about sexuality.

20. The Kinsey Institute for Reasearch in Sex, Gender, and Reproduction—*http://indiana.edu/~kinsey/*—The purpose of the Kinsey Institute's Web site is to support interdisciplinary research and the study of human sexuality. The institute was founded by Dr. Alfred Kinsey, 1894-1956, and this year celebrates its 50th anniversary.

21. American Association of University Women—*http://www.aauw.org/*—The American Association of University Women is a national organization that promotes education and equity for all women and girls.

22. The National Organization for Women (NOW) Home Page—*http://www.now.org/*—NOW is the largest organization of feminist activists in the United States. It has 250,000 members and 600 chapters in all 50 states and the District of Columbia. NOW's goal has been "to take action" to bring about equality for all women.

23. GLAAD: Gay and Lesbian Alliance Against Defamation—*http://www.glaad.org/*—GLAAD was formed in New York in 1985. Its mission is to improve the public's attitudes toward homosexuality and put an end to discrimination against lesbians and gay men.

Prejudice, Discrimination, and Stereotyping

24. NAACP Online: National Association for the Advancement of Colored People—*http://www.naacp.org/*—The NAACP is the oldest and largest civil rights organization in the United States. The principal objective of the NAACP is to ensure the political, educational, social, and economic equality of minority group citizens.

25. National Civil Rights Museum—*http://www.mecca.org/~crights/*—The National Civil Rights Museum, located at the Lorraine Motel, where Dr. Martin Luther King Jr. was tragically assassinated April 4, 1968, is the world's first and only comprehensive overview of the civil rights movement in exhibit form. The museum's goal is to instill in viewers an appreciation of the history, struggle, and important events and personalities of the movement.

26. United States Holocaust Memorial Museum—*http://www.ushmm.org/*—The United States Holocaust Memorial Museum is America's national institution for the documentation, study, and interpretation of Holocaust history, and serves as this country's memorial to the millions of people murdered during the Holocaust.

27. National Educational Association of Disabled Students—*http://indie.ca/neads/*—The National Educational Association of Disabled Students is a consumer organization with a mandate to encourage the self-empowerment of post-secondary students with disabilities. NEADS advocates for increased accessibility at all levels so that disabled students may gain equal access to education.

Aggression

28. National Consortium on Violence Research—*http://www.ncovr.heinz.cmu.edu/ncovr/home.htm*—The National Consortium on Violence Research is a newly established research and training institute founded in 1996, and dedicated to the scientific and advanced study of the factors contributing to interpersonal violence.

29. Contemporary Conflict—*http://www.cfcsc.dnd.ca/links/wars/index.html*—This site, maintained by the Canadian Forces College/Department of National Defence, has an interactive map listing all current world conflicts. Detailed information regarding each conflict can be accessed through this site.

30. MINCAVA: Minnesota Center Against Violence and Abuse—*http://www.umn.edu/mincava/index.html*—The Minnesota Center Against Violence and Abuse operates an electronic clearinghouse via the World Wide Web with access to thousands of Gopher servers, interactive discussion groups, newsgroups, and Web sites around the world. It's goal is to provide a quick and user-friendly access point to the extensive electronic resources on the topic of violence and abuse.

Helping

31. Americans with Disabilities Act Document Center—*http://janweb.icdi.wvu.edu/kinder/*—This Web site contains copies of the Americans with Disabilities Act of 1990 (ADA) and ADA regulations. This Web site also provides you with links to other Internet sources of information concerning disability issues.

32. University of Maryland Diversity Database—*http://www.inform.umd.edu/EdRes/Topic/Diversity/*—The University of Maryland's Diversity Database is sponsored by the Diversity Initiative Program, a program designed by the Office of Human Relations Programs. This database contains campus, local, national, and international academic material relating to these areas of diversity: age, class, disability, ethnicity, gender, national origin, race, religion, and sexual orientation.

33. Mandel Center for Nonprofit Organuizations—*http://www.cwru.edu/bulletin/mandel_center.html*—Located at Case Western Reserve University, the mission of the Mandel Center is to foster effective management, leadership, and governance of nonprofit organizations in human services, the arts, education, community development, religion, and other areas.

34. Give Five—*http://www.indepsec.org/give5/give5_1.html*—The Give Five Web site is a project of Independent Sector, a national coalition of foundations, voluntary organizations, and corporate giving programs working to encourage giving, volunteering, not-for-profit initiative, and citizen action.

35. HungerWeb—*http://www.brown.edu/Departments/World_Hunger_Program/*—The aim of this site is to help prevent and eradicate hunger by facilitating the free exchange of ideas and information regarding the causes of, and solutions to, hunger. It contains primary information, made available by the World Hunger Program—the prime sponsor of this site—as well as links to other sites.

Group Processes

36. TeamCenter.com—*http://teamcenter.com/main.html*—This page is intended specifically for people in organizations who are formed into, or will be forming into, teams. It is the online resource center of First Step Training and Consulting. There are some excellent free resources about teams located at this site.

37. Center for the Study of Work Teams—*http://www.workteams.unt.edu/*—The Center for the Study of Work Teams is a nonprofit organization whose vision is to become the premier center for research on collaborative work systems. Its mission is to create learning partnerships that support the design, implementation, and development of collaborative work systems.

38. Center for the Study of Group Processes—*http://www.uiowa.edu/~grpproc/*—The Center for the Study of Group Processes is part of the Department of Sociology of the University of Iowa. The mission of the center includes promoting basic research in the field of group processes and enhancing the professional development of faculty and students in the field of group processes.

We highly recommend that you review our Web site for expanded information and our other product lines. We are continually updating and adding links to our Web site in order to offer you the most usable and useful information that will support and expand the value of your Annual Editions. You can reach us at: *http://www. dushkin.com/annualeditions/.*

The Self

The Sense of Self (Articles 1 and 2)
Self-Concept (Articles 3–6)

What are you *really* like? Are you extraverted or introverted? Are you optimistic or pessimistic? Are you the kind of person who is spontaneous and impulsive, or the kind who is organized and orderly?

How do you define yourself? That is, if called upon to describe yourself to others, which characteristics would you mention first? Would it be personality characteristics, such as extraversion, shyness, impulsivity, and so on? Would it be physical characteristics such as your height, weight, speed, strength, or physical attractiveness? Would you mention social categories such as your sex, race, religion, or nationality? Finally, no matter which of these characteristics you focus on, what is your overall evaluation of yourself—that is, do you generally see yourself in a positive or negative light?

As you can see from these questions, there are many ways in which people can define themselves, and an issue of considerable interest to contemporary social psychologists is where these different views of the self come from and what implications they have for how we act. This interest in the individual self, however, is of relatively recent vintage; traditionally the field of social psychology placed more emphasis on the ways in which individuals are influenced by situations. That is, the traditional approach was to manipulate features of the situation to see what effect it had on behavior. Essentially, in this approach people were thought to be similar and interchangeable; the focus was on the role of environmental factors.

More recently, contemporary social psychology has recognized the important role played by stable characteristics of the individual. That is, not only do certain situations tend to make all people act alike, but some people act in consistent ways no matter what the situation. Thus, one feature of modern social psychology is the realization that personality variables—shyness, self-esteem, and many more—can be important influences on human behavior. This growing emphasis on the self has also coincided with modern social psychology devoting considerable attention to understanding the notion of self-concept: that is, how people go about acquiring self-knowledge, organizing and integrating such knowledge, and how self-information then influences our thoughts, feelings, and actions.

This unit is divided into two sections. The first subsection deals with what we might call the "sense of self." In essence, the question is this: How and why would humans ever develop the ability to think about the self? In "Evolutionary Necessity or Glorious Accident? Biologists Ponder the Self," Natalie Angier summarizes some recent thinking by biologists and psychologists about how such self-awareness might have evolved. In the second article in this section, "The Tarzan Syndrome," Karen Wright focuses on one such explanation for self-awareness—the "clambering hypothesis"—and considers it in detail.

The second unit subsection deals with the notion of self-concept. The first selection, "First Born, Later Born," describes Frank Sulloway's theory that one's birth order within the family has a substantial effect on the individual's later self-concept. According to Sulloway, first-born children tend to be more dominant and conscientious, while later borns tend to be more sociable and open to change. The second selection, "Race and the Schooling of Black Americans," argues that the components of self-concept frequently differ between white Americans and African Americans. Author Claude Steele contends that while performance in school is typically a significant in-

UNIT 1

fluence on the self-esteem of white children, it frequently is not for African American children. In essence, Steele believes, these children learn that there are few rewards for them in educational settings, and so they come to define their self-worth in nonacademic ways. The next selection in this section, "Who Is Happy?" takes a different approach to the issue of self-concept and examines the factors that contribute to a generally happy and satisfied outlook on the world. Finally, in "Team Spirit Spills Over into Real Life for Fans," Nathan Seppa examines the phenomenon of sports "fandom" and how it affects self-concept. Evidence indicates that for some individuals, self-concept, emotional reactions, and even self-esteem are intimately tied up with the fortunes of their favorite sports teams.

Looking Ahead: Challenge Questions

Where does our sense of self-awareness come from? Why would it ever have evolved? Frankly, what good is it to us?

Of what does a person's self-concept consist? Which characteristics are the most important in determining how a person views the self? Why would people differ in the kind of characteristics they use to define the self? In particular, what differences in self-concept would you expect to find between men and women? People of different ethnic groups? People of different socioeconomic status? People who are first born versus those who are later born?

Is there such a thing as a "true self" or are we all social chameleons, changing our behaviors to fit whatever situation we are in? How could you tell what your "true" self is? What would make it the "true" one?

Evolutionary Necessity or Glorious Accident? Biologists Ponder the Self

NATALIE ANGIER

THE self is like an irritating television jingle: you cannot get it out of your head. Whatever you do on this blue planet with your allotted three score and ten, whatever you taste, embrace, learn or create, all will be filtered through the self. Even sleep offers no escape, for who is it that struts through the center of every dream but you, yourself and id?

Call it self-awareness, self-identity, mind, consciousness, or even soul, but the sense of self, of being a particular individual set apart from others, seems intrinsic to the human condition. After all, Homo sapiens have large brains, and they are awfully good at taking stock of their surroundings. Sooner or later, they were bound to notice themselves, and the impermeable physical barrier between themselves and others. The invention of personal pronouns, philosophy and large-pore illuminating mirrors was bound to follow.

> For people, and other mammals, 'Know thyself' may be the key to living in a group.

Yet as natural and inevitable as human self-awareness may seem, evolutionary biologists and psychologists do not take its existence for granted. Instead, they are asking deceptively simple questions that cut to the core of selfhood. Among them: What good is the self, anyway? Has self-awareness been selected by evolutionary pressures, or is it, to borrow a phrase from Stephen Jay Gould, a "glorious accident," the by-product of a large intelligence that allows humans to build tools and otherwise manipulate their environment? Might humans not fare just as well operating like computers, which, cyberfantasy notwithstanding, do their jobs without mulling over why they are here?

The quest to understand the evolution of the self is part of the much larger and very fashionable study of consciousness, which has spawned enough scientific symposiums, Web sites and books to render even the most diligent student unconscious. But most consciousness research focuses on so-called proximate mechanisms, the question of how the brain knows itself and which neural pathways and patterns of synaptic firings might underlie self-awareness. Evolutionary researchers concern themselves with ultimate mechanisms, the whys and wherefores of self. They are taking a phylogenetic approach, seeking to understand when self-awareness arose in the evolutionary past, whether other species have a sense of self, and if so, how it can be demonstrated.

The researchers are aided in their efforts by recent advances in the study of infants, and improved tools for asking questions of subjects that lack language skills. The new work indicates that an infant's sense of self, once thought to develop only gradually over the first couple of years of life, may arise prenatally. Those insights, in turn, suggest that self-awareness is not limited to the species capable of growling, "I want to be alone."

A number of biologists now suspect that a robustly articulated sense of self, far from being an afterthought of abundant cortical tissue, is very much the point of the human brain. They propose that consciousness allows humans to manipulate the most important resource of all—themselves—and to use the invented self as a tool to advance their own interests among their peers. This theory, in turn, suggests that the sense of self, of being set apart like an island afloat in a dark cosmic sea, paradoxically may have arisen because humans evolved in a highly interdependent group—because, in fact, no human is an island.

The rudiments of selfhood are as ancient as the plasma membrane, the greasy coating that separates one single-celled organism from another. "Even something as simple as an amoeba has a boundary between the self and the outside world," said Dr. David Darling, a former computer researcher and author of "Soul Search" (Villard Books, 1995) about the nature of self-consciousness. "That physical and chemical border is the beginning of some kind of self." Most creatures are sufficiently self-aware to place themselves first on their list. "It would be unlikely for an insect to start grooming a neighbor's foot," said Dr. May R. Berenbaum, an entomologist at the University of Illinois in Urbana-Champaign and author of "Bugs in the System" (Addison-Wesley, 1995). 'You wouldn't want to waste energy promoting the well-being of somebody else."

Two-month-old babies may already have a sense of self and other.

But it is one thing to have a foot-jerk preference for No. 1, and another to be conscious of that preference, or to have some sense of the self's relationship to others. Dr. Stephen W. Porges, a neurobiology researcher at the University of Maryland in College Park, defines a sense of self as essentially self-actualization, of acting upon the world rather than being acted on. He sees the emergence of self-awareness reflected in the neuroanatomical differences between the reptilian and mammalian brains. Reptiles are sit-and-wait feeders, he explains, and their primary neural structures, the brainstem and hypothalamus, are driven by their viscera. "When there's food available, they eat," Dr. Porges said. "When there isn't, their brain reduces their metabolic demands and slows everything up." Moreover, reptiles must react defensively to fine-tune their physiology; for example, by moving into the shade to cool themselves, or into the sun for warmth. For the cold-bloods, Dr. Porges said, life is a perpetual case of matter over mind, and there is no room for mindfulness.

Mammals, by comparison, are dynamic foragers and explorers of their environment. Regardless of external circumstances, their core body temperature and metabolism are maintained stably by the brainstem and hypothalamus, thus freeing up neural circuits to permit an active as opposed to reactive stance in the world. With the development of the cortex, mammals, particularly primates, gained the ability to engage with others, vocalize, display facial expressions and otherwise show evidence of emotions, all of which Dr. Porges counts as aspects of self-awareness.

In describing the transition from the reptilian to the primate brain, Dr. Porges uses the metaphor of emergence from the Garden of Eden. "In the garden, food is available, but there is no awareness of self," he said. "When we leave the garden, we must search for food, and we are aware of self. That is the forbidden knowledge."

Many mammals give signs that they know themselves, at least well enough to know their place. A spotted hyena, for example, learns shortly after birth where it stands in the hierarchy of its clan, a position determined by its mother's status, and it behaves accordingly, bullying its subordinates and groveling up to its superiors. Yet many researchers are reluctant to attribute that sort of bureaucratic behavior to genuine consciousness. They seek evidence that an animal is aware of its individuality—that it has an internal life.

One classic method for testing an animal's degree of self-awareness is the mirror self-recognition test, which has been mainly used in primate studies. In the experiment, a

1 ❖ THE SELF: The Sense of Self

researcher sees how an animal reacts when confronted with its image in a mirror, and whether it recognizes that, for example, a bit of paint has been daubed on its face.

The initial results of such tests seemed to indicate an intellectual divide between the monkeys and the great apes, the primate group most closely related to humans, which includes chimpanzees, gorillas and orangutans. Apes were said to be able to recognize themselves in the mirror, while monkeys were not, supposed evidence that only apes have self-awareness. But recently, Dr. Marc D. Hauser, an associate professor of psychology and anthropology at Harvard University, and his colleagues showed that cotton-top tamarins, a South American monkey, can indeed recognize themselves in the mirror, staring in fascination after their shock of white hair had been dyed a punkish neon color. Yet Dr. Hauser and others dispute whether the results of this or any other mirror test are all that revealing. "The mirror test is not the be-all and end-all of self-recognition," he said. "People have been relying on it too much. What we need are a battery of tests to look at many aspects of self-awareness."

To that end, Dr. Hauser has lately borrowed a page from child development studies and begun subjecting nonhuman primates to the so-called false-belief test, a measure of how well one individual can appreciate that another individual might have a mental geography that differs from one's own. In a hypothetical example of such tests, three monkeys might be allowed to watch a trainer put a banana into a box. Two of the monkeys are then taken away, just long enough for the remaining monkey to see the trainer moving the banana from the box to a basket. Dr. Hauser's question: when its two fellows are returned to the training area, will the observing monkey show signs that it recognizes they now hold a false belief about the banana's location? Preliminary results with tamarins suggest that the monkeys do have something approaching a theory of mind: the observing monkey will look at the box seemingly in full expectation that the fooled monkeys will hunt for the banana there.

In this regard, at least, nonhuman primates seem to be like 3-year-old children, who show with their eye gaze that they, too, recognize another's false belief. Interestingly, though, when 3-year-olds are asked, as in the above example, where the benighted individuals will look, they say, "The basket." "Their eyes look at the right place, but they can't yet express their awareness of the deception," Dr. Hauser said. "They have implicit rather than explicit knowledge." By 4, the children make the correct response with language as well as with eye gaze.

Assuming that some nonhuman species have an implicit self-awareness, researchers expect that such intelligence is likely to be limited to, or at least most prominent in, highly social animals like primates, and possibly dolphins and a sprinkling of others. All research points to the importance of the group in giving birth to the self, and nowhere is the link more clearly seen than in humans. "Even before a baby is born, it has an identity, a place in the social hierarchy," said Dr. Roy F. Baumeister, a professor of psychology at Case Western Reserve University in Cleveland. "It may be given a name, a Social Security number, even a bank account, long before it has consciousness." The earliest contents of self-description are categorical ones, Dr. Baumeister said. By the age of 15 months or so, children identify themselves by their family, their sex and the fact that they are children rather than adults.

Dr. Alan Fogel of the University of Utah in Salt Lake City, who studies the development of the self in children, proposes that an infant first understands itself relationally, by registering its impact on others. Contrary to old notions that a young baby knows no distinction between itself and its mother, he said, recent work suggests that even newborns can tell the difference between when they move or touch themselves and when they are being moved or touched by others.

Dr. Fogel has found that babies see themselves as part of a "relational field," which they can alter with their behavior. For example, he said, it a mother smiles and coos at a 2-month-old, the baby will smile and gurgle in response, a seamless exchange of delight. But if the mother suddenly turns stony-faced, the baby will stop, turn away and then look back with a smile, as though trying to reinitiate the exchange. If that fails, the baby eventually turns away, apparently dejected.

"Some people argue that, well, it is just because the baby's expectations were upset," Dr. Fogel said. "But I argue that the baby has a sense of itself and its role in the relationship, as shown by the fact that the baby tries to re-establish communication. It doesn't wither away and do nothing at all."

In seeing itself as dependent on yet distinct from the mother, and in

> As psychology tests reveal, most people have a slightly inflated image of themselves and their talents.

seeking to manipulate the relationship with its behavior, a baby demonstrates, on a small scale, the benefits of self-awareness and offers insight into why humans are so full of themselves. Dr. Steven Pinker, professor of cognitive science at the Massachusetts Institute of Technology and author of "How the Mind Works," a book to be published this fall by W. W. Norton, points out that humans are the most elaborately social of all species, possibly as a result of environmental conditions pitting early humans against other hominids and apes. Self-awareness helps an individual maximize the benefits that he or she can reap from the group.

"Our fate depends on what other people think of us," Dr. Pinker said. "It would make sense to apply our intelligence to assuring that social interactions come out in our favor."

For example, he said, people want to form alliances with those they deem brave, honest and trustworthy. "It's to our advantage to be seen as brave, trustworthy, kind and so forth," Dr. Pinker said. "We have the ability to float above ourselves and look down at ourselves, to play back tapes of our own behavior to evaluate and manipulate it. Knowing thyself is a way of making thyself as palatable as possible to others."

Certain oddities of self-awareness support the theory that it has adaptive value, Dr. Pinker said. Self-deception is one of them. As psychology tests reveal, most people have a slightly inflated image of themselves and their talents. "There may be an advantage to believing that one is kinder, smarter and more in control than you really are," he said. "To the extent that all of us are at least occasional liars, the best liar is one who believes his own lies." Those with low self-esteem, then, may be the most truthful members of the tribe, but somehow that sort of honesty will not win you allies or a date on Saturday night.

The Tarzan Syndrome

BY KAREN WRIGHT

Only apes, it seems, alone among all the animals, can truly distinguish themselves from the world around them. But only the naked apes, apparently, can conceive of not just "self" but "other."

I'm the king of the swingers

The jungle VIP

I've reached the top and had to stop and

That's what's bothering me...

THUS BEGINS THE SYNCOPATED lament of an orangutan named King Louie in the animated film *The Jungle Book.* Louie is confiding his envy of the human race to the man-cub Mowgli, whom he has recently, if forcibly, befriended. *Ooh be dooh,* he explains. *I wanna be like you/I wanna walk like you/Talk like you, too....*

At the New Iberia Research Center in southwestern Louisiana, relations between humans and apes are far less flattering. Rather than serenade a visiting hominid, certain adolescent chimpanzees are likely to fill their mouths with water and then send the fluid out between their front teeth with a faucet-like force aimed at the visitor's face, chest, or notebook. Among with the water comes a generous helping of half-chewed food and saliva. *Ooh be dooh. Here's what we think of you.*

"Brandy, no. No. Stop that. Stop it. Kara, you too. C'mon guys. Cut it out." The demands come from Daniel Povinelli, director of the center's laboratory of comparative behavioral biology, who is wearing a smartly pressed white shirt and standing well within spitting range of the chimps' chain-link compound. He and a small crew of caretakers raised these seven apes from toddlerhood, but the animals ignore him and continue their spirited greeting. "Between the ages of four and five they start to figure out that they can control people's behavior at a distance," says Povinelli, dodging another aqueous salvo. "I used to be able to get them to stop. Now I can't even intimidate them."

It is hard to imagine Povinelli intimidating anyone. The lanky, towheaded 32-year-old seems barely removed from adolescence himself as he describes or, more often, acts out the behavior he has observed in a decade of research on ape cognition. Povinelli isn't interested in the behavior as such, but he is always on the lookout for clues to the mental lives of his charges. He has carried out dozens of experiments with the New Iberia chimps to explore the way their minds represent the world. In doing so, he has discovered differences between human and chimpanzee mentalities that defy expectations and even common sense.

Povinelli's work addresses the question of how—or whether—apes think about themselves and other beings. Researchers of animal behavior have long suspected that certain nonhuman primates may share with humans a trait as fundamental to our species as walking and talking: self-awareness, the quality of mind that recognizes its own existence. It is self-awareness that allows enlightened individuals like Mowgli and Louie to comprehend abstract notions such as "I" and "wanna"; in the human psyche, self-awareness is coupled with an awareness of the mental lives of others, giving rise to abstract notions such as compassion, pride, embarrassment, guilt, envy, and deceit.

Researchers have also assumed that apes, like humans, possess some awareness of the mental lives of others—that they have an inkling of what it means "to be like you." This assumption has shaped prevailing models of primate intelligence, which hold that complex social interactions, informed by an awareness of self and others, drove the evolution of mental acuity in human beings and their nearest phylogenetic relatives. The sociality theory has dominated studies of primate cognition for more than ten years.

2. Tarzan Syndrome

Povinelli believes that the key to the origins of self-awareness lies not in the social behavior of the much-celebrated chimpanzee but in the locomotive behavior of the solitary and elusive orangutan.

But Povinelli's investigations have led him to challenge that model and to propose a radical new theory of the evolutionary origins of self-awareness—one that would make King Louie proud. Povinelli believes that the key to the origins of self-awareness lies not in the social behavior of the much-celebrated chimpanzee but in the locomotive behavior of the solitary and elusive orangutan. He glimpses the dawning of self-conception not in the stresses of communal living but in the perils of traversing treetops. In 1995, Povinelli and physical anthropologist John Cant of the University of Puerto Rico School of Medicine elaborated this vision in an idea they call the clambering hypothesis. Their argument is subtle and recondite, combining elements of philosophy, psychology, evolutionary biology, and physical anthropology. Its principal tenet rests, however, on the observation that the orangutan truly is, in some sense, the king of the swingers.

ON A STEAMY SATURDAY IN APRIL, Povinelli lugs a three-by-three-foot mirror into the chimp compound and gives his apes a chance to eyeball themselves for the first time in about a year. Reactions vary. All the chimps are excited by the new arrivals, but some seem to understand better than others just who it is that has arrived. Apollo hoots and feints in an attempt to engage his reflection in play. Brandy fixes her gaze on the mirror while repeating a series of unusual gestures, apparently mesmerized by the simian mimic who can anticipate her every move.

It is Megan, the Einstein of the cohort, who performs an eerily familiar repertoire of activities before the looking glass. She opens her mouth wide and picks food from her teeth, tugs at a lower lid to inspect a spot on her eye, tries out a series of exaggerated facial expressions. Then, assuming a not-so-familiar posture that in another primate might be considered obscene, Megan uses the mirror to draw a bead on her privates. She pokes at them with one finger and proceeds to sniff the digit with enthusiasm.

"That's classic self-exploratory behavior—getting the butt right up against the mirror, where they can see, well, parts of themselves they can't ordinarily see," says Povinelli. "They never do that—get in that bizarre posture, pick at the genitals—unless there's a mirror there."

Povinelli and other researchers maintain that self-exploratory behavior in front of mirrors shows that the ape recognizes the self therein. And for an animal to recognize itself, they reason, it must have a sense of self—some form, however rudimentary, of self-awareness. Thus self-recognition in mirrors, they argue, can serve as an index of self-awareness in species other than our own.

The architect of this line of reasoning is psychologist Gordon Gallup of the State University of New York at Albany, who in the late 1960s devised a standard measure of self-recognition called the mark test. In the test, marks of bright red dye are applied to a chimpanzee's eyebrow ridge and opposite ear while the animal is anesthetized. The dye is odorless and nonirritating, so the chimp can't smell or feel it; nor can the chimp see the marks without the aid of a mirror. After the ape comes to, it is given a chance to check out its new look.

"When they see themselves in the mirror, they do a double take," says Gallup. "Then they touch the dyed areas, then smell and look at the fingers that have contacted the marks. That's the basic test of self-recognition." The fact that chimpanzees touch the marks and then inspect their fingers is the clincher, says Gallup, for it demonstrates that the animals know the blood red spots they see in the mirror are not "out there" on some unfortunate conspecific but on their own hairy selves.

Since Gallup originated this procedure, researchers have subjected dozens of animal species—including cats, dogs, elephants, and more than 20 species of monkeys—to the mark test. So far, the only subjects that have passed are the great apes: chimpanzees, orangutans, and one gorilla (the celebrated Koko). Even for members of this elite group, self-recognition is no instant achievement. They require prolonged exposure to mirrors—from minutes to days, depending on the individual—before they begin to display self-exploratory behavior.

WHEN THEY FIRST ENCOUNTER their reflections, chimps act very much as if they were confronting another chimp. Apollo's playful outbursts are typical of these social responses. Most chimps, though, soon abandon such tactics and, like Brandy, begin to perform simple, repetitive movements, such as swaying from side to side, while watching their mirrored doubles intently. At this stage, Povinelli believes, the animals may be apprehending the connection between their actions and those of the stranger in the glass; they may understand that they are causing or controlling the other's behavior. When they finally grasp the equivalence between their mirror images and themselves, they turn their attention on their own bodies, as Megan did.

In some sense, says Povinelli, these chimps may be recapitulating the evolutionary drama that produced self-awareness in some ape-human ancestor. In that drama, other species never get beyond the first act. Monkeys, like many animals, seem to "understand" how mirrors work; yet they cannot solve the riddle of their own reflections. In 1978, for example, Gallup introduced a pair of macaques to a mirror, and it's been in their cage ever since. If the monkeys espy a human image in the mirror, they immediately turn to confront the person directly. But each monkey still threatens its mirror image as it would a macaque intruder.

"It's not that they're incapable of responding to mirrored information—they can clearly detect the dualism as it applies to objects other than themselves," says Gallup. "But when they see themselves, they're at a complete loss."

Povinelli discovered Gallup's work as a teenager while photocopying an article in *American Scientist* magazine for a high school debate. Along with the last page of that article, he copied the first page of an article by Gallup; he read the beginning of Gallup's paper at home and then went back to the library to finish it.

"I was, I don't know, 15 or 16, and I started reading this stuff about chimps," says Povinelli. "The ape language experiments were really hot and heavy then, and I got caught up in the chimps-as-hairy-human-children zeitgeist."

The attitude of the time placed the cognitive faculties of monkeys, apes, and humans on a continuum, with differences between the species portrayed as matters of degree rather than kind. Koko, the captive gorilla, had done much to reinforce this view by learning American Sign Language in the early 1970s. And in the early 1980s, when young Povinelli began devouring the literature on chimp cognition, primate researchers began to document social interactions among monkeys and apes that rivaled aspects of complex human behavior. The most compelling of these interactions involve apparent deceptions—hiding food from a compatriot, for example, "crying wolf" to distract an aggressor, and concealing illicit sexual encounters.

The treachery, pettiness, and politicking seems to reach an apex, as it were, in societies of chimpanzees, our closest relatives. Gallup's self-recognition studies provided a conceptual framework for these observations. It was easy to see how a keen awareness of self—including the ability to plan your actions and anticipate their effects—might come in handy if you're bent on making a chump of your fellow chimp. Furthermore, many primate researchers argued that the elaborate deceptions practiced in chimpanzee social groups offered clear evidence that the animals appreciate one another's motives and intentions as well as their own. Gallup had speculated that self-recognition implied not only self-awareness but insight into the mental states of others, a capacity known as empathy.

Can tests be devised to measure empathy in primates in the same way the mark test plumbs self-awareness? That question has long preoccupied Povinelli. It became the topic of his dissertation at Yale and the principal focus of his subsequent work at the New Iberia center. The University of Southwestern Louisiana, which administers the primate center, hired the fledgling Ph.D. to set up a research program in 1991; Povinelli also established the university's Center for Child Studies, where he runs experiments that parallel his primate research—matching the wits, in effect, of apes and children. By comparing the performances of the two species on cognitive tasks, Povinelli hopes to clarify the features of mind that distinguish people from pongids.

In human beings, self-awareness and other-awareness are inextricably linked in a cognitive feature that psychologists call theory of mind. That lofty term describes the tendency to assume that other people—and also pets and even, sometimes, inanimate objects—experience desires, intentions, and beliefs just as they do. We use our assumptions about these subjective experiences to interpret behavior (as in, the dog is barking at the door because it wants to go out), to predict behavior (as in, he won't call because he's angry with me), and to judge behavior (as in, the killing was self-defense, not murder). And yes, human beings also use their theories about the minds of others to manipulate and deceive.

In toddlers, these conceptions of self and other as conscious, mental agents seem to develop in tandem. "We think that theory-of-mind skills are emerging in kids right around 18 to 24 months of age," says Povinelli. "That's where you see their first understanding of desire, reference, and attention. And that's also the age at which kids first recognize themselves in mirrors."

Children who can pass the mark test, for example, clearly understand conventions of nonverbal communication that require a concept of other. They understand pointing as a referential gesture—a gesture meant to connect, intangibly, two or more subjects with an object in space. And they recognize that the direction of a person's gaze indicates where that person's attention is directed as well.

Povinelli decided that such hallmarks of human cognitive development could serve as models for tests of empathy in primates. Could chimps understand, say, the intentions that underlie pointing and gazing in humans? He designed a series of experiments that yielded intriguing results. In one such test, a chimp has to choose between two overturned cups to find a treat underneath. An experimenter offers a hint by pointing at one cup. At first, it looked as though the apes could learn how to interpret the gesture; after several dozen trials, they picked the right cup almost every time. But additional experiments showed that the chimps were not taking their cue from the direction of the pointing finger. Instead they were choosing the cup closest to the experimenter's hand. If the experimenter held her pointing hand equidistant from the two cups, the chimps chose randomly. They seemed unable to learn the significance of pointing alone.

In another experiment, Povinelli tried to ascertain whether chimpanzees' ability to track another's gaze reflects a conscious understanding of another's point of view. This time the chimps had to choose which of two boxes contained a hidden treat. An experimenter gazed at a spot midway between the receptacles. A wooden partition blocked one box from the experimenter's view, and the chimp's task was to figure out which box he could be gazing at. Children know to pick the box in front of the partition. But chimps, while they clearly register the direction of the experimenter's gaze, tend to pick the box behind the barrier almost as often as the one in front of it.

"They'll follow your gaze, but there's no evidence that they understand your vision as a mental state of attention," says Povinelli. Another experiment confirmed this: given a choice between two experimenters, chimpanzees will beg for food from someone wearing a bucket over his head—someone who not only looks foolish but clearly cannot see their entreaties—as often as they will solicit a person carrying a bucket on his shoulder.

Why would an animal so adept at learning in the lab fail to respond to the cues in these experiments? Povinelli acknowledges the difficulty of probing the mind of another species. With such unorthodox experimental designs, it is not always clear who is testing whom. So far, though, the results of his experiments suggest that chimpanzees don't comprehend the intentions or points of view of others—though an anthropomorphic reading of their social behavior may suggest that they do.

Contrary to what Gallup believed about empathy among apes, chimpanzees may inhabit a cognitive realm that includes a subjective notion of "me" but not "you." Anecdotal accounts of chimpanzee deception, says Povinelli, can be explained without invoking the capacity for empathy—and should be, in light of his research. Chimpanzees are hard-wired to be ultrasensitive to social contexts and cues, he adds; they are expert at manipulating behavior—"just like spitting at you in the compound."

But while deception and manipulation indicate a powerful, specialized intelligence, they do not necessarily implicate a theory of mind. A chimpanzee can get a cheap thrill from watching a human being evade a projectile of water without knowing (or caring) why the human responds that way—without appreciating

2. Tarzan Syndrome

The pressures of navigating social hierarchies may have advanced some aspects of primate intelligence. But even extreme social pressures would not have driven the dawning of self-awareness.

the embarrassment, annoyance, and discomfort of conducting an interview in a spit-spattered blouse with a handful of soggy pulp for a notepad. As Povinelli sees it, chimps may be self-centered in the purest sense of the word.

POVINELLI'S PORTRAIT OF THE SELF-centered chimp recasts the question of how primate intelligence evolved. If his data accurately represent simian sensibilities—and he is not excluding the possibility that they don't—there is a deep cognitive chasm separating apes from humans. "It's possible that there's a disjunction, evolutionarily speaking, between self-conception on the one hand and a general theory of mind on the other," he says. "In other words, there was an understanding of self before there was an understanding of other.

"Maybe chimps have a pretty good theory of their own minds, in the sense that they can contemplate what their attention is focused on, what they want, that kind of thing. But maybe they simply don't have any understanding of that quality in others. And maybe humans, for some reason, have fused an understanding of self and other."

Povinelli's findings don't exactly refute the sociality theory; instead they render it somewhat less relevant. It is easy to imagine that the pressures of navigating primate social hierarchies—dodging the wrath of the dominant male, for example—may have advanced some aspects of intelligence in certain primates. Yet there is nothing about social pressures that would have driven the dawning of self-awareness per se, notes Povinelli. After all, monkeys have fairly complex social lives, and they fail the mark test. Orangutans, on the other hand, are among the most solitary of primates, yet they pass with flying colors.

"No one has ever explained why on earth sociality would have anything to do with this phylogenetic break in the self-concept," says Povinelli. In fact, there were no explanations at all for how a primitive sense of self may have evolved in the common ancestor of great apes and humans—until Povinelli went into the Indonesian jungle.

In 1989 and again in 1991, Povinelli spent a field season with John Cant documenting the movements of arboreal primates in the rain forests of northern Sumatra. Cant was studying the locomotion of monkeys, gibbons, and orangutans for his research on the evolution of the primate musculoskeletal system. Though such studies are outside his own area of interest, Povinelli was eager for field experience; in particular, he looked forward to watching orangutans, which are scarce in captivity.

Primatology lore holds that these large, solitary, and slow-moving apes are as smart as, if not smarter than, their phylogenetic cousins, the chummy chimpanzees. Yet if the orangutan's social life isn't responsible for its perspicacity, Povinelli began to wonder, what forces are responsible? Braving scorpions, leeches, and warm Bintang beer, he and Cant struck upon a way to explain not only the intelligence of orangutans but also the self-awareness of chimps and human beings. The clambering hypothesis was born.

The idea's ungainly name derives from an equally ungainly activity unique to orangutan locomotion. As Cant defines it, clambering is the slow, deliberate navigation by which an orangutan manages to move from tree to tree. In no way, Cant contends, does clambering resemble the more automatic and repetitive movements, such as running, leaping, and swinging, that are typical of other primates. And according to his observations, clambering is the method orangutans prefer for traveling through the treetops.

"When an orangutan is moving around up there," says Cant, "it sounds like a small tornado is going through the canopy—branches swaying back and forth, brushing against each other, some breaking. And if you look, quite often you see what you think is the animal stopping and making up its mind. It starts doing something, stops, pauses, and—whether or not it looks around in some befuddled human way—it then does something different."

There is much in navigating treetops to give an orangutan pause. Adult males of the species can weigh upwards of 180 pounds; tree trunks and branches bow mightily under their weight, and falls can be fatal. In spite of these risks, Sumatran orangutans rarely, if ever, travel on the ground. They climb from tree to tree like sluggish acrobats, using the exceptional mobility of their hip and shoulder joints to distribute their mass among multiple supports. It is not unusual to see an orangutan grasping a woody vine with one hand, holding a branch with the other, and bracing one foot against a tree trunk while the other reaches for a nearby limb. By shifting their weight back and forth, orangutans can bend a tree to their will, making it sway closer to its neighbors and thus aid passage.

None of these maneuvers were lost on Povinelli. While becoming acquainted with orangutan locomotion, he was also boning up on the work of Jean Piaget. The Swiss psychologist had described the dawning of self-conception in children as arising from the inadequacy, or "failure," as he put it, of the sensorimotor system. In Piaget's theory, this system governs the repetitive and seemingly instinctual movements of infants younger than 18 months or so. Before that age, Piaget argued, children are not conscious of causing their own actions. But as a child's mental life becomes more complex, those actions become more ambitious, and some will inevitably fail to provide the intended outcome. Confronted with such failures, children become conscious of both their actions and their intentions—they become, in a word, self-aware. Somewhere around the age of two they also enter a new stage of development, in which they learn to control and plan the outcome of their actions.

"When we got to the field and started talking about clambering," says Povinelli, "it suddenly struck me that that, in a way, may be the same damn thing. Clambering is the failure of the sensorimotor system, in an evolutionary sense."

In Povinelli and Cant's hypothesis, clambering represents the self-aware locomotive style of a common ancestor of humans, chimps, orangutans, and gorillas. Like orangutans, this ancestor probably lived in the trees and weighed at least three times as much as the most massive tree-dwelling monkey. Climbing procedures scripted by the sensorimotor system—exemplified by the limited repertoire of repetitive movements that characterize monkey locomotion—would most likely have failed the ancestor, much as they would fail present-day orangutans. And in this context, failure meant an express trip of 30 feet or more to the forest floor. Fall flat on your face from a height of a few dozen feet for a few million years, say Povinelli and Cant, and sooner or later you will evolve the capacity to figure out what went wrong. Figuring that out means conceiving of the self as a causal agent: understanding that the breaking of boughs and subsequent plummeting action is caused by one's own heft, inexpertly deployed.

"Once this sense of personal identity and agency emerges," the coauthors have written, "an understanding of that object (the self) can be elaborated and expanded upon almost indefinitely."

It is this budding awareness of the self as a causal agent that Povinelli sees in his chimpanzees' antics in front of mirrors. Reflections give the apes an opportunity to observe the direct consequences of their actions: "I caused that." Self-recognition occurs when an ape understands that it causes everything about its mirror double: "I *am* that."

For monkeys, it seems, there is no "I." Povinelli and Cant assert that tree-to-tree travel was never hazardous enough for monkey ancestors to warrant the evolution of a specialized cognitive coping mechanism. Because of these ancestors' low body weight, falls would have been infrequent and not particularly harmful.

"Monkeys jump onto the end of the branch, and when it bends on them they just hold on," says Povinelli. "It's the difference between assimilating the reaction of the environment into your behavior and actively using your behavior to plan how to change the environment in order to solve a particular problem. You don't need to have a sense of self to do what you have to do to be a monkey."

Having elaborated this distinction between monkeys and apes, however, Povinelli emphasizes that his claims for ape self-awareness are still quite modest.

"It's nothing like, 'My God, I'm an orangutan. I'm an orangutan, and gosh, I was born 17 years ago, and here I am, still up in the trees, climbing. I wonder what my fate is?'" says Povinelli. "We're just arguing that a combination of factors drove the evolution of an ability to objectify the self—the first step," he says, "along the road to self-discovery."

Qualifiers aside, Povinelli and Cant are well aware that they are out on a rather fragile limb themselves. The clambering hypothesis is by far Povinelli's most speculative piece of work to date, and it has garnered more than a few hoots from other naked apes.

"We hardly know what self-awareness is, let alone how it came about," says ethologist Frans de Waal, research scientist at the Yerkes Primate Center in Atlanta. "I am personally not convinced by the argument." De Waal believes that the climbing behaviors of several species of South American spider monkeys may be as complex and premeditated as the clambering of orangutans. "I don't think orangutans are doing anything that these monkeys don't do." De Waal also objects to defining self-awareness so narrowly. "I look at self-awareness as a kind of continuum that probably runs from fish to humans," he says. "The mirror test somehow taps into a higher level of it. But I cannot imagine that this is an all-or-nothing phenomenon."

"This is what I say to people who are extremely skeptical about the clambering hypothesis," says Povinelli. "I say, well, okay, fine. But there's a real problem here. Self-recognition in mirrors is restricted to the great ape–human clade. There's no other proposal on the table that explains why.

"That doesn't mean," he adds, "that the clambering hypothesis is right."

Indeed, even claims of mirror self-recognition in apes have come under fire of late. Using a modified version of the mark test, cognitive neuroscientist Marc Hauser of Harvard has prompted unusual behavior in tamarins that he says could be taken as a sign of self-recognition. "I want to remain kind of agnostic about what's actually going on," says Hauser. But he says his observations cast doubt on the long-standing notion that mirror self-recognition is a reliable marker for self-awareness.

Povinelli says he and Gallup have tried to replicate Hauser's work in marmosets, so far with no success. But he is the first to admit that he doesn't have the final word on either self-recognition studies or primates' concept of self.

"The problem seems so simple, you know? A mirror, a monkey . . . a mirror, a chimp. . . . But there's three decades' worth of work to be done in figuring out what the heck's going on.

"Anybody who thinks that they've got the final word on this"—Povinelli pauses to engage his own theory of mind—"I think they're stark raving mad."

First Born, Later Born

REBEL OR REACTIONARY?
A new book says it's due to your place in the family structure.

By Geoffrey Cowley

When 22-year-old Charles Darwin set out in 1831 to circle the globe on the HMS Beagle, his mind lay squarely in the mainstream. He assumed that life forms were fixed entities, each one handcrafted by God for its special place in nature. But during his travels, Darwin started noticing things that didn't fit the paradigm. Why, he wondered, would finches and iguanas assume distinct but related forms on adjacent islands? And when Darwin proposed a revolutionary solution—that all nature's variety stems from a simple process that preserves useful variations and discards harmful ones—the authorities were appalled. "A scientific mistake," thundered Louis Agassiz, then the world's leading naturalist—"untrue in its facts ... and mischievous in its tendency."

What drives people like Darwin to stick pins in conventional wisdom? And why do radical innovations so enrage people like Agassiz? To Frank Sulloway, a science historian at MIT, it's no coincidence that Darwin was the fifth of six kids in his family, or that Agassiz was the firstborn in his. Sulloway has spent two decades gathering data on thousands of people involved in historic controversies—from the Copernican revolution to the Protestant Reformation—and running statistical tests to see what sets rebels apart from reactionaries. His findings, due out this month in a new book titled "Born to Rebel" (*640 pages. Pantheon Books. $30*), suggest that "the foremost engine of historical change" is not the church, state or economy but family structure. Sulloway makes a compelling case that firstborns, whatever their age, sex, class or nationality, specialize in defending the status quo while later-borns specialize in toppling it. Indeed, he says, people with the same birthranks have more in common with each other than they do with their own siblings.

It's an audacious claim (Sulloway himself is a later-born), and not one that social scientists will flock to embrace. Birth-order research, for all its intuitive appeal, has a reputation for flakiness. "Both laypeople and experts tend to overinterpret the importance of birth order," says Joseph Rodgers, a psychologist at the University of Oklahoma. "There are very few birth-order effects." In a 1983 review of 2,000 studies dating to the 1940s, the Swiss psychologists Cecile Ernst and Jules Angst declared that

Bill Clinton

Firstborn: He's ambitious, extroverted and status-conscious. In private, he's famously short-tempered. Flirted with rebellion, but says he didn't inhale.

since most had failed to control for variables like social class and family size, none could be taken seriously. Sulloway agrees that much of the past research has been marred by weak hypotheses and poor methods. But his own study tackles many of the issues left unresolved by earlier ones, and some experts are raving about it. "It's a monumental work of scholarship," says Sarah Blaffer Hrdy, an anthropologist at the University of California, Davis. "I think it will change the way all of us think about ourselves and our families."

Most of us already have a seat-of-the-pants sense of how birthrank affects personality. Firstborns are by reputation the list makers and control freaks. "Show me a librarian who's not a firstborn," says pop psychologist Kevin Leman, author of "The Birth Order Book" and "Growing Up First Born." "They live by the Dewey Decimal System." Firstborns are supposedly at home in trades like accounting and architecture—and maybe airline piloting. Walter Cronkite, Peter Jennings and Ted Koppel are all firstborns or only children. Chevy Chase, Danny DeVito and Jay Leno are last-borns. Psychologists have theorized about sibling differences since the 1920s, when Freud's estranged disciple Alfred Adler alleged that firstborns spend their lives getting over their displacement by younger brothers and sisters. But the models have been vague enough to accommodate almost any real-world observation—or its opposite. Adler, for example, argued that last-borns are often spoiled and lazy because they don't have younger siblings challenging them. He also characterized them as go-getters, hardened by incessant competition with their elders. Take your pick.

Sulloway starts not by spinning random hypotheses but by thinking about the Darwinian pressures that foster sibling competition throughout the natural world. Parental support is often the key to a youngster's survival—and siblings are often the primary obstacle. When food is scarce, chicks in a nest may gang up to murder the youngest member of the brood, without a peep of parental protest. Humans harbor similar propensities. Many societies accord firstborns higher status than later-borns, and some still condone killing a newborn in times of scarcity, just to ensure an older child's survival. Sibling competition may take different forms in the New Jersey suburbs than it does among peasants facing starvation. But firstborns and later-borns still confront very different pressures and opportunities. And by Sulloway's reckoning, their experiences should foster very different qualities of character.

How, exactly, should they differ? Firstborns, who grow up knowing they're "bigger, stronger and smarter than their younger siblings," should be more assertive and dominant. They should also be more jealous and status-conscious, having seen their untrammeled turf invaded by newcomers. Their early experience as parents' lieutenants should make them more conscientious than later-borns. And the favoritism they enjoy should leave them more closely wedded to their parents' values and standards. Later-borns, since they can't get their way by force or bluster, should be more sociable and agreeable. And their lesser stake in the established family order should leave them more open to novelty and innovation.

SULLOWAY HAS FOUND INGENIOUS ways of testing these hypotheses. By sifting through the 2,000 studies that Ernst and Angst discarded in 1983, he found 196 in which researchers had factored out differences in social class and family size before looking for birth-order effects. And those studies, which included nearly 121,000 participants, supported his predictions about each of the five personality dimensions that psychological tests look for. Birth order was a lousy predictor of extroversion, a category so broad that it could encompass both a firstborn's assertiveness and a later-born's backslapping sociability. But most studies found that firstborns were more neurotic than were later-borns, and more conscientious (as in responsible, organized and achievement-oriented). Later-borns were consistently deemed more agreeable, and they were overwhelmingly more open to experience. People without siblings fell somewhere between firstborns and later-borns on most personality measures, but they were no more open to experience than were firstborns.

So far, so good. But did these psychological tests say anything about how people would behave out in the world? That's where Sulloway's historical surveys come into play. To get at the roots of real-life radicalism, he compiled biographical data on 6,566 people who have played public roles in scientific or political controversies over the past five centuries. By having panels of historians rate these players on their resistance or receptivity to the innovations they confronted, he was able to plot their "openness to experience" in relation to everything from birth order to age, sex, race, temperament, social class, family size and even the tenor of their family relationships.

In one case after another, the influence of birth order is remarkable. Later-borns were more likely than firstborns were to support each of the 61 liberal causes Sulloway surveyed, from the Protestant Reformation to the American civil-rights movement. Indeed birth order rivaled race as a predictor of who would support the abolition of slavery during the mid-1800s. Firstborns and later-borns differ more in their styles of thought than in their core beliefs—liberals can be rigidly doctrinaire and conservatives can be open to new ways of thinking. But the last-borns in Sulloway's survey were 18 times more likely to take up left-wing causes than to get involved in conservative ones, such as the temperance movement. Not surprisingly, Mahatma Gandhi and Martin Luther King Jr. were all later-borns, as were Leon Trotsky, Fidel Castro, Yasir Arafat and Ho Chi Minh. Rush Limbaugh, George Wallace and Newt Gingrich are all firstborns.

Howard Stern

Later-born: A professional rebel, the shock jock uses humor to get attention and subvert the status quo. 'Butt Bongo Fiesta' does not a president make.

The pattern was just as clear when Sulloway examined 28 scientific controversies. Later-borns were five times more likely than firstborns were to support the Copernican and Darwinian revolutions—and nine times more likely to embrace phrenology, a wacky 19th-century fad that involved divining character from the shape of a person's skull. By contrast, Sulloway found that "conservative innovations," such as the eugenics movement, have consistently been spearheaded by firstborns and opposed by later-borns.

This isn't to say that birth order is all that counts in life, or even in the contentious worlds of science and politics. "These are statistical patterns, not physical laws," says Harvard evolutionist Ernst Mayr. "There are always exceptions." Isaac Newton was a firstborn, for example, and Adolf Hitler wasn't. Sulloway is the first to admit that the effects of birth order can be offset, exaggerated or even overridden by other factors. Indeed, he devotes much of the new book to plotting the ways in which different influences interact. Gender has a huge and obvious impact on personality. But studies have found that firstborn girls are typically more confident, assertive and verbally aggressive than their younger brothers or sisters are. By the same token, age makes most people less open-minded, regardless of their birthrank. Within Sulloway's sample, young later-borns were more than twice as likely as elderly ones were to embrace the idea of evolution during the 19th century. But 80-year-old later-borns were still more receptive than 30-year-old firstborns.

Like age, certain features of a person's innate temperament can mask the effects of birth order. Congenital shyness, for example, tends to minimize birth-order differences. By placing a damper on other aspects of character, it makes firstborns less arch and later-borns less outwardly subversive. Likewise, extroversion tends to magnify the contrast. It might lead a firstborn to become a drill sergeant instead of a bank teller, and a lastborn to do stand-up comedy instead of writing poems.

Conflict with a parent can also offset a firstborn's conformist ways. Once estranged from the familial status quo and pushed into the underdog role, says Sulloway, anyone becomes more radical.

Sulloway's findings are sure to strike a chord with lay readers, but social scientists may not appreciate his chutzpah. In the years since Ernst and Angst declared birth order meaningless, few researchers have bothered to look at it, and many of those who have tried have been disappointed. In a recent book titled "Birth Order and Political Behavior," Alfred University political scientist Steven Peterson and two colleagues describe how they analyzed a huge list of eminent figures to see if it was dominated by firstborns. When they came up dry, they assumed there was nothing left to study. "There are always some people who are going to say, 'Gee, you just didn't look at enough variables'," says Peterson's collaborator Alan Arwine. "It's like trying to kill a vampire." But Arwine and Peterson's findings don't contradict Sulloway's. They merely answer a less interesting question. "The question isn't whether firstborns are more eminent than later-borns," Sulloway insists. "Eminence isn't even a personality trait. It's an outcome. What's interesting is that firstborns and later-borns become eminent in different ways."

Other critics will dismiss Sulloway's whole approach. "From what I read, it's not scientific," says Toni Falbo, a professor of educational psychology at the University of Texas at Austin. "He looks at special cases. If you're looking at special cases, particularly in history, you can find a case that fits almost any hypothesis you want." By her logic, history is just an endless series of special cases, not a lawful process that can be illuminated through hypothesis testing. Sulloway's real accomplishment is to show that's not the case. His "special cases" span five centuries and many countries, yet they repeatedly confirm his predictions. "Frank attacks questions that could not be more contingent," says John Tooby, an anthropologist at the University of California, Santa Barbara—"why some countries ended up Protestant, why France resisted Darwinism, who ended up in which faction in the French National Assembly—and shows that they fit into larger patterns."

Sulloway doesn't claim to have solved any ultimate questions. He plans to expand his database, test new predictions and publish a revised edition of the book every five years or so. "The publisher put that in my contract," he says. "It was the only way I could make myself stop and publish this." Anyone who can stomach a revolution should be glad that he did.

With KAREN SPRINGEN

Race and the Schooling of Black Americans

Claude Steele's article from the Atlantic Monthly *is a perceptive and troubling analysis of why black children are more likely than their white counterparts to fail in school. Steele notes the subtle and not-so-subtle ways that lead young blacks to "disidentify" with school, to resist measuring themselves against the values and goals of the classroom. He advocates the concept of "wise schooling," in which teachers and classmates see value and promise in black children rather than the opposite. Although he does not refer directly to them, note how Steele's analysis fits very well with modern social psychological theories about the development and maintenance of self-esteem.*

Claude M. Steele

My former university offered minority students a faculty mentor to help shepherd them into college life. As soon as I learned of the program, I volunteered to be a mentor, but by then the school year was nearly over. Undaunted, the program's eager staff matched me with a student on their waiting list—an appealing nineteen-year-old black woman from Detroit, the same age as my daughter. We met finally in a campus lunch spot just about two weeks before the close of her freshman year. I realized quickly that I was too late. I have heard that the best way to diagnose someone's depression is to note how depressed you feel when you leave the person. When our lunch was over, I felt as gray as the snowbanks that often lined the path back to my office. My lunchtime companion was a statistic brought to life, a living example of one of the most disturbing facts of racial life in America today: the failure of so many black Americans to thrive in school. Before I could lift a hand to help this student, she had decided to do what 70 percent of all black Americans at four-year colleges do at some point in their academic careers—drop out.

I sense a certain caving-in hope of America that problems of race can be solved. Since the sixties, when race relations held promise for the dawning of a new era, the issue has become one whose persistence causes "problem fatigue"—resignation to an unwanted condition of life.

This fatigue, I suspect, deadens us to the deepening crisis in the education of black Americans. One can enter any desegregated school in America, from grammar school to high school to graduate or professional school, and meet a persistent reality: blacks and whites in largely separate worlds. And if one asks a few questions or looks at a few records, another reality emerges: these worlds are not equal, either in the education taking place there or in the achievement of the students who occupy them.

As a social scientist, I know that the crisis has enough possible causes to give anyone problem fatigue. But at a personal level, perhaps because of my experience as a black in American schools, or perhaps just as the hunch of a myopic psychologist, I have long suspected a particular culprit—a culprit that can undermine black achievement as effectively as a lock on a schoolhouse door. The culprit I see is *stigma,* the endemic devaluation many blacks face in our society and schools. This status is its own condition of life, different from class, money, culture. It is capable, in the words of the late sociologist Erving Goffman, of "breaking the claim" that one's human attributes have on people. I believe that its connection to school achievement among black Americans has been vastly underappreciated.

This is a troublesome argument, touching as it does on a still unhealed part of American race relations. But it leads us to a heartening principle: if blacks are made less racially vulnerable in school, they can overcome even substantial obstacles. Before the good news, though, I must at least sketch in the bad: the worsening crisis in the education of black Americans.

Despite their socioeconomic disadvantages as a group, blacks begin school with test scores that are fairly close to the test scores of whites their age. The longer they stay in school, however, the more they fall behind; for example, by the sixth grade blacks in many school districts are two full grade levels behind whites in achievement. This pattern holds true in the middle class nearly as much as in the lower class. The record does not improve in high school. In 1980, for example, 25,500 minority students, largely black and Hispanic, entered high school in Chicago. Four years later only 9,500 graduated, and of those only 2,000 could read at grade level. The situation in other cities is comparable.

Even for blacks who make it to college, the problem doesn't go away. As I noted, 70 percent of all black students who enroll in four-year colleges drop out at some point, as compared with 45 percent of whites. At any given time nearly as many black males are incarcerated as are in college in this country. And the grades of black college students average half a letter below those of their white classmates. At one prestigious university I recently studied, only 18 percent of the graduating black students had grade averages of B or above, as compared with 64 percent of the whites. This pattern is the rule, not the exception, in even the most elite American colleges. Tragically, low grades can render a degree essentially "terminal" in the sense that they preclude further schooling.

Blacks in graduate and professional schools face a similarly worsening or stagnating fate. For example, from 1977 to 1990, though the number of Ph.D.s awarded to other minorities increased and the number awarded to whites stayed roughly the same, the number awarded to American blacks dropped from 1,116 to 828. And blacks needed more time to get those degrees.

Standing ready is a familiar set of explanations. First is societal disadvantage. Black Americans have had, and continue to have, more than their share: a history of slavery, segregation, and job ceilings; continued lack of economic opportunity; poor schools; and the related problems of broken families, drug-infested communities, and social isolation. Any of these factors—alone, in combination, or through accumulated effects—can undermine school achievement. Some analysts point also to black American culture, suggesting that, hampered by disadvantage, it doesn't sustain the values and expectations critical to education, or that it fosters learning orientations ill suited to school achievement, or that it even "opposes" mainstream achievement. These are the chestnuts, and I had always thought them adequate. Then several facts emerged that just didn't seem to fit.

For one thing, the achievement deficits occur even when black students suffer no major financial disadvantage—among middle-class students on wealthy college campuses and in graduate school among black students receiving substantial financial aid. For another thing, survey after survey shows that even poor black Americans value education highly, often more than whites. Also, as I will demonstrate, several programs have improved black school achievement without addressing culturally specific learning orientations or doing anything to remedy socioeconomic disadvantage.

Neither is the problem fully explained, as one might assume, by deficits in skill or preparation which blacks might suffer because of background disadvantages. I first doubted that such a connection existed when I saw flunk-out rates for black and white students at a large, prestigious university. Two observations surprised me. First, for both blacks and whites the level of preparation, as measured by Scholastic Aptitude Test scores, didn't make much difference in who flunked out; low scorers (with combined verbal and quantitative SATs of 800) were no more likely to flunk out than high scorers (with combined SATs of 1,200 to 1,500). The second observation was racial: whereas only two percent to 11 percent of the whites flunked out, 18 percent to 33 percent of the blacks flunked out, even at the highest levels of preparation (combined SATs of 1,400). Dinesh D'Souza has argued recently that college affirmative-action programs cause failure and high dropout rates among black students by recruiting them to levels of college work for which they are inadequately prepared. That was clearly not the case at this school; black students flunked out in large numbers even with preparation well above average.

And, sadly, this proved the rule, not the exception. From elementary school to graduate school, something depresses black achievement *at every level of preparation, even the highest*. Generally, of course, the better prepared achieve better than the less prepared, and this is about as true for blacks as for whites. But given any level of school preparation (as measured by tests and earlier grades), blacks somehow achieve less in subsequent schooling than whites (that is, have poorer grades, have lower graduation rates, and take longer to graduate), no matter how strong that preparation is. Put differently, the same achievement level requires better preparation for blacks than for whites—far better: among students with a C+ average at the university I just described, the mean American College Testing Program (ACT) score for blacks was at the 98th percentile, while for whites it was at only the 34th percentile. This pattern has been documented so broadly across so many regions of the country, and by so many investigations (literally hundreds), that it is virtually a social law in this society—as well as a racial tragedy.

Clearly, something is missing from our understanding of black underachievement. Disadvantage contributes, yet blacks underachieve even when they have ample resources, strongly value education, and are prepared better than adequately in terms of knowledge and skills. Something else has to be involved. That something else could be of just modest importance—a barrier that simply adds its effect to that of other disadvantages—or it could be pivotal, such that were it corrected, other disadvantages would lose their effect.

That something else, I believe, has to do with the process of identifying with school. I offer a personal example:

I remember conducting experiments with my research adviser early in graduate school and awaiting the results with only modest interest. I struggled to meet deadlines. The research enterprise—the core of what one does as a social psychologist—just wasn't *me* yet. I was in school for other reasons—I wanted an advanced degree, I was vaguely ambitious for intellectual work, and being in graduate school made my parents proud of me. But as time passed, I began to like the work. I also began to grasp the value system that gave it meaning, and the faculty treated me as if they thought I might even be able to do it. Gradually I began to think of myself as a social psychologist. With this change in self-concept came a new accountability; my self-esteem was affected now by what I did as a social psychologist, something that hadn't been true before. This added a new motivation to my work; self-respect, not just parental respect, was on the line. I noticed changes in myself. I worked without deadlines. I bored friends with applications of arcane theory to their daily lives. I went to conventions. I lived and died over how experiments came out.

Before this transition one might have said that I was handicapped by my black working-class background and lack of motivation. After the transition the same observer might say that even though my background was working-class, I had special advantages: achievement oriented parents, a small and attentive college. But these facts alone would miss the importance of the identification process I had experienced: the change in self-definition and in the activities on which I based my self-esteem. They would also miss a simple condition necessary for me to make this identification: treatment as a valued person with good prospects.

I believe that the "something else" at the root of black achievement problems is the failure of American schooling to meet this simple condition for many of its black students. Doing well in school requires a belief that school achievement can be a promising basis of self-esteem, and that belief needs constant reaffirmation even for advantaged students. Tragically, I believe, the lives of black Americans are still haunted by a specter that threatens this belief and the identification that derived from it at every level of schooling.

The Specter of Stigma and Racial Vulnerability

I have a good friend, the mother of three, who spends considerable time in the public school classrooms of Seattle, where she lives. In her son's third-grade room, managed by a teacher of unimpeachable good will and competence, she noticed over many visits that the extraordinary art work of a small black boy named Jerome was ignored—or, more accurately perhaps, its significance was ignored. As a genuine art talent has a way of doing—even in the third grade—his stood out. Yet the teacher seemed hardly to notice. Moreover, Jerome's reputation, as it was passed along from one grade to the next, included only the slightest mention of his talent. Now, of course, being ignored like this could happen to anyone—such is the overload in our public schools. But my friend couldn't help wondering how the school would have responded to this talent had the artist been one of her own, middle-class white children.

Terms like "prejudice" and "racism" often miss the full scope of racial devaluation in our society, implying as they do that racial devaluation comes primarily from the strongly prejudiced, not from "good people" like Jerome's teacher. But the prevalence of racists—deplorable though racism is—misses the full extent of Jerome's burden, perhaps even the most profound part.

He faces a devaluation that grows out of our images of society and the way those images catalogue people. The catalogue need never be taught. It is implied by all we see around us: the kinds of people revered in advertising (consider the unrelenting racial advocacy of Ralph Lauren ads) and movies (black women are rarely seen as romantic partners, for example); media discussions of whether a black can be President; invitation lists to junior high school birthday parties; school curricula; literary and musical canons. These details create an image of society in which black Americans simply do not fare well. When I was a kid, we captured it with the saying "If you're white you're right, if you're yellow you're mellow, if you're brown stick around, but if you're black get back."

In ways that require no fueling from strong prejudice or stereotypes, these images expand the devaluation of black Americans. They act as mental standards against which information about blacks is evaluated: that which fits these images we accept; that which contradicts them we suspect. Had Jerome had a reading problem, which fits these images, it might have been accepted as characteristic more readily than his extraordinary art work, which contradicts them.

These images do something else as well, something especially pernicious in the classroom. They set up a jeopardy of double devaluation for blacks, a jeopardy that does not apply to whites. Like anyone, blacks risk devaluation for a particular incompetence, such as a failed test or a flubbed pronunciation. But they further risk that such performances will confirm the broader, racial inferiority they are suspected of. Thus, from the first grade through graduate school, blacks have the extra fear that in the eyes of those around them their full humanity could fall with a poor answer or a mistaken stroke of the pen.

Moreover, because these images are conditioned in all of us, collectively held, they can spawn racial devaluation in all of us, not just in the strongly prejudiced. They can do this even in blacks themselves: a majority of black children recently tested said they like and prefer to play with white rather than black dolls—almost fifty years after Kenneth and Mamie Clark, conducting similar experiments, documented identical findings and so paved the way for *Brown v. Topeka Board of Education*. Thus Jerome's devaluation can come from a circle of people in his world far greater than the expressly prejudiced—a circle that apparently includes his teacher.

In ways often too subtle to be conscious but sometimes overt, I believe, blacks remain devalued in American schools, where, for example, a recent national survey shows that through high school they are still more than twice as likely as white children to receive corporal punishment, be suspended from school, or be labeled mentally retarded.

Tragically, such devaluation can seem inescapable. Sooner or later it forces on its victims two painful realizations. The first is that society is preconditioned to see the worst in them. Black students quickly learn that acceptance, if it is to be won at all, will be hard-won. The second is that even if a black student achieves exoneration in one setting—with the teacher and fellow students in one classroom, or at one level of schooling, for example—this approval will have to be rewon in the next classroom, at the next level of schooling. Of course, individual characteristics that enhance one's value in society—skills, class status, appearance, and success—can diminish the racial devaluation one faces. And sometimes the effort to prove oneself fuels achievement. But few from any group could hope to sustain so daunting and everlasting a struggle. Thus, I am afraid, too many black students are left hopeless and deeply vulnerable in America's classrooms.

"Disidentifying" with School

I believe that in significant part the crisis in black Americans' education stems from the power of this vulnerability to undercut identification with schooling, either before it happens or after it has bloomed.

Jerome is an example of the first kind. At precisely the time when he would need to see school as a viable source of self-esteem, his teachers fail to appreciate his best work. The devalued status of his race devalues him and his work in the classroom. Unable to entrust his sense of himself to this place, he resists measuring himself against its values and goals. He languishes there, held by the law, perhaps even by his parents, but not allowing achievement to affect his view of himself. This psychic alienation—the act of not caring—makes him less vulnerable to the specter of devaluation that haunts him. Bruce Hare, an educational researcher, has documented this process among fifth-grade boys in several schools in Champaign, Illinois. He found that although the black boys had considerably lower achievement-test scores than their white classmates, their overall self-esteem was just as high. This stunning imperviousness to poor academic performance was accomplished, he found, by their deemphasizing school achievement as a basis of self-esteem and giving preference to peer-group relations—a domain in which their esteem prospects were better. They went where they had to go to feel good about themselves.

But recall the young reader whose mentor I was. She had already identified with school, and wanted to be a doctor. How can racial vulnerability break so developed an achievement identity? To see, let us follow her steps onto campus: Her recruitment and admission stress her minority status perhaps more strongly than it has been stressed at any other time in her life. She is offered academic and social support services, further implying that she is "at risk" (even though, contrary to common belief, the vast majority of black college students are admitted with qualifications well above the threshold for whites). Once on campus, she enters a socially circumscribed world in which blacks—still largely separate from whites—have lower status; this is reinforced by a sidelining of minority material and interests in the curriculum and in university life. And she can sense that everywhere in this new world her skin color places her under suspicion of intellectual inferiority. All of this gives her the double vulnerability I spoke of: she risks confirming a particular incompetence, at chemistry or a foreign language, for example; but she also risks confirming the racial inferiority she is suspect of—a judgment that can feel as close at hand as a mispronounced word or an ungrammatical sentence. In reaction, usually to some modest setback, she withdraws, hiding her troubles from instructors, counselors, even other students. Quickly, I believe, a psychic defense takes over. She *disidentifies* with achievement; she changes her self-conception, her outlook and values, so that achievement is no longer so important to her self-esteem. She may continue to feel pressure to stay in school from her parents, even from the potential advantages of a college degree. But now she is psychologically insulated from her academic life, like a disinterested visitor. Cool, unperturbed. But, like a pain-killing drug, disidentification undoes her future as it relieves her vulnerability.

The prevalence of this syndrome among black college students has been documented extensively, especially on predominantly white campuses. Summarizing this work, Jacqueline Fleming, a psychologist, writes, "The fact that black students must matriculate in an atmosphere that feels hostile arouses defensive reactions that interfere with intellectual performance. . . . They display academic demotivation and think less of their abilities. They profess losses of energy." Among a sample of blacks on one predominantly white campus, Richard Nisbett and Andrew Reaves, both psychologists, and I found that attitudes related to disidentification were more strongly predictive of grades than even academic preparation (that is, SATs and high school grades).

To make matters worse, once disidentification occurs in a school, it can spread like the common cold. Blacks who identify and try to achieve embarrass the strategy by valuing the very thing the strategy denies the value of. Thus pressure to make it a group norm can evolve quickly and become fierce. Defectors are called "oreos" or "incognegroes." One's identity as an authentic black is held hostage, made incompatible with school identification. For black students, then, pressure to disidentify with school can come from the already demoralized as well as from racial vulnerability in the setting.

Stimatization of the sort suffered by black Americans is probably also a barrier to the school achievement of other groups in our society, such as lower-class whites, Hispanics, and women in male-dominated fields. For example, at a large midwestern university I studied women match men's achievement in the liberal arts, where they suffer no marked stigma, but underachieve compared with men (get lower grades than men with the same ACT scores) in engineering and premedical programs, where they, like blacks across the board, are more vulnerable to suspicions of inferiority.

"Wise" Schooling

"When they approach me they see . . . everything and anything except me. . . . [This] invisibility occurs because of a peculiar disposition of the eyes. . . ."

Ralph Ellison, *Invisible Man*

Erving Goffman, borrowing from gays of the 1950s, used the term "wise" to describe people who don't themselves bear the stigma of a given group but who are accepted by the group. These are people in whose eyes the full humanity of the stigmatized is visible, people in whose eyes they feel less vulnerable. If racial vulnerability undermines black school achievement, as I have argued, then this achievement should improve significantly if schooling is made "wise"—that is, made to see value and promise in black students and to act accordingly.

And yet, although racial vulnerability at school may undermine black achievement, so many other factors seem to contribute—from the debilitations of poverty to the alleged dysfunctions of black American culture—that one might expect "wiseness" in the classroom to be of little help. Fortunately, we have considerable evidence to the contrary. Wise schooling may indeed be the missing key to the schoolhouse door.

In the mid-seventies black students in Philip Uri Treisman's early calculus courses at the University of California at Berkeley consistently fell to the bottom of every class. To help, Treisman developed the Mathematics Workshop Program, which, in a surprisingly short time, reversed their fortunes, causing them to outperform their white and Asian counterparts. And although it is only a freshman program, black students who take it graduate at a rate comparable to the Berkeley average. Its central technique is group study of calculus concepts. But it is also wise; it does things that allay the racial vulnerabilities of these students. Stressing their potential to learn, it recruits them to a challenging "honors" workshop tied to their first calculus course. Building on their skills, the workshop gives difficult work, often beyond course content, to students with even modest preparation (some of their math SATs dip to the 300s). Working together, students soon understand that everyone knows something and nobody knows everything, and learning is speeded through shared understanding. The wisdom of these tactics is their subtext message: "You are valued in this program because of your academic potential—regardless of your current skill level. You have no more to fear than the next person, and since the work is difficult, success is a credit to your ability, and a setback is a reflection only of the challenge." The black students' double vulnerability around failure—the fear that they lack ability, and the dread that they will be devalued—is thus reduced. They can relax and achieve. The movie *Stand and Deliver* depicts Jaime Escalante using the same techniques of assurance and challenge to inspire advanced calculus performance in East Los Angeles Chicano high schoolers. And, explaining Xavier University's extraordinary success in producing black medical students, a spokesman said recently, "What doesn't work is saying, 'You need remedial work.' What does work is saying, 'You may be somewhat behind at this time but you're a talented person. We're going to help you advance at an accelerated rate.' "

The work of James Comer, a child psychiatrist at Yale, suggests that wiseness can minimize even the barriers of poverty. Over a fifteen-year period he transformed the two worst elementary schools in New Haven, Connecticut, into the third and fifth best in the city's thirty-three-school system without any change in the type of students—largely poor and black. His guiding belief is that learning requires a strongly accepting relationship between teacher and student. "After all," he notes, "what is the difference between scribble and a letter of the alphabet to a child? The only reason the letter is meaningful, and worth learning and remembering, is because a *meaningful* other wants him or her to learn and remember it." To build these relationships Comer focuses on the over-all school climate, shaping it not so much to transmit specific skills, or to achieve order per se, or even to improve achievement, as to establish a valuing and optimistic atmosphere in which a child can—to use his term—"identify" with learning. Responsibility for this lies with a team of ten to fifteen members, headed by the principal and made up of teachers, parents, school staff, and child-development experts (for example, psychologists or special-education teachers). The team develops a plan of specifics: teacher training, parent workshops, coordination of information about students. But at base I believe it tries to ensure that the students—vulnerable on so many counts—get treated essentially like middle-class students, with conviction about their value and promise. As this happens, their vulnerability diminishes, and with it the companion defenses of disidentification and misconduct. They achieve, and apparently identify, as their achievement gains persist into high school. Comer's genius, I believe, is to have recognized the importance of these vulnerabilities as barriers to *intellectual* development, and the corollary that schools hoping to educate such students must learn first how to make them feel valued.

These are not isolated successes. Comparable results were observed, for example, in a Comer-type program in Maryland's Prince Georges County, in the Stanford economist Henry Levin's accelerated-schools program, and in Harlem's Central Park East Elementary School, under the principalship of Deborah Meier. And research involving hundreds of programs and schools points to the same conclusion: black achievement is consistently linked to conditions of schooling that reduce racial vulnerability. These include relatively harmonious race relations among students; a commitment by teachers and schools to seeing minority-group members achieve; the instructional goal that students at all levels of preparation achieve; desegregation at the classroom as well as the school level; and a de-emphasis on ability tracking.

That erasing stigma improves black achievement is perhaps the strongest evidence that stigma is what depresses it in the first place. This is no happy realization. But it lets in a ray of hope: whatever other factors also depress black achievement—poverty, social isolation, poor preparation—they may be substantially overcome in a schooling atmosphere that reduces racial and other vulnerabilities, not through unrelenting niceness or ferocious regimentation but by wiseness, by *seeing* value and acting on it.

What Makes Schooling Unwise

But if wise schooling is so attainable, why is racial vulnerability the rule, not the exception, in American schooling?

One factor is the basic assimilationist offer that schools make to blacks: You can be valued and rewarded in school (and society), the schools say to these students, but you must first master the culture and ways of the American mainstream, and since that mainstream (as it is represented) is essentially white, this means you must give up many particulars of being black—styles of speech and appearance, value priorities, preferences—at least in mainstream settings. This is asking a lot.

4. Race and the Schooling of Black Americans

But it has been the "color-blind" offer to every immigrant and minority group in our nation's history, the core of the melting-pot ideal, and so I think it strikes most of us as fair. Yet non-immigrant minorities like blacks and Native Americans have always been here, and thus are entitled, more than new immigrants, to participate in the defining images of the society projected in school. More important, their exclusion from these images denies their contributive history and presence in society. Thus, whereas immigrants can tilt toward assimilation in pursuit of the opportunities for which they came, American blacks may find it harder to assimilate. For them, the offer of acceptance in return for assimilation carries a primal insult: it asks them to join in something that has made them invisible.

Now, I must be clear. This is not a criticism of Western civilization. My concern is an omission of image-work. In his incisive essay "What America Would Be Like Without Blacks," Ralph Ellison showed black influence on American speech and language, the themes of our finest literature, and our most defining ideals of personal freedom and democracy. In *The World They Made Together,* Mechal Sobel described how African and European influences shaped the early American South in everything from housing design and land use to religious expression. The fact is that blacks are not outside the American mainstream but, in Ellison's words, have always been "one of its major tributaries." Yet if one relied on what is taught in America's schools, one would never know this. There blacks have fallen victim to a collective self-deception, a society's allowing itself to assimilate like mad from its constituent groups while representing itself to itself as if the assimilation had never happened, as if progress and good were almost exclusively Western and white. A prime influence of American society on world culture is the music of black Americans, shaping art forms from rock-and-roll to modern dance. Yet in American schools, from kindergarten through graduate school, these essentially black influences have barely peripheral status, are largely outside the canon. Thus it is not what is taught but what is *not* taught, what teachers and professors have never learned the value of, that reinforces a fundamental unwiseness in American schooling, and keeps black disidentification on full boil.

Deep in the psyche of American educators is a presumption that black students need academic remediation, or extra time with elemental curricula to overcome background deficits. This orientation guides many efforts to close the achievement gap—from grammar school tutoring to college academic-support programs—but I fear it can be unwise. Bruno Bettelheim and Karen Zelan's article "Why Children Don't Like to Read" comes to mind: apparently to satisfy the changing sensibilities of local school boards over this century, many books that children like were dropped from school reading lists; when children's reading scores also dropped, the approved texts were replaced by simpler books; and when reading scores dropped again, these were replaced by even simpler books, until eventually the children could hardly read at all, not because the material was too difficult but because they were bored stiff. So it goes, I suspect, with a great many of these remediation efforts. Moreover, because so many such programs target blacks primarily, they virtually equate black identity with substandard intellectual status, amplifying racial vulnerability. They can even undermine students' ability to gain confidence from their achievement, by sharing credit for their successes while implying that their failures stem from inadequacies beyond the reach of remediation.

The psychologist Lisa Brown and I recently uncovered evidence of just how damaging this orientation may be. At a large, prestigious university we found that whereas the grades of black graduates of the 1950s improved during the students' college years until they virtually matched the school average, those of blacks who graduated in the 1980s (we chose only those with above-average entry credentials, to correct for more-liberal admissions policies in that decade) worsened, ending up considerably below the school average. The 1950s graduates faced outward discrimination in everything from housing to the classroom, whereas the 1980s graduates were supported by a phalanx of help programs. Many things may contribute to this pattern. The Jackie Robinson, "pioneer spirit of the 1950s blacks surely helped them endure. And in a pre-affirmative-action era, they may have been seen as intellectually more deserving. But one cannot ignore the distinctive fate of the 1980s blacks: a remedial orientation put their abilities under suspicion, deflected their ambitions, distanced them from their successes, and painted them with their failures. Black students on today's campuses may experience far less overt prejudice than their 1950s counterparts but, ironically, may be more racially vulnerable.

The Elements of Wiseness

For too many black students school is simply the place where, more concertedly, persistently, and authoritatively than anywhere else in society, they learn how little valued they are.

Clearly, no simple recipe can fix this, but I believe we now understand the basics of a corrective approach. Schooling must focus more on reducing the vulnerabilities that block identification with achievement. I believe that four conditions, like the legs of a stool, are fundamental.

- If what is meaningful and important to a teacher is to become meaningful and important to a student, the student must feel valued by the teacher for his or her potential and as a person. Among the more fortunate in society, this relationship is often taken for granted. But it is precisely the relationship that race can still undermine in American society. As Comer, Escalante, and Treisman have shown, when one's students bear race and class vulnerabilities, building this relationship is the first order of business—at all levels of schooling. No tactic of instruction, no matter how ingenious, can succeed without it.
- The challenge and the promise of personal fulfillment, not remediation (under whatever guise), should guide the education of these students. Their present skills should be taken into account, and they should be moved along at a pace that is demanding but doesn't defeat them. Their

ambitions should never be scaled down but should instead be guided to inspiring goals even when extraordinary dedication is called for. Frustration will be less crippling than alienation. Here psychology is everything: remediation defeats, challenge strengthens—affirming their potential, crediting them with their achievements, inspiring them.

But the first condition, I believe, cannot work without the second, and vice versa. A valuing teacher-student relationship goes nowhere without challenge, and challenge will always be resisted outside a valuing relationship. (Again, I must be careful about something: in criticizing remediation I am not opposing affirmative-action recruitment in the schools. The success of this policy, like that of school integration before it, depends, I believe, on the tactics of implementation. Where students are valued and challenged, they generally succeed.)

- Racial integration is a generally useful element in this design, if not a necessity. Segregation, whatever its purpose, draws out group differences and makes people feel more vulnerable when they inevitably cross group lines to compete in the larger society. This vulnerability, I fear, can override confidence gained in segregated schooling unless that confidence is based on strongly competitive skills and knowledge—something that segregated schooling, plagued by shortages of resources and access, has difficulty producing.
- The particulars of black life and culture—art, literature, political and social perspective, music—must be presented in the mainstream curriculum of American schooling, not consigned to special days, weeks, or even months of the year, or to special-topic courses and programs aimed essentially at blacks. Such channeling carries the disturbing message that the material is not of general value. And this does two terrible things: it wastes the power of this material to alter our images of the American mainstream—continuing to frustrate black identification with it—and it excuses in whites and others a huge ignorance of their own society. The true test of democracy, Ralph Ellison has said, is "the inclusion—not assimilation—of the black man."

Finally, if I might be allowed a word specifically to black parents, one issue is even more immediate: our children may drop out of school before the first committee meets to accelerate the curriculum. Thus, although we, along with all Americans, must strive constantly for wise schooling, I believe we cannot wait for it. We cannot yet forget our essentially heroic challenge: to foster in our children a sense of hope and entitlement to mainstream American life and schooling, even when it devalues them.

WHO IS HAPPY?

David G. Myers and Ed Diener
Hope College and University of Illinois

Address correspondence to David G. Myers, Hope College, Holland, MI 49422-9000, e-mail: myers@hope.edu, or Ed Diener, University of Illinois, Department of Psychology, 603 East Daniel St., Champaign, IL 61820, e-mail: ediener@s.psych.uiuc.edu.

A flood of new studies explores people's subjective well-being (SWB). Frequent positive affect, infrequent negative affect, and a global sense of satisfaction with life define high SWB. These studies reveal that happiness and life satisfaction are similarly available to the young and the old, women and men, blacks and whites, the rich and the working-class. Better clues to well-being come from knowing about a person's traits, close relationships, work experiences, culture, and religiosity. We present the elements of an appraisal-based theory of happiness that recognizes the importance of adaptation, cultural worldview, and personal goals.

Books, books, and more books have analyzed human misery. During its first century, psychology focused far more on negative emotions, such as depression and anxiety, than on positive emotions, such as happiness and satisfaction. Even today, our texts say more about suffering than about joy. That is now changing. During the 1980s, the number of *Psychological Abstract* citations of "well-being," "happiness," and "life satisfaction" quintupled, to 780 articles annually. Social scientists, policymakers, and laypeople express increasing interest in the conditions, traits, and attitudes that define quality of life.

Studies (see Diener & Diener, 1994) reveal that happiness is more abundant than believed by writers from Samuel Johnson ("That man is never happy for the present is so true"; Boswell, 1776/1973, Vol. 2, p. 37) to John Powell ("Professionals estimate that only 10 to 15 percent of Americans think of themselves as truly happy"; Powell, 1989, p. 4). Thomas Szasz (quoted by Winokur, 1987) summed up the assumption of many people: "Happiness is an imaginary condition, formerly attributed by the living to the dead, now usually attributed by adults to children, and by children to adults" (p. 133).

Recognizing that most people are reasonably happy, but that some people are happier than others, researchers are offering a fresh perspective on an old puzzle: Who are the happy people? Does happiness favor those of a particular age, sex, or race? Does wealth enhance well-being? Does happiness come with having certain traits? a particular job? close friends? an active faith?

The scientific study of emotional well-being is new, but theories about happiness are ages old. The philosophers of ancient Greece believed that happiness accompanies a life of intelligent reflection. "There is no fool who is happy, and no wise man who is not," echoed the Roman philosopher Cicero (in *De Finibus*). The Epicurean and Stoic philosophers offered variations on this song of happy wisdom. Aristotle regarded happiness as the *summum bonum*, the supreme good. Virtue, he believed, is synonymous with happiness. In the centuries since, sages have offered contrasting ideas about the roots of happiness. They have told us that happiness comes from knowing the truth, and from preserving healthy illusions; that it comes from restraint, and from purging ourselves of pent-up emotions; that it comes from being with other people, and from living in contemplative solitude. The list goes on, but the implication is clear: Discerning the actual roots of subjective well-being requires rigorous scientific inquiry.

MEASURING SUBJECTIVE WELL-BEING

Psychological investigations of well-being complement long-standing measures of physical and material well-being with assessments of subjective well-being (SWB). Researchers have, for example, asked people across the industrialized world to reflect on their happiness and life satisfaction. Measures range from multi-item scales to single questions, such as "How satisfied are you with your life as a whole these days? Are you very satisfied? satisfied? not very satisfied? not at all satisfied?"

Self-reports of global well-being have temporal stability in the 0.5 to 0.7 range over periods from 6 months to 6 years (Diener, 1994; Magnus & Diener, 1991). But can we believe people's answers? Or are "happy" people often "in denial" of their actual misery? It is reassuring, first, that response artifacts, such as the effects of social desirability and current mood, do not invalidate the SWB measures (Diener, Sandvik, Pavot, & Gallagher, 1991; Diener, Suh, Smith, & Shao, in press). For example, social desirability scores do correlate modestly with self-reported SWB scores, but they predict non-self-report SWB measures (such as peer reports) equally well, suggesting that social desirability is a substantive characteristic that enhances well-being.

Second, people's self-reported well-being converges with other measures (e.g., Pavot, Diener, Colvin, &

Sandvik, 1991; Sandvik, Diener, & Seidlitz, 1993). Those who describe themselves as happy and satisfied with life seem happy to their friends and to their family members. Their daily mood ratings reveal mostly positive emotions. They recall more positive events and fewer negative events (Seidlitz & Diener, 1993). And ratings derived from clinical interviews converge well with their SWB scores.

Third, SWB measures exhibit construct validity. They are responsive to recent good and bad events and to therapy (e.g., Headey & Wearing, 1992; Sandvik et al., 1993). They correlate inversely with feeling ill (Sandvik et al., 1993). And they predict other indicators of psychological well-being. Compared with depressed people, happy people are less self-focused, less hostile and abusive, and less vulnerable to disease. They also are more loving, forgiving, trusting, energetic, decisive, creative, helpful, and sociable (Myers, 1993a; Veenhoven, 1988).

Finally, the research concerns *subjective* well-being, for which the final judge is whoever lives inside a person's skin. For all these reasons, researchers take seriously people's reports of their subjective unhappiness (or happiness), especially when supported by converging reports from informants and by observations of accompanying dysfunction (or social competence).

THE COMPONENTS OF WELL-BEING

High SWB reflects a preponderance of positive thoughts and feelings about one's life. At the cognitive level, SWB includes a global sense of satisfaction with life, fed by specific satisfactions with one's work, marriage, and other domains. At the affective level, people with high SWB feel primarily pleasant emotions, thanks largely to their positive appraisal of ongoing events. People with low SWB appraise their life circumstances and events as undesirable, and therefore feel unpleasant emotions such as anxiety, depression, and anger.

Surprisingly, positive and negative emotions correlate with different predictor variables (e.g., Costa & McCrae, 1980; Magnus & Diener, 1991). Moreover, positive and negative emotions are only weakly correlated with each other (Bradburn, 1969; Diener & Emmons, 1985). Knowing the global amount of good feeling a person experiences over time does not indicate the global amount of bad feeling the person experiences. How could this be? If good feelings exclude bad feelings at the same moment in time, then the more time one spends up the less time one can spend down. Thus, the frequencies of good and bad moods are inversely related. People who experience their good moods intensely, however, tend similarly to experience intense bad moods. For some people, high highs alternate with low lows. Others are characteristically happy, or melancholy, or unemotional.

Thus, positive and negative affect seem not to be bipolar opposites. Positive well-being is not just the absence of negative emotions. Rather, SWB is defined by three correlated but distinct factors: the relative presence of positive affect, absence of negative affect, and satisfaction with life.

MYTHS OF HAPPINESS

So, who are the happy people? By identifying predictors of happiness and life satisfaction, psychologists and sociologists have exploded some myths.

Is Happiness Being Young? Middle-Aged? Newly Retired?

Many people believe there are notably unhappy times of life—typically the stress-filled teen years, the "midlife crisis" years, or the declining years of old age. But interviews with representative samples of people of all ages reveal that no time of life is notably happier or unhappier than others (Latten, 1989; Stock, Okun, Haring, & Witter, 1983). This conclusion is reinforced by a 1980s survey of 169,776 people representatively sampled in 16 nations (Inglehart, 1990; see Fig. 1). The predictors of happiness do change with age (e.g., satisfaction with social relations and health become more important in later life; Herzog, Rogers, & Woodworth, 1982). And the emotional terrain varies with age (teens, unlike adults, usually come up from gloom or down from elation within an hour's time; Csikszentmihalyi & Larson, 1984). Yet knowing someone's age gives no clue to the person's average sense of well-being.

Nor does one find in rates of depression, suicide, ca-

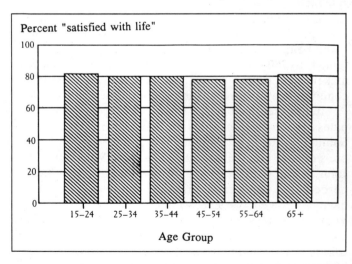

Fig. 1. Age and well-being in 16 nations. Data from 169,776 people, representatively sampled from 1980 to 1986, and reported by Inglehart (1990).

reer change, or divorce any evidence of increased personal upheaval during the supposed early 40s "midlife crisis" years. People do face crisis times, but not at any predictable age (Hunter & Sundel, 1989; McCrae &

Costa, 1990). The "empty nest syndrome"—a sense of despondency and lost meaning when children leave home—also turns out to be rare (Adelmann, Antonucci, Crohan, & Coleman, 1989; Glenn, 1975). For most couples, the empty nest is a happy place—often a place where marital happiness rebounds after the stresses of child rearing.

Does Happiness Have a Favorite Sex?

There are striking gender gaps in misery: Women are twice as vulnerable as men to disabling depression and anxiety, and men are five times as vulnerable as women to alcoholism and antisocial personality disorder (Robins & Regier, 1991). Women's more intense sadness, given bad circumstances, must be considered in light of their greater capacity for joy under good circumstances (Diener, Sandvik, & Larsen, 1985; Fujita, Diener, & Sandvik, 1991). Although women report slightly greater happiness than men when only positive emotions are assessed (Wood, Rhodes, & Whelan, 1989), the net result is roughly equal hedonic balance for women and men. In a meta-analysis of 146 studies, gender therefore accounted for less than 1% of people's global well-being (Haring, Stock, & Okun, 1984). The finding generalizes worldwide. In the 1980s collaborative survey of 16 nations, 80% of men and 80% of women said that they were at least "fairly satisfied" with life (Inglehart, 1990; see Fig. 2). A similar result appeared in a study of 18,032 university students surveyed in 39 countries (Michalos, 1991).

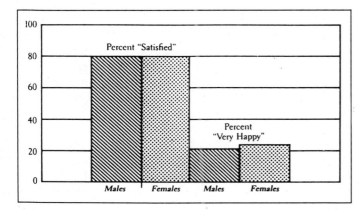

Fig. 2. Gender and well-being in 16 nations. Data from 169,776 people, representatively sampled from 1980 to 1986, and reported by Inglehart (1990).

Does Happiness Vary by Race?

Knowing someone's race or ethnic group also gives little clue to the person's psychological well-being. African-Americans, for example, report nearly as much happiness as European-Americans and are actually slightly less vulnerable to depression (Diener, Sandvik, Seidlitz, & Diener, 1993; Robins & Regier, 1991; Stock, Okun, Haring, & Witter, 1985). Blacks and whites, like women and men, and people with and without disabilities, also score similarly on tests of self-esteem (Crocker & Major, 1989). Despite discrimination, noted Crocker and Major, people in disadvantaged groups maintain self-esteem by valuing the things at which they excel, by making comparisons within their own groups, and by attributing problems to external sources such as prejudice.

Does Happiness Vary by Culture?

Interestingly, nations differ strikingly in happiness, ranging from Portugal, where about 10% of people say they are very happy, to the Netherlands, where about 40% of people say the same (Inglehart, 1990). Nations differ markedly in happiness even when income differences are controlled for (Diener, Diener, & Diener, 1994). Although national levels of SWB covary with whether basic physical needs are met, countries such as Japan have much lower SWB than one would expect based only on material considerations. In general, collectivist cultures report lower SWB than do individualistic cultures, where norms more strongly support experiencing and expressing positive emotions (Diener, Suh, Smith, & Shao, in press).

National differences appear not to reflect mere differences in the connotations of the translated questions. For example, regardless of whether they are German-, French-, or Italian-speaking, the Swiss rank high on self-reported life satisfaction—significantly higher than their German, French, and Italian neighbors (Inglehart, 1990).

Does Money Buy Happiness?

The American dream seems to have become life, liberty, and the purchase of happiness. In 1993, 75% of America's entering collegians declared that an "essential" or "very important" life goal was "being very well off financially"—nearly double the 39% who said the same in 1970 (Astin, Green, & Korn, 1987; Astin, Korn, & Riggs, 1993). This goal topped a list of 19 possible life objectives, exceeding the rated importance even of "raising a family" and "helping others in difficulty." Most adults share this materialism, believing that increased income would make them happier (Strumpel, 1976). Few agree that money can buy happiness, but many agree that a little more money would make them a little happier.

Are wealth and well-being indeed connected? We can make the question more specific: First, are people in rich countries more satisfied than those in not-so-rich countries? As Figure 3 illustrates, the correlation between national wealth and well-being is positive (+.67, despite curious reversals, such as the Irish reporting greater life satisfaction than the wealthier West Germans). But national wealth is confounded with other variables, such as number of continuous years of democracy, which correlates +.85 with average life satisfaction (Inglehart, 1990).

Second, within any country, are rich individuals happiest? Having food, shelter, and safety is basic to well-being. Thus, in poor countries, such as Bangladesh and India, satisfaction with finances is a moderate predictor of SWB (Diener & Diener, in press). But once people are able to afford life's necessities, increasing levels of affluence matter surprisingly little. Although the correlation between income and happiness is not negative, it is modest. In the United States, one study (Diener et al., 1993) found a mere +.12 correlation between income and happiness; increases or decreases in income had no long-term influence on SWB. And Inglehart (1990) noted that in Europe, income "has a surprisingly weak (indeed, virtually negligible) effect on happiness" (p. 242). Although satisfaction with income predicts SWB better than actual income, there is only a slight tendency for people who

Fig. 4. Inflation-adjusted income and happiness in the United States. National Opinion Research Center happiness data from Niemi, Mueller, and Smith (1989) and T. Smith (personal communication, November 1993). Income data from Bureau of the Census (1975) and *Economic Indicators*.

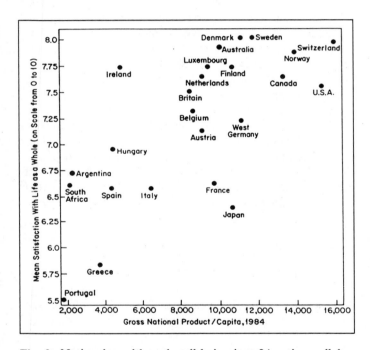

Fig. 3. National wealth and well-being in a 24-nation collaborative survey. Euro-Barometer and World Values Survey data reported by Inglehart (1990).

make a great deal of money to be more satisfied with what they make (Campbell, 1981).

Wealth, it seems, is like health: Its absence can breed misery, yet having it is no guarantee of happiness. In one survey, people on *Forbes*'s list of wealthiest Americans reported only slightly greater happiness than other Americans; 37% were less happy than the average American (Diener, Horwitz, & Emmons, 1985). Even lottery winners gain only a temporary jolt of joy (Argyle, 1986; Brickman, Coates, & Janoff-Bulman, 1978). The emo-

tional effects of some tragedies are likewise temporary: After a period of adaptation, people with disabilities usually report a near-normal level of well-being (Diener, 1994). Thus, concluded Kammann (1983), "Objective life circumstances have a negligible role to play in a theory of happiness" (p. 18). Satisfaction is less a matter of getting what you want than wanting what you have.

Third, over time, as cultures become more affluent, do their people become happier? In 1957, as economist John Galbraith was about to describe America as *The Affluent Society*, Americans' per person income, expressed in today's dollars, was less than $8,000. Today it is more than $16,000, making America "the doubly affluent society"—with double what money buys. Compared with 1957, Americans have twice as many cars per person—plus microwave ovens, color TVs, VCRs, air conditioners, answering machines, and $12 billion worth of new brand-name athletic shoes a year.

So, are Americans happier than they were in 1957? They are not (see Fig. 4). In 1957, 35% told the National Opinion Research Center that they were "very happy." In 1993, with doubled affluence, 32% said the same (Smith, 1979, and personal communication, November 1993). To judge by soaring rates of depression (Cross-National Collaborative Group, 1992), a quintupled rate of reported violent crime since 1960, a doubled divorce rate, a slight decline in marital happiness among the marital survivors (Glenn, 1990), and a tripled teen suicide rate, Americans are richer and no happier. Easterlin (in press) has reported the same for European countries and Japan. Thus, although policymakers and economists are wedded to the assumption that SWB rises with income (Easterlin, in press), the data indicate that economic growth in affluent countries gives little boost to human morale.

HAPPY PEOPLE

If happiness is similarly available to people of any age, sex, or race, and to those of most income levels, who is happiest? Through life's ups and downs, some people's capacity for joy persists undiminished. In one National Institute of Aging study of 5,000 adults, the happiest of people in 1973 were still relatively happy a decade later, despite changes in their work, their residence, and their family status (Costa, McCrae, & Zonderman, 1987). Who are these chronically happy people?

The Traits of Happy People

In study after study, four inner traits mark happy people: self-esteem, a sense of personal control, optimism, and extraversion.

First, happy people like themselves (Campbell, 1981). On tests of self-esteem, they agree with such statements as "I'm a lot of fun to be with" and "I have good ideas." Indeed, happy people often exhibit a self-serving bias by believing themselves more ethical, more intelligent, less prejudiced, better able to get along with others, and healthier than average (Janoff & Bulman, 1989; Myers, 1993b; Taylor & Brown, 1988). (The findings bring to mind Freud's joke about the man who said to his wife, "If one of us should die, I think I would go live in Paris.") Most people do express positive self-esteem. This helps explain why, contrary to those who would have us believe that happy people are rare, 9 in 10 North Americans describe themselves as at least "pretty happy." The strong link between self-esteem and SWB so often found in individualistic Western cultures is, however, weaker in collectivist cultures, where the group is given priority over the self (Diener & Diener, in press).

Second, happy people typically feel personal control (Campbell, 1981; Larson, 1989). Those who feel empowered rather than helpless typically do better in school, cope better with stress, and live more happily. When deprived of control over their own lives—an experience studied in prisoners, nursing home patients, and people living under totalitarian regimes—people suffer lower morale and worse health. Severe poverty demoralizes when it erodes people's sense of control over their life circumstances (Dumont, 1989).

Third, happy people are usually optimistic. Optimists—those who agree, for example, that "when I undertake something new, I expect to succeed"—tend to be more successful, healthier, and happier than are pessimists (Dember & Brooks, 1989; Seligman, 1991).

Fourth, happy people tend to be extraverted (Costa & McCrae, 1980; Diener, Sandvik, Pavot, & Fujita, 1992; Emmons & Diener, 1986a, 1986b; Headey & Wearing, 1992). Compared with introverts, extraverts are happier both when alone and with other people (Pavot, Diener, & Fujita, 1990), whether they live alone or with others, whether they live in rural or metropolitan areas, and whether they work in solitary or social occupations (Diener et al., 1992).

Reasons for the trait-happiness correlations are not yet fully understood. The causal arrow may go from traits to SWB, or the reverse. Extraversion, for example, may predispose happiness, perhaps because of the social contacts extraversion entails. Or happiness may produce outgoing behavior. Outgoing people, for example, usually appear temperamentally high-spirited and relaxed about reaching out to others, which may explain why they marry sooner, get better jobs, and make more friends (Magnus & Diener, 1991). Twin studies indicate genetic influences on SWB (Tellegen et al., 1988).

The Relationships of Happy People

One could easily imagine why close relationships might exacerbate illness and misery. Close relationships are fraught with stress. "Hell is other people," mused Jean-Paul Sartre (1944/1973, p. 47). Fortunately, the benefits of close relationships with friends and family usually outweigh the strains. People who can name several intimate friends with whom they share their intimate concerns freely are healthier, less likely to die prematurely, and happier than people who have few or no such friends (Burt, 1986; Cohen, 1988; House, Landis, & Umberson, 1988). People report higher positive affect when they are with others (Pavot et al., 1990). In experiments, people relax as they confide painful experiences. In one study, 33 Holocaust survivors spent 2 hr recalling their experiences, often revealing intimate details never before disclosed. Fourteen months later, those who were most self-disclosing had the most improved health (Pennebaker, 1990).

Seligman (1991) contended that today's epidemic levels of depression stem partly from impoverished social connections in increasingly individualistic Western societies. Individualistic societies offer personal control, harmony between the inner and outer person, and opportunity to express one's feelings and talents, though with the risks of a less embedded, more detached self. Today, 25% of Americans live alone, up from 8% half a century ago.

For more than 9 in 10 people, the most significant alternative to aloneness is marriage. As with other close social bonds, broken marital relationships are a source of much self-reported unhappiness, whereas a supportive, intimate relationship is among life's greatest joys (Glenn, 1990). To paraphrase Henry Ward Beecher, "Well-married a person is winged; ill-matched, shackled." Three out of 4 married people say that their spouse is their best friend, and 4 out of 5 say they would marry the same person again (Greeley, 1991). Such feelings help explain why over the 1970s and 1980s, 24% of never-married adults, but 39% of married adults, told the National Opinion Research Center that they were "very happy" (Lee, Seccombe, & Shehan, 1991; see Fig. 5).

The traffic between marriage and happiness, however, appears to be two-way: Happy people are more appealing as potential marriage partners and more likely to marry (Masteekaasa, 1992; Scott, 1992).

Is marriage, as is so often supposed, more strongly associated with men's happiness than women's? The happiness gap between married and never-married people (Fig. 5) was slightly greater among men (37.7% vs. 20.1%, for a 17.6% difference) than women (41.6% vs. 25.7%, for a 15.9% difference). In European surveys, and in a meta-analysis of 93 other studies, the happiness gap between the married and never-married was virtually identical for men and women (Inglehart, 1990; Wood et al., 1989). Although a bad marriage may indeed be more depressing to a woman than a man, the myth that "single

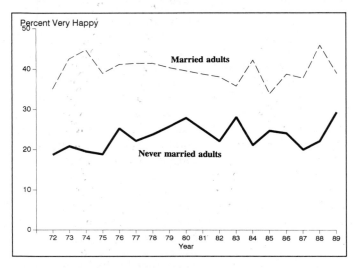

Fig. 5. Percentage of people who reported they were "very happy" among married and never-married U.S. adults. Derived from National Opinion Research Center data reported by Lee, Seccombe, and Shehan (1991).

women report greater life satisfaction than married women" can be laid to rest. Throughout the Western world, married people of both sexes report more happiness than those never married, divorced, or separated.

The "Flow" of Happy People

Turn-of-the-century Russian writer Maksim Gorky anticipated recent studies of work satisfaction: "When work is a pleasure, life is a joy! When work is a duty, life is slavery." Work satisfaction affects life satisfaction (Crohan, Antonucci, Adelmann, & Coleman, 1989; Freedman, 1978; Michalos, 1986). Why? And why are out-of-work people less likely to feel satisfied with life than those productively engaged?

For many people, work provides personal identity: It helps people define who they are. Work also adds to a sense of community: It offers people a network of supportive relationships and a "we feeling." This sense of pride and belonging to a group helps people construct their social identity. And work can add focus and purpose—a sense that one's life matters. Studs Terkel (1972) described "the Chicago piano tuner, who seeks and finds the sound that delights; the bookbinder, who saves a piece of history; the Brooklyn fireman, who saves a piece of life.... There is a common attribute here: a meaning to their work well over and beyond the reward of the paycheck" (p. xi).

Work is, however, sometimes unsatisfying, for two reasons. We can be overwhelmed: When challenges exceed our available time and skills, we feel anxious, stressed. Or we can be underwhelmed: When challenges do not engage our time and skills, we feel bored. Between anxiety and boredom lies a middle ground where challenges engage and match skills. In this zone, we enter an optimal state that Csikszentmihalyi (1990) termed "flow" (Fig. 6).

To be in flow is to be un-self-consciously absorbed. In such times, one gets so caught up in an activity that the mind does not wander, one becomes oblivious to surroundings, and time flies. Csikszentmihalyi formulated the flow concept after studying artists who would spend hour after hour painting or sculpting with enormous concentration. Immersed in a project, they worked as if nothing else mattered. The artists seemed driven less by the external rewards of doing art—money, praise, promotion—than by the intrinsic rewards of creating the work.

Csikszentmihalyi conducted studies in which people reported on their activities and feelings when paged with electronic beepers. He discovered that happiness comes not from mindless passivity but from engagement in mindful challenge. Whether at work or at leisure, people enjoyed themselves more when absorbed in the flow of an activity than when doing nothing meaningful. Thus,

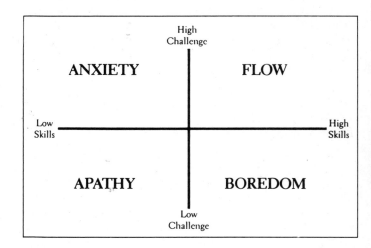

Fig. 6. The flow model. When a challenge engages skills, people often become so absorbed in the flow of an activity that they lose consciousness of self and time. Adapted from Csikszentmihalyi and Csikszentmihalyi (1988, p. 251).

involvement in interesting activities, including engaging work, is a major source of well-being. As playwright Noel

Coward observed, interesting work "is more fun than fun."

The Faith of Happy People

The links between religion and mental health are impressive. Religious people (often defined as those who attend church regularly) are much less likely than irreligious people to become delinquent, to abuse drugs and alcohol, to divorce or be unhappily married, and to commit suicide (Batson, Schoenrade, & Ventis, 1993; Colasanto & Shriver, 1989). Religiously active people even tend to be physically healthier and to live longer, in part because of their healthier smoking, eating, and drinking habits (Koenig, Smiley, & Gonzales, 1988; Levin & Schiller, 1987; McIntosh & Spilka, 1990).

Across North America and Europe, religious people also report higher levels of happiness and satisfaction with life (e.g., Poloma & Pendleton, 1990). Religious people are slightly less vulnerable to depression (Brown, 1993; Gartner, Larson, Allen, & Gartner, 1991). The most striking finding, however, comes from the Gallup Organization (Gallup, 1984), which compared people low in "spiritual commitment" with highly spiritual people (who consistently agree with statements such as "My religious faith is the most important influence in my life."). The highly spiritual were twice as likely to say they were "very happy." Other surveys, in the United States and across 14 Western nations, found that happiness and life satisfaction rise with strength of religious affiliation and frequency of worship attendance (Inglehart, 1990; Witter, Stock, Okun, & Haring, 1985). One meta-analysis among the elderly revealed that the two best predictors of well-being among older persons were health and religiousness (Okun & Stock, 1987).

Other studies have probed the connection between faith and coping with a crisis. Compared with religiously inactive widows, recently widowed women who worshipped regularly reported more joy in their lives (Harvey, Barnes, & Greenwood, 1987; McGloshen & O'Bryant, 1988; Siegel & Kuykendall, 1990). Among mothers of disabled children, those with a deep religious faith were less vulnerable to depression than were those who were irreligious (Friedrich, Cohen, & Wilturner, 1988). People with a strong faith also retained greater happiness after suffering divorce, unemployment, serious illness, or bereavement (Ellison, 1991; McIntosh, Silver, & Wortman, 1993).

What explains these positive links between faith and well-being? Is it the supportive close relationships often enjoyed by people who are active in local congregations (of which there are 258,000 in the United States)? Is it the sense of meaning and purpose that many people derive from their faith? Is it a religious worldview that offers answers to life's deepest questions and an optimistic appraisal of life events? Is it the hope that faith affords when people suffer or face what social psychologists Solomon, Greenberg, and Pyszczynski (1991) called "the terror resulting from our awareness of vulnerability and death" (p. 97)? Such proposed explanations await more rigorous exploration.

Elements of a Theory of Happiness

A viable theory of happiness must, first, recognize the importance of adaptation. Over time, the immediate affective response to significant life events inevitably fades. Thus, variables such as income (Diener et al., 1993), physical attractiveness (Diener, Wolsic, & Fujita, in press), and health (Okun & George, 1984) have minimal long-term influence on SWB despite having powerful effects on people's lives. Although lottery winners are initially elated, their euphoria soon wanes. "Continued pleasures wear off," noted Frijda (1988, p. 353). "Pleasure is always contingent upon change and disappears with continuous satisfaction."

Likewise, the agony of most bad events gradually subsides. Even the initial psychological trauma of paralyzing car accidents typically gives way to a return of normal happiness (Wortman & Silver, 1987). Reflecting on the successes and mental health of American Jews who survived horrific Holocaust experiences, Helmreich (1992) noted that "the story of the survivors is one of courage and strength, of people who are living proof of the indomitable will of human beings to survive and of their tremendous capacity for hope. It is not a story of remarkable people. It is a story of just how remarkable people can be" (p. 276).

In a recent longitudinal study, only life events within the last 3 months influenced SWB (Suh, Diener, & Fujita, in press). The more recent an event, the greater its emotional effect. Studies of daily moods (e.g., Clark & Watson, 1988; Stone & Neale, 1984) confirm Benjamin Franklin's surmise that happiness "is produced not so much by great pieces of good fortune that seldom happen as by little advantages that occur every day." Thanks to our human capacity for adaptation, the affect system is most attuned to the information value of new events.

In addition to adaptation, a second component of a theory of happiness is cultural worldview. Some cultures construe the world as benevolent and controllable. Other cultures emphasize the normality of negative emotions, such as anxiety, anger, and guilt (Diener, Suh, Smith, & Shao, in press). Cultural templates for interpreting life events predispose varying SWB in the absence of differing objective life circumstances. Likewise, some individuals appear habitually to interpret many of life's events negatively, whereas others tend to interpret events positively.

A third component of a theory of happiness is values and goals. Emmons (1986) found that having goals, making progress toward goals, and freedom from conflict among one's goals were all predictors of SWB. Diener and Fujita (in press) discovered that resources such as money, social skills, and intelligence were predictive of SWB only if they were relevant to a person's goals. This finding helps explain why income predicts SWB in very poor nations and why self-esteem predicts SWB in wealthy, individualistic nations. Happiness grows less from the passive experience of desirable circumstances than from involvement in valued activities and progress toward one's goals (Diener & Larsen, 1993).

CONCLUSION

Who is happy? Knowing a person's age, sex, race, and income (assuming the person has enough to afford life's necessities) hardly gives a clue. Better clues come from knowing a person's traits, whether the person enjoys a supportive network of close relationships, whether the person's culture offers positive interpretations for most daily events, whether the person is engaged by work and leisure, and whether the person has a faith that entails social support, purpose, and hope.

This new research on psychological well-being is a welcome complement to long-standing studies of depression and anxiety, and of physical and material well-being. By asking who is happy, and why, we can help people rethink their priorities and better understand how to build a world that enhances human well-being.

REFERENCES

Adelmann, P.K., Antonucci, T.C., Crohan, S.F., & Coleman, L.M. (1989). Empty nest, cohort, and employment in the well-being of midlife women. *Sex Roles, 20,* 173–189.

Argyle, M. (1986). *The psychology of happiness.* London: Methuen.

Astin, A.W., Green, K.C., & Korn, W.S. (1987). *The American freshman: Twenty year trends.* Los Angeles: University of California at Los Angeles, Graduate School of Education, Higher Education Research Institute.

Astin, A.W., Korn, W.S., & Riggs, E.R. (1993). *The American freshman: National norms for fall 1993.* Los Angeles: University of California at Los Angeles, Graduate School of Education, Higher Education Research Institute.

Batson, C.D., Schoenrade, P.A., & Ventis, W.L. (1993). *Religion and the individual: A social-psychological perspective.* New York: Oxford.

Boswell, J. (1973). *The life of Samuel Johnson.* London: Dent. (Original work published 1776)

Bradburn, N. (1969). *The structure of psychological well-being.* Chicago: Aldine.

Brickman, P., Coates, D., & Janoff-Bulman, R.J. (1978). Lottery winners and accident victims: Is happiness relative? *Journal of Personality and Social Psychology, 36,* 917–927.

Brown, L.B. (Ed.). (1993). *Religion, personality and mental health.* New York: Springer-Verlag.

Bureau of the Census. (1975). *Historical statistics of the United States, colonial times to 1970.* Washington, DC: Superintendent of Documents.

Burt, R.S. (1986). *Strangers, friends and happiness* (GSS Technical Report No. 72). Chicago: University of Chicago, National Opinion Research Center.

Campbell, A. (1981). *The sense of well-being in America.* New York: McGraw-Hill.

Clark, L.A., & Watson, D. (1988). Mood and the mundane: Relations between daily life events and self-reported mood. *Journal of Personality and Social Psychology, 54,* 296–308.

Cohen, S. (1988). Psychosocial models of the role of social support in the etiology of physical disease. *Health Psychology, 7,* 269–297.

Colasanto, D., & Shriver, J. (1989, May). Mirror of America: Middle-aged face marital crisis. *Gallup Report,* pp. 34–38.

Costa, P.T., Jr., & McCrae, R.R. (1980). Influence of extraversion and neuroticism on subjective well-being: Happy and unhappy people. *Journal of Personality and Social Psychology, 38,* 668–678.

Costa, P.T., Jr., McCrae, R.R., & Zonderman, A.B. (1987). Environmental and dispositional influences on well-being: Longitudinal follow-up of an American national sample. *British Journal of Psychology, 78,* 299–306.

Crocker, J., & Major, B. (1989). Social stigma and self-esteem: The self-protective properties of stigma. *Psychological Review, 96,* 608–630.

Crohan, S.E., Antonucci, T.C., Adelmann, P.K., & Coleman, L.M. (1989). Job characteristics and well-being at midlife. *Psychology of Women Quarterly, 13,* 223–235.

Cross-National Collaborative Group. (1992). The changing rate of major depression. *Journal of the American Medical Association, 268,* 3098–3105.

Csikszentmihalyi, M. (1990). *Flow: The psychology of optimal experience.* New York: Harper & Row.

Csikszentmihalyi, M., & Csikszentmihalyi, I.S. (1988). *Optimal experience: Psychological studies of flow in consciousness.* New York: Cambridge University Press.

Csikszentmihalyi, M., & Larson, R. (1984). *Being adolescent: Conflict and growth in the teenage years.* New York: Basic Books.

Dember, W.N., & Brooks, J. (1989). A new instrument for measuring optimism and pessimism: Test-retest reliability and relations with happiness and religious commitment. *Bulletin of the Psychonomic Society, 27,* 365–366.

Diener, E. (1994). Assessing subjective well-being: Progress and opportunities. *Social Indicators Research, 31,* 103–157.

Diener, E., & Diener, C. (1994). *Most people in the United States experience positive subjective well-being.* Unpublished manuscript, University of Illinois, Champaign.

Diener, E., & Diener, M. (in press). Cross-cultural correlates of life satisfaction and self-esteem. *Journal of Personality and Social Psychology.*

Diener, E., Diener, M., & Diener, C. (1994). *Factors predicting the subjective well-being of nations.* Manuscript submitted for publication.

Diener, E., & Emmons, R.A. (1985). The independence of positive and negative affect. *Journal of Personality and Social Psychology, 47,* 71–75.

Diener, E., & Fujita, F. (in press). Resources, personal strivings, and subjective well-being: A nomothetic and ideographic approach. *Journal of Personality and Social Psychology.*

Diener, E., Horwitz, J., & Emmons, R.A. (1985). Happiness of the very wealthy. *Social Indicators, 16,* 263–274.

Diener, E., & Larsen, R.J. (1993). The experience of emotional well-being. In M. Lewis & J.M. Haviland (Eds.), *Handbook of emotions* (pp. 404–415). New York: Guilford Press.

Diener, E., Sandvik, E., & Larsen, R.J. (1985). Age and sex effects for emotional intensity. *Developmental Psychology, 21,* 542–548.

Diener, E., Sandvik, E., Pavot, W., & Fujita, F. (1992). Extraversion and subjective well-being in a U.S. national probability sample. *Journal of Research in Personality, 26,* 205–215.

Diener, E., Sandvik, E., Pavot, W., & Gallagher, D. (1991). Response artifacts in the measurement of subjective well-being. *Social Indicators Research, 24,* 35–56.

Diener, E., Sandvik, E., Seidlitz, L., & Diener, M. (1993). The relationship between income and subjective well-being: Relative or absolute? *Social Indicators Research, 28,* 195–223.

Diener, E., Suh, E., Smith, H., & Shao, L. (in press). National and cultural differences in reported well-being: Why do they occur? *Social Indicators Research.*

Diener, E., Wolsic, B., & Fujita, F. (in press). Physical attractiveness and subjective well-being. *Journal of Personality and Social Psychology.*

Dumont, M.P. (1989, September). An unfolding memoir of community mental health. *Readings: A Journal of Reviews and Commentary in Mental Health,* pp. 4–7.

Easterlin, R.A. (in press). Will raising the incomes of all increase the happiness of all? *Journal of Economic Behavior and Organization.*

Ellison, C.G. (1991). Religious involvement and subjective well-being. *Journal of Health and Social Behavior, 32,* 80–99.

Emmons, R.A. (1986). Personal strivings: An approach to personality and subjective well-being. *Journal of Personality and Social Psychology, 51,* 1058–1068.

Emmons, R.A., & Diener, E. (1986a). Influence of impulsivity and sociability on subjective well-being. *Journal of Personality and Social Psychology, 50,* 1211–1215.

Emmons, R.A., & Diener, E. (1986b). An interactional approach to the study of personality and emotion. *Journal of Personality, 54,* 371–384.

Freedman, J. (1978). *Happy people.* New York: Harcourt, Brace, Jovanovich.

Friedrich, W.N., Cohen, D.S., & Wilturner, L.T. (1988). Specific beliefs as moderator variables in maternal coping with mental retardation. *Children's Health Care, 17,* 40–44.

Frijda, N. (1988). The laws of emotion. *American Psychologist, 43,* 349–358.

Fujita, F., Diener, E., & Sandvik, E. (1991). Gender differences in dysphoria and well-being: The case for emotional intensity. *Journal of Personality and Social Psychology, 61,* 427–434.

Gallup, G., Jr. (1984, March). *Religion in America. Gallup Report.*

Gartner, J., Larson, D.B., Allen, G.D., & Gartner, A.F. (1991). Religious commitment and mental health: A review of the empirical literature. *Journal of Psychology and Theology, 19,* 6–25.

Glenn, N.D. (1975). Psychological well-being in the postparental stage: Some evidence from national surveys. *Journal of Marriage and the Family, 37,* 105–110.

Glenn, N.D. (1990). The social and cultural meaning of contemporary marriage. In B. Christensen (Ed.), *The retreat from marriage* (pp. 33–54). Rockford, IL: Rockford Institute.

Greeley, A.M. (1991). *Faithful attraction.* New York: Tor Books.

Haring, M.J., Stock, W.A., & Okun, M.A. (1984). A research synthesis of gender and social class as correlates of subjective well-being. *Human Relations, 37,* 645–657.

Harvey, C.D., Barnes, G.E., & Greenwood, L. (1987). Correlates of morale among Canadian widowed persons. *Social Psychiatry, 22,* 65–72.

Headey, B., & Wearing, A. (1992). *Understanding happiness: A theory of well-being.* Melbourne: Longman Cheshire.

Helmreich, W.B. (1992). *Against all odds: Holocaust survivors and the successful lives they made in America.* New York: Simon & Schuster.

Herzog, A.R., Rogers, W.L., & Woodworth, J. (1982). *Subjective well-being among different age groups.* Ann Arbor: University of Michigan, Survey Research Center.

House, J.S., Landis, K.R., & Umberson, D. (1988). Social relationships and health. *Science, 241,* 540–545.

Hunter, S., & Sundel, M. (Eds.). (1989). *Midlife myths: Issues, findings, and practice implications.* Newbury Park, CA: Sage.

Inglehart, R. (1990). *Culture shift in advanced industrial society.* Princeton, NJ: Princeton University Press.

Janoff-Bulman, R. (1989). The benefits of illusions, the threat of disillusionment, and the limitations of inaccuracy. *Journal of Social and Clinical Psychology, 8,* 158–175.

Kammann, R. (1983). Objective circumstances, life satisfactions, and sense of well-being: Consistencies across time and place. *New Zealand Journal of Psychology, 12,* 14–22.

Koenig, H.G., Smiley, M., & Gonzales, J.A.P. (1988). *Religion, health, and aging: A review and theoretical integration.* Westport, CT: Greenwood Press.

Larson, R. (1989). Is feeling "in control" related to happiness in daily life? *Psychological Reports, 64,* 775–784.

Latten, J.J. (1989). Life-course and satisfaction, equal for every-one? *Social Indicators Research, 21,* 599–610.

Lee, G.R., Seccombe, K., & Shehan, C.L. (1991). Marital status and personal happiness: An analysis of trend data. *Journal of Marriage and the Family, 53,* 839–844.

Levin, J.S., & Schiller, P.L. (1987). Is there a religious factor in health? *Journal of Religion and Health, 26,* 9–36.

Magnus, K., & Diener, E. (1991, May). *A longitudinal analysis of personality, life events, and well-being.* Paper presented at the annual meeting of the Midwestern Psychological Association, Chicago.

Mastekaasa, A. (1992). Marriage and psychological well-being: Some evidence on selection into marriage. *Journal of Marriage and the Family, 54,* 901–911.

McCrae, R.R., & Costa, P.T., Jr. (1990). *Personality in adulthood.* New York: Guilford Press.

McGloshen, T.H., & O'Bryant, S.L. (1988). The psychological well-being of older, recent widows. *Psychology of Women Quarterly, 12,* 99–116.

McIntosh, D.N., Silver, R.C., & Wortman, C.B. (1993). Religion's role in adjustment to a negative life event: Coping with the loss of a child. *Journal of Personality and Social Psychology, 65,* 812–821.

McIntosh, D.N., & Spilka, B.B. (1990). Religion and physical health: The role of personal faith and control beliefs. In M.L. Lynn & D.O. Moberg (Eds.), *Research on the social scientific study of religion* (Vol. 2, pp. 167–194). Greenwich, CT: JAI Press.

Michalos, A.C. (1986). Job satisfaction, marital satisfaction, and the quality of life: A review and a preview. In F.M. Andrews (Ed.), *Research on the quality of life* (pp. 57–83). Ann Arbor: University of Michigan, Survey Research Center.

Michalos, A.C. (1991). *Global report on student well-being: Vol. 1. Life satisfaction and happiness.* New York: Springer-Verlag.

Myers, D.G. (1993a). *The pursuit of happiness.* New York: Avon Books.

Myers, D.G. (1993b). *Social psychology* (4th ed.). New York: McGraw-Hill.

Niemi, R.G., Mueller, J., & Smith, T.W. (1989). *Trends in public opinion: A compendium of survey data.* New York: Greenwood Press.

Okun, M.A., & George, L.K. (1984). Physician- and self-ratings of health, neuroticism and subjective well-being among men and women. *Personality and Individual Differences, 5,* 533–539.

Okun, M.A., & Stock, W.A. (1987). Correlates and components of subjective well-being among the elderly. *Journal of Applied Gerontology, 6,* 95–112.

Pavot, W., Diener, E., Colvin, C.R., & Sandvik, E. (1991). Further validation of the Satisfaction With Life Scale: Evidence for the cross-method convergence of well-being measures. *Journal of Personality Assessment, 57,* 149–161.

Pavot, W., Diener, E., & Fujita, F. (1990). Extraversion and happiness. *Personality and Individual Differences, 11,* 1299–1306.

Pennebaker, J. (1990). *Opening up: The healing power of confiding in others.* New York: William Morrow.

Poloma, M.M., & Pendleton, B.F. (1990). Religious domains and general well-being. *Social Indicators Research, 22,* 255–276.

Powell, J. (1989). *Happiness is an inside job.* Valencia, CA: Tabor.

Robins, L., & Regier, D. (Eds.). (1991). *Psychiatric disorders in America.* New York: Free Press.

Sandvik, E., Diener, E., & Seidlitz, L. (1993). Subjective well-being: The convergence and stability of self-report and non-self-report measures. *Journal of Personality, 61,* 317–342.

Sartre, J.-P. (1973). *No exit.* New York: Vintage Books. (Original work published 1944)

Scott, C. (1992). *Personality versus the situational effect in the relation between marriage and subjective well-being.* Unpublished doctoral dissertation, University of Illinois, Champaign.

Seidlitz, L., & Diener, E. (1993). Memory for positive versus negative life events: Theories for the differences between happy and unhappy persons. *Journal of Personality and Social Psychology, 64,* 654–664.

Seligman, M.E.P. (1991). *Learned optimism.* New York: Random House.

Siegel, J.M., & Kuykendall, D.H. (1990). Loss, widowhood, and psychological distress among the elderly. *Journal of Consulting and Clinical Psychology, 58,* 519–524.

Smith, T.W. (1979). Happiness: Time trends, seasonal variations, intersurvey differences, and other mysteries. *Social Psychology Quarterly, 42,* 18–30.

Solomon, S., Greenberg, J., & Pyszczynski, T. (1991). A terror management theory of social behavior: The psychological functions of self-esteem and cultural world-views. *Advances in Experimental Social Psychology, 24,* 93–159.

Stock, W.A., Okun, M.A., Haring, M.J., & Witter, R.A. (1983). Age and subjective well-being: A meta-analysis. In R.J. Light (Ed.), *Evaluation studies: Review annual* (Vol. 8, pp. 279–302). Beverly Hills, CA: Sage.

Stock, W.A., Okun, M.A., Haring, M.J., & Witter, R.A. (1985). Race and subjective well-being in adulthood. *Human Development, 28,* 192–197.

Stone, A.A., & Neale, J.M. (1984). Effects of severe daily events on mood. *Journal of Personality and Social Psychology, 46,* 137–144.

Strumpel, B. (1976). Economic lifestyles, values, and subjective welfare. In B. Strumpel (Ed.), *Economic means for human needs* (pp. 19–65). Ann Arbor: University of Michigan, Survey Research Center.

Suh, E., Diener, E., & Fujita, F. (in press). Events and subjective well-being: Only recent events matter. *Journal of Personality and Social Psychology.*

Taylor, S.E., & Brown, J.D. (1988). Illusion and well-being: A social psychological perspective on mental health. *Journal of Personality and Social Psychology, 103,* 193–210.

Tellegen, A., Lykken, D.T., Bouchard, T.J., Wilcox, K.J., Segal, N.C., & Rich, S. (1988). Personality similarity in twins reared apart and together. *Journal of Personality and Social Psychology, 54,* 1031–1039.

Terkel, S. (1972). *Working: People talk about what they do all day and how they feel about what they do.* New York: Pantheon Books.

Veenhoven, R. (1988). The utility of happiness. *Social Indicators Research, 20,* 333–354.

Winokur, J. (1987). *The portable curmudgeon.* New York: New American Library.

Witter, R.A., Stock, W.A., Okun, M.A., & Haring, M.J. (1985). Religion and subjective well-being in adulthood: A quantitative synthesis. *Review of Religious Research, 26,* 332–342.

Wood, W., Rhodes, N., & Whelan, M. (1989). Sex differences in positive well-being: A consideration of emotional style and marital status. *Psychological Bulletin, 106,* 249–264.

Wortman, C.B., & Silver, R.C. (1987). Coping with irrevocable loss. In G.R. VandenBos & B.K. Bryant (Eds.), *Cataclysms, crises, and catastrophes: Psychology in action* (pp. 185–235). Washington, DC: American Psychological Association.

(Received 2/1/94; Revision accepted 9/9/94)

Team spirit spills over into real life for fans

Sports enthusiasts' loyalty to their favorite teams can give them a sense of belonging and may even ward off depression.

By Nathan Seppa

Monitor staff

Some sports fans identify so closely with their favorite team that game outcomes can affect their self-esteem and even their testosterone levels, research shows.

And even though some teams rarely win championships—such as baseball's Chicago Cubs—die-hard fans stick with them apparently to maintain a sense of belonging to a group, psychologists believe.

A raft of studies over the past 20 years has probed the ardent sports aficionado—an enigmatic figure ranging from the well-dressed basketball fan at court-side to young hooligans clashing after a soccer game. The psychological thread connecting these fans, studies show, is strong identification with their team and an intense interest in the game at hand.

"This is not some light diversion to be enjoyed for its inherent beauty," said Robert Cialdini, PhD, an Arizona State University psychology professor. "The self is involved."

As early as 1975, Cialdini found that on Monday mornings after a college sports team had won, students in classes wore clothes with the team logo more often than when the team had lost. This is part of what Cialdini came to call "basking in reflected glory," the feeling of well-being a fan gets from identifying strongly with a winning team. Such "highly identified" fans used victories to enhance their own self-image and public image, he found.

But all teams lose, too, and subsequent research has shown how wins and losses can change the outlook of highly identified fans.

In one study, Edward Hirt, PhD, associate professor of psychology at Indiana University, asked college-age fans—some after a win and some after a loss—to look at pictures of persons of the opposite sex and estimate their own chances of going on a date with that person.

Highly identified fans who were flush from watching a victory were quite optimistic about their chances with attractive persons, he found. But in defeat, this optimism was greatly reduced.

Reflected failure

Research by Cialdini in the mid-1980s showed that fans with a low self-concept identified more closely with a team when describing a victory—"we won"—than after a defeat—"they lost."

But Hirt suspected that the effects of a team's loss would not be so easily sloughed off by ardent fans—that they would carry a loss around like baggage. And in his research, they did. Hirt had fans fill out questionnaires before games, to gauge their interest in the game. After a loss, those less caught up in the sport didn't fall as far in the self-esteem "dating" test as the highly identified fans did, Hirt found.

Such fans are often so highly identified with teams that they mimic the players with gestures, said Daniel Wann, PhD, assistant professor of psychology at Murray State University in Murray, Ky. In a win, such fans sometimes even seek to share the credit. When asked to list factors in a victory, some fervid college basketball fans told Wann, "We helped out the team; we cheered really well."

After a loss, average fans cut off any "reflected failure" given off by the team, Wann said. But highly identified fans are the opposite.

"The result is you go down with the ship," he said.

These people are, simply put, more intense about it. "They are more likely to say we lost because of the referees," or some other reason apart from the team itself, Wann said.

Hormones involved

New research indicates that testosterone levels in male fans rise markedly after a win and drop just as sharply after a loss.

Paul Bernhardt, a psychology graduate student at the University of Utah, and James Dabbs, PhD, a psychology professor at Georgia State University, used saliva samples taken from four different groups of sports fans before and after four games. They used the saliva samples to measure the fans' testosterone. In one test, samples were taken from 21 men from the Italian and Brazilian communities of Atlanta before and after they watched on television Brazil's victory over Italy in the 1994 World Cup soccer championship.

The results showed the Brazilians' testosterone rose 28 percent on average; the Italians' average levels dropped 27 percent. The researchers found similar results in men watching college basketball.

Another test, of Psychology 101 students, found that those male fans whose questionnaire responses indicated low self-esteem levels but high interest in basketball also registered the highest testosterone surges after a win, Bernhardt said.

Samples sizes of the four studies ranged from eight to 29 subjects. "The sample sizes were regrettably small, but there were such consistent results across the studies we still feel the results are meaningful," Bernhardt said. "It tells us that fans are vicariously experiencing the competition; it is psychologically similar to the actual competition to such an extent that it's even reflected in their physiology." The study has been submitted for publication in the *Personality and Social Psychology Bulletin*.

Let's go Cubs!

"All things being equal," author and scientist Isaac Asimov once said, "you root for your own sex, your own culture, your own locality. And what you want to prove is that you are better than the other person. Whomever you root for represents you, and when he or she wins, you win."

Cialdini, who began researching the psychology of sports fans in the 1970s, noted that Asimov's remark always leads back to the self. Thus, for highly identified sports fans, attending a game is not like going to the theater, he said.

When the New Orleans Saints football team was losing, some fans appeared at games with paper bags over their heads. "You don't want to be connected [with a losing team]," Cialdini said. "Your public image is involved." When the Saints started winning, the bags came off.

"The self is bolstered or damaged, and the self is at stake [in the] perception of those around you who might associate you with the team," he said. "It hooks into our very primitive conditions of who we are."

This close attachment of the self with a sports team—coupled with the dynamics of crowd behavior—helps to explain fan violence at soccer matches, Cialdini said. "It's because [the fans] are *involved*," he said.

Beyond this interest in the self, however, lies a group phenomenon, Hirt said. Sports fans frequently go to bars or games together. "There is a sense of belonging to a group, an allegiance to the group," he said.

Some psychologists believe this may explain why some fans root for hopeless teams: It may not matter whether they win. The Chicago Cubs last won a championship in 1908, yet Wrigley Field is consistently full.

"The Chicago Cubs are the most salient counter-example to the 'basking in reflected glory' [theory]," Hirt said.

Many fans abandon a team when it starts losing, Wann said. "But highly identified fans—even if the team's struggling—maintain the association with the team," he said. "It's so central to their identity, they can't distance themselves."

Whether it's good to be highly identified with a team is an open question. But Wann and psychologist Nyla Branscombe, PhD, a University of Kansas associate professor, found in a study that such a connection buffers the individual from depression and alienation, while fostering feelings of self-worth and belonging.

The closer these fans live to the team geographically, the more they sense it, Wanna and Branscombe found. Even if the team is losing, they are surrounded by the crowds, the banners, the hype of a team—the sense of belonging.

But when a highly identified fan moves far away from the team, this can change. The fan may require more team success to maintain the bond. "You don't get this sense of belonging," Wann said. "You need the wins."

Social Cognition

Pretend that I have just asked you your position on gun control, the name of your favorite television program, and how many children you plan on having. Now assume that I also ask you to estimate what proportion of the U.S. population holds the same attitude about guns, likes the same program, or plans on having that same number of children. If you are like most people, there is a good chance that your estimates of what the general population thinks on an issue will be influenced by your own opinion. In short, most of us believe that our own attitudes and preferences are relatively common in the population, and that alternate attitudes and preferences are less common. This tendency to see our own preferences as being widely shared by others is referred to as the "false consensus effect."

This phenomenon is just one example of the kinds of topics that fall under the heading of social cognition, a broad area that may loosely be defined as how people think about the social world. That is, the emphasis in this area is on the thought processes people engage in when they think about others. The emphasis in social cognition research, then, is usually on *how* people think, rather than on the *content* of those thoughts. For example, one issue of importance to those who study social cognition is what happens to the information we acquire about other people. How is such information about people stored and organized in memory? How is it accessed and retrieved later on? After retrieval, how is it used to help us understand and interpret the world?

In response to questions such as these, considerable evidence now suggests that information about the self, other individuals, groups, places, and activities is stored in memory in the form of schemas—mental structures that contain information relevant to some concept or stimulus. These schemas are extremely important to us in a number of ways. For example, they influence the way in which we interpret and encode new information; in many instances, we are especially likely to notice and remember new information if it is consistent with information in existing schemas. Schemas also appear to exert an influence on the kinds of judgments we make about other people. Attitudes toward a new acquaintance who is a member of some identifiable group (for example, used car salesmen) can be significantly influenced if our preexisting schema for used car salesmen contains negative information (for example, "sneaky" or "slimy"). Much of the research in social cognition has been devoted, then, to understanding how cognitive structures such as schemas are formed, how they change, and how they affect our thoughts, feelings, and actions.

The four articles included in this unit illustrate the wide variety of issues that have been addressed within this area. The first selection, "Like Goes with Like: The Role of Representativeness in Erroneous and Pseudo-scientific Beliefs," describes how a particular mental shortcut that we all use, known as the representativeness heuristic, can actually lead us to accept incorrect beliefs. Because certain things just seem to us to "go together," we are at risk of ignoring real evidence that they do not. The second selection, "Creating False Memories," considers another kind of cognitive process that can produce inaccurate thinking. Noted psychologist Elizabeth Loftus describes recent research that indicates how easy it is to create false memories in people. Simply by

UNIT 2

having participants imagine that something happened to them in the past, researchers are able to induce these participants to actually believe that the experiences have in fact occurred.

The other two selections address an important issue in contemporary social psychology, the distinction between automatic and controlled mental processes. In "The Process of Explanation," Douglas Krull and Craig Anderson present a general model describing how people produce explanations for the events that they perceive. Some parts of this process occur rather quickly and automatically, while others are more effortful and deliberate. The final selection, "Influences from the Mind's Inner Layers," treats the automatic versus controlled distinction in a different way. Author Beth Azar summarizes recent research that indicates that existing schemas can be activated and influence our later judgments without any conscious awareness at all; in fact, stimuli presented too briefly to be consciously perceived (subliminally) can nevertheless activate cognitive structures and influence our behavior.

Looking Ahead: Challenge Questions

Why does the representativeness heuristic so strongly affect our judgments? Why would such a heuristic even exist? Can you think of any ways to counteract its effects?

How does the automatic/controlled distinction presented in the Douglas Krull and Craig Anderson model compare with the automatic/controlled distinction described by Beth Azar? Are the authors talking about the same thing? If not, how are they different?

Like Goes with Like:
The Role of Representativeness in Erroneous and Pseudoscientific Beliefs

The misguided premise that effects should resemble their causes underlies a host of erroneous beliefs, from folk wisdom about health and the human body to elaborate pseudoscientific belief systems.

THOMAS GILOVICH and KENNETH SAVITSKY

It was in 1983, at an infectious-disease conference in Brussells, that Barry Marshall, an internal-medicine resident from Perth, Australia, first staked his startling claim. He argued that the peptic ulcer, a painful crater in the lining of the stomach or duodenum, was not caused by a stressful lifestyle as everyone had thought. Instead, the malady that afflicts millions of adults in the United States alone was caused by a simple bacterium, and thus could be cured using antibiotics (Hunter 1993; Monmaney 1993; Peterson 1991; Wandycz 1993).

Although subsequent investigations have substantiated Marshall's claim (e.g., Hentschel et al. 1993), his colleagues initially were highly skeptical. Martin Blaser, director of the Division of Infectious Diseases at the Vanderbilt University School of Medicine, described Marshall's thesis as "the most preposterous thing I'd ever heard" (Monmaney 1993).

What made the idea so preposterous? Why were the experts so resistant to Marshall's suggestion? There were undoubtedly many reasons. For one, the claim contradicted what most physicians, psychiatrists, and psychologists knew (or thought they knew): Ulcers were caused by stress. As one author noted, "No physical ailment has ever been more closely tied to psychological turbulence" (Monmaney 1993, p. 64). In addition, science is necessarily and appropriately a rather conservative enterprise. Although insight, creativity, and even leaps of faith are vital to the endeavor, sound empirical evidence is the true coin of the realm. Much of the medical establishment's hesitation doubtless stemmed from the same healthy skepticism that readers of the SKEPTICAL INQUIRER have learned to treasure. After all, Marshall's results at the time were suggestive at best—no cause-effect relationship had yet been established.

But there may have been a third reason for the reluctance to embrace Marshall's contention, a reason we explore in this article. The belief that ulcers derive from stress is particularly seductive—for physicians and laypersons alike—because it flows from a general tendency of human judgment, a tendency to employ what psychologists Amos Tversky and Daniel Kahneman have called the "representativeness heuristic" (Kahneman and Tversky 1972, 1973; Tversky and Kahneman 1974, 1982). Indeed, we believe that judgment by representativeness plays a role in a host of erroneous beliefs, from beliefs about health and the human body to handwriting analysis and astrology (Gilovich 1991). We consider a sample of these beliefs in this article.

The Representativeness Heuristic

Representativeness is but one of a number of heuristics that people use to render complex problems manageable. Heuristics are often described as judgmental shortcuts that generally get us where we need to go—and quickly— but at the cost of occasionally sending us off course. Kahneman and Tversky liken them to perceptual cues, which generally enable

Brad Marshall

Thomas Gilovich, professor of psychology at Cornell University and a Fellow of CSICOP, is the author of How We Know What Isn't So: The Fallibility of Human Reason in Everyday Life. *Kenneth Savitsky is a doctoral student in social psychology at Cornell University.*

us to perceive the world accurately, but occasionally give rise to misperception and illusion. Consider their example of using clarity as a cue for distance. The clarity of an object is one cue people use to decide how far away it is. The cue typically works well because the farther away something is, the less distinct it appears. On a particularly clear day, however, objects can appear closer than they are, and on hazy days they can appear farther away. In some circumstances, then, this normally accurate cue can lead to error.

Representativeness works much the same way. The representativeness heuristic involves a reflexive tendency to assess the similarity of objects and events along salient dimensions and to organize them on the basis of one overarching rule: "Like goes with like." Among other things, the representativeness heuristic reflects the belief that a member of a given category ought to resemble the category prototype, and that an effect ought to resemble the cause that produced it. Thus, the representativeness heuristic is often used to assess whether a given instance belongs to a particular category, such as whether an individual is likely to be an accountant or a comedian. It is also used in assigning causes to effects, as when deciding whether a meal of spicy food caused a case of heartburn or determining whether an assassination was the product of a conspiracy.[1]

Note that judgment by representativeness often works well. Instances often resemble their category prototypes and causes frequently resemble their effects. Members of various occupational groups, for example, frequently do resemble the group prototype. Likewise, "big" effects (such as the development of the atomic bomb) are often brought about by "big" causes (such as the Manhattan Project).

Still, the representativeness heuristic is only that—a heuristic or shortcut. As with all shortcuts, the representativeness heuristic should be used with caution. Although it can help us to make some judgments with accuracy and ease, it can also lead us astray. Not all members fit the category prototype. Some comedians are shy or taciturn, and some accountants are wild and crazy. And although causes are frequently representative of their effects, this relationship does not always hold: Tiny viruses give rise to devastating epidemics like malaria or AIDS; and splitting the nucleus of an atom releases an awesome amount of energy. In some cases, then, representativeness yields inaccuracy and error. Or even superstition. A nice example is provided by craps shooters, who roll the dice gently to coax a low number, and more vigorously to encourage a high one (Hanslin 1967). A small effect (low number) requires a small cause (gentle roll), and a big effect (high number) requires a big cause (vigorous roll).

How might the belief in a stress-ulcer link derive from the conviction that like goes with like? Because the burning feeling of an ulcerated stomach is not unlike the gut-wrenching, stomach-churning feeling of extreme stress (albeit more severe), the link seems natural: Stress is a representative cause of an ulcer.[2] But as Marshall suggested (and subsequent research has borne out), the link may be overblown. Stress alone does not appear to cause ulcers (Glavin and Szabo 1992; Soll 1990).

Representativeness and the Conjunction Fallacy

One of the most compelling demonstrations of how the representativeness heuristic can interfere with sound judgment comes from a much-discussed experiment in which participants were asked to consider the following description (Tversky and Kahneman 1982, 1983):

> Linda is 31 years old, single, outspoken, and very bright. She majored in philosophy. As a student, she was deeply concerned with issues of discrimination and social justice, and also participated in anti-nuclear demonstrations.
> Now, based on the above description, rank the following statements about Linda, from most to least likely:
> a. Linda is an insurance salesperson.
> b. Linda is a bank teller.
> c. Linda is a bank teller and is active in the feminist movement.

If you are like most people, you probably thought it was more likely that "Linda is a bank teller and is active in the feminist movement" than that "Linda is a bank teller." It is easy to see why: A feminist bank teller is much more representative of the description of Linda than is "just" a bank teller. It reflects the political activism, social-consciousness, and left-of-center politics implied in the description.

It may make sense, but it cannot be. The category "bank teller" subsumes the category "is a bank teller and is active in the feminist movement." The latter therefore cannot be more likely than the former. Anyone who is a bank teller and is active in the feminist movement is automatically also a bank teller. Indeed, even if one thinks it is impossible for someone with Linda's description to be solely a bank teller (that is, one who is not a feminist), being a bank teller is still *as* likely as being both. This error is referred to as the "conjunction fallacy" because the probability of two events co-occurring (i.e., their conjunction) can never exceed the individual probability of either of the constituents (Tversky and Kahneman 1982, 1983; Dawes and Mulford 1993).

> "Heuristics are often described as judgmental shortcuts that generally get us where we need to go—and quickly—but at the cost of occasionally sending us off course."

Such is the logic of the situation. The psychology we bring to bear on it is something else. If we start with an unrepresentative outcome (being a bank teller) and then add a representative element (being active in the feminist movement), we create a description that is at once more psychologically compelling but objectively less likely. The rules of representativeness do not follow the laws of probability. A detailed description can seem compelling precisely because of the very details that, objectively speaking, actually make it less likely. Thus, someone may be less concerned about dying during a trip to the Middle East than about dying in a terrorist attack while there, even though the probability of death due to a *particular* cause is obviously lower than the probability of death due to the set of all possible causes. Likewise, the probability of global economic collapse can seem remote until one sketches a detailed scenario in which such a collapse follows, say, the destruction of the oil fields in the Persian Gulf. Once again, the additional details make the outcome less likely at the same time that they make it more psychologically compelling.

Representativeness and Causal Judgments

Most of the empirical research on the representativeness heuristic is similar to the work on the conjunction fallacy in that the judgments people make are compared to a normative standard—in this case, to the laws of probability. The deleterious effect of judgment by representativeness is thereby established by the failure to meet such a standard. Previous work conducted in this fashion has shown, for example, that judgment by representativeness leads people to commit the "gambler's fallacy," to overestimate the reliability of small samples of data, and to be insufficiently "regressive" in making predictions under conditions of uncertainty.

The ulcer example with which we began this article does not have this property of being obviously at variance with a clear-cut normative standard. The same is true of nearly all examples of the impact of representativeness on causal judgments: It can be difficult to establish with certainty that a judgmental error has been made. Partly for this reason, there has been less empirical research on representativeness and causal judgments than on other areas, such as representativeness and the conjunction fallacy. This is not because representativeness is thought to have little impact on causal judgments, but because without a clear-cut normative standard it is simply more difficult to conduct research in this domain. The research that has been conducted, furthermore, is more suggestive than definitive. Nonetheless, the suggestive evidence is rather striking, and it points to the possibility that representativeness may exert at least as much influence over causal judgments as it does over other, more exhaustively researched types of judgments. To see how much, we discuss some examples of representativeness-thinking in medicine, in pseudoscientific systems, and in psychoanalysis.

Representativeness and Medical Beliefs

One area in which the impact of representativeness on causal judgments is particularly striking is the domain of health and medicine. Historically, people have often assumed that the symptoms of a disease should resemble either its cause or its cure (or both). In ancient Chinese medicine, for example, people with vision problems were fed ground bat in the mistaken belief that bats had particularly keen vision and that some of this ability might be transferred to the recipient (Deutsch 1977). Evans-Pritchard (1937) noted many examples of the influence of representativeness among the African Azande (although he discussed them in the context of magical-thinking, not representativeness). For instance, the Azande used the ground skull of the red bush monkey to cure epilepsy. Why? The cure should resemble the disease, so the herky-jerky movements of the monkey make the essence of monkey appear to be a promising candidate to settle the violent movements of an epileptic seizure. As Evans-Pritchard (quoted in Nisbett and Ross 1980, p. 116) put it:

> Generally the logic of therapeutic treatment consists in the selection of the most prominent external symptoms, the naming of the disease after some object in nature it resembles, and the utilization of the object as the principal ingredient in the drug administered to cure the disease. The circle may even be completed by belief that the external symptoms not only yield to treatment by the object which resembles them but are caused by it as well.

Western medical practice has likewise been guided by the representativeness heuristic. For instance, early Western medicine was strongly influenced by what was known as the "doctrine of signatures," or the belief that "every natural substance which possesses any medicinal virtue indicates by an obvious and well-marked external character the disease for which it is a remedy, or the object for which it should be employed" (quoted in Nisbett and Ross 1980, p. 116). Thus, physicians prescribed the lungs of the fox (known for its endurance) for asthmatics, and the yellow spice turmeric for jaundice. Again, disease and cure are linked because they resemble one another.

Or consider the popularity of homeopathy, which derives from the eighteenth century work of the German physician Samuel Hahnemann (Barrett 1987). One of the bedrock principles of homeopathy is Hahnemann's "law of similars," according to which the key to discovering what substance will cure a particular disorder lies in noting the effect that various substances have on healthy people. If a substance causes a particular reaction in an unafflicted person, then it is seen as a likely cure for a disease characterized by those same symptoms. As before, the external symptoms of a disease are used to identify a cure for the disease—a cure that manifests the same external characteristics.

Of course, there are instances in which substances that cause particular symptoms *are* used effectively as part of a therapeutic regimen to cure, alleviate, or prevent those very symptoms. Vaccines deliver small quantities of disease-causing viruses to help individuals develop immunities. Likewise, allergy sufferers sometimes receive periodic doses of the exact substance to which they are allergic so that they will develop a tolerance over time. The problem with the dubious medical practices described above is the *general* assumption that the symptoms of a disease should resemble its cause, its cure, or both. Limiting the scope of possible cures to those that are representative of the disease can seriously impede scientific discovery. Such a narrow focus, for example, would have

> "In ancient Chinese medicine, for example, people with vision problems were fed ground bat in the mistaken belief that bats had particularly keen vision and that some of this ability might be transferred to the recipient."

inhibited the discovery of the two most significant developments of modern medicine: sanitation and antibiotics.

Representativeness-thinking continues to abound in modern "alternative" medicine, a pursuit that appears to be gaining in perceived legitimacy (Cowley, King, Hager, and Rosenberg 1995). An investigation by Congress into health fraud and quackery noted several examples of what appear to be interventions inspired by the superficial appeal of representativeness (U.S. Congress, House Subcommittee on Health and Long-Term Care 1984). In one set of suggested treatments, patients are encouraged to eat raw organ concentrates corresponding to the dysfunctional body part: e.g., brain concentrates for mental disorders, heart concentrates for cardiac conditions, and raw stomach lining for ulcers. Similarly, the fingerprints of representativeness are all over the practice of "rebirthing," a New Age therapeutic technique in which individuals attempt to reenact their own births in an effort to correct personality defects caused by having been born in an "unnatural" fashion (Ward 1994). One person who was born breech (i.e., feet first) underwent the rebirthing procedure to cure his sense that his life was always going in the wrong direction and that he could never seem to get things "the right way round." Another, born Caesarean, sought the treatment because of a lifelong difficulty with seeing things to completion, and always relying on others to finish tasks for her. As one author quipped, "God knows what damage forceps might inflict . . . a lifelong neurosis that you're being dragged where you don't want to go?" (Ward 1994, p. 90).

A more rigorous examination of the kind of erroneous beliefs about health and the human body that can arise from the appeal of representativeness has dealt with the adage, "You are what you eat." Just how far do people take this idea? In certain respects, the saying is undeniably true: Bodies are composed to a large extent of the molecules that were once ingested as food. Quite literally, we are what we have eaten. Indeed, there are times when we take on the character of what we ingest: People gain weight by eating fatty foods, and a person's skin can acquire an orange tint from the carotene found in carrots and tomatoes. But the notion that we develop the characteristics of the food we eat sometimes goes beyond such examples to almost magical extremes. The Hua of Papua New Guinea, for example, believe that individuals will grow quickly if they eat rapidly growing food (Meigs 1984, cited by Nemeroff and Rozin 1989).

But what about a more "scientifically minded" population? Psychologists Carol Nemeroff and Paul Rozin (1989) asked college students to consider a hypothetical culture known as the "Chandorans," who hunt wild boar and marine turtles. Some of the students learned that the Chandorans hunt turtles for their shells, and wild boar for their meat. The others heard the opposite: The tribe hunts turtles for their meat, and boar for their tusks.

After reading one of the two descriptions of the

"The representativeness heuristic should be used with caution. Although it can help us to make some judgments with accuracy and ease, it can also lead us astray."

Chandorans, the students were asked to rate the tribe members on numerous characteristics. Their responses reflected a belief that the characteristics of the food that was eaten would "rub off" onto the tribe members. Boar-eaters were thought to be more aggressive and irritable than their counterparts—and more likely to have beards! The turtle-eaters were thought to live longer and be better swimmers.

However educated a person may be (the participants in Nemeroff and Rozin's experiment were University of Pennsylvania undergraduates), it can be difficult to get beyond the assumption that like goes with like. In this case, it leads to the belief that individuals tend to acquire the attributes of the food they ingest. Simple representativeness.

Representativeness and Pseudoscientific Beliefs

A core tenet of the field of astrology is that an individual's personality is influenced by the astrological sign under which he or she was born (Huntley 1990). A glance at the personality types associated with the various astrological signs reveals an uncanny concordance between the supposed personality of someone with a particular sign and the characteristics associated with the sign's namesake (Huntley 1990; Howe 1970; Zusne and Jones 1982). Those born under the sign of the goat (Capricorn) are said to be tenacious, hardworking, and stubborn; whereas those born under the lion (Leo) are proud, forceful leaders. Likewise, those born under the sign of Cancer (the crab) share with their namesake a tendency to appear hard on the outside; while inside their "shells" they are soft and vulnerable. One treatment of astrology goes so far as to suggest that, like the crab, those born under the sign of Cancer tend to be "deeply attached to their homes" (Read et al. 1978).

What is the origin of these associations? They are not empirically derived, as they have been shown time and time again to lack validity (e.g., Carlson 1985; Dean 1987; for reviews see Abell 1981; Schick and Vaughn 1995; Zusne and Jones 1982). Instead, they are conceptually driven by simple, representativeness-based assessments of the personalities that *should* be associated with various astrological signs. After all, who is more likely to be retiring and modest than a Virgo (the virgin)? Who better to be well balanced, harmonious, and fair than a Libra (the scales)? By taking advantage of people's reflexive associations, the system gains plausibility among those disinclined to dig deeper.

And it doesn't stop there. Consider another elaborate "scientific" system designed to assess the "secrets" of an individual's personality—graphology, or handwriting analysis. Corporations pay graphologists sizable fees to help screen job applicants by developing personality profiles of those who apply for jobs (Neter and Ben-Shakhar 1989). Graphologists are also called upon to provide "expert" testimony in trial proceedings, and to help the Secret Service determine if any real danger is posed by threatening letters to government officials (Scanlon and Mauro 1992). How much stock can we put in the work of handwriting analysts?

Unlike astrology, graphology is not worthless. It has been, and continues to be, the subject of careful empirical investigation (Nevo 1986), and it has been shown that people's handwriting can reveal certain things about them. Particularly shaky writing can be a clue that an individual suffers from some neurological disorder that causes hand tremors; whether a person is male or female is often apparent from his or her writing. In general, however, what handwriting analysis can determine most reliably tends to be things that can be more reliably ascertained through other means. As for the "secrets" of an individual's personality, graphology has yet to show that it is any better than astrology.

This has not done much to diminish the popularity of handwriting analysis, however. One reason for this is that graphologists, like astrologers, gain some surface plausibility or "face validity" for their claims by exploiting the tendency for people to employ the representativeness heuristic. Many of their claims have a superficial "sensible" quality, rarely violating the principle that like goes with like. Consider, for instance, the "zonal theory" of graphology, which divides a person's handwriting into the upper, middle, and lower regions. A person's "intellectual," "practical," and "instinctual" qualities supposedly correspond to the different regions (Basil 1989). Can you guess which is which? Could our "lower" instincts be reflected anywhere other than the lower region, or our "higher" intellect anywhere other than the top?

The list of such representativeness-based "connections" goes on and on. Handwriting slants to the left? The person must be holding something back, repressing his or her true emotions. Slants to the right? The person gets carried away by his or her feelings. A signature placed far below a paragraph suggests that the individual wishes to distance himself or herself from what was written (Scanlon and Mauro 1992). Handwriting that stays close to the left margin belongs to individuals attached to the past, whereas writing that hugs the right margin comes from those oriented toward the future.

What is ironic is that the very mechanism that many graphologists rely upon to argue for the persuasive value of their endeavor—that the character of the handwriting resembles the character of the person—is what ultimately betrays them: They call it "common sense"; we call it judgment by representativeness.

Representativeness and Psychoanalysis

Two prominent social psychologists, Richard Nisbett and Lee Ross, have argued that "the enormous popularity of Freudian theory probably lies in the fact that, unlike all its competitors among contemporary views, it encourages the layperson to do what comes naturally in causal explanation, that is, to use the representativeness heuristic" (Nisbett and Ross 1980, p. 244). Although this claim would be difficult to put to empirical test, there can be little doubt that much of the interpretation of symbols that lies at the core of psychoanalytic theory is driven by representativeness. Consider the interpretation of dreams, in which the images a client reports from his or her dreams are considered indicative of underlying motives. An infinite number of potential relationships exist between dream content and underlying psychodynamics, and it is interesting that virtually all of the "meaningful" ones identified by psychodynamically oriented clinicians are ones in which there is an obvious fit or resemblance between the reported image and inner dynamics. A man who dreams of a snake or a cigar is thought to be troubled by his penis or his sexuality. People who dream of policemen are thought to be concerned about their fathers or authority figures. Knowledge of the representativeness heuristic compels one to wonder whether such connections reflect something important about the psyche of the client, or whether they exist primarily in the mind of the therapist.

One area of psychodynamic theorizing in which the validity of such superficially plausible relationships has been tested and found wanting is the use of projective tests. The most widely known projective test is the Rorschach, in which clients report what they "see" in ambiguous blotches of ink on cards. As in all projective tests, the idea is that in responding to such an unstructured stimulus, a person must "project," and thus reveal, some of his or her inner dynamics. Countless studies, however, have failed to produce evidence that the test is valid—that is, that the assessments made about people on the basis of the test correspond to the psychopathological conditions from which they suffer (Burros 1978).[3]

The research findings notwithstanding, clinicians frequently report the Rorschach to be extremely helpful in clinical practice. Might representativeness contribute to this paradox of strongly held beliefs coexisting with the absence of any real relationship? You be the judge. A person who interprets the whole Rorschach card, and not its specific details, is con-

> "Although skepticism is a vital component of critical thought, it should not be based on an excessive adherence to the principle that like goes with like."

sidered by clinicians to suffer from a need to form a "big picture," and a tendency toward grandiosity, even paranoia. In contrast, a person who refers only to small details of the ink blots is considered to have an obsessive personality—someone who attends to detail at the expense of the more important holistic aspects (Dawes 1994). Once again, systematic research has failed to find evidence for these relationships, but the sense of representativeness gives them some superficial plausibility.

Conclusion

We have described numerous erroneous beliefs that appear to derive from the overuse of the representativeness heuristic. Many of them arise in domains in which the reach for solutions to important problems exceeds our grasp—such as the attempt to uncover (via astrology or handwriting analysis) simple cues to the complexities of human motivation and personality. In such domains in which no simple solutions exist, and yet the need or desire for such solutions remains strong, people often let down their guard. Dubious cause-effect links are then uncritically accepted because they satisfy the principle of like goes with like.

Representativeness can also have the opposite effect, inhibiting belief in valid claims that violate the expectation of resemblance. People initially scoffed at Walter Reed's suggestion that malaria was carried by the mosquito. From a representativeness standpoint, it is easy to see why: The cause (a tiny mosquito) is not at all representative of the result (a devastating disease). Reed's claim violated the notion that big effects should have big causes, and thus was difficult to accept (Nisbett and Ross 1980). Although skepticism is a vital component of critical thought, it should not be based on an excessive adherence to the principle that like goes with like.

Indeed, it is often those discoveries that violate the expected resemblance between cause and effect that are ultimately hailed as significant breakthroughs, as with the discovery of *Helicobacter pylori,* as the ulcer-causing bacterium is now named. As one author put it, "The discovery of *Helicobacter* is no crummy little shift. It's a mindblower—tangible, reproducible, unexpected, and, yes, revolutionary. Just the fact that a bug causes peptic ulcers, long considered the cardinal example of a psychosomatic illness, is a spear in the breast of New Age medicine" (Monmaney 1993, p. 68). Given these stakes, one might be advised to avoid an overreliance on the shortcut of representativeness, and instead to devote the extra effort needed to make accurate judgments and decisions. (But not too much effort—you wouldn't want to give yourself an ulcer.)

Notes

We thank Dennis Regan for his helpful comments on an earlier draft of this article.

1. The reason that the heuristic has been dubbed "representativeness" rather than, say, "resemblance" or "similarity" is that it also applies in circumstances in which the assessment of "fit" is not based on similarity. For example, when assessing whether a series of coin flips was produced by tossing a fair coin, people's judgments are influenced in part by whether the sequence is representative of one produced by a fair coin. A sequence of five heads and five tails is a representative outcome, but a sequence of nine heads and one tail is not. Note, however, that a fifty-fifty split does not make the sequence "similar" to a fair coin, but it does make it representative of one.

2. Some theories of the link between stress and ulcers are even more tinged with representativeness. Since the symptoms of an ulcer manifest themselves in the stomach, the cause "should" involve something that is highly characteristic of the stomach as well, such as hunger and nourishment. Thus, one theorist asserts, "The critical factor in the development of ulcers is the frustration associated with the wish to receive love—when this wish is rejected, it is converted into a wish to be fed," leading ultimately "to an ulcer." Echoing such ideas, James Masterson writes in his book *The Search for the Real Self* that ulcers affect those who are "hungering for emotional supplies that were lost in childhood or that were never sufficient to nourish the real self" (both quoted in Monmaney 1993).

3. Actually, a nonprojective use of the Rorschach, called the Exner System, has been shown to have some validity (Exner 1986). The system is based on the fact that some of the inkblots *do* look like various objects, and a person's responses are scored for the number and proportion that fail to reflect this correspondence. Unlike the usual Rorschach procedure, which is subjectively scored, the Exner system is a standardized test.

References

Abell, G. O. 1981. Astrology. In *Science and the Paranormal: Probing the Existence of the Supernatural,* ed. by G. O. Abell and B. Singer. New York: Charles Scribner's Sons.

Barrett, S. 1987. Homeopathy: Is it medicine? SKEPTICAL INQUIRER 12(1) (Fall): 56-62.

Basil, R. 1989. Graphology and personality: Let the buyer beware. SKEPTICAL INQUIRER 13 (3) (Spring): 241-243.

Burros, O. K. 1978. *Mental Measurement Yearbook.* 8th ed. Highland Park, N.J.: Gryphon Press.

Carlson, S. 1985. A double-blind test of astrology. *Nature* 318: 419-425.

Cowley, G., P. King, M. Hager, and D. Rosenberg. 1995. Going mainstream. *Newsweek* June 26: 56-57.

Dawes, R. M. 1994. *House of Cards: Psychology and Psychotherapy Built on Myth.* New York: Free Press.

Dawes, R. M., and M. Mulford. 1993. Diagnoses of alien kidnappings that result from conjunction effects in memory. SKEPTICAL INQUIRER 18(1) (Fall): 50-51.

Dean, G. 1987. Does astrology need to be true? Part 2: The answer is no. SKEPTICAL INQUIRER 11(3) (Spring): 257-273.

Deutsch, R.M. 1977. *The New Nuts among the Berries: How Nutrition Nonsense Captured America.* Palo Alto, Calif.: Ball Publishing.

Evans-Pritchard, E. E. 1937. *Witchcraft, Oracles and Magic among the Azande.* Oxford: Clarendon.

Exner, J. E. 1986. *The Rorschach: A Comprehensive System.* 2d ed. New York: John Wiley.

Gilovich, T. 1991. *How We Know What Isn't So: The Fallibility of Human Reason in Everyday Life.* New York: The Free Press.

Glavin, G. B., and S. Szabo. 1992. Experimental gastric mucosal injury: Laboratory models reveal mechanisms of pathogenesis and new therapeutic strategies. *FASEB Journal* 6: 825-831.

Hanslin, J. M. 1967. Craps and magic. *American Journal of Sociology* 73: 316-330.

Hentschel, E., G. Brandstatter, B. Dragosics, A. M. Hirschel, H. Nemec, K. Schutze, M. Taufer, and H. Wurzer. 1993. Effect of ranitidine and amoxicillin plus metronidazole on the eradication of Helicobacter pylori and the recurrence of duodenal ulcer. *New England Journal of Medicine* 328: 308-312.

Howe, E. 1970. Astrology. In *Man, Myth, and Magic: An Illustrated Encyclopedia of the Supernatural,* ed. by R. Cavendish. New York: Marshall Cavendish.

Hunter, B. T. 1993. Good news for gastric sufferers. *Consumer's Research* 76 (October): 8-9.

Huntley, J. 1990. *The Elements of Astrology.* Shaftesbury, Dorset, Great Britain: Element Books.

Kahneman, D., and A. Tversky. 1972. Subjective probability: A judgment of representativeness. *Cognitive Psychology* 3: 430-454.

Kahneman, D., and A. Tversky. 1973. On the psychology of prediction. *Psychological Review* 80: 237-251.

Meigs, A.S. 1984. *Food, Sex, and Pollution: A New Guinea Religion.* New Brunswick, N.J.: Rutgers University Press.

Monmaney, T. 1993. Marshall's hunch. *The New Yorker* 69 (September 20): 64-72.

Nemeroff, C., and P. Rozin. 1989. 'You are what you eat': Applying the demand-free 'impressions' technique to an unacknowledged belief. *Ethos* 17: 50-69.

Neter, E., and G. Ben-Shakhar. 1989. The predictive validity of graphological inferences: A meta-analytic approach. *Personality and Individual Differences* (10) 737-745.

Nevo, B. 1986. ed. *Scientific Aspects of Graphology: A Handbook.* Springfield, Ill.: Charles C. Thomas.

Nisbett, R., and L. Ross. 1980. *Human Inference: Strategies and Shortcomings of Social Judgment.* Englewood Cliffs, N.J.: Prentice-Hall.

Peterson, W. L. 1991. Helicobacter pylori and peptic ulcer disease. *New England Journal of Medicine* 324: 1043-1048.

Read, A. W. et al. eds. 1978. *Funk and Wagnall's New Comprehensive International Dictionary of the English Language.* New York: Publishers Guild Press.

Scanlon, M., and J. Mauro. 1992. The lowdown on handwriting analysis: Is it for real? *Psychology Today* (November/December): 46-53; 80.

Schick, T., and L. Vaughn. 1995. *How to Think about Weird Things: Critical Thinking for a New Age.* Mountain View, Calif.: Mayfield Publishing Company.

Soll, A. H. 1990. Pathogenesis of peptic ulcer and implications for therapy. *New England Journal of Medicine* 322: 909-916.

Tversky, A., and D. Kahneman. 1974. Judgment under uncertainty: Heuristics and biases. *Science* 185: 1124-1131.

Tversky, A., and D. Kahneman. 1982. Judgments of and by representativeness. In *Judgment under Uncertainty: Heuristics and Biases,* ed. by D. Kahneman, P. Slovic, and A. Tversky. Cambridge: Cambridge University Press.

Tversky, A., and D. Kahneman. 1983. Extensional versus intuitive reasoning: The conjunction fallacy in probability judgment. *Psychological Review* 90: 293-315.

U.S. Congress. 1984. *Quackery: A $10 Billion Scandal: A Report by the Chairman of the (House) Subcommittee on Health and Long-Term Care.* Washington, D.C.: United States Government Printing Office.

Wandycz, K. 1993. The H. pylori factor. *Forbes* 152 (August 2): 128.

Ward, R. 1994. Maternity ward. *Mirabella* (February): 89-90.

Zusne, L. and W. H. Jones 1982. *Anomalistic Psychology.* Hillsdale, N.J.: Lawrence Erlbaum Associates.

Creating False Memories

Researchers are showing how suggestion and imagination can create "memories" of events that did not actually occur

by Elizabeth F. Loftus

In 1986 Nadean Cool, a nurse's aide in Wisconsin, sought therapy from a psychiatrist to help her cope with her reaction to a traumatic event experienced by her daughter. During therapy, the psychiatrist used hypnosis and other suggestive techniques to dig out buried memories of abuse that Cool herself had allegedly experienced. In the process, Cool became convinced that she had repressed memories of having been in a satanic cult, of eating babies, of being raped, of having sex with animals and of being forced to watch the murder of her eight-year-old friend. She came to believe that she had more than 120 personalities—children, adults, angels and even a duck—all because, Cool was told, she had experienced severe childhood sexual and physical abuse. The psychiatrist also performed exorcisms on her, one of which lasted for five hours and included the sprinkling of holy water and screams for Satan to leave Cool's body.

When Cool finally realized that false memories had been planted, she sued the psychiatrist for malpractice. In March 1997, after five weeks of trial, her case was settled out of court for $2.4 million.

Nadean Cool is not the only patient to develop false memories as a result of questionable therapy. In Missouri in 1992 a church counselor helped Beth Rutherford to remember during therapy that her father, a clergyman, had regularly raped her between the ages of seven and 14 and that her mother sometimes helped him by holding her down. Under her therapist's guidance, Rutherford developed memories of her father twice impregnating her and forcing her to abort the fetus herself with a coat hanger. The father had to resign from his post as a clergyman when the allegations were made public. Later medical examination of the daughter revealed, however, that she was still a virgin at 22 and had never been pregnant. The daughter sued the therapist and received a $1-million settlement in 1996.

About a year earlier two juries returned verdicts against a Minnesota psychiatrist accused of planting false memories by former patients Vynnette Hamanne and Elizabeth Carlson, who under hypnosis and sodium amytal, and after being fed misinformation about the workings of memory, had come to remember horrific abuse by family members. The juries awarded Hammane $2.67 million and Carlson $2.5 million for their ordeals.

In all four cases, the women developed memories about childhood abuse in therapy and then later denied their authenticity. How can we determine if memories of childhood abuse are true or false? Without corroboration, it is very difficult to differentiate between false memories and true ones. Also, in these cases, some memories were contrary to physical evidence, such as explicit and detailed recollections of rape and abortion when medical examination confirmed virginity. How is it possible for people to acquire elaborate and confident false memories? A growing number of investigations demonstrate that under the right circumstances false memories can be instilled rather easily in some people.

My own research into memory distortion goes back to the early 1970s, when I began studies of the "misinformation effect." These studies show that when people who witness an event are later exposed to new and misleading information about it, their recollections often become distorted. In one example, participants viewed a simulated automobile accident at an intersection with a stop sign. After the viewing, half the participants received a suggestion that the traffic sign was a yield sign. When asked later what traffic sign they remembered seeing at the intersection, those who had been given the suggestion tended to claim that they had seen a yield sign. Those who had not received the phony information were much more accurate in their recollection of the traffic sign.

My students and I have now conducted more than 200 experiments involving over 20,000 individuals that document how exposure to misinformation induces memory distortion. In these studies, people "recalled" a conspicuous barn in a bucolic scene that contained no buildings at all, broken glass and tape recorders that were not in the scenes they viewed, a white instead of a blue vehicle in a crime scene, and Minnie Mouse when they actually saw Mickey Mouse. Taken together, these studies show that misinformation can change an individual's recollection in predictable and sometimes very powerful ways.

Misinformation has the potential for invading our memories when we talk to other people, when we are suggestively interrogated or when we read or view media coverage about some event that we may have experienced ourselves. After more than two decades of exploring the power of misinformation, researchers have learned a great deal about the conditions that make people susceptible to memory modification. Memories are more easily modified, for instance, when the passage of time allows the original memory to fade.

False Childhood Memories

It is one thing to change a detail or two in an otherwise intact memory but quite another to plant a false memory of an event that never happened. To study false memory, my students and I first had to find a way to plant a pseudomemory that would not cause our subjects undue emotional stress, either in the process of creating the false memory or when we revealed that they had been intentionally deceived. Yet we wanted to try to plant a memory that would be at least mildly traumatic, had the experience actually happened.

My research associate, Jacqueline E. Pickrell, and I settled on trying to plant a specific memory of being lost in a shopping mall or large department store at about the age of five. Here's how we did it. We asked our subjects, 24 individuals ranging in age from 18 to 53, to try to remember childhood events that had been recounted to us by a parent, an older sibling or another close relative. We prepared a booklet for each participant containing one-paragraph stories about three events that had actually happened to him or her and one that had not. We constructed the false event using information about a plausible shopping trip provided by a relative, who also verified that the participant had not in fact been lost at about the age of five. The lost-in-the-mall scenario included the following elements: lost for an extended period, crying, aid and comfort by an elderly woman and, finally, reunion with the family.

After reading each story in the booklet, the participants wrote what they remembered about the event. If they did not remember it, they were instructed to write, "I do not remember this." In two follow-up interviews, we told the participants that we were interested in examining how much detail they could remember and how their memories compared with those of their relative. The event paragraphs were not read to them verbatim, but rather parts were provided as retrieval cues. The participants recalled something about 49 of the 72 true events (68 percent) immediately after the initial reading of the booklet and also in each of the two follow-up interviews. After reading the booklet, seven of the 24 participants (29 percent) remembered either partially or fully the false event constructed for them, and in the two follow-up interviews six participants (25 percent) continued to claim that they remembered the fictitious event. Statistically, there were some differences between the true memories and the false ones: participants used more words to describe the true memories, and they rated the true memories as being somewhat more clear. But if an onlooker were to observe many of our participants describe an event, it would be difficult indeed to tell whether the account was of a true or a false memory.

Of course, being lost, however frightening, is not the same as being abused. But the lost-in-the-mall study is not about real experiences of being lost; it is about planting false memories of being lost. The paradigm shows a way of instilling false memories and takes a step toward allowing us to understand how this might happen in real-world settings. Moreover, the study provides evidence that people can be led to remember their past in different ways, and they can even be coaxed into "remembering" entire events that never happened.

Studies in other laboratories using a similar experimental procedure have produced similar results. For instance, Ira Hyman, Troy H. Husband and F. James Billing of Western Washington University asked college students to recall childhood experiences that had been recounted by their parents. The researchers told the students that the study was about how people remember shared experiences differently. In addition to actual events reported by parents, each participant was given one false event—either an overnight hospitalization for a high fever and a possible ear infection, or a birthday party with pizza and a clown—that supposedly happened at about the age of five. The parents confirmed that neither of these events actually took place.

Hyman found that students fully or partially recalled 84 percent of the true events in the first interview and 88 percent in the second interview. None of the participants recalled the false event during the first interview, but 20 percent said they remembered something about the false event in the second interview. One participant who had been exposed to the emergency hospitalization story later remembered a male doctor, a female nurse and a friend from church who came to visit at the hospital.

In another study, along with true events Hyman presented different false events, such as accidentally spilling a bowl of punch on the parents of the bride at a wedding reception or having to evacuate a grocery store when the overhead sprinkler systems erroneously activated. Again, none of the participants recalled the false event during the first interview, but 18 percent remembered something about it in the second interview and 25 percent in the third interview. For example, during the first interview, one participant, when asked about the fictitious wedding event, stated, "I have no clue. I have never heard that one before." In the second interview, the participant said, "It was an outdoor wedding, and I think we were running around and knocked something over like the punch bowl or something and made a big mess and of course got yelled at for it."

Imagination Inflation

The finding that an external suggestion can lead to the construction of false childhood memories helps us understand the process by which false memories arise. It is natural to wonder whether this research is applicable in real situations such as being interrogated by law officers or in psychotherapy. Although strong suggestion may not routinely occur in police questioning or therapy, suggestion in the form of an imagination exercise sometimes does. For instance, when trying to obtain a confession, law officers may ask a suspect to imagine having participated in a criminal act. Some mental health professionals encourage patients to imagine childhood events as a way of recovering supposedly hidden memories.

Surveys of clinical psychologists reveal that 11 percent instruct their clients to "let the imagination run wild," and 22 percent tell their clients to "give free rein to the imagination." Therapist Wendy Maltz, author of a popular book on childhood sexual abuse, advocates telling the patient: "Spend time imagining that you were sexually abused, without worrying about accuracy, proving anything, or having your ideas make sense.... Ask yourself...these questions: What time of day is it? Where are you? Indoors or outdoors? What kind of things are happening? Is there one or more person with you?" Maltz further recommends that therapists continue to ask questions such as "Who would have been likely perpetrators? When were you most vulnerable to sexual abuse in your life?"

The increasing use of such imagination exercises led me and several colleagues to wonder about their consequences. What happens when people imagine childhood experiences that did not happen to them? Does imagining a childhood event increase confidence that it occurred? To explore this, we designed a three-stage procedure. We first asked individuals to indicate the likelihood that certain events happened to them during their childhood. The list contains 40 events, each rated on a scale ranging from "definitely did not happen" to "definitely did happen." Two weeks later we asked the participants to imagine that they had experienced some of these events. Different subjects were asked to imagine different events. Sometime later the participants again were asked to respond to the original list of 40 childhood events, indicating how likely it was that these events actually happened to them.

Consider one of the imagination exercises. Participants are told to imagine playing inside at home after school, hearing a strange noise outside, running toward the window, tripping, falling, reaching out and breaking the window with their hand. In addition, we asked participants questions such as "What did you trip on? How did you feel?"

In one study 24 percent of the participants who imagined the broken-window scenario later reported an increase in confidence that the event had occurred, whereas only 12 percent of those who were not asked to imagine the incident reported an increase in the likelihood that it had taken place. We found this "imagination inflation" effect in each of the eight events that participants were asked to imagine. A number of possible explanations come to mind. An obvious one is that an act of imagination simply makes the event seem more familiar and that familiarity is mistakenly related to childhood memories rather than to the act of imagination. Such source confusion—when a person does not remember the source of information—can be especially acute for the distant experiences of childhood.

Studies by Lyn Goff and Henry L. Roediger III of Washington University of recent rather than childhood experiences more directly connect imagined actions to the construction of false memory. During the initial session, the researchers instructed participants to perform the stated action, imagine doing it or just listen to the statement and do nothing else. The actions were simple ones: knock on the table, lift the stapler, break the toothpick, cross your fingers, roll your eyes. During the second session, the participants were asked to imagine some of the actions that they had not previously performed. During the final session, they answered questions about what actions they actually performed during the initial session. The investigators found that the more times participants imagined an unperformed action, the more likely they were to remember having performed it.

Impossible Memories

It is highly unlikely that an adult can recall genuine episodic memories from the first year of life, in part because the hippocampus, which plays a key role in the creation of memories, has not matured enough to form and store long-lasting memories that can be retrieved in adulthood. A procedure for planting "impossible" memories about experiences that occur shortly after birth has been developed by the late Nicholas Spanos and his collaborators at Carleton University. Individuals are led to believe that they have well-coordinated eye movements and visual exploration skills probably because they were born in hospitals that hung swinging, colored mobiles over infant cribs. To confirm whether they had such an experience, half the participants are hypnotized, age-regressed to the day after birth and asked what they remembered. The other half of the group participates in a "guided mnemonic restructuring" procedure that uses age regression as well as active encouragement to re-create the infant experiences by imagining them.

Spanos and his co-workers found that the vast majority of their subjects were susceptible to these memory-planting procedures. Both the hypnotic and guided participants reported infant memories. Surprisingly, the guided group did so somewhat more (95 versus 70 percent). Both groups remembered the colored mobile at a relatively high rate (56 percent of the guided group and 46 percent of the hypnotic subjects). Many participants who did not remember the mobile did recall other things, such as doctors, nurses, bright lights, cribs and masks. Also, in both groups, of those who reported memories of infancy, 49 percent felt that they were real memories, as opposed to 16 percent who claimed that they were merely fantasies. These findings confirm earlier studies that many individuals can be led to construct complex, vivid and detailed false memories via a rather simple procedure. Hypnosis clearly is not necessary.

How False Memories Form

In the lost-in-the-mall study, implantation of false memory occurred when another person, usually a family member, claimed that the incident happened. Corroboration of an event by another person can be a powerful technique for instilling a false memory. In fact, merely claiming to have seen a person do something can lead that person to make a false confession of wrongdoing.

This effect was demonstrated in a study by Saul M. Kassin and his colleagues at Williams College, who investigated the reactions of individuals falsely accused of damaging a computer by pressing the wrong key. The innocent participants initially denied the charge, but when a confederate said that she had seen them perform the action, many participants signed a confession, internalized guilt for the act and went on to confabulate details that were consistent with that belief. These findings show that false incriminating evidence can induce people to accept guilt for a crime they did not commit and even to develop memories to support their guilty feelings.

Research is beginning to give us an understanding of how false memories of complete, emotional and self-participatory experiences are created in adults. First, there are social demands on individuals to remember; for instance, researchers exert some pressure on participants in a study to come up with memories. Second, memory construction by imagining events can be explicitly encouraged when people are having trouble remembering. And, finally, individuals can be encouraged not to think about whether their constructions are real or not. Creation of false memories is most likely to occur when these external factors are present, whether in an experimental setting, in a therapeutic setting or during everyday activities.

False memories are constructed by combining actual memories with the content of suggestions received from others. During the process, individuals may forget the source of the information. This is a classic example of source confusion, in which the content and the source become dissociated.

Of course, because we can implant false childhood memories in some individuals in no way implies that all memories that arise after suggestion are necessarily false. Put another way, although experimental work on the creation of false memories may raise doubt about the validity of long-buried memories, such as repeated trauma, it in no way disproves them. Without corroboration, there is little that can be done to help even the most experienced evaluator to differentiate true memories from ones that were suggestively planted.

The precise mechanisms by which such false memories are constructed await further research. We still have much to learn about the degree of confidence and the characteristics of false memories created in these ways, and we need to discover what types of individuals are particularly susceptible to these forms of suggestion and who is resistant.

As we continue this work, it is important to heed the cautionary tale in the data we have already obtained: mental health professionals and others must be aware of how greatly they can influence the recollection of events and of the urgent need for maintaining restraint in situations in which imagination is used as an aid in recovering presumably lost memories.

The Author

ELIZABETH F. LOFTUS is professor of psychology and adjunct professor of law at the University of Washington. She received her Ph.D. in psychology from Stanford University in 1970. Her research has focused on human memory, eyewitness testimony and courtroom procedure. Loftus has published 18 books and more than 250 scientific articles and has served as an expert witness or consultant in hundreds of trials, including the McMartin preschool molestation case. Her book *Eyewitness Testimony* won a National Media Award from the American Psychological Foundation. She has received honorary doctorates from Miami University, Leiden University and John Jay College of Criminal Justice. Loftus was recently elected president of the American Psychological Society.

Further Reading

THE MYTH OF REPRESSED MEMORY. Elizabeth F. Loftus and Katherine Ketcham. St. Martin's Press, 1994.
THE SOCIAL PSYCHOLOGY OF FALSE CONFESSIONS: COMPLIANCE, INTERNALIZATION, AND CONFABULATION. Saul M. Kassin and Katherine L. Kiechel in *Psychological Science,* Vol. 7, No. 3, pages 125–128; May 1996.
IMAGINATION INFLATION: IMAGINING A CHILDHOOD EVENT INFLATES CONFIDENCE THAT IT OCCURRED. Maryanne Garry, Charles G. Manning, Elizabeth F. Loftus and Steven J. Sherman in *Psychonomic Bulletin and Review,* Vol. 3, No. 2, pages 208–214; June 1996.
REMEMBERING OUR PAST: STUDIES IN AUTOBIOGRAPHICAL MEMORY. Edited by David C. Rubin. Cambridge University Press, 1996.
SEARCHING FOR MEMORY: THE BRAIN, THE MIND, AND THE PAST. Daniel L. Schacter. BasicBooks, 1996.

The Process of Explanation

Douglas S. Krull and Craig A. Anderson[1]

Department of Psychology, University of Missouri, Columbia, Missouri

People are constantly generating explanations. "Perhaps that 17-car accident on Interstate 35 occurred because people in Austin aren't used to driving on icy roads." "I think Jim was promoted to executive vice president because he's such a good conversationalist." "I can't believe that a good kid like Michelle would have broken that vase on purpose; it must have been an accident." People generate explanations to help them understand their social worlds, as when they explain the apparently altruistic actions of someone they dislike by invoking ulterior motives. People also generate explanations to increase feelings of prediction and control, as when they explain that an assault victim should have known better than to walk through the park alone at night. What cognitive operations are involved when people generate explanations such as these? A variety of different mechanisms have been suggested, from substantially automatic[2] perceptual processes (e.g., McArthur & Baron, 1983) to substantially deliberate and effortful processes (e.g., Pennington & Hastie, 1991). Instead of attempting to show which of these views is correct, our model integrates several different theoretical perspectives.

Two definitions will clarify the discussion. First, the term *event* refers to the incident or condition that is to be explained. For example, people may seek to explain why the moon appears smaller overhead than it does near the horizon. Second, the term *explanation* refers to a judgment about causality, a chaining backward from an event to its cause. This term is similar to but broader than the term *attribution*, in that attribution theory focuses primarily on a subtype of explanation, the causes of events involving people. In contrast, our model is designed to apply to explanations about the actions and characteristics of galaxies, pendulums, zebras, and so on, as well as peoples' behaviors.[3]

A GENERAL MODEL OF THE EXPLANATION PROCESS

As depicted in Figure 1, the explanation process is initiated when an event occurs. The event may be an unexpected personal failure or success. It may be the headline of a newspaper, the peculiar behavior of a pet, or a piece of significant evidence in a trial. Before an event can be explained, however, it must first be noticed.

Noticing the Event

Many factors influence whether a person will notice an event. Event features such as loudness and brightness are important. A silent, unmarked police car is much less likely to attract attention than a marked police car with screeching sirens and flashing lights. Characteristics of the person also play a role. Arthur Conan Doyle's Sherlock Holmes trained himself to notice details (or their absence) that other perceivers would overlook. In addition, the importance or self-relevance of the event to the perceiver will influence its noticeability. For instance, one's name may capture one's attention when equally loud but less self-relevant stimuli do not. Finally, activation of particular cognitive categories or affective states may influence the noticeability of an event (e.g., Higgins, 1989). For example, perceivers more easily recognize success- or failure-related words, respectively, after learning that they have succeeded or failed (Postman & Brown, 1952).

Similarly, the noticeability of potential causes influences the likelihood that they will be adopted as explanations of events. Stimuli that are particularly novel, visually dominant, unusual, or relevant to one's goals are more likely to be assigned a causal role than less attention-grabbing stimuli. For instance, perceivers are more likely to attribute causality to actors who are salient than to those who are

Recommended Reading

Abraham, S.C.S. (1988). Seeing the connections in lay causal comprehension. In D.J. Hilton (Ed.), *Contemporary science and natural explanation: Commonsense conceptions of causality* (pp. 175–203). Brighton, England: Harvester Press.

Anderson, C.A., Krull, D.S., & Weiner, B. (1996). (See References)

Kruglanski, A.W. (1989). (See References)

Kunda, Z. (1987). Motivated inference: Self-serving generation and evaluation of causal theories. *Journal of Personality and Social Psychology, 53*, 636–647.

Novick, L.R., Fratianne, A., & Cheng, P.W. (1992). Knowledge-based assumptions in causal attribution. *Social Cognition, 10*, 299–334.

Sedikides, C., & Anderson, C.A. (1992). Causal explanations of defection: A knowledge structure approach. *Personality and Social Psychology Bulletin, 18*, 420–429.

Weiner, B. (1986). *An attributional theory of motivation and emotion*. New York: Springer-Verlag.

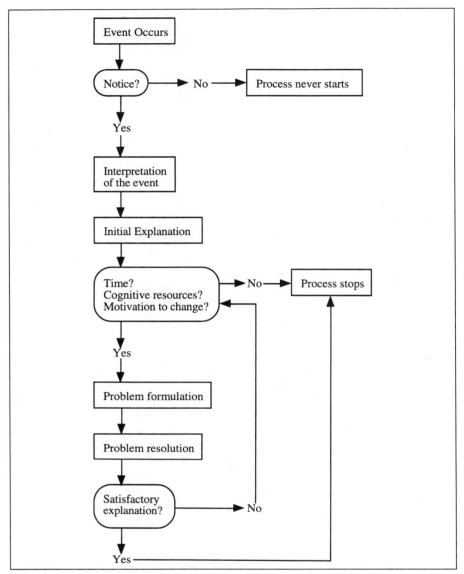

Fig. 1. A general model of the explanation process. Adapted from Anderson, Krull, and Weiner (1996).

not (e.g., Taylor & Fiske, 1978; Zebrowitz, 1990).

Interpreting the Event

After perceivers notice an event, they must decide what it is that they have noticed. This interpretation is influenced by the perceivers' expectations. However, this influence of expectations is difficult to recognize. People may often think that they do not "call 'em as they see 'em," but "call 'em as they are" (Ross & Nisbett, 1991, p. 82). Events tend to be interpreted in the direction of perceivers' expectations, although contrast effects (in which events are interpreted as being less like perceivers' expectations than is actually the case) may also occur under certain conditions. Thus, perceivers may be more likely to interpret a shove as hostile if the actor is black rather than white, a facial expression as fear if it occurs in the presence of a charging rhinoceros, and a blind date as "warm" if he or she had previously been described that way (e.g., Manis, Nelson, & Shedler, 1988; Martin, Seta, & Crelia, 1990; Sagar & Schofield, 1980).

Initial Explanation

After interpreting an event, the person generates an initial explanation. When you see a rapidly traveling baseball strike a window and break it, how is it that you immediately recognize the baseball as the cause of the broken window? Your prior experience tells you that windows are comparatively fragile, and that baseballs are not. In addition, you know that the arrival of the baseball was spatially and temporally contiguous with the breaking of the window. Thus, the combination of prior knowledge about windows and baseballs with the application of the perceptual causal principles of spatial and temporal contiguity produces the initial explanation immediately. The use of such perceptual causal principles may be the most automatic mechanism by which explanations are generated, and may well be the first type of explanation process to emerge developmentally (e.g., White, 1988).

Explanations may also be generated in a very automatic manner when an event activates a knowledge structure (e.g., explanation prototype, schema, script, intuitive causal theory) that contains an explanation about why the event occurs. Thus, when people learn that an outspoken ambassador was found dead shortly before an important and controversial meeting with a foreign diplomat, the possibility of foul play might immediately pop into their heads. In this example, the event simply activates a stored explanation. In other instances, a more general rule or theory may be used to generate an explanation. For example, people who learn that an individual defected from a war-torn and poverty-stricken country to a prosperous one might well select the difference between the countries as the explanation for the individual's defection. In contrast, if another individual emigrates in the opposite direction, aspects of that individual's personality might be invoked in explaining the event. In both cases, people use their intuitive theory that most people desire to move from unfavorable situations to favorable ones, and that only atypical people move from favorable situations to unfavorable ones.

Of course, in many cases, a prepackaged knowledge structure, complete with a single explanation, is not available. Many events require the effortful gathering of information to test alternative explanations. For example, when explaining a plane crash, one needs to know about weather conditions, aircraft maintenance records, and the pilot's actions. In explaining a death by gunshot wounds, a jury needs to know about motives, alibis, and means. In many such cases, a variety of constraints become important.

Constraints

After an initial explanation is generated (or if an explanation cannot be reached quickly and easily), constraints play a significant role. If insufficient cognitive or informational resources are available, or if the explainer is unmotivated to continue either because the event is unimportant or because the initial explanation is satisfactory, the process stops (e.g., Kruglanski, 1989). In this case, the initial explanation is adopted. Of course, in many instances people desire to continue, either because they do not like the initial explanation or because the event is important and accuracy is crucial. If sufficient time and cognitive resources are available, a more effortful problem-based process begins.

Problem-Based Explanation

Problem-based explanation is what people typically think of when they think about the explanation process. Problem-based explanation may make use of processes based on perceptions and knowledge structures, but it is more effortful and deliberate. This type of explanation is more likely to occur to the extent that the event is unexpected or puzzling, the event is very important, or the data to be considered are too difficult or too substantial for the explainer to generate a "top of the head" explanation. The juror's task is a prototypical example of problem-based explanation. Sitting on a jury is a novel task for most people, the amount of information may be substantial and challenging, legal jargon or aspects of the case may be perplexing, and yet accuracy is at a premium. When people are faced with such a challenging task, their first step is to formulate the problem.

Problem Formulation

Problem formulation is controlled by a guiding knowledge structure that contains information about the event, possible explanations for the event, types of information needed to evaluate the explanations, and the probable implications of these explanations for oneself and for other people who may eventually be told of the final explanation. This knowledge structure may recruit relevant information from memory, may direct a search for information in the immediate environment, and may suggest more effortful search procedures for relevant information, such as consulting other people or going to the library (e.g., Anderson & Slusher, 1986).

Several guiding knowledge structures may be relevant to a given event. The similarity of a knowledge structure to the event strongly influences whether it is selected, but characteristics of the explainer and situation also play a role. Chronically or temporarily accessible knowledge structures are more likely to be selected than less accessible ones (e.g., Higgins, 1989). Similarly, the goals of the explainer influence which guiding knowledge structure is used. One type of knowledge structure may be selected when the goal is accuracy; another may be selected when the explainer desires to reach an explanation quickly. Political candidates who expect their explanations to be made public may recruit knowledge structures that contain information about how to create a favorable impression.

Frequently, people desire to believe a particular explanation. This desire can itself influence which guiding knowledge structure is selected. For instance, students who desire to believe that their poor grades in a psychology course are due to the instructor's incompetence might selectively search for information that supports this explanation. Upon finding such information, they might readily adopt the "incompetent instructor" explanation despite the fact that information that supports the "unmotivated student" explanation might also be available.

Although some aspects of problem formulation may be very complex and resource intensive, other aspects may take place more automatically. Indeed, such automatic effects make it especially valuable to have people with different perspectives working together to generate explanations. One cannot easily correct for biases that one's own cognitive system unconsciously introduces, but different individuals have different biases, and so the biases of one individual may be compensated for by those of another.

Of course, biases can also be introduced by effortful processes.

For instance, research demonstrates that people often seek information that is consistent with their hypotheses, rather than seeking disconfirming information (e.g., Klayman & Ha, 1987; Snyder & Swann, 1978). Consequently, even the information available for their consideration may be biased.

Problem Resolution

In the problem resolution stage, the information collected during problem formulation is integrated into a "best" explanation. The potential explanations of the event identified in the problem formulation stage are evaluated using the available evidence. The most well supported explanation is adopted as a tentative explanation of the event.

Read and Miller's model of social perception (e.g., Read & Miller, 1993) provides an excellent mechanism by which the best explanation might be selected. They propose that after concepts related to an event are activated, the activated information and possible explanations are evaluated repeatedly using principles of explanatory coherence (e.g., breadth, parsimony). For example, suppose Robert is hired as an executive vice president of Smith-Lincoln Investments, Inc., immediately after finishing his M.B.A. Several explanations are possible. Perhaps Robert was hired because he is an extremely talented business professional, or perhaps Robert was hired because he is well liked by a powerful partner in the company. As the explainer considers these and other possible explanations, some pieces of information might support one explanation (e.g., Robert graduated at the top of his class), some might support another (e.g., Robert is the favorite nephew of Smith-Lincoln's most important client), and some might support both or neither. As this information is evaluated and new concepts are activated, some possible explanations will be discarded (e.g., because they conflict with the available information, because they are unparsimonious) until a coherent explanation is reached. Note, however, that the quality of an explanation is relative; people may be willing to accept a poor explanation if no better explanation is available.

Satisfaction

At least one additional judgment is then made: The explainer must decide whether the best explanation produced in the problem resolution stage is satisfactory. (This judgment could be construed as a part of problem resolution, but for the purpose of clarity, we discuss it separately.) If this explanation is unsatisfactory, either because none of the explanatory possibilities sufficiently fits the information or because other goals of the explainer are not met, then the explainer cycles back to the constraint step. If time, resources, and the motivation to achieve a better explanation are sufficient, then the problem may be reformulated. Additional explanatory possibilities may be generated and additional information may be gathered, or the explainer may simply reexecute the process with relaxed standards. Problem resolution is engaged in once again, and a new "best" explanation is produced. This explanation must also undergo the satisfaction test. As in the Rolling Stones song, if "... I can't get no satisfaction," then "I try, and I try, and I try, and I try...." Eventually, either the explainer arrives at a satisfactory explanation or the cognitive or motivational constraints cause the cycling to stop.

CONCLUSION

The generation of explanations is an important and ubiquitous process. It is of interest to researchers, practitioners, and laypeople alike. How do people explain their successes and failures, or the successes and failures of others? How do people make sense of the behavior of others and of major positive or negative events with which they come into contact either directly or indirectly on a daily basis? What influences people toward particular conclusions about the actions of politicians, defendants, groups, or nations? The vast array of domains in which explanation processes have been investigated attests to their importance in everyday life.

There can be no doubt that there is considerable room for advancement in the study of explanation processes. Numerous questions about, for example, automaticity, the interplay of motivation and cognition, and the stages at which a variety of personal and situational influences exert the greatest impact await additional investigation and theory development. We hope that our attempts at integration will serve as useful starting points for additional research, and will serve to increase collaboration and lead to important advances across the various areas that can all be sheltered under the "explanation" umbrella.

Acknowledgments—We wish to thank Jody C. Dill, Karen E. Dill, Lori A. Krull, and several reviewers for their valuable comments on this manuscript.

Notes

1. Address correspondence to either Douglas S. Krull, Department of Psychology, BEP 353, Northern Kentucky University, Highland Heights, KY 41099, or Craig A. Anderson, Department of Psychology, University of Missouri, Columbia, MO 65211; e-mail: krull@nku.edu or psycaa@showme.missouri.edu.

2. We view automatic and controlled processes as endpoints of a con-

tinuum, rather than dichotomous categories. For discussions of automaticity and its characteristics, see Bargh (1989, 1996).

3. It should be noted that there may be important differences in how people explain social and nonsocial events. For example, the actions of people may be produced and guided by internal motivations, but such internal explanations are typically not invoked for the actions of baseballs, electrons, or hurricanes. For a relevant discussion, see Ostrom (1984).

References

Anderson, C.A., Krull, D.S., & Weiner, B. (1996). Explanations: Processes and consequences. In E.T. Higgins & A.W. Kruglanski (Eds.), *Social psychology: Handbook of basic principles* (pp. 271–296). New York: Guilford Press.

Anderson, C.A., & Slusher, M.P. (1986). Relocating motivational effects: An examination of the cognition-motivation debate on attributions for success and failure. *Social Cognition, 4,* 270–292.

Bargh, J.A. (1989). Conditional automaticity: Varieties of automatic influence in social perception and cognition. In J.S. Uleman & J.A. Bargh (Eds.), *Unintended thought* (pp. 3–51). New York: Guilford Press.

Bargh, J.A. (1996). Automaticity in social psychology. In E.T. Higgins & A.W. Kruglanski (Eds.), *Social psychology: Handbook of basic principles* (pp. 169–183). New York: Guilford Press.

Higgins, E.T. (1989). Knowledge accessibility and activation: Subjectivity and suffering from unconscious sources. In J.S. Uleman & J.A. Bargh (Eds.), *Unintended thought* (pp. 75–123). New York: Guilford Press.

Klayman, J., & Ha, Y.-W. (1987). Confirmation, disconfirmation, and information in hypothesis testing. *Psychology Review, 94,* 211–228.

Kruglanski, A.W. (1989). *Lay epistemics and human knowledge: Cognitive and motivational bases.* New York: Plenum Press.

Manis, M., Nelson, T.E., & Shedler, J. (1988). Stereotypes and social judgment: Extremity, assimilation, and contrast. *Journal of Personality and Social Psychology, 55,* 28–36.

Martin, L.L., Seta, J.J., & Crelia, R.A. (1990). Assimilation and contrast as a function of people's willingness and ability to expend effort in forming an impression. *Journal of Personality and Social Psychology, 59,* 27–37.

McArthur, L.Z., & Baron, R. (1983). Toward an ecological theory of social perception. *Psychological Review, 90,* 215–238.

Ostrom, T.M. (1984). The sovereignty of social cognition. In R.S. Wyer, Jr., & T.K. Srull (Eds.), *Handbook of social cognition* (Vol. 1, pp. 1–38). Hillsdale, NJ: Erlbaum.

Pennington, N., & Hastie, R. (1991). A cognitive theory of juror decision making: The story model. *Cardozo Law Review, 13,* 519–557.

Postman, L., & Brown, D.R. (1952). The perceptual consequences of success and failure. *Journal of Abnormal and Social Psychology, 47,* 213–221.

Read, S.J., & Miller, L.C. (1993). Rapist or "regular guy": Explanatory coherence in the construction of mental models of others. *Personality and Social Psychology Bulletin, 19,* 526–540.

Ross, L., & Nisbett, R.E. (1991). *The person and the situation: Perspectives of social psychology.* New York: McGraw-Hill.

Sagar, H.A., & Schofield, J.W. (1980). Racial and behavioral cues in black and white children's perceptions of ambiguously aggressive acts. *Journal of Personality and Social Psychology, 39,* 590–598.

Snyder, M., & Swann, W.B. (1978). Hypothesis-testing processes in social interaction. *Journal of Personality and Social Psychology, 36,* 1202–1212.

Taylor, S.E., & Fiske, S.T. (1978). Salience, attention, and attribution: Top of the head phenomena. In L. Berkowitz (Ed.), *Advances in experimental social psychology* (Vol. 11, pp. 249–288). New York: Academic Press.

White, P.A. (1988). Causal processing: Origins and development. *Psychological Bulletin, 104,* 36–52.

Zebrowitz, L.A. (1990). *Social perception.* Pacific Grove, CA: Brooks-Cole.

Influences from the Mind's Inner Layers

Research unveils the power that the unconscious mind has on judgment and behavior.

Beth Azar

Monitor staff

Without our knowledge, a force is at work tainting our perceptions and altering our behavior: That provocateur is our unconscious, and it plays a role in our attitudes, our demeanor and even our movements.

A decade's-worth of psychological research has documented that the mind reacts automatically to environmental cues before we consciously perceive them. These automatic reactions can influence our judgments and alter our behavior. Such findings counter the social-psychology assumption that thinking and behavior are consciously controlled.

"That unconsciously motivated thoughts can impact the manner in which we judge ourselves and others is still surprising," said psychologist Mahzarin Banaji, PhD, of Yale University. "These discoveries will change our view of human nature," giving the unconscious much more credit for our behavior.

Automatic Evaluations

Nothing is safe from the scrutinizing eye of the unconscious. The unconscious mind subtly evaluates whatever it perceives and colors our perception without us knowing it, argue psychologists John Bargh, PhD, and Shelly Chaiken, PhD, of New York University.

To study this automatic evaluation, researchers use a technique called priming. By exposing subjects to a prime—a stimulus such as a word or face—they trigger thoughts, feelings or ideas associated with the prime. They then examine how the prime unconsciously influences responses to another stimulus.

For example, researchers may present subjects with pairs of words or pictures. They flash the first item at the subjects for a quarter of a second, long enough for people to perceive it but not long enough for them to consciously form an opinion.

The second item is taken from a list of items that researchers know people find either pleasing or displeasing. For example, people universally rate the word "beautiful" as positive and the word "terrible" as negative.

After viewing or hearing the second item, subjects press a button indicating whether they regard it as positive or negative or, in some experiments, they pronounce the words "good" or "bad."

If people like or dislike both objects, they respond quickly. But if they like one and dislike the other, subjects respond detectably slower.

In her dissertation, graduate student Magda Garcia worked with Bargh and Chaiken to test how people evaluate novel words or pictures, such as "glojkrot," "gumok" or "taleer." When they paired "taleer"—a made up word--with "beautiful," reaction time was quicker than when they paired "taleer" with "terrible." This implies that when subjects see taleer, they unconsciously evaluate it positively and so are more ready to respond positively when they see the second word. If the word is obviously negative, they hesitate, causing the delay, Bargh said. It also turns out that English speakers like "wehsee" and "taleer" but dislike "glojkrot" and "gumok."

Bargh and Chaiken have yet to identify a word or object that people don't automatically evaluate as good or bad. Bargh believes these automatic evaluations may play a role in do-or-die situations where we must make a decision quicker than our conscious brains can act. It's unknown, however, whether they influence subsequent conscious judgments but there's no evidence to prove that, he added.

Gender Judgments

People make gender-biased judgments too, according to research by Banaji and Anthony Greenwald, PhD, of the University of Washington. In a series of studies, they found that words trigger unconscious gender stereotypes in men and women.

Subjects read a list of 72 names, presumably to judge how easy each name was to pronounce. Half of the list contained famous names, the other half nonfamous names, and each group contained equal numbers of male and female names. Two days later, subjects read a second list of 144 names, which contained the 72 names from the previous list and 72 new famous and nonfamous names, again half male and half female. Subjects had to judge each name on the second list as famous or nonfamous.

Although there were equal numbers of famous males and females, subjects consistently identified more men than women as famous. They most often mistakenly tagged nonfamous male names as famous if they saw the names on the first day.

Banaji and Greenwald's analysis revealed that subjects held men to a lower standard then women, said Banaji. "We have discovered that this bias is rooted in stricter criterion being set for judging female fame," she said.

Unconscious stereotypes can also influence behavior, such as body movement and manners, according to work by Bargh and his colleagues. He and graduate student Mark Chen began with the finding from previous experiments that the stereotypical image of an elderly person conveys notions of slowness and physical weakness. They secretly primed subjects with nonphysical elements of the elderly stereotype—forgetful, Florida, bingo—through what students thought was a language-ability test.

Unbeknownst to the subjects, the researchers timed them as they walked down a hallway after what they thought was the end of the experiment. Subjects primed with words related to the elderly stereotype walked slower than control subjects who saw unrelated words.

Bargh and Chen conducted a second experiment using polite or rude primes. After performing a language test that secretly primed subjects for one or the other behavior, subjects had to locate the experimenter outside the room. When they found the researcher, he was engaged in conversation with another student—who was clandestinely working for the researcher.

The two kept talking for up to 10 minutes or until the subject interrupted.

Sixty-seven percent of subjects primed with rude words interrupted within the allotted time, while 84 percent of the patience-primed subjects waited the entire 10 minutes. Subjects claimed they were unaware that the priming task influenced their behavior.

The priming words activate the same concepts that real-life events—such as seeing another person act rude or polite—would spark, said Bargh. These findings show that our surroundings can have striking unconscious influences on our behavior.

Approach or Avoid?

Our automatic reactions to environmental cues might be linked to an evolutionary need to quickly assess whether to approach or avoid a situation, suggests Bargh. Research by him and others find that our positive or negative evaluations of situations enhance arm-muscle movements toward or away from the body respectively.

For example, in priming tasks, people hesitate to pull a lever toward them in response to a negative word, but are quick to pull it toward them in response to a positive word.

Immediate avoidance reactions—that appear unconsciously—can be viewed by others as condescending facial expressions and can seriously affect an interaction, said Bargh. Picture this: you meet someone and because of his or her gender, race or even shirt color, you have an automatic, unconscious avoidance reaction that shows up on your face. That person may notice and react in kind and you're left wondering why they're so cold. Your unconscious reaction just colored the entire interaction.

Bargh and his colleagues say that these types of experiments point to a parallel-processing model of action and reaction. The environment triggers three forms of preconscious analysis: perceptual, evaluative and motivational.

Words, people and events trigger stereotypes that color our perceptions and our behavior. We automatically and unconsciously evaluate even novel or nonsense stimuli as bad or good, and our evaluation affects whether we approach or avoid.

"A large portion of our everyday thinking and feeling and actions must be guided by factors that operate outside conscious awareness," said Banaji. Understanding how such unconscious reactions operate will help us better understand how to control them or apply them to our benefit.

Social Perception

Perception Processes (Articles 11 and 12)
Perception and Accuracy (Articles 13 and 14)

A personnel director has the job of interviewing hundreds of prospective employees for her company every year. The total amount of time and money that will be invested in these new employees will be enormous; thus, the consequences of hiring the wrong people will be serious. In each interview, then, the personnel director tries to answer a number of important questions: How honest is this candidate? How dependable? How will he or she fit in with the other employees?

Sally has been dating Harry for several months, and things are starting to become more serious between them. As she begins to seriously consider the possibility that he may be "the one," Sally starts to think with extra care about what kind of person Harry really is: Is he just being especially nice during courtship, or is he a genuinely kind and considerate person? Was that time when he got really angry at another driver just an isolated incident, or does it indicate that Harry is someone who has the potential for violence?

Both of these examples are instances of social perception, or the process by which one individual makes inferences about another individual. As you might imagine, this is a very important ability for humans to have, because there are many times when it is important to reach an accurate understanding about what kind of person someone else is. When the behavior of others, such as employees and spouses, has important implications for us, the ability to successfully predict how such people will act in the future can be critical. It should not be surprising, then, to discover that social psychology has been interested in this topic for decades.

One approach to this topic has been to study "impression formation"—the process by which we form an initial impression of someone with whom we are not familiar. Research indicates that we form such impressions quite quickly, often on the basis of very little information. One kind of information that is often available in such situations—and which is therefore frequently used—is group membership; that is, the person's sex, race, age, social class, and so on. Beyond such obvious kinds of information, we also use the person's words and actions to reach an initial impression.

There are problems facing us, however, when using another's actions in this way. It is not always easy to know the real cause of someone's behavior: Is it a reflection of his or her underlying personality, or was the behavior caused by factors outside the individual's control? Attempts to answer questions such as these are what social psychology calls making "attributions," and a number of theories have been proposed to help us understand how people make such determinations. Most of these approaches have emphasized the view that humans often act like scientists as they try to logically figure out the causes of events.

The subsections that make up this unit approach the question of social perception from two different angles. The first unit subsection focuses on the actual processes by which social perception occurs. In the first article, "Inferential Hopscotch: How People Draw Social Inferences from Behavior," the authors review recent research that indicates that drawing inferences actually consists of multiple steps. The initial step is typically rather quick and automatic; in it, the behavior is immediately interpreted as evidence of an underlying trait. In the more conscious and effortful second step, however, we deliberately try to take into account other factors that might have influenced the behavior. The second article, "Motivational Approaches to Expectancy Confirmation," deals with an interesting phenomenon known as the self-fulfilling prophecy—when our expectancies about people lead us

UNIT 3

to act differently toward them, and this behavior then prompts them to act in ways that confirm the expectancy. In this selection, John Copeland reviews recent research on motivational factors that can either make this phenomenon more likely, or less likely, to occur.

The unit's second subsection is concerned with the question of accuracy in social perception. The first selection, "The Truth about Lying," examines the phenomenon of deceit in everyday life and reviews research evidence that bears on such questions as: how common is lying, who engages in it, and what kind of deceptions are most common? In "Spotting Lies: Can Humans Learn to Do Better?" Bella DePaulo considers the question of whether humans are able to distinguish truthful statements from lies and finds that the evidence for such an ability is not very strong. Despite humans' generally poor performance as lie detectors, however, DePaulo also argues that such performance might be improved through practice.

Looking Ahead: Challenge Questions

What does it mean to say that some parts of the social inference process are "automatic" and some are "controlled"? Why is that distinction important for our understanding of the perception process?

How would you summarize the phenomenon known as "behavioral confirmation"? What is actually being "confirmed"? What circumstances make behavioral confirmation more likely to occur? Less likely? Why?

How do people go about detecting deception in others? What cues do we use to distinguish between someone telling the truth and someone telling a lie? Why aren't we more accurate in making such distinctions? How would you specifically go about improving the ability to detect deceit in others?

Inferential Hopscotch: How People Draw Social Inferences From Behavior

Douglas S. Krull and Darin J. Erickson

Douglas S. Krull is an Assistant Professor of Psychology at Northern Kentucky University, Highland Heights. **Darin J. Erickson** is a graduate student at the University of Missouri, Columbia. Address correspondence to Douglas S. Krull, Department of Psychology, Northern Kentucky University, Highland Heights, KY 41099; e-mail: krull@nku.edu.

Tim and Sue observe an anxious-looking man in a dentist's waiting room. Tim decides that the man must have an anxious personality (a trait inference). In contrast, Sue decides that the man is anxious because he is waiting to see the dentist (a situational inference). Why might Tim and Sue have drawn such different inferences? Social inference researchers have long been interested in the different inferences that people draw when they view the same behavior. Early work on social inference focused on the tendency for peoples' inferences to be biased in favor of trait inferences. For example, when members of a debate team are assigned to argue for a particular political position, observers often infer that the debaters' true attitudes match their assigned position.[1] More recently, research has focused not only on *what* people infer (i.e., the final inference), but also on *how* they infer (i.e., the process by which inferences are drawn).

THE TRAIT INFERENCE PROCESS

The vast majority of recent work on social inference has investigated the process by which people draw inferences about an actor's personality. Research suggests that the trait inference process can be thought of as composed of three stages: behavior interpretation, trait inference, and situational revision.[2] First, people interpret, or derive meaning from, the actor's behavior ("John seems to be behaving in a very anxious manner"); next, they draw a trait inference that corresponds to the behavior ("John must have a very anxious personality"); finally, they may revise this inference to a greater or lesser degree by taking into account the situational forces that may have contributed to the actor's behavior ("John is waiting to see the dentist; perhaps he isn't such an anxious person after all"). These three stages seem to differ in the amount of effort required. Behavior interpretation and trait inference seem to be relatively spontaneous and effortless, whereas situational revision seems to be relatively effortful.[3] This process is depicted in Figure 1.

Stage 1: Behavior Interpretation

People tend to see what they expect to see.[4] Thus, many people in American society tend to interpret an ambiguous shove as more hostile when given by a black person than by a white person. However, people's expectations have less impact on their interpretations of behavior if the behavior is unambiguous. Trope[5] conducted an experiment in which participants interpreted facial expressions after being informed about the context in which the expressions took place. If the facial expressions were ambiguous, participants' context-based expectations influenced their interpretations of the emotions (e.g., participants interpreted a facial expression as happier if the context was "winning in a TV game show" and more fearful if the context was "a swarm of bees flying into the room"). If the facial expressions were unambiguous, participants' expectations had significantly less impact.

Stage 2: Trait Inference

People often think that you can judge a book by its cover, that people's actions reflect their personalities. Uleman, Winter, and their colleagues[6] conducted a series of investigations which suggest that when people view behavior, they may spontaneously draw inferences about the actor's personality. In these studies, participants read sentences (e.g., "The secretary solved the mystery halfway through the book") that suggest a particular trait (e.g., clever). Uleman and Winter proposed that if people spontaneously draw trait inferences upon reading the sentences (at encoding), then these traits should facilitate recall for the sentences (at retrieval). Studies of this hypothesis have found repeatedly that participants' recall is superior with trait cues than with no cues, and occasionally better with trait cues than with other types of

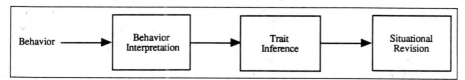

Fig. 1. The trait inference process.

cues (semantic), even when participants were not aware when reading the sentences that their memory for the sentences would be tested.

In a similar paradigm, Lupfer, Clark, and Hutcherson[7] conducted an experiment which suggests that trait inferences may be substantially effortless as well as spontaneous. If trait inference is substantially effortless, then people should be able to perform it even when their conscious resources are limited (i.e., when they are cognitively busy). Participants read sentences while they simultaneously rehearsed an easy set of numbers (which should not make people cognitively busy) or a difficult set of numbers (which should make people cognitively busy). Not only did trait-cued participants recall more sentences than noncued participants, but the trait-cued recall of participants in the difficult condition was not significantly different from the trait-cued recall of participants in the easy condition. This and other research suggests that when people view behavior, they may spontaneously and effortlessly interpret the behavior and infer that the actor's personality corresponds to the behavior ("John behaved in an anxious manner; John must have an anxious personality") even when they are distracted or preoccupied.

A relearning paradigm developed by Carlston and Skowronski[8] looks particularly promising for the further investigation of spontaneous trait inferences. These researchers first presented participants with person photos paired with personal statements that implied traits. For example, the following statement implies that the person in the photo is cruel: "I hate animals. Today I was walking to the pool hall and I saw this puppy. So I kicked it out of my way." Some participants were instructed to draw a trait inference (specific-impression condition), others were instructed to form an impression (general-impression condition), and others were told to simply look at the photos and statements (ostensibly to familiarize themselves with these materials for a later phase of the experiment; no-instruction condition). If these latter participants inferred traits, this would be evidence for spontaneity.

After a filler task, all participants were given photo–trait pairs and were instructed explicitly to memorize the trait associated with each photo. In some cases (relearning trials), these pairs corresponded to the photo–statement pairs presented earlier (e.g., the photo previously presented with the statement about kicking the puppy was paired with the word *cruel*). Thus, if the participants had previously inferred traits from the statements, they would be relearning the associations between the photos and the traits instead of learning these associations for the first time. In other cases, the photo–trait pairs did not correspond to the previous photo–statement pairs (control trials). Finally, participants were shown the photos and asked to recall the traits. Recall was higher for relearning trials than for control trials, suggesting that participants had inferred traits from the initial photo–statement pairs. In addition, this finding was similar across all three conditions (specific impression, general impression, no instruction), which suggests that trait inferences had occurred in the impression conditions, and spontaneous trait inferences had occurred in the no-instruction condition. Carlston and Skowronski also ruled out several alternative explanations. Thus, these results provide strong evidence that trait inferences can be drawn spontaneously.

Stage 3: Situational Revision

People may consider the situation in which the behavior took place when they draw trait inferences, but it is not easy for them to do so. Unlike behavior interpretation and trait inference, situational revision seems to be a relatively effortful process, and so people may not complete it when they lack either the ability or the motivation to do so. A program of research conducted by Gilbert and his colleagues[3] suggests that people may be unable to complete the situational revision stage sufficiently when they are cognitively busy (when they have limited conscious resources). In one study, participants viewed several videotape clips of an anxious-appearing woman who was ostensibly discussing anxiety-provoking topics (sexual fantasies) or calm topics (world travel) with an interviewer. The film was silent, but the discussion topics appeared in subtitles. Half the participants were required to memorize these topics (cognitively busy participants), and half were not. One might expect that participants would recognize that most people would be more anxious when discussing anxiety-provoking topics than calm topics, but, remarkably, participants who attempted to memorize the discussion topics were less able than the other participants to consider the effects of the topics when drawing inferences about the target. Thus, this study suggests that when people are preoccupied or distracted, they may draw biased trait inferences because they fail to sufficiently consider the situation in which the behavior took place.

An experiment by Webster[9] suggests that people may also revise their trait inferences insufficiently when they are unmotivated. Participants expected to answer questions about their impression of a speaker who expressed a negative view toward student exchange programs. Before viewing the speaker, participants were informed that she was required to express a negative view, but Webster predicted that unmotivated participants would be less likely than motivated participants to consider this fact, and would be more likely to infer that the speaker's view reflected her true attitude. Half of the participants expected to perform a task involving multivariate statistics after the impression formation task, whereas the other half expected to perform a task involving comedy clips after the impression formation task. Webster predicted that participants who expected to view the statistics lecture would be motivated to "stretch the fun" on the (comparatively attractive) impression formation task, whereas participants who expected to view the comedy clips would be motivated to "get the (comparatively boring) impression formation task over with." As Webster predicted, participants in the statistics condition were better able to revise their inferences than were participants in the comedy clips condition, and were less likely to infer that the speaker's expressed view reflected her true attitude.

THE SITUATIONAL INFERENCE PROCESS

When people want to know about people, they seem to infer traits. What if people want to know about situations? Social inference researchers have learned much about the process by which people infer traits. Considerably less work has investigated how social inference proceeds when people are interested in learning about a situation, but some work suggests that situational inference may be a mirror image of the trait inference process.[10] In an experiment very similar to Gilbert's aforementioned anxious-woman experiment, participants viewed a silent videotape of an anxious-appearing interviewee. Half the participants attempted to estimate the interviewee's trait anxiety (trait goal); half attempted to estimate the degree of anxiety provoked by the interview topics (situational goal). Half of the participants in each of these conditions were made cognitively busy. For people with a trait goal, the results mirrored Gilbert's; that is, in an analysis that combined the dispositional and situational anxiety measures, busy participants inferred more dispositional anxiety than did nonbusy participants. However, the results were reversed for participants with a situational goal; that is, busy participants in this condition inferred more situational anxiety than did nonbusy participants. These results suggest that when people are interested in situations (rather than traits), they may spontaneously and effortlessly draw situational inferences (rather than trait inferences) from behavior. If people have the ability and motivation, they may revise these inferences by considering the actor's personality.

THE SOCIAL INFERENCE PROCESS

Considerable research suggests that when people have a trait goal, they interpret the actor's behavior, spontaneously and effortlessly draw a trait inference, and, if they have sufficient conscious resources and motivation, revise this inference by considering the situation in which the behavior took place. When people have a situational goal, they interpret the actor's behavior, may spontaneously and effortlessly draw a situational inference, and, if they have sufficient conscious resources and motivation, revise this inference by considering the actor's personality (see Fig. 2). It seems that people are able to draw either trait inferences or situational inferences from behavior when they are given either trait goals or situational goals, but what might create these goals in people's day-to-day lives? Social inference researchers have long maintained that people draw inferences to increase their ability to predict other people's behavior. Thus, a trait goal may be invoked when someone expects to interact with a person in the future ("I just met our new neighbors. They seem like friendly people."). When someone expects to enter a situation, a situational goal may be invoked ("Did you hear those people laughing? I can hardly wait to see that movie.").

Even when goals are not invoked by the immediate circumstances or people's current needs and motives, people may be predisposed to either trait inference or situational inference by their culture or personality.[11] A number of cross-cultural investigations have found that non-Westerners tend to form judgments that are more situational than those of Westerners. Shweder and Bourne[12] have suggested that non-Western people may be "culturally primed to see context and social relationships as a necessary condition for behavior," whereas Westerners may be "culturally primed to search for abstract summaries of the autonomous individual." Thus, Westerners' default process may be the trait inference process, whereas non-Westerners' default process may be the situational inference process. Even within a culture, some types of individuals may think more in terms of traits, and others may think more in terms of situational forces. For instance, Newman[13] has found that

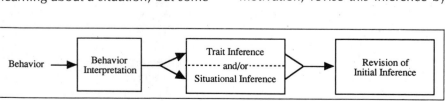

Fig. 2. The social inference process.

people who are high in idiocentrism (an individualistic view) are more likely than people who are low in idiocentrism to infer traits spontaneously from behavior.

CONCLUSION

In the past decade or so, social inference researchers have increased their attention on the process by which people draw inferences from behavior, particularly the trait inference process. This research suggests that when people are interested in learning about another person, they may spontaneously and effortlessly interpret behavior and draw an inference about the actor's personality. They may then revise their initial inference by considering the situation in which the behavior took place if they have the ability and motivation to do so. Less research has investigated how people draw inferences when they are interested in learning about situations. However, people with a situational goal may spontaneously and effortlessly interpret behavior and draw an inference about the situation, and may revise this inference by considering the actor's personality if they have the ability and motivation to do so. Thus, it seems that the social inference process may be flexible in that people may not be compelled to always travel the same inferential road. Social inference researchers have begun to investigate factors that might influence people's tendency to initially draw either trait or situational inferences (or perhaps both); some research suggests that people's current goals and motives may influence the process, and that individual differences and cultural factors may predispose people to either trait or situational inferences.

Further advances in the understanding of social inference processes and the influence of cultural factors and individual differences will have important implications at many levels of social science. Important benefits will accrue for psychologists, but also for political scientists and sociologists. For example, in politics, it may be that the tendency for conservatives to blame the poor for their plight and for liberals to blame the system reflects differences in social inference. Similarly, the default social inference process for an entire culture may influence its members' inferences and proposed solutions with regard to such ubiquitous social problems as homelessness, injustice, and violence.

Acknowledgments—We wish to thank Craig A. Anderson, Lori A. Krull, Jody C. Dill, and David Dubois for their valuable comments on earlier drafts of this manuscript.

Notes

1. This tendency to draw unwarranted trait inferences has been called correspondence bias, the fundamental attribution error, and overattribution bias. For a review, see E.E. Jones, *Interpersonal Perception* (Macmillan, New York, 1990).
2. See, e.g., D.T. Gilbert, B.W. Pelham, and D.S. Krull, On cognitive busyness: When person perceivers meet persons perceived, *Journal of Personality and Social Psychology*, 54, 733–740 (1988); Y. Trope, Identification and inferential processes in dispositional attribution, *Psychological Review*, 93, 239–257 (1986).
3. See, e.g., D.T. Gilbert, Thinking lightly about others: Automatic components of the social inference process, in *Unintended Thought: Limits of Awareness, Intention, and Control*, J.S. Uleman and J.A. Bargh, Eds. (Guilford Press, New York, 1989).
4. See, e.g., H.A. Sagar and J.W. Schofield, Racial and behavioral cues in black and white children's perceptions of ambiguously aggressive acts, *Journal of Personality and Social Psychology*, 39, 590–598 (1980). Note that contrast effects may also occur; e.g., L.L. Martin, J.J. Seta, and R.A. Crelia, Assimilation and contrast as a function of people's willingness and ability to expend effort in forming an impression, *Journal of Personality and Social Psychology*, 59, 27–37 (1990).
5. Trope, note 2.

6. For a review, see J.S. Uleman, Consciousness and control: The case of spontaneous trait inferences, *Personality and Social Psychology Bulletin*, 13, 337–354 (1987). Note that more recent work suggests that these spontaneous inferences may often be better thought of as summaries of behavior; e.g., J.N. Bassili, Traits as action categories versus traits as person attributes in social cognition, in *On-Line Cognition in Person Perception*, J.N. Bassili, Ed. (Erlbaum, Hillsdale, NJ, 1989).
7. M.B. Lupfer, L.F. Clark, and H.W. Hutcherson, Impact of context on spontaneous trait and situational attributions, *Journal of Personality and Social Psychology*, 58, 239–249 (1990). Note that trait inferences do require some conscious resources; see J.S. Uleman, L.S. Newman, and L. Winter, Can personality traits be inferred automatically? Spontaneous inferences require cognitive capacity at encoding, *Consciousness and Cognition*, 1, 72–90 (1992). See Bassili, note 6.
8. D.E. Carlston and J.J. Skowronski, Savings in the relearning of trait information as evidence for spontaneous inference generation, *Journal of Personality and Social Psychology*, 66, 840–856 (1994).
9. D.M. Webster, Motivated augmentation and reduction of the overattribution bias, *Journal of Personality and Social Psychology*, 65, 261–271 (1993).
10. D.S. Krull, Does the grist change the mill?: The effect of perceiver's goal on the process of social inference, *Personality and Social Psychology Bulletin*, 19, 340–348 (1993). See also G.A. Quattrone, Overattribution and unit formation: When behavior engulfs the person, *Journal of Personality and Social Psychology*, 42, 593–607 (1982); J.D. Vorauer and M. Ross, Making mountains out of molehills: An informational goals analysis of self- and social perception, *Personality and Social Psychology Bulletin*, 19, 620–632 (1993).
11. See, e.g., G.J.O. Fletcher and C. Ward, Attribution theory and processes: A cross-cultural perspective, in *The Cross-Cultural Challenge to Social Psychology*, M.H. Bond, Ed. (Sage, Beverly Hills, CA, 1988); J.G. Miller, Culture and the development of everyday social explanation, *Journal of Personality and Social Psychology*, 46, 961–978 (1984). Although the terms Western and non-Western have been used for simplicity, the cultural difference is perhaps better thought of as a distinction between cultures with an independent and with an interdependent view of the self.
12. R.A. Shweder and E. Bourne, Does the concept of the person vary cross-culturally? in *Cultural Conceptions of Mental Health and Therapy*, A.J. Marsella and G. White, Eds. (Reidel, Boston, 1982), pp. 129–130.
13. L.S. Newman, How individualists interpret behavior: Idiocentrism and spontaneous trait inference, *Social Cognition*, 11, 243–269 (1993). See Bassili, note 6.

Recommended Reading

Trope, Y., and Higgins, E.T., Eds. (1993). Special Issue: On Inferring Personal Dispositions From Behavior. *Personality and Social Psychology Bulletin*, 19.

Motivational Approaches to Expectancy Confirmation

John T. Copeland

John T. Copeland is an Assistant Professor of Psychology at Wabash College. Address correspondence to John T. Copeland, Wabash College, Crawfordsville, IN 47933; e-mail: copelanj@wabash.bitnet.

For some time now, social, personality, and cognitive psychologists have been interested in how our interpersonal expectations affect our thoughts, feelings, and behavior. A provocative finding in this research suggests that people often act in ways that preferentially confirm their expectations of others. Specifically, an individual who holds some expectation (who is generally referred to as a perceiver) about some other person (who is generally referred to as a target), through the course of their interaction, will often form expectancy-confirming impressions of the target (a phenomenon referred to as *perceptual confirmation*) and elicit expectancy-confirming behavior from the target (a phenomenon referred to as *behavioral confirmation*). Thus, expecting Jody to be a warm and friendly person, I may elicit warm and friendly behavior from her and form similar impressions of her. This expectancy confirmation is the essence of Merton's self-fulfilling prophecy and has been the subject of considerable laboratory and field studies by social psychologists.[1]

In a widely cited investigation of expectancy confirmation, Snyder, Tanke, and Berscheid had male perceivers engage in a dyadic, getting-acquainted conversation with female targets.[2] Before the conversation, each man was given a randomly assigned photograph, ostensibly of his woman partner. For half of the men, the picture portrayed the target woman as physically attractive; for the other half of the men, the picture portrayed the target as physically unattractive. In reality, the pictures were not of the targets, but of women who had participated in an earlier study. Snyder, Tanke, and Berscheid wanted to see if the beliefs, expectations, and stereotypes associated with physical attractiveness—namely, "what is beautiful is good"—would have an influence on the conversations between perceivers and targets.

Perceivers' reports indicated that the photo-induced expectations did indeed affect perceivers' postconversation impressions of targets. Men given attractive photos found their women partners to be more warm, open, and friendly than did men given unattractive photos—evidence of the perceptual confirmation of the men's physical attractiveness-based expectations. Additionally, independent judges, blind to experimental conditions, listened to only the targets' portion of the conversations. Judges' reports of targets' behavior indicated that the women in the attractive-photo condition actually behaved in a more warm and friendly manner than the women in the unattractive-photo condition—providing evidence of behavioral confirmation of perceivers' expectations. Analyses of perceivers' portions of the conversation, also by independent judges, indicated that the observed confirmation effects were due to differential behavior of the perceivers during the conversations. Specifically, men who expected to interact with attractive, warm, and friendly women behaved in a warm and friendly manner themselves, thus helping to elicit such behavior from those women. Thus, Snyder, Tanke, and Berscheid demonstrated that a "what is beautiful is good" stereotype can be self-fulfilling—behaviorally confirmed by targets because of perceivers' biased behavior.

Although this expectancy confirmation effect has important moderators and boundary conditions, it has been demonstrated in a variety of social settings, including the classroom, the workplace, and the psychological clinic. In addition to physical appearance, researchers have examined the confirmatory effects of other interpersonal expectations, such as those based on gender, race, and academic ability.[1] Although recent reviews and theoretical models have questioned the pervasiveness and extent of behavioral expectancy effects, most accounts of expectancy-influenced social encounters affirm the potential of such expectancies for producing biased outcomes.[3] Furthermore, expectancy confirmation phenomena have been linked to important deleterious social phenomena such as prejudice, discrimination, and the perpetuation of stereotypes. Thus, previous work on expectancy confirmation has focused on questions of the process, outcomes, and boundary conditions of the phenomenon—the "how" and "how much" of expectancy confirmation.

The purpose of this review is to highlight a newly emerging theme in theory and research on expectancy confirmation. Recently, researchers interested in expectancy confirmation processes have turned their attention toward understanding the motivational antecedents of these processes—the "why" of expectancy confirmation. These efforts reflect an attempt to understand and explain, at a more parsimonious level, the diverse psychological and behavioral mechanisms that affect expectancy-influenced social interactions. Additionally, this motivational focus coincides with a renewed interest in motivational theories of social thinking and social behavior—theories being developed and explored in many psychological domains. Such theories postulate that much of thinking and behavior is purposeful and directed at achieving some more or less specific end. Thus, understanding psychological and behavioral processes requires understanding the needs, motives, goals, and plans that underlie such processes.

This review presents a sample of the emerging theory and research on the motivational moderators of expectancy confirmation. First, the role of impression formation goals—the extent to which people are concerned with gathering and integrating information about other people—is considered. Work on motives dealing with the regulation and facilitation of social interaction is then presented, including work on the moderating effects of self-presentation (e.g., ingratiation, self-promotion). Finally, the motivational and confirmatory implications of the social relationship between interactants is considered. Although covering the steps in the expectancy confirmation process and the pervasiveness of that process is beyond the scope of the current review, it does represent a taste of the current motivational work in this area.

PERSON PERCEPTION AND IMPRESSION FORMATION

Impression formation is generally defined as the process of perceiving pieces of information about an individual (e.g., prior expectations, verbal and nonverbal behaviors) and integrating them into some coherent summary impression. Already a process of considerable study by cognitive and social psychologists for some time, impression formation as a motivational goal has recently become a focus of researchers interested in expectancy confirmation processes. These researchers postulate that social interactants' person perception and impression formation concerns moderate the extent of expectancy influences.

Snyder and his colleagues have taken a functional approach to studying the motivational foundations of expectancy confirmation.[4] At a general level, a functional approach is concerned with understanding the psychological functions served by an individual's beliefs and behaviors. A functional analysis of expectancy confirmation focuses on the psychological functions served by the beliefs and behaviors of a perceiver and a target. According to Snyder, perceivers motivated to form stable, predictable impressions of their target partners—perceivers whose behaviors serve the psychological function of acquiring and using social knowledge—are likely to confirm their expectations of targets.

In one study, Snyder and Haugen had male perceivers engage in a getting-acquainted conversation with female targets.[5] This was a conceptual replication of the earlier study by Snyder, Tanke, and Berscheid, but with a focus on obesity stereotypes. Each man was given a photograph, ostensibly of his partner, but, again, in reality, obtained in an earlier study. The picture portrayed the partner as being either obese or of normal weight. Independent of the picture manipulation, each man was given one of three sets of motivational instructions. One third of the men were told to try to "get to know" their partners during their conversations—to form stable, predictable impressions of their partners. Another third of the men were told to "get along" well with their partners—to have smooth and pleasant conversations with them and try to avoid awkward points during their talk. Finally, one third of the men were given no specific motivational instructions for the conversations (a motivational control condition consisting of the traditional paradigmatic components but without any specific interaction objectives delivered to perceivers).

Analyses of perceivers' postconversation impression ratings revealed that relative to the men in the other motivational conditions, the men who were instructed to form stable, predictable impressions of their partners were more likely to form expectancy-confirming impressions of those targets. Specifically, for the men in this motivational condition, those given a picture of an obese target found their partners to be more unfriendly, reserved, and unenthusiastic than those given a picture of a normal-weight target found their partners. Additionally, the behavior of the women in this motivational condition was found by independent judges to be expectancy-consistent. In contrast, there was no evidence of either perceptual or behavioral confirmation in the other two motivational conditions. Perceivers who were instructed to "get along" with their targets as well as perceivers lacking any specific motivational instructions for their interaction neither formed confirming impressions nor elicited confirming behavior. Thus, perceivers whose behaviors served the psychological function of acquiring and using social knowledge were more likely to confirm their preinteraction expectations of targets.

Neuberg has focused on how accuracy motives in person perception moderate expectancy confirmation.[6] Neuberg contrasts the goal of forming an accurate impression of a person with the goal of forming a rapid impression of a person. He believes that a perceiver motivated to form an accurate impression of a target will be less biased in information gathering about the target than will a perceiver motivated to form a rapid impression. As a result, the tendency for expectancy-confirming outcomes will be reduced for the former perceiver.

In a test of this hypothesis, Neuberg had perceivers serve as interviewers for a hypothetical job, with targets serving as applicants. Each interviewer talked with two targets, one at a time, and assessed their suitability for the job. Prior to the conversations, perceivers were led to believe that one of the targets was not well suited for the job, but no such information was given about the other target. Independent of the expectations, perceivers were given instructions either to form accurate impressions of the targets (accuracy goal) or to form impressions sufficient to decide on their suitability for the job (sufficiency goal).

Results indicated that accuracy motives had the predicted effects. Perceivers' postinterview impressions showed that expectancy confirmation occurred only in the sufficiency-goal condition, in which negative-expectancy targets were assessed less favorably than control targets. In contrast, perceivers motivated to form accurate impressions did not differ significantly in their impressions of the two targets. A substantially similar pattern of results was found from analyses of targets' actual behavior. Behavioral confirmation of perceivers' expectations occurred only in the sufficiency-goal condition. Indeed, in the accuracy-goal condition, there was evidence of behavioral disconfirmation: In the eyes of the independent judges, negative-expectancy targets performed better than the control targets.

These researchers have demonstrated that the extent to which perceivers are concerned with arriving at some understanding of their target partners will moderate expectancy effects. One distinction within this research seems to be between forming a stable, predictable impression of a target, as in the work of Snyder and Haugen, and forming an accurate impression of a target, as in Neuberg's work. When perceivers are motivated to form stable, predictable impressions of targets, we see the traditional expectancy confirmation effects. However, when perceivers are motivated to form accurate impressions, the effects are attenuated. The distinction between stability and accuracy appears to be important and has drawn the attention of these researchers.[5] Indeed, some recent theoretical accounts of expectancy confirmation highlight the potential accuracy of expectations and call into question the degree of confirmatory biases in social interaction.[7]

SELF-PRESENTATION AND INTERACTION FACILITATION

Researchers interested in the motivational antecedents of expectancy confirmation are also examining how interactants' self-presentational concerns and concerns with facilitating their social interactions affect the expectancy confirmation process. Briefly, self-presentational motives are concerns associated with managing one's image, one's appearance in the eyes of other people, or one's self-perception. Concerns about interaction facilitation center on having pleasant interactions with others, interactions unencumbered by awkward or uncomfortable exchanges. Both types of motives appear to play important roles in the moderation of expectancy effects.

In the previously discussed study by Snyder and Haugen, one third of the perceivers were instructed to get along well with their target partners.[5] As a result of this manipulation, there was no evidence of expectancy confirmation either in perceivers' postinteraction impressions of targets or in judges' ratings of targets' behavior. Perceivers whose behaviors served the psychological function of regulating and facilitating their social interaction avoided the cognitive and behavioral processes that generally lead to expectancy-confirming interaction outcomes.

In an investigation of the moderating role of ingratiation—a self-presentational goal—Neuberg, Judice, Virdin, and Carrillo had perceivers interview targets for a hypothetical job.[8] Half of the targets were portrayed in a negative light, and the other half were given no such portrayal. Independent of the expectancy manipulation, half of the interviewers were encouraged to get the applicants to like them (self-presentation), while the other half of the interviewers were given no explicit goal.

In the no-goal condition, the traditional expectancy confirmation effects were obtained. Interviewers were relatively cold and more challenging toward the negative-expectancy targets, causing these targets to perform less favorably during the interviews. However, in the liking-goal condition, interviewers behaved in a more warm and friendly manner toward the negative-expectancy targets than toward the no-expectancy targets, which led these interviewers to form expectancy-disconfirming impressions of the negatively labeled targets.

These studies suggest that perceivers motivated either to manage the impressions they give to targets or to have enjoyable social encounters will be less likely to effect a self-fulfilling prophecy than perceivers motivated to form impressions of targets. The interactions seem to be qualitatively different. Self-presentational and facilitative motives appear to inhibit both the tendency for perceivers to engage in expectancy-biased information seeking and targets' behavioral confirmation of perceivers' expectations.

THE PERCEIVER–TARGET RELATIONSHIP

Other researchers interested in the motivational underpinnings of expectancy confirmation focus on the relationship between a perceiver and a target in a particular interaction setting. These researchers claim that the interactants' roles, their relative power in the interaction setting, and the formality and structure of the interaction setting may affect both the motives of the interactants and the likelihood of expectancy-confirming outcomes.

Elsewhere, I have suggested that the relative power of perceiver and target moderates both motivation and expectancy confirmation.[9] In an investigation of this hypothesis, each perceiver was given one of two expectations about the target. Independent of the expectancy manipulation, one of the participants (either the perceiver or the target, as determined by random assignment to experimental conditions) had the power to choose whether the other would be a participant in a subsequent reward-laden phase of the study. When the perceivers had the power to affect the targets' outcomes, perceivers reported they were motivated primarily to acquire knowledge about targets, and targets reported they were motivated primarily to facilitate favorable interaction outcomes. These interactions resulted in both the perceptual and the behavioral confirmation of perceivers' experimentally delivered expectations about targets. However, when targets had control over perceivers' outcomes, the motive reports were reversed: Perceivers reported a primary concern with facilitating favorable interaction outcomes, and targets reported a primary concern with the acquisition of knowledge about perceivers. In these interactions, there were no signs of perceptual or behavioral confirmation. Thus, power affected both subjects' motivations (at least, self-reported motivations) and the likelihood of subsequent expectancy confirmation.

In her situational taxonomy of expectancy situations, Harris has suggested that the formality and degree of structure in an interaction affect the extent to which expectancies will be influential.[10] Formality refers to the social formality of an interaction setting, the extent of adherence to explicit and fixed customs or social rules. Structure refers to how highly scripted an interaction is, the extent to which the roles are highly specified and articulated. Although these two dimensions are related, they are probably not redundant, as not all socially structured situations are formal (e.g., the players of a board game have structured roles, but they need not be formal roles).

Indirect support for Harris's hypothesis about the degree of structure was found in a study in which grade-school boys were paired for two different tasks.[11] For the structured task, the boys worked together to complete a color-by-number picture; for the less structured task, the boys worked together to plan and build their own Lego block design. Perceiver boys in this study also either were told that their partner would be difficult to work with or were given no such expectancy. Expectancy effects were weaker in the more structured task. During the color-by-number task, perceivers were less likely to form expectancy-confirming impressions and elicit expectancy-confirming behavior from targets than during the Lego task. From a motivational perspective, this result may have been due to perceivers' greater concern with completing the formal requirements of the more structured task. This concern may have kept perceivers too cognitively and behaviorally busy to engage in the expectancy confirmation processes that the less structured Lego task afforded.

Thus, aspects of the social relationship between a perceiver and a target can have motivational ramifications and subsequent moderating effects on expectancy influences. The effects of these relationship factors are important to a thorough understanding of expectancy confirmation phenomena. Perceivers' and targets' motives may often be induced specifically because of the nature of the social relationship in a given interaction setting. When perceivers and targets will be concerned with impression formation or self-presentation may depend in large part on the nature of their social setting and the roles they are required to play.

DISCUSSION

Although most of the work covered in this review focuses on a perceiver's motives, other work not covered here focuses on the moderating role of a target's motives. To the extent that the same motives operate in other social contexts, these motivational approaches may add not only to our understanding of expectancy confirmation processes in particular, but also to what we know about social thinking and social behavior in general.

Acknowledgments—Support for the author's research described in this article was provided by a Dissertation Research Award from the American Psychological Association. The author would like to thank the anonymous reviewer who provided valuable comments on an earlier version of the manuscript. Preparation of the manuscript was aided through a Byron K. Trippet stipend.

Notes

1. J.M. Darley and R.H. Fazio, Expectancy-confirmation processes arising in the social interaction sequence, *American Psychologist, 35,* 867–881 (1980); R. Rosenthal, *On the Social Psychology of the Self-Fulfilling Prophecy: Further Evidence for Pygmalion Effects and Their Mediating Mechanisms* (M.S.S. Information Corporation Modular Publications, New York, 1974); M. Snyder, When belief creates reality, in *Advances in Experimental Social Psychology,* Vol. 18, L. Berkowitz, Ed. (Academic Press, Orlando, FL, 1984).

2. M. Snyder, E.D. Tanke, and E. Berscheid, Social perception and interpersonal behavior: On the self-fulfilling nature of social stereotypes, *Journal*

of Personality and Social Psychology, 35, 656–666 (1977).

3. L. Jussim, Social perception and social reality: A reflection-construction model, *Psychological Review, 98,* 54–73 (1991); E.E. Jones, *Interpersonal Perception* (W.H. Freeman, New York, 1990).

4. M. Snyder, Motivational foundations of behavioral confirmation, in *Advances in Experimental Social Psychology,* Vol. 25, M. Zanna, Ed. (Academic Press, San Diego, 1992).

5. M. Snyder and J.A. Haugen, *Why does behavioral confirmation occur? A functional perspective,* paper presented at the annual meeting of the American Psychological Association, Boston (August 1990).

6. S.L. Neuberg, The goal of forming accurate impressions during social interactions: Attenuating the impact of negative expectancies, *Journal of Personality and Social Psychology, 56,* 374–386 (1989).

7. Jussim, note 3.

8. S.L. Neuberg, T.N. Judice, L.M. Virdin, and M.A. Carrillo, Perceiver self-presentational goals as moderators of expectancy influences: Ingratiation and the disconfirmation of negative expectancies, *Journal of Personality and Social Psychology, 64,* 409–420 (1993).

9. J.T. Copeland, *Motivational implications of social power for behavioral confirmation,* paper presented at the annual meeting of the Midwestern Psychological Association, Chicago (May 1992).

10. M.J. Harris, Issues in studying the mediation of interpersonal expectancy effects: A taxonomy of expectancy situations, in *Interpersonal Expectations: Theory, Research, and Applications,* P.D. Blank, Ed. (Cambridge University Press, London, in press).

11. M.J. Harris, R. Milich, E.M. Corbitt, D.W. Hoover, and M. Brady, Self-fulfilling effects of stigmatizing information on children's social interactions, *Journal of Personality and Social Psychology, 63,* 41–50 (1992).

Recommended Reading

Hilton, J.L., and Darley, J.M. (1991). The effects of interaction goals on person perception. In *Advances in Experimental Social Psychology,* Vol. 24, M.P. Zanna, Ed. (Academic Press, San Diego).

Jussim, L. (1991). Social perception and social reality: A reflection-construction model. *Psychological Review, 98,* 54–73.

Snyder, M. (1992). Motivational foundations of behavioral confirmation. In *Advances in Experimental Social Psychology,* Vol. 25, M. Zanna, Ed. (Academic Press, San Diego).

Article 13

THE TRUTH about LYING

Has lying gotten a bad rap?

WE DO IT AS OFTEN AS WE BRUSH OUR TEETH, YET UNTIL RECENTLY LYING RECEIVED LITTLE ATTENTION FROM PSYCHOLOGISTS. COULD WE REALLY GET THROUGH LIFE WITHOUT IT?

By Allison Kornet

If, as the cliche has it, the 1980s was the decade of greed, then the quintessential sin of the 1990s might just be lying. After all, think of the accusations of deceit leveled at politicians like Bob Packwood, Marion Barry, Dan Rostenkowski, Newt Gingrich, and Bill Clinton.

And consider the top-level Texaco executives who initially denied making racist comments at board meetings; the young monk who falsely accused Cardinal Bernardin of molestation; Susan Smith, the white woman who killed her young boys and blamed a black man for it; and Joe Klein, the *Newsweek* columnist who adamantly swore for months that he had nothing to do with his anonymously-published novel *Primary Colors*. Even Hollywood has noticed our apparent deception obsession: witness recent films like *Quiz Show, True Lies, The Crucible, Secrets & Lies,* and comedian Jim Carrey's latest release, *Liar, Liar.*

What's going on here? Nothing out of the ordinary, insists Leonard Saxe, Ph.D., a polygraph expert and professor of psychology at Brandeis University. "Lying has long been a part of everyday life," he says. "We couldn't get through the day without being deceptive." Yet until recently lying was almost entirely ignored by psychologists, leaving serious discussion of the topic in the hands of ethicists and theologians. Freud wrote next to nothing about deception; even the 1500-page *Encyclopedia of Psychology*, published in 1984, mentions lies only in a brief entry on detecting them. But as psychologists delve deeper into the details of deception, they're finding that lying is a surprisingly common and complex phenomenon.

For starters, recent work by Bella DePaulo, Ph.D., a psychologist at the University of Virginia, confirms Nietzche's assertion that the lie is a condition of life. In a 1996 study, DePaulo and her colleagues had 147 people between the ages of 18 and 71 keep a diary of all the falsehoods they told over the course of a week. Most people, she found, lie once or twice a day—almost as often as they snack from the refrigerator or brush their teeth. Both men and women lie in approximately a fifth of their social exchanges lasting 10 or more minutes; over the course of a week they deceive about 30 percent of those with whom they interact one-on-one. Furthermore, some types of relationships, such as those between parents and teens, are virtual magnets for deception: "College students lie to their mothers in one out of two conversations," reports DePaulo. (Incidentally, when researchers refer to lying, they don't include the mindless pleasantries or polite equivocations we offer each other in passing, such as "I'm fine, thanks" or "No trouble at all." An "official" lie actually misleads, deliberately conveying a false impression. So complimenting a friend's awful haircut or telling a creditor that the check is in the mail both qualify.)

Saxe points out that most of us receive conflicting messages about lying. Although we're socialized from the time we can speak to believe that it's always better to tell the truth, in reality society often encourages and even rewards deception. Show up late for an early morning meeting at work and it's best

> **THE AVERAGE PERSON LIES ONCE OR TWICE A DAY.**

not to admit that you overslept. "You're punished far more than you would be if you lie and say you were stuck in traffic," Saxe notes. Moreover, lying is integral to many occupations. Think how often we see lawyers constructing farfetched theories on behalf of their clients or reporters misrepresenting themselves in order to gain access to good stories.

Of Course I Love You

Dishonesty also pervades our romantic relationships, as you might expect from the titles of books like *101 Lies Men Tell Women* (Harper Collins), by Missouri psychologist Dory Hollander, Ph.D. (Hollander's nomination for the #1 spot: "I'll call you.") Eighty-five percent of the couples interviewed in a 1990 study of college students reported that one or both partners had lied about past relationships or recent indiscretions. And DePaulo finds that dating couples lie to each other in about a third of their interactions—perhaps even more often than they deceive other people.

Fortunately, marriage seems to offer some protection against deception: Spouses lie to each other in "only" about 10 percent of their major conversations. The bad news? That 10 percent just refers to the typically minor lies of everyday life. DePaulo recently began looking at the less frequent "big" lies that involve deep betrayals of trust, and she's finding that the vast majority of them occur between people in intimate relationships. "You save your really big lies," she says, "for the person that you're closest to."

Sweet Little Lies

Though some lies produce interpersonal friction, others may actually serve as a kind of harmless social lubricant. "They make it easier for people to get along," says DePaulo, noting that in the the diary study one in every four of the participants' lies were told solely for the benefit of another person. In fact, "fake positive" lies—those in which people pretend to like someone or something more than they actually do ("Your muffins are the best ever")—are about 10 to 20 times more common than "false negative" lies in which people pretend to like someone or something *less* ("That two-faced rat will never get my vote").

Certain cultures may place special importance on these "kind" lies. A survey of residents at 31 senior citizen centers in Los Angeles recently revealed that only about half of elderly Korean Americans believe that patients diagnosed with life-threatening metastatic cancer should be told the truth about their condition. In contrast, nearly 90 percent of Americans of European or African descent felt that the terminally ill should be confronted with the truth.

Not surprisingly, research also confirms that the closer we are to someone, the more likely it is that the lies we tell them will be altruistic ones. This is particularly true of women: Although the sexes lie with equal frequency, women

> **DATING COUPLES LIE TO EACH OTHER IN ABOUT A THIRD OF THEIR INTERACTIONS.**

are especially likely to stretch the truth in order to protect someone else's feelings, DePaulo reports. Men, on the other hand, are more prone to lying about themselves—the typical conversation between two guys contains about eight times as many self-oriented lies as it does falsehoods about other people.

Men and women may also differ in their ability to deceive their friends. In a University of Virginia study, psychologists asked pairs of same-sex friends to try to detect lies told by the other person. Six months later the researchers repeated the experiment with the same participants. While women had become slightly better at detecting their friends' lies over time, men didn't show any improvement—evidence, perhaps, that women are particularly good at learning to read their friends more accurately as a relationship deepens.

Who Lies?

Saxe believes that anyone under enough pressure, or given enough incentive, will lie. But in a study published in the *Journal of Personality and Social Psychology*, DePaulo and Deborah A. Kashy, Ph.D., of Texas A&M University, report that frequent liars tend to be manipulative and Machiavellian, not to mention overly concerned with the impression they make on others. Still, DePaulo warns that liars "don't always fit the stereotype of caring only about themselves." Further research reveals that extroverted, sociable people are slightly more likely to lie, and that some personality and physical traits—notably self-confidence and physical attractiveness—have been linked to an individual's skill at lying when under pressure.

On the other hand, the people *least* likely to lie are those who score high on psychological scales of responsibility and those with meaningful same-sex friendships. In his book *Lies! Lies!!*

> **SAXE BELIEVES THAT ANYONE UNDER ENOUGH PRESSURE, OR GIVEN ENOUGH INCENTIVE, WILL LIE.**

Lies!!! The Psychology of Deceit (American Psychiatric Press, Inc.), psychiatrist Charles Ford, M.D., adds depressed people to that list. He suggests that individuals in the throes of depression seldom deceive others—or are deceived themselves—because they seem to perceive and describe reality with greater accuracy than others. Several studies show that depressed people delude themselves far less than their nondepressed peers about the amount of control they have over situations, and also about the effect they have on other people. Researchers such as UCLA psychologist Shelley Taylor, Ph.D., have even cited such findings as evidence that a certain amount of self-delusion—basically, lying to yourself—is essential to good mental health. (Many playwrights, including Arthur Miller and Eugene O'Neill, seem to share the same view about truth-telling. In *Death of a Salesman* and *The Iceman Cometh*, for example, lies are life sustaining: The heroes become tragic figures when their lies are stripped away.)

Detecting Lies

Anyone who has played cards with a poker-faced opponent can appreciate how difficult it is to detect a liar. Surprisingly, technology doesn't help very much. Few experts display much confidence in the deception-detecting abilities of the polygraph, or lie detector. Geoffrey C. Bunn, Ph.D., a psychologist and polygraph historian at Canada's York University, goes so far as to describe the lie detector as "an entertainment device" rather than a scientific instrument. Created around 1921 during one of the first collaborations between scientists and police, the device was quickly popularized by enthusiastic newspaper headlines and by the element of drama it bestowed in movies and novels.

But mass appeal doesn't confer legitimacy. The problem with the polygraph, say experts like Bunn, is that it detects fear, not lying; the physiological responses that it measures—most often heart rate, skin conductivity, and rate of respiration—don't necessarily accompany dishonesty.

"The premise of a lie detector is that a smoke alarm goes off in the brain when we lie because we're doing something wrong," explains Saxe. "But sometimes we're completely comfortable with our lies." Thus a criminal's lie can easily go undetected if he has no fear of telling it. Similarly, a true statement by an innocent individual could be misinterpreted if the person is sufficiently afraid of the examination circumstances. According to Saxe, the best-controlled research suggests that lie detectors err at a rate anywhere from 25 to 75 percent. Perhaps this is why most state and federal courts won't allow polygraph "evidence."

Some studies suggest that lies can be detected by means other than a polygraph—by tracking speech hesitations or changes in vocal pitch, for example, or by identifying various nervous adaptive habits like scratching, blinking, or fidgeting. But most psychologists agree that lie detection is destined to be imperfect. Still, researchers continue to investigate new ways of picking up lies. While studying how language patterns are associated with improvements in physical health, James W. Pennebaker, Ph.D., a professor of psychology at Southern Methodist University, also began to explore whether a person's choice of words was a sign of deception. Examining data gathered from a text analysis program, Pennebaker and SMU colleague Diane Berry, Ph.D., determined that there are certain language patterns that predict when someone is being less than honest. For example, liars tend to use fewer first-person words like *I* or *my* in both speech and writing. They are also less apt to use emotional words, such as *hurt* or *angry*, cognitive words, like *understand* or *realize*, and so-called exclusive words, such as *but* or *without*, that distinguish between what is and isn't in a category.

Not Guilty

While the picture of lying that has emerged in recent years is far more favorable than that suggested by its biblical "thou shalt not" status, most liars remain at least somewhat conflicted about their behavior. In DePaulo's studies, participants described conversations in which they lied as less intimate and pleasant than truthful encounters, suggesting that people are not entirely at ease with their deceptions. That may explain why falsehoods are more likely to be told over the telephone, which provides more anonymity than a face-to-face conversation. In most cases, however, any mental distress that results from telling an everyday lie quickly dissipates. Those who took part in the diary study said they would tell about 75 percent of their lies again if given a second chance—a position no doubt bolstered by their generally high success rate. Only about a fifth of their falsehoods were discovered during the one-week study period.

> **FALSEHOODS ARE ESPECIALLY LIKELY TO BE TOLD OVER THE TELEPHONE.**

Certainly anyone who insists on condemning all lies should ponder what would happen if we could reliably tell when our family, friends, colleagues, and government leaders were deceiving us. It's tempting to think that the world would become a better place when purged of the deceptions that seem to interfere with our attempts at genuine communication or intimacy. On the other hand, perhaps our social lives would collapse under the weight of relentless honesty, with unveiled truths destroying our ability to connect with others. The ubiquity of lying is clearly a problem, but would we want to will away all of our lies? Let's be honest.

Spotting Lies: Can Humans Learn to Do Better?

Bella M. DePaulo

Bella M. DePaulo is Professor of Psychology at the University of Virginia and recipient of a Research Scientist Development Award from the National Institute of Mental Health. Address correspondence to Bella DePaulo, Department of Psychology, Gilmer Hall, University of Virginia, Charlottesville, VA 22903; e-mail: bmd@virginia.edu.

Though cynicism may seem rampant, the empirical fact is that most people seem to believe most of what they hear most of the time. I have seen this repeatedly in the studies my colleagues and I have conducted on the detection of deception.[1] To determine whether people can separate truths from lies, we show them videotapes we have made of people we know to be lying or telling the truth. The topics of these lies and truths vary widely. For example, sometimes the people on the tape are talking about their feelings about other people they know; other times, the speakers are describing their opinions about controversial issues; in still other studies, they are talking to an artist about their preferences for various paintings, some of which are the artist's own work. When we show people ("judges") these tapes, we ask them to tell us, for each segment that they watch, whether they think the person on the tape (the "speaker") was lying or telling the truth. We also ask them to indicate, on rating scales, just how deceptive or truthful the speaker seemed to be. We might also ask them how they think the speaker really did feel and what impression the speaker was trying to convey about how he or she felt. For example, it might seem that the speaker was politely trying to give the impression that she liked the person she was describing, when in fact she detested that person.

Typically, the tapes that we play for our judges include equal numbers of truths and lies. Yet when judges watch or hear the tapes, they almost always think that many more of the messages are truths than lies. (One of the rare exceptions was a study in which the speakers on the tape were experienced salespersons pitching the kinds of products that they sell; in that study, the judges more often thought that the salespersons were lying.[2]) Similarly, judges typically believe that the speakers really do feel the way they are claiming to feel. When a speaker claims to like a painting, the judges are more inclined to believe that he or she really does like it than to infer that the kind words are a facade to cover genuine loathing.

Despite this compelling inclination to take what other people say at face value, judges are not totally blind to the differences between truths and lies. When we ask them to indicate just how deceptive or truthful the speakers seemed to be, judges reliably rate the lies as somewhat more deceptive than the truths. The ratings of both the lies and the truths are almost always on the truthful end of the scale; still, the lies seem to the judges to be a little less truthful than the truths.[3] When we study humans' ability to detect lies, it is this ability to distinguish truths from lies that we examine.

WOULD PEOPLE BE BETTER LIE DETECTORS IF THEY WERE LESS TRUSTING?

Generally, then, people seem to take each other at their word more often than they should. Carol Toris and I did a simple study to see whether people would be better lie detectors if they were forewarned of the possibility that another person might be lying to them.[4] Subjects played the role of interviewers and either were or were not forewarned that the applicants might lie to them. The forewarned interviewers did indeed become less trusting: They thought the applicants were generally more deceptive than did the interviewers whose suspicions had not been aroused. But the suspicious interviewers did not become any more accurate at distinguishing liars from truth tellers. That is, they did not rate the applicants who really were lying as any more deceptive than the ones who were telling the truth.

Robert Rosenthal and I have seen the same pattern in our studies of sex differences in detecting deceit.[5] In the way that they perceive the liars and the truth tellers on our videotapes, men are generally less trusting than women. For example, when judges watch subjects who are talking to an art student about paintings, the male judges are more likely than the female judges to think that the subjects are exaggerating their liking for the paintings; the women, in contrast, are more inclined to believe that the liking expressed by the subjects is genuine. Again, though, men and women do not differ in their abilities to distinguish liars from truth tellers, that is, to see the liars as relatively less trustworthy than the truth tellers.

WOULD PEOPLE BE BETTER LIE DETECTORS IF THEY HAD MORE EXPERIENCE AT IT?

To distinguish truths from lies may require some knowledge or sensitivity about the ways that lies differ from truths. Perhaps this sort of understanding comes with endless practice at trying to detect deceit. Roger Pfeifer and I studied the lie detection skills of federal law enforcement officers who had worked for years at jobs that routinely involved attempts to detect deceit.[6] These officers and undergraduate students who had no special experience or training at detecting deceit both listened to the same audiotapes of students who were lying or telling the truth about their opinions about controversial issues. Across this test of 32 lies and 32 truths, the officers were no more accurate than the students at discriminating truths from lies—they only thought they were. That is, the officers were more confident than the students, and their confidence increased over the course of the test, although their accuracy did not. A study of experienced customs inspectors told the same tale: They were no better than laypersons at discerning which potential "smugglers" to search in a mock customs inspection conducted at an airport.[7] Similarly, in studies of special groups of people who should be especially skilled lie detectors—members of the U.S. Secret Service, federal polygraphers, judges, police, psychiatrists, and special interest groups (e.g., business people and lawyers)—as well as students, Paul Ekman and Maureen O'Sullivan have found generally unimpressive levels of accuracy at detecting deceit.[8] Of those groups, only the Secret Service did particularly well.

Another kind of experience that intuitively might seem to predict skill at knowing when someone is lying is the kind that comes from getting to know someone over the course of a deepening relationship. Should not dating partners, spouses, and close friends be much more perceptive than strangers at spotting each other's lies? Once again, research has shown that experience is no guarantee of sensitivity to deceit. Compared with strangers, relational partners are more trusting of each other's truthfulness and more certain that their impressions of each other's truthfulness or deceptiveness are correct. But unless that trust is severed somehow, they are ordinarily not more accurate at detecting each other's deceit.[9]

Perhaps there is still another way in which experience might predict skill at detecting deception. Maybe any special skills that people have at detecting deceit are specific to the kinds of lies they are most experienced at hearing—the "I've heard that one before" phenomenon. My colleagues and I already knew from prior work in our lab that people lie differently to attractive people than to unattractive people. Interestingly, they lie more transparently to the former. We wanted to know whether the lies told to attractive people are especially transparent to judges who are themselves attractive. To test this idea, we asked judges who were themselves either attractive or unattractive to watch tapes of speakers who were lying and telling the truth to attractive and unattractive listeners.[10] The judges, however, could see only the speakers; they did not even know that the listeners varied systematically in attractiveness. Further, the speakers all lied and told the truth about the same topics—their opinions on controversial issues. These were not the stereotypical "gee, what beautiful eyes you have" kinds of lies. We found, once again, that the lies told to attractive listeners were easier to detect than were the lies told to unattractive listeners. More important, the lies told to attractive listeners were especially obvious to the judges who were themselves attractive. The unattractive judges, in contrast, did relatively better at detecting the lies told to the unattractive listeners.

There is other evidence, too, that skill at detecting lies may be specific to particular kinds of lies. For example, we have found that the ability to detect lies when liars are trying to hide their fond feelings is not related to the ability to detect lies when liars are trying to conceal ill will. We have also found that skill at detecting women's lies is unrelated to skill at detecting men's lies.[11] There is another interesting bit of evidence of specificity, which comes from a study in which Miron Zuckerman and his colleagues tried to train judges to be more accurate detectors of deceit.[12] The training procedure was very straightforward. Judges watched a segment in which a speaker was lying or telling the truth, and then they recorded their judgment as to whether the speaker was lying. Next, they were told whether the segment was in fact a lie or a truth. This procedure was repeated for several lies and truths told by the same speaker. Judges who were "trained" in this way did indeed become better at detecting deception, but only when watching the speaker they were trained on. Their new and improved deception detection skills did not generalize to different liars.

There is even evidence for specificity at a cultural level. Charles Bond and his colleagues have shown that both Americans and Jordanians can distinguish lies from truths when judging members of their own culture; however, they cannot differentiate each other's truths and lies.[13]

HOW DO LIES DIFFER FROM TRUTHS?

Intuitively, it may seem that the best way to train people to detect deceit is to instruct them about the kinds of behaviors that really do distinguish truths from lies and to give them practice at recognizing such behaviors. This approach assumes that there are known differences between truths and lies, and in fact there are.[1]

Meta-analyses of the many studies of cues to deception reported in the literature indicate that when people are lying, they blink more, have more dilated pupils, and show more *adaptors* (self-manipulating gestures, such as rubbing or scratching) than they do when they are telling the truth. They also give shorter responses that are more negative, more irrelevant, and more generalized. They speak in a more distancing way (as if they do not really want to commit themselves to what they are saying), and they speak in a higher pitch. Though people who are about to tell a lie take more time to plan what they are about to say than do people who are about to tell the truth, the resulting statements tend to be more internally discrepant and more marred by hesitations, repetitions, grammatical errors, slips of the tongue, and other disfluencies. The lies seem rehearsed and lacking in spontaneity.[14]

There are, then, some important behavioral cues to deception. But for a variety of reasons, I am not optimistic about the prospects of teaching these cues directly, despite the fact that some limited successes have been reported. First, although these findings were obtained across a variety of studies, they are qualified in important ways. For example, it is possible to divide the studies into categories based on whether the liars were more or less motivated to get away with their lies. When this is done, it becomes apparent that the cues to deception differ. When people are more highly motivated to get away with their lies (compared with when they do not care as much), they shift their postures less, move their heads less, show fewer adaptors, gaze less, and even blink less when they are lying than when they are telling the truth. Their answers are also shorter and spoken more slowly. The overall impression they seem to convey is one of inhibition and rigidity, as if they are trying too hard to control their behavior and thereby overcontrolling it. (It may be this dampening of expressiveness that accounts for another counterintuitive finding documented repeatedly in my lab—that is, that people who are most motivated to get away with their lies are, ironically, least likely to be successful at doing so when other people can see or hear any of their nonverbal cues.) Degree of liars' motivation is just one of the factors that will qualify conclusions about cues to deceit. There will be many others. For example, cues to deceit should vary with emotional state. The liar who feels guilty about a grave offense, for example, will probably lie in different ways than will a friend bubbling over with glee in an attempt to conceal a surprise birthday celebration.

Second, all these cues are associated with deceit only probabilistically. There is no one cue that always indicates that a person is lying. And each of the cues that is associated with deceit is also associated with other psychological states and conditions. For example, people speak in a higher pitch not only when they are lying but also when they are talking to children.

Third, as suggested by the training study in which improvement did not generalize to different liars, there are important individual differences in the ways that people lie. When Machiavellian people are rightly accused of lying, for example, they look their accusers in the eye while denying they have lied. It is the "low-Mach" types who conform to the cultural stereotype about lying and instead look away. Further, to determine when a person is lying, it is important to understand that person's usual ways of behaving. For instance, although halting and disfluent speech can be a sign of deceit, there are people who characteristically speak haltingly and disfluently; for them, verbal clutter is unlikely to indicate deceit unless it is even more marked than usual. Moreover, some people may be so skilled at lying that it is virtually impossible for anyone to distinguish their lies from their truths. In the study of experienced salespersons, for example, the same kinds of judges (introductory psychology students) who could detect differences between the truths and lies of inexperienced liars could see no differences at all between the truths and lies told by experienced salespersons.[2] Even when the judges were given a hint that improved their lie detection success when they were observing inexperienced liars (namely, to pay special attention to tone of voice), they still could not differentiate the salespersons' lies and truths.

Does this mean that it is hopeless to try to refine people's sensitivity to the differences between truths and lies? Perhaps not. I think people know more about deception than it appears when experimenters ask them directly whether they think someone is lying. Sometimes people who cannot distinguish truths from lies by their ratings of deceptiveness can make a distinction by their ratings of some other attribute, such as ambivalence. Also, when people talk out loud as they try to decide whether someone is lying or not, they sound less confident when the message they are considering is a lie than when it is a truth; further, they are more likely to mention the possibility that the message is a lie when it really is.[15] Interviewers sometimes behave differently toward liars than toward truth tellers; for example, they might ask liars more questions that sound suspicious.[16] I think, then, that people have implicit knowledge about deception that they do not quite know how to access. Just how they can learn to access it is the question my students and I are currently pursuing.

Notes

1. B.M. DePaulo, J.I. Stone, and G.D. Lassiter, Deceiving and detecting deceit, in *The Self and Social Life*, B.R. Schlenker, Ed. (McGraw-Hill, New York, 1985).
2. P.J. DePaulo and B.M. DePaulo, Can at-

tempted deception by salespersons and customers be detected through nonverbal behavioral cues? *Journal of Applied Social Psychology, 19,* 1552–1577 (1989).

3. In studies in which judges simply indicate whether they think the speaker was lying or telling the truth, and lies and truths occur equally often, accuracy rarely exceeds 60%. A chance level of accuracy would be 50% in those studies.

4. C. Toris and B.M. DePaulo, Effects of actual deception and suspiciousness of deception on interpersonal perceptions, *Journal of Personality and Social Psychology, 47,* 1063–1073 (1984).

5. R. Rosenthal and B.M. DePaulo, Sex differences in eavesdropping on nonverbal cues, *Journal of Personality and Social Psychology, 37,* 273–285 (1979).

6. B.M. DePaulo and R.L. Pfeifer, On-the-job experience and skill at detecting deception, *Journal of Applied Social Psychology, 16,* 249–267 (1986).

7. R.E. Kraut and D. Poe, Behavioral roots of person perception: The deception judgments of customs inspectors and laypersons, *Journal of Personality and Social Psychology, 39,* 784–798 (1980).

8. P. Ekman and M. O'Sullivan, Who can catch a liar? *American Psychologist, 46,* 913–920 (1991).

9. S.A. McCornack and T.R. Levine, When lovers become leery: The relationship between suspiciousness and accuracy in detecting deception, *Communication Monographs, 57,* 219–230 (1990).

10. B.M. DePaulo, J. Tang, and J.I. Stone, Physical attractiveness and skill at detecting deception, *Personality and Social Psychology Bulletin, 13,* 177–187 (1987).

11. B.M. DePaulo and R. Rosenthal, Telling lies, *Journal of Personality and Social Psychology, 37,* 1713–1722 (1979).

12. M. Zuckerman, R. Koestner, and A.O. Alton, Learning to detect deception, *Journal of Personality and Social Psychology, 46,* 519–528 (1984).

13. C.F. Bond, Jr., A. Omar, A. Mahmoud, and R.N. Bonser, Lie detection across cultures, *Journal of Nonverbal Behavior, 14,* 189–204 (1990).

14. Other behavioral cues to deception have also been documented, but are based on fewer studies. For example, Ekman and his colleagues showed that nurses who were pretending to watch a pleasant film when the film was actually very gory smiled in different ways than the nurses who really were watching a pleasant film and telling the truth about it. The lying nurses were less likely to show smiles of genuine enjoyment ("Duchenne" smiles) and more likely to show "masking" smiles in which traces of their negative feelings were discernible. These data were reported in P. Ekman, W.V. Friesen, and M. O'Sullivan, Smiles while lying, *Journal of Personality and Social Psychology, 54,* 414–420 (1988).

15. K. Hurd and P. Noller, Decoding deception: A look at the process, *Journal of Nonverbal Behavior, 12,* 217–233 (1988).

16. D.B. Buller, K.D. Strzyzewski, and J. Comstock, Interpersonal deception: I. Deceivers' reactions to receivers' suspicions and probing, *Communication Monographs, 58,* 1–24 (1991).

Recommended Reading

DePaulo, B.M., Stone, J.I., and Lassiter, G.D. (1985). Deceiving and detecting deceit. In *The Self and Social Life,* B.R. Schlenker, Ed. (McGraw-Hill, New York).

Lewis, M., and Saarni, C., Eds. (1993). *Lying and Deception in Everyday Life* (Guilford Press, New York).

Attitudes

Every year during professional football's Super Bowl, advertisers pay untold millions of dollars in order to show their commercials for beer, chips, beer, tires, beer, computers, and beer. The network showing the game also takes the opportunity to air countless advertisements promoting other programs on that network.

Every 4 years, during the presidential election, the airwaves are crowded with political advertisements in which candidates tout their own accomplishments, pose with cute children and cheering crowds, and display ominous, unflattering, black and white photographs of their opponents, as grim-voiced announcers catalog the opponents' shortcomings.

The underlying reason for both of these phenomena is that the advertisers, networks, and candidates all share a common assumption: that attitudes are important. If attitudes toward a particular brand of beer can be made more favorable through cute commercials involving talking frogs, then people will buy more of that beer. If attitudes toward a television program can be made more favorable by showing funny clips from it every 12 minutes, then more people will watch the program. If atti-

UNIT 4

tudes toward a candidate can be made more positive—or attitudes toward the opponent more negative—then people will be more likely to vote for the candidate. To change someone's behavior, this argument goes, you must first change that person's attitude.

To one degree or another, social psychology has shared this view for decades. The study of attitudes and attitude change has been a central concern of the field for half a century—in fact, for a while that seemed to be *all* that social psychology studied. One major approach during this time has been to focus on where attitudes come from. The evidence from this research suggests that we acquire attitudes not only from careful consideration of the facts, but also through processes that are much less conscious and deliberate. Merely being exposed to some object frequently enough, for example, generally leads to a more favorable attitude toward it. It also appears that we sometimes arrive at our attitudes by looking at our behaviors, and then simply inferring what our attitudes must be based on our actions.

Another approach to the topic of attitudes has been to examine directly the basic assumption mentioned above, namely that attitudes are strongly associated with actual behavior. As it turns out, the link between attitudes and behavior is not as powerful or reliable as you might think, although under the right circumstances it is still possible to predict behavior from attitudes with considerable success. In fact, it is because of this link between attitudes and behavior that the last major approach to the topic—studying the factors that influence attitude *change*—has been popular for so long. The first two articles in this unit, in fact, focus on the issue of persuasion; in short, how does one person convince others to change their attitudes?

In "Mindless Propaganda, Thoughtful Persuasion," Anthony Pratkanis and Elliot Aronson discuss an influential theory in contemporary social psychology, the elaboration likelihood model. According to this approach, audiences react to persuasion attempts in two basic ways—either by thinking carefully about the message and attending to its arguments, or through a much more superficial processing of the message and its content. In "How to Sell a Pseudoscience," Anthony Pratkanis outlines how someone could use social psychological principles to persuade others to accept as valid a pseudoscientific belief system. He claims that existing pseudosciences use precisely these techniques in their quest for new members.

The final article, "In Work on Intuition, Gut Feelings Are Tracked to Source: The Brain," discusses some recent research illustrating how we sometimes have unconscious emotional responses to a person or an object before we ever have a conscious awareness of our attitude.

Looking Ahead: Challenge Questions

When someone is paying careful attention to a persuasive message, what implications does this have for the message's success? That is, what factors will be especially important, or unimportant, in such cases? What are the implications when the audience is *not* carefully attending to the message? Could persuasion still occur? What would determine whether it did or not?

How would you go about "selling" a pseudoscientific belief system to someone? Which techniques do you think would be most effective? Least effective? Can you think of any examples from real life of such techniques being used? How could you use the individual's own behaviors as a means of increasing commitment?

Can you think of any times in your life when you have had a "gut" feeling—either positive or negative—about someone or something? Was this feeling based on anything that you could identify? Describe whether or not the feeling turned out to be accurate.

Mindless Propaganda, Thoughtful Persuasion

Anthony Pratkanis and Elliot Aronson

Here are a five facts that professional persuaders have learned about modern propaganda:[1]

> Ads that contain the words *new, quick, easy, improved, now, suddenly, amazing,* and *introducing* sell more products.
>
> In supermarkets, merchandise placed on shelves at eye level sells best. Indeed, one study found that sales for products at waist level were only 74% as great and sales for products at floor level were only 57% as great as for those products placed at eye level.
>
> Ads that use animals, babies, or sex appeal are more likely to sell the product than those that use cartoon characters and historical figures.
>
> Merchandise placed at the end of a supermarket aisle or near the checkout aisle is more likely to be purchased.
>
> Bundle pricing—for example, selling items at 2 for $1 instead of 50¢ each—often increases the customer's perception of product "value."

Why do these five techniques work? When you think about it, it makes little sense to purchase an item because it happens to be placed at the end of a supermarket aisle or on a shelf at eye level. You may not really need this conveniently located product, or the item you really want may be located on a top shelf. It makes little sense to be convinced by an ad because it uses a baby or contains certain words; such "information" is of little value in determining the quality of the product. A subtle rewording of the price does not add any value to the product. But that is the point—we consumers often don't think about the reasons we make the decisions we do. Studies show that about half of purchases in a supermarket are impulse buys and that upwards of 62% of all shoppers in discount stores buy at least one item on an unplanned basis.[2]

We often respond to propaganda with little thought and in a mindless fashion. Consider the experiments on mindlessness conducted by Ellen Langer and her colleagues.[3] Langer's collaborators walked up to persons busily using a university copy machine and said: "Excuse me: may I use the Xerox machine?" What would you do in such a situation? If you are like most people, it would depend on your mood. On some occasions you might think: *"Sure, why not? I'm a helpful person."* At other times, you might say to yourself: *"Is this person nuts or what? I got here first and have lots of work to do."* Indeed Langer's results indicate that both types of thinking were going on—a little over half of the people complied with this request.

Now, here's the interesting part. Langer found that she could get almost everyone to agree to let another person cut in front of them at the copy machine by adding one detail to the request—a *reason* for why the machine was needed. This makes sense. It takes a cold heart to deny someone, perhaps panic-stricken with an urgent need, the simple use of a copy machine. The odd thing about Langer's study is that although some of the reasons given made no sense at all, nearly everyone let the person cut in. For example, on some occasions Langer's collaborators would say, "Excuse me: May I use the Xerox machine, because I have to make copies." When you think about it, this is a pretty silly thing to say: Why would you need a copy machine if you were not planning to make copies? It is the same as no reason at all. But that is the point. Most of the people in the study did not think about it and mindlessly complied with the request.

We can also be influenced when we are being thoughtful. For example, most of us, at one time or another, have been panhandled, that is, stopped on the street by a passerby who asks for a quarter or any spare change. A common response is to ignore the request and continue to walk *mindlessly* down the street. Recently, we were panhandled in a novel manner. The panhandler asked, "Excuse me, do you have 17 cents that I could have?" What thoughts would run through your head in this situation? When it happened to us, our immediate thought was: *"Why does this person need exactly 17 cents? Is it for bus fare? Is it for a specific food purchase? Maybe the person came up short at the*

From Age of Propaganda: The Everyday Use and Abuse of Persuasion by Anthony Pratkanis and Elliot Aronson, pp. 25-32. © 1992 by W. H. Freeman and Company. Reprinted by permission.

market." Suddenly the panhandler was a real individual with real needs, not someone we could mindlessly pass by. We were persuaded to part with a handful of change. Intrigued, we later sent our students out on the streets to panhandle for a local charity. They found that almost twice as many people contributed when asked for 17 or 37 cents compared to those who were asked for a quarter or any spare change.[4]

People can be persuaded both when they are in a mindless state *and* when they are thoughtful, but exactly how they are influenced in either of these two states differs considerably. Richard Petty and John Cacioppo argue that there are two routes to persuasion—*peripheral* and *central*.[5] In the peripheral route, a message recipient devotes little attention and effort to processing a communication. Some examples might include watching television while doing something else or listening to a debate on an issue that you don't care much about. In the peripheral route, persuasion is determined by simple cues, such as the attractiveness of the communicator, whether or not the people around you agree with the position presented, or the pleasure and pain associated with agreeing with the position. In contrast, in the central route, a message recipient engages in a careful and thoughtful consideration of the true merits of the information presented. For example, in the central route the person may actively argue against the message, may want to know the answer to additional questions, or may seek out new information. The persuasiveness of the message is determined by how well it can stand up to this scrutiny.

Let's see how the two routes to persuasion could be used to process one of the most influential and controversial television ads of the 1988 presidential election. This ad, prepared by the Bush campaign, told the story of Willie Horton, a black man who had been sent to prison for murder. During the time when Michael Dukakis, Bush's Democratic opponent, was governor of Massachusetts, Horton was released on a prison furlough program. While on furlough, Horton fled to Maryland, where he raped a white woman after stabbing her male companion.

The ad was influential because it required little thought for a person in the peripheral route to get the point. A typical response elicited by the ad went something like this: *"Dukakis let Horton out of prison to rape and kill. Dukakis is weak on crime, especially those committed by bad, black guys."* Although the response is simple, it was nonetheless effective for George Bush. Michael Dukakis was painted as a weak leader who was soft on crime; by comparison, George Bush looked strong and tough, capable of protecting us from the likes of Willie Horton.

However, no one was forced to think about this ad in the peripheral route. For example, in the central route to persuasion, the viewer might have asked *"Just how unusual is the Massachusetts prison furlough program? Do other states have similar programs? What is the success rate of such programs? Have instances like the Horton case happened in other states and with other governors? Can Dukakis really be held personally responsible for the decision to release Horton? How many prisoners were furloughed in Massachusetts without incident? Given that the cost of imprisoning someone for four years is approximately $88,000, or equal to the cost of four years of tuition for a student at Harvard with enough left over to buy the student a BMW upon graduation, is the furlough release program worth trying?"* In the central route, the Horton ad is potentially less effective (and might even have had the potential to damage the Bush campaign). The ad addressed few questions that a thoughtful viewer might raise.

This raises a crucial question: What determines which route to persuasion will be adopted? One factor identified by Petty and Cacioppo is the recipient's motivation to think about the message. In one experiment, Petty and Cacioppo, along with their student Rachel Goldman,[6] investigated the role of personal involvement in determining how we think about a message. Students at the University of Missouri heard a message advocating that their university adopt an exam that all students would need to pass in their senior year in order to graduate. Half of the students were told that their university's chancellor was considering adopting the comprehensive exam the following year, thereby making the issue of adopting the exam personally relevant for these students. The other half were told that the changes would not take effect for ten years and thus would not affect them personally.

To see how the personal relevance of an issue influenced thinking about a communication, Petty, Cacioppo, and Goldman prepared four different versions of the comprehensive exam message. Half of the messages were attributed to a source low in expertise—a local high school class. The other half of the messages were attributed to a source high in expertise—the Carnegie Commission on Higher Education. The researchers also varied the quality of arguments in the message, with half of the messages containing weak arguments (personal opinions and anecdotes) and the other half consisting of strong arguments (statistics and other data about the value of the exam).

This simple study can tell us a lot about the way people think about a persuasive message. Suppose someone was operating in the central route to persuasion and was carefully scrutinizing the communication. When would that person be most persuaded? Given that the person was thinking carefully, he or she would not be persuaded by weak arguments and the source of the communication would not matter much; however, a strong message that stood up to close examination would be very effective. In contrast, the content of the message would not matter much to someone who was not thinking too much about the issue; instead, someone using the peripheral route would be most persuaded by a simple device such as a source that appears to be expert.

What did Petty, Cacioppo, and Goldman find? The personal relevance of the issue determined the route to persuasion. For those students for whom the issue of comprehensive exams was personally relevant, the strength of the message's argument was the most important factor determining whether or not they were persuaded. In contrast, for those students for whom the issue of the comprehensive exam was not personally relevant, the source of the communication mattered—the source high in expertise convinced; the one from the high school class failed to do so.

Petty and Cacioppo's two routes to persuasion should alert us to two important points—one about ourselves as human beings and one about propaganda in our modern world. In many ways, we are *cognitive misers*—we are forever trying to conserve our cognitive energy.[7] Given our finite ability to process information, we often adopt the strategies of the peripheral route for simplifying complex problems; we mindlessly accept a conclusion or proposition—not for any good reason but because it is accompanied by a simplistic persuasion device.

Modern propaganda promotes the use of the peripheral route to persuasion and is designed to take advantage of the limited processing capabilities of the cognitive miser. The characteristics of modern persuasion—the message-dense environment, the thirty-second ad, the immediacy of persuasion—make it increasingly more difficult to think deeply about important issues and decisions. Given that we often operate in the peripheral route, professional propagandists have free rein to use the type of tactics described at the beginning of this chapter and throughout this book to achieve, with impunity, whatever goal they may have in mind.

We have a state of affairs that may be called the *essential dilemma of modern democracy*. On the one hand, we, as a society, value persuasion; our government is based on the belief that free speech and discussion and exchange of ideas can lead to fairer and better decision making. On the other hand, as cognitive misers we often do not participate fully in this discussion, relying instead not on careful thought and scrutiny of a message, but on simplistic persuasion devices and limited reasoning. Mindless propaganda, not thoughtful persuasion, flourishes.

The antidote to the dilemma of modern democracy is not a simple one. It requires each of us to take steps to minimize the likelihood of our processing important information in the peripheral route. This might include increasing our ability to think about an issue through education or improving our ability to detect and understand propaganda by learning more about persuasion. It may mean alerting others to the personal importance of an issue so that many more citizens are encouraged to think deeply about a proposition. It could involve restructuring the way information is presented in our society so that we have the time and the ability to think before we decide. . . . Given the stakes, it behooves each of us to think carefully about how this dilemma can best be resolved.

Notes

1. Burton, P. W. (1981). *Which ad pulled best?* Chicago: Crain; Caples, J. (9174). *Tested advertising methods.* Englewood Cliffs, NJ: Prentice-Hall; Loudon, D. L., & Della Bitta, A. J. (1984). *Consumer behavior.* New York: McGraw-Hill; Ogilvy, D. (1983). *Ogilvy on advertising.* New York: Crown.
2. Ibid.
3. Langer, E., Blank, A., & Chanowitz, B. (1978). The mindlessness of ostensibly thoughtful action: The role of "placebic" information in interpersonal interaction. *Journal of Personality and Social Psychology, 36*, 635–642.
4. Santos, M., Leve, C., & Pratkanis, A. R. (August 1991). *Hey buddy, can you spare 17 cents? Mindfulness and persuasion.* Paper presented at the annual meeting of the American Psychological Association, San Francisco.
5. Petty, R. E., & Cacioppo, J. T. (1986). The elaboration likelihood model of persuasion. In L. Berkowitz (Ed.), *Advances in experimental social psychology* (Vol. 19; pp. 123–205). New York: Academic Press; Petty, R. E., & Cacioppo, J. T. (1986). *Communication and persuasion: Central and peripheral routes to attitude change.* New York: Springer-Verlag. See also Chaiken, S. (1980). Heuristic versus systematic information processing and the use of source versus message cues in persuasion. *Journal of Personality and Social Psychology, 39*, 752–766; Chaiken, S., Liberman, A., & Eagly, A. (1989). Heuristic versus systematic information processing within and beyond the persuasion context. In J. S. Uleman & J. A. Bargh (Eds.), *Unintended thought* (pp. 212–252). New York: Guilford.
6. Petty, R. E., Cacioppo, J. T., & Goldman, R. (1981). Personal involvement as a determinant of argument-based persuasion. *Journal of Personality and Social Psychology, 41*, 847–855.
7. Fiske, S. T., & Taylor, S. E. (1991). *Social cognition.* New York: McGraw-Hill.

How to Sell a Pseudoscience

ANTHONY R. PRATKANIS

Want your own pseudoscience? Here are nine effective persuasion tactics for selling all sorts of flimflam.

Every time I read the reports of new pseudosciences in the SKEPTICAL INQUIRER or watch the latest "In Search Of"-style television show I have one cognitive response, "Holy cow, how can anyone believe that?" Some recent examples include: "Holy cow, why do people spend $3.95 a minute to talk on the telephone with a 'psychic' who has never foretold the future?" "Holy cow, why do people believe that an all uncooked vegan diet is natural and therefore nutritious?" "Holy cow, why would two state troopers chase the planet Venus across state lines thinking it was an alien spacecraft?" "Holy cow, why do people spend millions of dollars each year on subliminal tapes that just don't work?"

There are, of course, many different answers to these "holy cow" questions. Conjurers can duplicate pseudoscientific feats and thus show us how sleights of hand

and misdirections can mislead (e.g., Randi 1982a, 1982b, 1989). Sociologists can point to social conditions that increase the prevalence of pseudoscientific beliefs (e.g., Lett 1992; Padgett and Jorgenson 1982; Victor 1993). Natural scientists can describe the physical properties of objects to show that what may appear to be supernatural is natural (e.g., Culver and Ianna 1988; Nickell 1983, 1993). Cognitive psychologists have identified common mental biases that often lead us to misinterpret social reality and to conclude in favor of supernatural phenomena (e.g., Blackmore 1992; Gilovich 1991; Hines 1988). These perspectives are useful in addressing the "holy cow" question; all give us a piece of the puzzle in unraveling this mystery.

I will describe how a social psychologist answers the holy cow question. Social psychology is the study of social influence—how human beings and their institutions influence and affect each other (see Aronson 1992; Aronson and Pratkanis 1993). For the past seven decades, social psychologists have been developing theories of social influence and have been testing the effectiveness of various persuasion tactics in their labs (see Cialdini 1984; Pratkanis and Aronson, 1992). It is my thesis that many persuasion tactics discovered by social psychologists are used every day, perhaps not totally consciously, by the promoters of pseudoscience (see Feynman 1985 or Hines 1988 for a definition of pseudoscience).

To see how these tactics can be used to sell flimflam, let's pretend for a moment that we wish to have our very own pseudoscience. Here are nine common propaganda tactics that should result in success.

Anthony R. Pratkanis is associate professor of psychology, University of California, Santa, Cruz, CA 95064. This article is based on a paper presented at the conference of the Committee for the Scientific Investigation of Claims of the Paranormal, June 23-26, 1994, in Seattle, Washington.

Gerald Fried

1. Create a Phantom

The first thing we need to do is to create a phantom—an unavailable goal that looks real and possible; it looks as if it might be obtained with just the right effort, just the right belief, or just the right amount of money, but in reality it can't be obtained. Most pseudosciences are based on belief in a distant or phantom goal. Some examples of pseudoscience phantoms: meeting a space alien, contacting a dead relative at a séance, receiving the wisdom of the universe from a channeled dolphin, and improving one's bowling game or overcoming the trauma of rape with a subliminal tape.

Phantoms can serve as effective propaganda devices (Pratkanis and Farquhar 1992). If I don't have a desired phantom, I feel deprived and somehow less of a person. A pseudoscientist can take advantage of these feelings of inferiority by appearing to offer a means to obtain that goal. In a rush to enhance self-esteem, we suspend better judgment and readily accept the offering of the pseudoscience.

The trick, of course, is to get the new seeker to believe that the phantom is possible. Often the mere mention of the delights of a phantom will be enough to dazzle the new pseudoscience recruit (see Lund's 1925 discussion of wishful thinking). After all, who wouldn't want a better sex life, better health, and peace of mind, all from a $14.95 subliminal tape? The fear of loss of a phantom also can motivate us to accept it as real. The thought that I will never speak again to a cherished but dead loved one or that next month I may die of cancer can be so painful as to cause me to suspend my better judgment and hold out hope against hope that the medium can contact the dead or that Laetrile works. But at times the sell is harder, and that calls for our next set of persuasion tactics.

2. Set a Rationalization Trap

The rationalization trap is based on the premise: Get the person committed to the cause as soon as possible. Once a commitment is made, the nature of thought changes. The committed heart is not so much interested in a careful evaluation of the merits of a course of action but in proving that he or she is right.

To see how commitment to a pseudoscience can be established, let's look at a bizarre case—mass suicides at the direction of cult leader Jim Jones. This is the ultimate "holy cow" question: "Why kill yourself and your children on another's command?" From outside the cult, it appears strange, but from the inside it seems natural. Jones began by having his followers make easy commitments (a gift to the church, attending Wednesday night service) and then increased the level of commitment—more tithes, more time in service, loyalty oaths, public admission of sins and punishment, selling of homes, forced sex, moving to Guyana, and then the suicide. Each step was really a small one. Outsiders saw the strange end-product; insiders experienced an ever increasing spiral of escalating commitment. (See Pratkanis and Aronson 1992 for other tactics used by Jones.)

This is a dramatic example, but not all belief in pseudoscience is so extreme. For example, there are those who occasionally consult a psychic or listen to a subliminal tape. In such cases, commitment can be secured by what social psychologists call the foot-in-the-door technique (Freedman and Fraser 1966). It works this way: You start with a small request, such as accepting a free chiropractic spine exam (Barrett 1993a), taking a sample of vitamins, or completing a free personality inventory. Then a larger request follows—a $1,000 chiropractic realignment, a vitamin regime, or an expensive seminar series. The first small request sets the commitment: Why did you get that bone exam, take those vitamins, or complete that test if you weren't interested and didn't think there might be something to it? An all too common response, "Well gosh, I guess I am interested." The rationalization trap is sprung.

Now that we have secured the target's commitment to a phantom goal, we need some social support for the newfound pseudoscientific beliefs. The next tactics are designed to bolster those beliefs.

3. Manufacture Source Credibility and Sincerity

Our third tactic is to manufacture source credibility and sincerity. In other words, create a guru, leader, mystic, lord, or other generally likable and powerful authority, one who people would be just plain nuts if they didn't believe. For example, practitioners of alternative medicine often have "degrees" as chiropractors or in homeopathy. Subliminal tape sellers claim specialized knowledge and training in such arts as hypnosis. Advocates of UFO sightings often become directors of "research centers." "Psychic detectives" come with long résumés of police service. Prophets claim past successes. For example, most of us "know" that Jeane Dixon predicted the assassination of President Kennedy but probably don't know that she also predicted a Nixon win in 1960. As modern public relations has shown us, credibility is easier to manufacture than we might normally think (see Ailes 1988; Dilenschneider 1990).

Source credibility is an effective propaganda device for at least two reasons. First, we often process persuasive messages in a half-mindless state—either because we are not motivated to think, don't have the time to consider, or lack the abilities to understand the issues (Petty and Cacioppo 1986). In such cases, the presence of a credible source can lead one to quickly infer that the message has merit and should be accepted.

Second, source credibility can stop questioning (Kramer and Alstad 1993). After all, what gives you the right to question a guru, a prophet, the image of the Mother Mary, or a sincere seeker of life's hidden potentials? I'll clarify this point with an example. Suppose I told you that the following statement is a prediction of the development of the atomic bomb and the fighter aircraft (see Hines 1988):

> They will think they have seen the Sun at night
> When they will see the pig half-man:
> Noise, song, battle fighting in the sky perceived,
> And one will hear brute beasts talking.

You probably would respond: "Huh? I don't see how you get the atomic bomb from that. This could just as well be a prediction of an in-flight showing of the Dr. Doolittle movie or the advent of night baseball at Wrigley field." However, attribute the statement to Nostradamus and the dynamics change. Nostradamus was a man who supposedly cured plague victims, predicted who would be pope, foretold the future of kings and queens, and even found a poor dog lost by the king's page (Randi 1993). Such a great seer and prophet can't be wrong. The implied message: The problem is with you; instead of questioning, why don't you suspend your faulty, linear mind until you gain the needed insight?

4. Establish a Granfalloon

Where would a leader be without something to lead? Our next tactic supplies the answer: Establish what Kurt Vonnegut (1976) terms a "granfalloon," a proud and meaningless association of human beings. One of social psychology's most remarkable findings is the ease with which granfalloons can be created. For example, the social psychologist Henri Tajfel merely brought subjects into his lab, flipped a coin, and randomly assigned them to be labeled either Xs or Ws (Tajfel 1981; Turner 1987). At the end of the study, total strangers were acting as if those in their granfalloon were their close kin and those in the other group were their worst enemies.

Granfalloons are powerful propaganda devices because they are easy to create and, once established, the granfalloon defines social reality and maintains social identities. Information is dependent on the granfalloon. Since most granfalloons quickly develop outgroups, criticisms can be attributed to those "evil ones" outside the group, who are thus stifled. To maintain a desired social identity, such as that of a seeker or a New Age rebel, one must obey the dictates of the granfalloon and its leaders.

The classic séance can be viewed as an ad-hoc granfalloon. Note what happens as you sit in the dark and hear a thud. You are dependent on the group led by a medium for the interpretation of this sound. "What is it? A knee against the table or my long lost Uncle Ned? The group believes it is Uncle Ned. Rocking the boat would be impolite. Besides, I came here to be a seeker."

Essential to the success of the granfalloon tactic is the creation of a shared social identity. In creating this identity, here are some things you might want to include:

(a) rituals and symbols (e.g., a dowser's rod, secret symbols, and special ways of preparing food): these not only create an identity, but provide items for sale at a profit.

(b) jargon and beliefs that only the in-group understands and accepts (e.g., thetans are impeded by engrams, you are on a cusp with Jupiter rising): jargon is an effective means of social control since it can be used to frame the interpretation of events.

(c) shared goals (e.g., to end all war, to sell the faith and related products, or to realize one's human potential): such goals not only define the group, but motivate action as believers attempt to reach them.

(d) shared feelings (e.g., the excitement of a prophecy that might appear to be true or the collective rationalization of strange beliefs to others): shared feelings aid in the *we* feeling.

(e) specialized information (e.g., the U.S. government is in a conspiracy to cover up UFOs): this helps the target feel special because he or she is "in the know."

(f) enemies (e.g., alternative medicine opposing the AMA and the FDA, subliminal-tape companies spurning academic psychologists, and spiritualists condemning Randi and other investigators): enemies are very important because you as a pseudoscientist will need scapegoats to blame for your problems and failures.

5. Use Self-Generated Persuasion

Another tactic for promoting pseudoscience and one of the most powerful tactics identified by social psychologists is self-generated persuasion—the subtle design of the situation so that the targets persuade themselves. During World War II, Kurt Lewin (1947) was able to get Americans to eat more sweetbreads (veal and beef organ meats) by having them form groups to discuss how they could persuade others to eat sweetbreads.

Retailers selling so-called nutritional products have discovered this technique by turning customers into salespersons (Jarvis and Barrett 1993). To create a multilevel sales organization, the "nutrition" retailer recruits customers (who recruit still more customers) to serve as sales agents for the product. Customers are recruited as a test of their belief in the product or with the hope of making lots of money (often to buy more products). By trying to sell the product, the customer-turned-salesperson becomes more convinced of its worth. One multilevel leader tells his new sales agents to "answer all objections with testimonials. That's the secret to motivating people" (Jarvis and Barrett 1993), and it is also the secret to convincing yourself.

6. Construct Vivid Appeals

Joseph Stalin once remarked: "The death of a single Russian soldier is a tragedy. A million deaths is a statistic." (See Nisbett and Ross 1980.) In other words, a vividly presented case study or example can make a lasting impression. For example, the pseudosciences are replete with graphic stories of ships and planes caught in the Bermuda Triangle, space aliens examining the sexual parts of humans, weird goings-on in Borley Rectory or Amityville, New York, and psychic surgeons removing cancerous tumors.

A vivid presentation is likely to be very memorable and hard to refute. No matter how many logical arguments can be mustered to counter the pseudoscience claim, there remains that one graphic incident that comes quickly to mind to prompt the response: "Yeah, but what about that haunted house in New York? Hard to explain that." By the way, one of the best ways to counter a vivid appeal is with an equally vivid counter appeal. For example, to counter stories about psychic surgeons in the Philippines, Randi (1982a) tells an equally vivid story of a psychic surgeon palming chicken guts and then pretending to remove them from a sick and now less wealthy patient.

7. Use Pre-persuasion

Pre-persuasion is defining the situation or setting the stage so you win, and sometimes without raising so much as a valid argument. How does one do this? At least three steps are important.

First, establish the nature of the issue. For example, to avoid the wrath of the FDA, advocates of alternative medicine define the issue as health freedom (you should have the right to the health alternative of your choice) as opposed to consumer protection or quality care. If the issue is defined as freedom, the alternative medicine advocate will win because "Who is opposed to freedom?" Another example of this technique is to create a problem or disease, such as reactive hypoglycemia or yeast allergy, that then just happens to be "curable" with whatever quackery you have to sell (Jarvis and Barrett 1993).

Another way to define an issue is through differentiation. Subliminal-tape companies use product differentiation to respond to negative subliminal-tape studies. The claim: "Our tapes have a special technique that makes them superior to other tapes that have been used in studies that failed to show the therapeutic value of subliminal tapes." Thus, null results are used to make a given subliminal tape look superior. The psychic network has taken a similar approach—"Tired of those phoney psychics? Ours are certified," says the advertisement.

Second, set expectations. Expectations can lead us to interpret ambiguous information in a way that supports an original hypothesis (Greenwald, Pratkanis, Leippe, and Baumgardner 1986). For example, a belief in the Bermuda Triangle may lead us to interpret a plane crash off the coast of New York City as evidence for the Triangle's sinister effects (Kusche 1986; Randi 1982a). We recently conducted a study that showed how an expectation can lead people to think that subliminal tapes work when in fact they do not (Greenwald, Spangenberg, Pratkanis, and Eskenazi 1991; Pratkanis, Eskenazi, and Greenwald 1994; for a summary see Pratkanis 1992). In our study, expectations were established by mislabeling half the tapes (e.g., some subjects thought they had a subliminal tape to improve memory but really had one designed to increase self-esteem). The results showed that about half the subjects thought they improved (though they did not) based on how the tape was labeled (and not the actual content). The label led them to interpret their behavior in support of expectations, or what we termed an "illusory placebo" effect.

A third way to pre-persuade is to specify the decision criteria. For example, psychic supporters have developed guidelines on what should be viewed as acceptable evidence for paranormal abilities—such as using personal experiences as data, placing the burden of proof on the critic and not the claimant (see Beloff 1985), and above all else keeping James Randi and other psi-inhibitors out of the testing room. Accept these criteria and one must conclude that psi is a reality. The collaboration of Hyman and Honorton is one positive attempt to establish a fair playing field (Hyman and Honorton 1986).

8. Frequently Use Heuristics and Commonplaces

My next recommendation to the would-be pseudoscientist is to use heuristics and commonplaces. Heuristics are simple if-then rules or norms that are widely accepted; for example, if it costs more it must be more valuable. Commonplaces are widely accepted beliefs that can serve as the basis of an appeal; for example, government health-reform should be rejected because politicians are corrupt (assuming political corruption is a widely accepted belief). Heuristics and commonplaces gain their power because they are widely accepted and thus induce little thought about whether the rule or argument is appropriate.

To sell a pseudoscience, liberally sprinkle your appeal with heuristics and commonplaces. Here are some common examples.

(a) The *scarcity heuristic,* or if it is rare it is valuable. The Psychic Friends Network costs a pricey $3.95 a minute and therefore must be valuable. On the other hand, an average University of California professor goes for about 27 cents per minute and is thus of little value.[1]

(b) The *consensus or bandwagon* heuristic, or if everyone agrees it must be true. Subliminal tapes, psychic phone ads, and quack medicine (Jarvis and Barrett 1993) feature testimonials of people who have found what they are looking for (see Hyman 1993 for a critique of this practice).

> **"Source credibility can stop questioning. After all, what gives you the right to question a guru, a prophet, the image of the Mother Mary, or a sincere seeker of life's hidden potentials?"**

(c) The *message length* heuristic, or if the message is long it is strong. Subliminal-tape brochures often list hundreds of subliminal studies in support of their claims. Yet most of these studies do not deal with subliminal influence and thus are irrelevant. An uninformed observer would be impressed by the weight of the evidence.

(d) The *representative* heuristic or if an object resembles another (on some salient dimension) then they act similarly. For example, in folk medicines the cure often resembles the apparent cause of the disease. Homeopathy is based on the notion that small amounts of substances that can cause a disease's symptoms will cure the disease (Barrett 1993b). The Chinese Doctrine of Signatures claims that similarity of shape and form determine therapeutic value; thus rhinoceros horns, deer antlers, and ginseng root

look phallic and supposedly improve vitality (Tyler 1993).

(e) The *natural* commonplace, or what is natural is good and what is made by humans is bad. Alternative medicines are promoted with the word "natural." Psychic abilities are portrayed as natural, but lost, abilities. Organic food is natural. Of course mistletoe berries are natural too, and I don't recommend a steady diet of these morsels.

(f) The *goddess-within* commonplace, or humans have a spiritual side that is neglected by modern materialistic science. This commonplace stems from the medieval notion of the soul, which was modernized by Mesmer as animal magnetism and then converted by psychoanalysis into the powerful, hidden unconscious (see Fuller 1982, 1986). Pseudoscience plays to this commonplace by offering ways to tap the unconscious, such as subliminal tapes, to prove this hidden power exists through extrasensory perception (ESP) and psi, or to talk with the remnants of this hidden spirituality through channeling and the séance.

(g) The *science* commonplaces. Pseudosciences use the word "science" in a contradictory manner. On the one hand, the word "science" is sprinkled liberally throughout most pseudosciences: subliminal tapes make use of the "latest scientific technology"; psychics are "scientifically tested"; health fads are "on the cutting edge of science." On the other hand, science is often portrayed as limited. For example, one article in *Self* magazine (Sharp 1993) reported our subliminal-tapes studies (Greenwald et al. 1992; Pratkanis et al. 1994) showing no evidence that the tapes worked and then stated: "Tape makers dispute the objectivity of the studies. They also point out that science can't always explain the results of mainstream medicine either" (p. 194). In each case a commonplace about science is used: (1) "Science is powerful" and (2) "Science is limited and can't replace the personal." The selective use of these commonplaces allows a pseudoscience to claim the power of science but have a convenient out should science fail to promote the pseudoscience.

9. Attack Opponents Through Innuendo and Character Assassination

Finally, you would like your pseudoscience to be safe from harm and external attack. Given that the best defense is a good offense, I offer the advice of Cicero: "If you don't have a good argument, attack the plaintiff."

Let me give a personal example of this tactic in action. After our research showing that subliminal tapes have no therapeutic value was reported, my co-authors, Tony Greenwald, Eric Spangenberg, and Jay Eskenazi, and I were the target of many innuendoes. One subliminal newsletter edited by Eldon Taylor, Michael Urban, and others (see the *International Society of Peripheral Learning Specialists Newsletter,* August 1991) claimed that our research was a marketing study designed not to test the tapes but to "demonstrate the influence of marketing practices on consumer perceptions." The article points out that the entire body of data presented by Greenwald represents a marketing dissertation by Spangenberg and questions why Greenwald is even an author. The newsletter makes other attacks as well, claiming that our research design lacked a control group, that we really found significant effects of the tapes, that we violated American Psychological Association ethics with a hint that an investigation would follow, that we prematurely reported our findings in a manner similar to those who prematurely announced cold fusion, and that we were conducting a "Willie Horton"-style smear campaign against those who seek to help Americans achieve their personal goals.

Many skeptics can point to similar types of attacks. In the fourteenth century, Bishop Pierre d'Arcis, one of the first to contest the authenticity of the Shroud of Turin, was accused by shroud promoters as being motivated by jealousy and a desire to possess the shroud (Nickell 1983: 15). Today, James Randi is described by supporters of Uri Geller as "a powerful psychic trying to convince the world that such powers don't exist so he can take the lead role in the psychic world" (Hines 1988: 91).

Why is innuendo such a powerful propaganda device? Social psychologists point to three classes of answers. First, innuendoes change the agenda of discussion. Note the "new" discussion on subliminal tapes isn't about whether these tapes are worth your money or not. Instead, we are discussing whether I am ethical or not, whether I am a competent researcher, and whether I even did the research.

Second, innuendoes raise a glimmer of doubt about the character of the person under attack. That doubt can be especially powerful when there is little other information on which to base a judgment. For example, the average reader of the subliminal newsletter I quoted probably knows little about me—knows little about the research and little about the peer review process that evaluated it, and doesn't know that I make my living from teaching college and not from the sale of subliminal tapes. This average reader is left with the impression of an unethical and incompetent scientist who is out of control. Who in their right mind would accept what that person has to say?

Finally, innuendoes can have a chilling effect (Kurtz 1992). The recipient begins to wonder about his or her reputation and whether the fight is worth it. The frivolous lawsuit is an effective way to magnify this chilling effect.

Can Science Be Sold with Propaganda?

I would be remiss if I didn't address one more issue: Can we sell science with the persuasion tactics of pseudoscience? Let's be honest; science sometimes uses these tactics. For example, I carry in my wallet a membership card to the Monterey Bay Aquarium with a picture of the cutest little otter you'll ever see. I am in the otter granfalloon. On some occasions skeptics have played a little loose with their arguments and their name-calling. As just one example, see George Price's (1955) *Science* article attacking Rhine's and Soal's work on ESP—an attack that went well beyond the then available data. (See Hyman's [1985] discussion.)

I can somewhat understand the use of such tactics. If a cute otter can inspire a young child to seek to understand nature, then so be it. But we should remember that such tactics can be ineffective in promoting science if they are not followed up by involvement in the process of science—the process of questioning and discovering. And we should be mindful that the use of propaganda techniques has its costs. If we base our claims on cheap propaganda tactics, then it is an easy task for the pseudoscientist to develop even more effective propaganda tactics and carry the day.

More fundamentally, propaganda works best when we are half mindless, simplistic thinkers trying to rationalize our behavior and beliefs to ourselves and others. Science works best when we are thoughtful and critical and scrutinize claims carefully. Our job should be to promote such thought and scrutiny. We should be careful to select our persuasion strategies to be consistent with that goal.

Notes

I thank Craig Abbott, Elizabeth A. Turner, and Marlene E. Turner for helpful comments on an earlier draft of this article.

1. Based on 50 weeks a year at an average salary of $49,000 and a work week of 61 hours (as reported in recent surveys of the average UC faculty work load). Assuming a work week of 40 hours, the average faculty makes 41 cents a minute.

References

Ailes, R. 1988. *You Are the Message.* New York: Doubleday.
Aronson, E. 1992. *The Social Animal,* 6th ed. New York: W. H. Freeman.
Aronson, E., and A. R. Pratkanis. 1993. "What Is Social Psychology?" In *Social Psychology,* vol. 1, ed. by E Aronson and A. R. Pratkanis, xiii-xx. Cheltenham, Gloucestershire: Edward Elgar Publishing.
Barrett, S. 1993a. "The Spine Salesmen." In *The Health Robbers,* ed. by S. Barrett and W. T. Jarvis, 161-190. Buffalo, N.Y.: Prometheus Books.
———. 1993b. "Homeopathy: Is it Medicine?" In *The Health Robbers,* ed. by S. Barrett and W. T. Jarvis, 191-202. Buffalo, N.Y.: Prometheus Books.
Beloff, J. 1985. "What Is Your Counter-explanation? A Plea to Skeptics to Think Again." In *A Skeptic's Handbook of Parapsychology,* ed. by P. Kurtz, 359-377. Buffalo, N.Y.: Prometheus Books.
Blackmore, S. 1992. Psychic experiences: Psychic illusions. SKEPTICAL INQUIRER, 16: 367-376.
Cialdini, R. B. 1984. *Influence.* New York: William Morrow.
Culver, R. B., and P. A. Ianna. 1988. *Astrology: True or False?* Buffalo, N.Y.: Prometheus Books.
Dilenschneider, R. L. 1990. *Power and Influence.* New York: Prentice-Hall.
Feynman, R. P. 1985. *Surely You're Joking Mr. Feynman.* New York: Bantam Books.
Freedman, J., and S. Fraser. 1966. Compliance without pressure: The foot-in-the-door technique. *Journal of Personality and Social Psychology,* 4: 195-202.
Fuller, R. C. 1982. *Mesmerism and the American Cure of Souls.* Philadelphia: University of Pennsylvania Press.
———. 1986. *Americans and the Unconscious.* New York: Oxford University Press.
Gilovich, T. 1991. *How We Know What Isn't So.* New York: Free Press.
Greenwald, A. G., E. R. Spangenberg, A. R. Pratkanis, and J. Eskenazi. 1991. Double-blind tests of subliminal self-help audiotapes. *Psychological Science,* 2: 119-122.
Greenwald, A. G., A. R. Pratkanis, M. R. Leippe, and M. H. Baumgardner. 1986. Under what conditions does theory obstruct research progress? *Psychological Review,* 93: 216-229.
Hines, T. 1988. *Pseudoscience and the Paranormal.* Buffalo, N.Y.: Prometheus Books.
Hyman, R. 1985. "A Critical Historical Overview of Parapsychology." In *A Skeptic's Handbook of Parapsychology,* ed. by P. Kurtz, 3-96. Buffalo, N.Y.: Prometheus Books.
———. 1993. Occult health practices. In *The Health Robbers,* ed. by S. Barrett and W. T. Jarvis, 55-66. Buffalo, N.Y.: Prometheus Books.
Hyman, R., and C. Honorton. 1986. A joint communique: The Psi Ganzfeld controversy. *Journal of Parapsychology,* 56: 351-364.
Jarvis, W. T., and S. Barrett. 1993. "How Quackery Sells." In *The Health Robbers,* ed. by S. Barrett and W. T. Jarvis, 1-22. Buffalo, N.Y.: Prometheus Books.
Kramer, J., and D. Alstad. 1993. *The Guru Papers: Masks of Authoritarian Power,* Berkeley, Calif.: North Atlantic Books/ Frog Ltd.
Kurtz, P. 1992. On being sued: The chilling of freedom of expression. SKEPTICAL INQUIRER, 16: 114-117.
Kusche, L. 1986. *The Bermuda Triangle Mystery Solved.* Buffalo, N.Y.: Prometheus Books.
Lett, J. 1992. The persistent popularity of the paranormal. SKEPTICAL INQUIRER, 16, 381-388.
Lewin, K. 1947. "Group Decision and Social Change." In *Readings in Social Psychology,* ed. by T. M. Newcomb and E. L. Hartley, 330-344. New York: Holt.
Lund, F. H. 1925. The psychology of belief. *Journal of Abnormal and Social Psychology,* 20: 63-81, 174-196.
Nickell, J. 1983. *Inquest on the Shroud of Turin.* Buffalo, N.Y.: Prometheus Books.
———. 1993. *Looking for a Miracle.* Buffalo, N.Y.: Prometheus Books.
Nisbett, R., and L. Ross. 1980. *Human Inference: Strategies and Shortcomings of Social Judgment.* Englewood Cliffs, N.J.: Prentice-Hall.
Padgett, V. R., and D. O. Jorgenson. 1982. Superstition and economic threat: Germany 1918-1940. *Personality and Social Psychology Bulletin,* 8: 736-741.
Petty, R. E., and J. T. Cacioppo. 1986. *Communication and Persuasion: Central and Peripheral Routes to Attitude Change.* New York: Springer-Verlag.
Pratkanis, A. R. 1992. The cargo-cult science of subliminal persuasion. SKEPTICAL INQUIRER, 16: 260-272.
Pratkanis, A. R., and E. Aronson. 1992. *Age of Propaganda: Everyday Use and Abuse of Persuasion.* New York: W. H. Freeman.
Pratkanis, A. R., J. Eskenazi, and A. G. Greenwald. 1994. What you expect is what you believe (but not necessarily what you get): A test of the effectiveness of subliminal self-help audiotapes. *Basic and Applied Social Psychology,* 15: 251-276.
Pratkanis, A. R., and P. H. Farquhar. 1992. A brief history of research on phantom alternatives: Evidence for seven empirical generalizations about phantoms. *Basic and Applied Social Psychology,* 13: 103-122.
Price, G. R. 1955. Science and the supernatural. *Science,* 122: 359-367.
Randi, J. 1982a. *Flim-Flam!* Buffalo, N.Y.: Prometheus Books.
———. 1982b. *The Truth About Uri Geller.* Buffalo, N.Y.: Prometheus Books.
———. 1989. *The Faith Healers.* Buffalo, N.Y.: Prometheus Books.
———. 1993. *The Mask of Nostradamus.* Buffalo, N.Y.: Prometheus Books.
Sharp, K. 1993. The new hidden persuaders. *Self,* March, pp. 174-175, 194.
Tajfel, H. 1981. *Human Groups and Social Categories.* Cambridge, U.K.: Cambridge University Press.
Turner, J. C. 1987. *Rediscovering the Social Group.* New York: Blackwell.
Tyler, V. E. 1993. "The Overselling of Herbs." In *The Health Robbers,* ed. by S. Barrett and W. T. Jarvis, 213-224. Buffalo, N.Y.: Prometheus Books.
Victor, J. S. 1993. *Satanic Panic: The Creation of a Contemporary Legend.* Chicago, Ill.: Open Court.
Vonnegut, K. 1976. *Wampeters, Foma, and Granfalloons.* New York: Dell.

In Work on Intuition, Gut Feelings Are Tracked to Source: The Brain

In a rigged game, people knew more than they thought.

By SANDRA BLAKESLEE

In an experiment with broad implications for human behavior, scientists have shown that people have a covert system in their brains for telling them when decisions are good or bad and that the system, which draws upon emotional memories, is activated long before people are consciously aware that they have decided anything.

Intuition and gut feelings have a firm biological basis, said Dr. Antonio Damasio, the lead author of a paper describing the experiment in the current issue of the journal Science. Dr. Damasio, a neuroscientist at the University of Iowa College of Medicine in Iowa City, carried out the research with his wife, Dr. Hanna Damasio and two colleagues, Dr. Antoine Becahra and Dr. Daniel Tranel.

These are the first experiments on humans to show that specific brain regions help lead to anticipation about rewards and punishments, said Dr. Read Montague, a neuroscientist at the Baylor College of Medicine in Houston.

In the experiment, 16 players were each presented with four decks of cards, $2,000 in play money and a simple set of instructions. They were told to turn over cards from all the decks, in any order they liked, and to try to minimize their losses and maximize their winnings. Most cards were worth money (usually $50 or $100), but there were also penalty cards.

> For life's big decisions, hunches may add to the power of logic.

Players had no way of predicting when a penalty would arise, no way to calculate with precision the net gain or loss from each deck and no knowledge of how many cards they needed to turn over in order to end the game.

The players did not know that the game had been rigged so two "good decks" produced lower immediate rewards but a higher total payout, Dr. Antonio Damasio said. Two "bad decks" gave the thrill of large earnings but greater total losses.

While people played, their palms were wired to a machine that, like a polygraph, detected changes in the electrical conductance of the skin—a kind of microsweating that is thought to reflect flickers of emotion that do not reach conscious awareness. The players were also interrupted occasionally and asked to say what they thought was going on.

Two groups of people played the game—10 normal subjects and 6 patients with bilateral damage to a brain region behind the eyeballs involved in making decisions.

Normal subjects soon reached a hunch stage, Dr. Antonio Damasio said. They said things like, "I don't know what's going on here, but there may be some kind of hidden rule or spacing of cards." After turning about 50 cards, most of them reached a conclusion: "Hey, two decks are good, and two are bad."

But their actions anticipated the conclusions they voiced later. At the hunch stage, normal players were already making more selections from the good decks than from the bad

17. Gut Feelings Are Tracked to Source

decks. And their bodies reflected some unconscious perception. Early in the game, every time they reached for a card in a "bad deck," their palms sweated, as if they already expected excess punishment from the bad decks.

A couple of normal players, he said, never reached a point where they voiced a conclusion, the conceptual stage, even though they played correctly, guided by the covert system.

The brain-damaged patients never got to the hunch stage, Dr. Damasio said, and none of them experienced microsweating in their palms before turning over cards in the "bad decks." But three out of six of the patients did reach the point at which they consciously knew there were good and bad decks, he said. Despite this knowledge, they continued choosing cards from the bad decks, he said, saying that it was more exciting to play from the risky decks or that one could never tell when the rules might change.

Such self-destructive behavior mirrors what happens to these patients in real life, Dr. Damasio said. After their injury, they tend to make poor financial and personal decisions and have difficulty with all ethical judgments.

Dr. Damasio said he viewed the card game as a metaphor for the game of life. Most important things in life are riddled with uncertainty, including decisions about relationships, jobs, buying a house or a future course of action. While people use facts, logic and pure reasoning to make decisions, these inputs are not enough, he said. Decisions are also influenced by what has happened to a person in previous situations, he added, and he speculated that stored emotional memories came percolating up through a circuit in the prefrontal lobes, the region of the brain involved in decision making.

Most of the time, these emotional memories are covert, Dr. Damasio said, but these intuitions help guide decision-making on an unconscious level. If covert memories make it into consciousness, he said, they remain enigmatic but are given a name: gut feelings.

Social Influence

After World War II, members of the Nazi high command were put on trial for war crimes, in particular their genocidal slaughter of millions of "undesirables"—Jews, Gypsies, and homosexuals, among others. One argument that they offered in their defense was that they were "only following orders"—that is, as soldiers during wartime they had no choice but to obey the orders of their superior officers. As a result, so the argument went, they did not bear the ultimate responsibility for their actions. This argument was not especially effective, however, and many of the defendants were convicted and, in some cases, executed for their crimes. In essence, then, the war crimes judges rejected the notion that people can give up their individual moral responsibility when they are given immoral orders.

A decade later, in one of the most famous social psychological investigations ever, Stanley Milgram reexamined this issue, and his results were highly disturbing. Milgram found that normal everyday Americans—not Nazi monsters—would follow the orders of an experimenter to administer what they thought were extremely intense electric shocks to an innocent victim as part of a research

UNIT 5

project. In some cases, a substantial percentage of the participants would administer what they thought were 450-volt shocks to a man with a heart condition who was screaming hysterically to be released from the experiment. Although many of the participants were in a state of extreme anxiety and discomfort over their terrible behavior, they nevertheless continued to obey the experimenter. As had the Nazis during World War II, these American citizens seemed to give up their moral responsibility when they decided to follow the orders of the experimenter.

This research is just one example, although a highly dramatic one, of the phenomenon that social psychologists call social influence—the ability of a person or group to change the behavior of others. Traditionally, a distinction has been drawn among three different types of social influence: conformity, compliance, and obedience. *Conformity* refers to those times when individuals will change their attitudes or behaviors because of perceived group pressure—that is, they feel pressure to conform to the attitude or behavior of some group that is at least somewhat important to them. If, for instance, everyone in your group of friends adopts a particular style of clothing, or adopts a particular attitude toward another group, you may feel some pressure to conform your behavior to theirs, even if no one in the group ever asks you to. *Compliance*, on the other hand, refers to those times when individuals change their behavior in response to a direct request from others. We are often faced with direct requests intended to change our behavior, whether they come from family, friends, teachers, bosses, or door-to-door salespeople. Considerable research has been conducted to determine what kinds of strategies by "requesters" are the most effective in prompting actual compliance. Finally, *obedience* refers to those times when individuals change their behavior in response to a direct order from another person; thus, unlike compliance, in which you are asked to make a behavioral change, in obedience you are commanded to do so. The research by Milgram is a good example of an obedience situation.

The three selections in this unit illustrate, sometimes dramatically, the powerful ways in which social influence can operate. In "Making Sense of the Nonsensical: An Analysis of Jonestown," Neal Osherow analyzes one of the most horrific and bewildering events of the past quarter century: the 1978 mass suicide of over 900 followers of the cult leader Jim Jones. What could lead so many people to end their lives in order to follow the wishes of this man? Osherow argues that a variety of social psychological processes, including some that were also considered in other units, probably operated to produce this bizarre event.

In "Reciprocation: The Old Give and Take . . . and Take," Robert Cialdini describes another compliance-inducing strategy: the use of the reciprocity norm. By doing something for you initially (such as giving you a flower), other people can invoke the powerful reciprocity norm, which holds that we should return favors that are done for us. As a result, we become more likely to comply with a subsequent request from the one who has done us the favor.

In the final selection, "Suspect Confessions," Richard Jerome profiles a social psychologist who specializes in investigating a particular kind of compliance situation—the police interrogation. The work of social psychologist Richard Ofshe suggests that some of the techniques used by police during questioning can be so powerful that suspects will sometimes comply (confess) even when they are innocent of the crimes! This article provides a fascinating glimpse into just how powerful some compliance-inducing tactics can be.

Looking Ahead: Challenge Questions

Which social psychological principles of social influence can you identify in the typical operation of cults? For example, what evidence is there for *conformity* pressures? How are such pressures created? Which strategies for inducing *compliance* are commonly used in cult groups? Are there any other societal groups (ones we would not label as cults) that use the same kind of techniques?

Are the techniques described in "Suspect Confessions" fair tactics for the police to use? Why or why not? More generally, what sort of restrictions, if any, should be placed on the use of social influence techniques in our society?

Making Sense of the Nonsensical: An Analysis of Jonestown

Neal Osherow

University of California, Santa Cruz

> Those who do not remember the past are condemned to repeat it.
> —quotation on placard over Jim Jones's rostrum at Jonestown

Close to one thousand people died at Jonestown. The members of the Peoples Temple settlement in Guyana, under the direction of the Reverend Jim Jones, fed a poison-laced drink to their children, administered the potion to their infants, and drank it themselves. Their bodies were found lying together, arm in arm; over 900 perished.

How could such a tragedy occur? The image of an entire community destroying itself, of parents killing their own children, appears incredible. The media stories about the event and full-color pictures of the scene documented some of its horror but did little to illuminate the causes or to explain the processes that led to the deaths. Even a year afterwards, a CBS Evening News broadcast asserted that "it was widely assumed that time would offer some explanation for the ritualistic suicide/murder of over 900 people.... One year later, it does not appear that any lessons have been uncovered" (CBS News, 1979).

The story of the Peoples Temple is not enshrouded in mystery, however. Jim Jones had founded his church over twenty years before, in Indiana. His preaching stressed the need for racial brotherhood and integration, and his group helped feed the poor and find them jobs. As his congregation grew, Jim Jones gradually increased the discipline and dedication that he required from the members. In 1965, he moved to northern California; about 100 of his faithful relocated with him. The membership began to multiply, new congregations were formed, and the headquarters was established in San Francisco.

Behind his public image as a beloved leader espousing interracial harmony, "Father," as Jones was called, assumed a messiah-like presence in the Peoples Temple. Increasingly, he became the personal object of the members' devotion, and he used their numbers and obedience to gain political influence and power. Within the Temple, Jones demanded absolute loyalty, enforced a taxing regimen, and delivered sermons forecasting nuclear holocaust and an apocalyptic destruction of the world, promising his followers that they alone would emerge as survivors. Many of his harangues attacked racism and capitalism, but his most vehement anger focused on the "enemies" of the Peoples Temple—its detractors and especially its defectors. In mid-1977, publication of unfavorable magazine articles, coupled with the impending custody battle over a six-year-old Jones claimed as a "son," prompted emigration of the bulk of Temple membership to a jungle outpost in Guyana.

In November, 1978, Congressman Leo Ryan responded to charges that the Peoples Temple was holding people against their will at Jonestown. He organized a trip to the South American settlement; a small party of journalists and "Concerned Relatives" of Peoples Temple members accompanied him on his investigation. They were in Jonestown for one evening and part of the following day. They heard most residents praise the settlement, expressing their joy at being there and indicating their desire to stay. Two families, however, slipped messages to Ryan that they wanted to leave with him. After the visit, as Ryan's party and these defectors tried to board planes to depart, the group was ambushed and fired upon by Temple gunmen—five people, including Ryan, were murdered.

As the shootings were taking place at the jungle airstrip, Jim Jones

---

I am very grateful to Elliot Aronson for his assistance with this essay. His insights, suggestions, and criticism were most valuable to its development. Also, my thanks to Elise Bean for her helpful editing.

gathered the community at Jonestown. He informed them that the Congressman's party would be killed and then initiated the final ritual: the "revolutionary suicide" that the membership had rehearsed on prior occasions. The poison was brought out. It was taken.

Jonestown's remoteness caused reports of the event to reach the public in stages. First came bulletins announcing the assassination of Congressman Ryan along with several members of his party. Then came rumors of mass-deaths at Jonestown, then confirmations. The initial estimates put the number of dead near 400, bringing the hope that substantial numbers of people had escaped into the jungle. But as the bodies were counted, many smaller victims were discovered under the corpses of larger ones—virtually none of the inhabitants of Jonestown survived. The public was shocked, then horrified, then incredulous.

Amid the early stories about the tragedy, along with the lurid descriptions and sensational photographs, came some attempts at analysis. Most discussed the charisma of Jim Jones and the power of "cults." Jones was described as "a character Joseph Conrad might have dreamt up (Krause, 1978), a "self-appointed messiah" whose "lust for dominion" led hundreds of "fanatic" followers to their demise (Special Report: The Cult of Death, Newsweek, 1978a).

While a description in terms of the personality of the perpetrator and the vulnerability of the victims provides some explanation, it relegates the event to the category of being an aberration, a product of unique forces and dispositions. Assuming such a perspective distances us from the phenomenon. This might be comforting, but I believe that it limits our understanding and is potentially dangerous. My aim in this analysis is not to blunt the emotional impact of a tragedy of this magnitude by subjecting it to academic examination. At the same time, applying social psychological theory and research makes it more conceivable and comprehensible, thus bringing it closer (in kind rather than in degree) to processes each of us encounters. Social psychological concepts can facilitate our understanding: The killings themselves, and many of the occurrences leading up to them, can be viewed in terms of obedience and compliance. The processes that induced people to join and to believe in the Peoples Temple made use of strategies involved in propaganda and persuasion. In grappling with the most perplexing questions—Why didn't more people leave the Temple? How could they actually kill their children and themselves?—the psychology of self-justification provides some insight.

Conformity

The character of a church... can be seen in its attitude toward its detractors.
—Hugh Prather, Notes to Myself

At one level, the deaths at Jonestown can be viewed as the product of obedience, of people complying with the orders of a leader and reacting to the threat of force. In the Peoples Temple, whatever Jim Jones commanded, the members did. When he gathered the community at the pavilion and the poison was brought out, the populace was surrounded by armed guards who were trusted lieutenants of Jones. There are reports that some people did not drink voluntarily but had the poison forced down their throats or injected (Winfrey, 1979). While there were isolated acts of resistance and suggestions of opposition to the suicides, excerpts from a tape, recorded as the final ritual was being enacted, reveal that such dissent was quickly dismissed or shouted down:

JONES: I've tried my best to give you a good life. In spite of all I've tried, a handful of people, with their lies, have made our life impossible. If we can't live in peace then let's die in peace. (Applause)... We have been so terribly betrayed.
What's going to happen here in the matter of a few minutes is that one of the people on that plane is going to shoot the pilot—I know that. I didn't plan it, but I know it's going to happen.... So my opinion is that you be kind to children, and be kind to seniors, and take the potion like they used to in ancient Greece, and step over quietly, because we are not committing suicide—it's a revolutionary act.... We can't go back. They're now going back to tell more lies....
FIRST WOMAN: I feel like that as long as there's life, there's hope.
JONES: Well, someday everybody dies.
CROWD: That's right, that's right!
JONES: What those people gone and done, and what they get through will make our lives worse than hell.... But to me, death is not a fearful thing. It's living that's cursed.... Not worth living like this.
FIRST WOMAN: But I'm afraid to die.
JONES: I don't think you are. I don't think you are.
FIRST WOMAN: I think there were too few who left for 1,200 people to give them their lives for those people who left.... I look at all the babies and I think they deserve to live.
JONES: But don't they deserve much more—they deserve peace. The best testimony we can give is to leave this goddam world. (Applause)
FIRST MAN: It's over, sister.... We've made a beautiful day. (Applause)
SECOND MAN: If you tell us we have to give our lives now, we're ready. (Applause) [Baltimore Sun, 1979.]

Above the cries of babies wailing, the tape continues, with Jones insisting upon the need for suicide and urging the people to complete the act:

JONES: Please get some medication. Simple. It's simple. There's no convulsions with it.... Don't be afraid to die. You'll see people land out here. They'll torture our people.
SECOND WOMAN: There's nothing to worry about. Everybody keep calm and try to keep your children calm.... They're not crying from pain; it's just a little bitter tasting...
THIRD WOMAN: This is nothing to cry about. This is something we could all rejoice about. (Applause)

JONES: Please, for God's sake, let's get on with it.... This is a revolutionary suicide. This is not a self-destructive suicide. (Voices praise "Dad." Applause)
THIRD MAN: Dad has brought us this far. My vote is to go with Dad....
JONES: We must die with dignity. Hurry, hurry, hurry. We must hurry.... Stop this hysterics. Death is a million times more preferable to spending more days in this life.... If you knew what was ahead, you'd be glad to be stepping over tonight...
FOURTH WOMAN: It's been a pleasure walking with all of you in this revolutionary struggle.... No other way I would rather go than to give my life for socialism. Communism, and I thank Dad very much.
JONES: Take our life from us.... We didn't commit suicide. We committed an act of revolutionary suicide protesting against the conditions of an inhuman world [*Newsweek*, 1978b, 1979].

If you hold a gun at someone's head, you can get that person to do just about anything. As many accounts have attested,[1] by the early 1970s the members of the Peoples Temple lived in constant fear of severe punishment—brutal beatings coupled with public humiliation—for committing trivial or even inadvertent offenses. But the power of an authority need not be so explicitly threatening in order to induce compliance with its demands, as demonstrated by social psychological research. In Milgram's experiments (1963), a surprisingly high proportion of subjects obeyed the instructions of an experimenter to administer what they thought were very strong electric shocks to an-

[1] The reports of ex-Peoples Temple members who defected create a very consistent picture of the tactics Jim Jones employed in his church. Jeanne Mills (1979) provides the most comprehensive personal account, and there are affidavits about the Peoples Temple sworn to by Deborah Blakey (May 12, 1978 and June 15, 1978) and Yolanda Crawford (April 10, 1978). Media stories about the Peoples Temple, which usually rely on interviews with defectors, and about Jonestown, which are based on interviews with survivors, also corroborate one another. (See especially Kilduff and Tracy (1977), *Newsweek* (1978a), Lifton (1979), and Cahill (1979).

other person. Nor does the consensus of a group need be so blatantly coercive to induce agreement with its opinion, as Asch's experiments (1955) on conformity to the incorrect judgments of a majority indicate.

Jim Jones utilized the threat of severe punishment to impose the strict discipline and absolute devotion that he demanded, and he also took measures to eliminate those factors that might encourage resistance or rebellion among his followers. Research showed that the presence of a "disobedient" partner greatly reduced the extent to which most subjects in the Milgram situation (1965) obeyed the instructions to shock the person designated the "learner." Similarly, by including just one confederate who expressed an opinion different from the majority's, Asch (1955) showed that the subject would also agree far less, even when the "other dissenter's" judgment was also incorrect and differed from the subject's. In the Peoples Temple, Jones tolerated no dissent, made sure that members had no allegiance more powerful than to himself, and tried to make the alternative of leaving the Temple an unthinkable option.

Jeanne Mills, who spent six years as a high-ranking member before becoming one of the few who left the Peoples Temple, writes: "There was an unwritten but perfectly understood law in the church that was very important: 'No one is to criticize Father, his wife, or his children' " (Mills, 1979). Deborah Blakey, another long-time member who managed to defect, testified:

> Any disagreement with [Jim Jones's] dictates came to be regarded as "treason."... Although I felt terrible about what was happening, I was afraid to say anything because I knew that anyone with a differing opinion gained the wrath of Jones and other members. [Blakey, June 15, 1978.]

Conditions in the Peoples Temple became so oppressive, the discrepancy between Jim Jones's stated aims and his practices so pronounced,

that it is almost inconceivable that members failed to entertain questions about the church. But these doubts went unreinforced. There were no allies to support one's disobedience of the leader's commands and no fellow dissenters to encourage the expression of disagreement with the majority. Public disobedience or dissent was quickly punished. Questioning Jones's word, even in the company of family or friends, was dangerous—informers and "counselors" were quick to report indiscretions, even by relatives.

The use of informers went further than to stifle dissent; it also diminished the solidarity and loyalty that individuals felt toward their families and friends. While Jones preached that a spirit of brotherhood should pervade his church, he made it clear that each member's personal dedication should be directed to "Father." Families were split: First, children were seated away from parents during services; then, many were assigned to another member's care as they grew up; and ultimately, parents were forced to sign documents surrendering custody rights. "Families are part of the enemy system," Jones stated, because they hurt one's total dedication to the "Cause" (Mills, 1979). Thus, a person called before the membership to be punished could expect his or her family to be among the first and most forceful critics (Cahill, 1979).

Besides splitting parent and child, Jones sought to loosen the bonds between wife and husband. He forced spouses into extramarital sexual relations, which were often of a homosexual or humiliating nature, or with Jones himself. Sexual partnerships and activities not under his direction and control were discouraged and publicly ridiculed.

Thus, expressing any doubts or criticism of Jones—even to a friend, child, or partner—became risky for the individual. As a consequence, such thoughts were kept to oneself, and with the resulting impression that nobody else shared them. In addition to limiting one's access to information, this "fallacy of uniqueness" precluded the sharing of support. It is interesting that among the few who successfully defected from the Peoples Temple were couples such as Jeanne and Al Mills, who kept together, shared their doubts, and gave each other support.

Why didn't more people leave? Once inside the Peoples Temple, getting out was discouraged; defectors were hated. Nothing upset Jim Jones so much; people who left became the targets of his most vitriolic attacks and were blamed for any problems that occurred. One member recalled that after several teen-age members left the Temple, "We hated those eight with such a passion because we knew any day they were going to try bombing us. I mean Jim Jones had us totally convinced of this" (Winfrey, 1979).

Defectors were threatened: Immediately after she left, Grace Stoen headed for the beach at Lake Tahoe, where she found herself looking over her shoulder, checking to make sure that she hadn't been tracked down (Kilduff and Tracy, 1977). Jeanne Mills reports that she and her family were followed by men in cars, their home was burglarized, and they were threatened with the use of confessions they had signed while still members. When a friend from the Temple paid a visit, she quickly examined Mills' ears—Jim Jones had vowed to have one of them cut off (Mills, 1979). He had made ominous predictions concerning other defectors as well: Indeed, several ex-members suffered puzzling deaths or committed very questionable "suicides" shortly after leaving the Peoples Temple (Reiterman, 1977; Tracy, 1978).

Defecting became quite a risky enterprise, and, for most members, the potential benefits were very uncertain. They had little to hope for outside of the Peoples Temple; what they had, they had committed to the church. Jim Jones had vilified previous defectors as "the enemy" and had instilled the fear that, once outside of the Peoples Temple, members' stories would not be believed by the "racist, fascist" society, and they would be subjected to torture, concentration camps, and execution. Finally, in Guyana, Jonestown was surrounded by dense jungle, the few trails patrolled by armed security guards (Cahill, 1979). Escape was not a viable option. Resistance was too costly. With no other alternatives apparent, compliance became the most reasonable course of action.

The power that Jim Jones wielded kept the membership of the Peoples Temple in line, and the difficulty of defecting helped to keep them in. But what attracted them to join Jones's church in the first place?

Persuasion

Nothing is so unbelievable that oratory cannot make it acceptable.
—Cicero

Jim Jones was a charismatic figure, adept at oratory. He sought people for his church who would be receptive to his messages and vulnerable to his promises, and he carefully honed his presentation to appeal to each specific audience.

The bulk of the Peoples Temple membership was comprised of society's needy and neglected: the urban poor, the black, the elderly, and a sprinkling of ex-addicts and ex-convicts (Winfrey, 1979). To attract new members, Jones held public services in various cities. Leaflets would be distributed:

PASTOR JIM JONES ... Incredible! ... Miraculous! ... Amazing! ... The Most Unique Prophetic Healing Service You've Ever Witnessed! Behold the Word Made Incarnate In Your Midst!
God works as tumorous masses are passed in every service. ... Before your eyes, the crippled walk, the blind see! [Kilduff and Javers, 1978.]

Potential members first confronted an almost idyllic scene of blacks and whites living, working, and worshipping together. Guests were greeted and treated most warmly and were invited to share in the group's meal. As advertised, Jim Jones also gave them miracles. A number of members would recount how Jones had cured them of cancer or other dread diseases; during the service Jones or one of his nurses would reach into the member's throat and emerge with a vile mass of tissue—the "cancer" that had been passed as the person gagged. Sometimes Jim Jones would make predictions that would occur with uncanny frequency. He also received revelations about members or visitors that nobody but those individuals could know—what they had eaten for dinner the night before, for instance, or news about a far-off relative. Occasionally, he performed miracles similar to more well-established religious figures:

> There were more people than usual at the Sunday service, and for some reason the church members hadn't brought enough food to feed everyone. It became apparent that the last fifty people in line weren't going to get any meat. Jim announced, "Even though there isn't enough food to feed this multitude, I am blessing the food that we have and multiplying it—just as Jesus did in biblical times."
> Sure enough, a few minutes after he made this startling announcement, Eva Pugh came out of the kitchen beaming, carrying two platters filled with fried chicken. A big cheer came from the people assembled in the room, especially from the people who were at the end of the line.
> The "blessed chicken" was extraordinarily delicious, and several of the people mentioned that Jim had produced the best-tasting chicken they had ever eaten. [Mills, 1979.]

These demonstrations were dramatic and impressive; most members were convinced of their authenticity and believed in Jones's "powers." They didn't know that the "cancers" were actually rancid chicken gizzards, that the occurrences Jones "forecast" were staged, or that sending people to sift through a person's garbage could reveal packages of certain foods or letters of out-of-town relatives to serve as grist for Jones' "revelations" (Kilduff and Tracy, 1977; Mills, 1979). Members were motivated to believe in Jones; they appreciated the racial harmony, sense of purpose, and relief from feelings of worthlessness that the Peoples Temple provided them (Winfrey, 1979; Lifton, 1979). Even when suspecting that something was wrong, they learned that it was unwise to voice their doubts:

> One of the men, Chuck Beikman... jokingly mentioned to a few people standing near him that he had seen Eva drive up a few moments earlier with buckets from the Kentucky Fried Chicken stand. He smiled as he said, "The person that blessed this chicken was Colonel Sanders."
> During the evening meeting Jim mentioned the fact that Chuck had made fun of his gift. "He lied to some of the members here, telling them that the chicken had come from a local shop," Jim stormed. "But the Spirit of Justice has prevailed. Because of his lie Chuck is in the men's room right now, wishing that he was dead. He is vomiting and has diarrhea so bad he can't talk!"
> An hour later a pale and shaken Chuck Beikman walked out of the men's room and up to the front, being supported by one of the guards. Jim asked him, "Do you have anything you'd like to say?"
> Chuck looked up weakly and answered, "Jim, I apologize for what I said. Please forgive me."
> As we looked at Chuck, we vowed in our hearts that we would never question any of Jim's "miracles"—at least not out loud. Years later, we learned that Jim had put a mild poison in a piece of cake and given it to Chuck. [Mills, 1979.]

While most members responded to presentations that were emotional, one-sided, and almost sensational in tone, those who eventually assumed positions of responsibility in the upper echelons of the Peoples Temples were attracted by different considerations. Most of these people were white and came from upper-middle-class backgrounds—they included lawyers, a medical student, nurses, and people representing other occupations that demanded education and reflected a strong social consciousness. Jones lured these members by stressing the social and political aspects of the church, its potential as an idealistic experiment with integration and socialism. Tim Stoen, who was the Temple's lawyer, stated later, "I wanted utopia so damn bad I could die" (Winfrey, 1979). These members had the information and intelligence to see through many of Jones's ploys, but, as Jeanne Mills explains repeatedly in her book, they dismissed their qualms and dismissed Jones's deception as being necessary to achieve a more important aim—furthering the Cause: "For the thousandth time, I rationalized my doubts. 'If Jim feels it's necessary for the Cause, who am I to question his wisdom?'" (Mills, 1979).

It turned out to be remarkably easy to overcome their hesitancy and calm their doubts. Mills recalls that she and her husband initially were skeptical about Jones and the Peoples Temple. After attending their first meeting, they remained unimpressed by the many members who proclaimed that Jones had healed their cancers or cured their drug habits. They were annoyed by Jones' arrogance, and they were bored by most of the long service. But in the weeks following their visit, they received numerous letters containing testimonials and gifts from the Peoples Temple, they had dreams about Jones, and they were attracted by the friendship and love they had felt from both the black and the white members. When they went back for their second visit, they took their children with them. After the long drive, the Mills's were greeted warmly by many members and by Jones himself. "This time... my mind was open to hear his message because my own beliefs had become very shaky" (Mills, 1979). As they were driving home afterwards, the children begged their parents to join the church:

> We had to admit that we enjoyed the service more this time and we told the children that we'd think it over. Somehow, though, we knew that it was only a matter of time before we were going to become members of the Peoples Temple. [Mills, 1979.]

Jim Jones skillfully manipulated the impression that his church would convey to newcomers. He carefully managed its public image. He used the letter-writing and political clout of hundreds of members to praise and impress the politicians and press that supported the Peoples Temple, as well as to criticize and intimidate its opponents (Kasindorf, 1978). Most importantly, Jones severely restricted the information that was available to the members. In addition to indoctrinating members into his own belief system through extensive sermons and lectures, he inculcated a distrust of any contradictory messages, labelling them the product of enemies. By destroying the credibility of their sources, he inoculated the membership against being persuaded by outside criticism. Similarly, any contradictory thoughts that might arise within each member were to be discredited. Instead of seeing them as having any basis in reality, members interpreted them as indications of their own shortcomings or lack of faith. Members learned to attribute the apparent discrepancies between Jones's lofty pronouncements and the rigors of life in the Peoples Temple to their personal inadequacies rather than blaming them on any fault of Jones. As ex-member Neva Sly was quoted: "We always blamed ourselves for things that didn't seem right" (Winfrey, 1979). A unique and distorting language developed within the church, in which "the Cause" became anything that Jim Jones said (Mills, 1979). It was spoken at Jonestown, where a guard tower was called the "playground" (Cahill, 1979). Ultimately, through the clever use of oratory, deception, and language, Jones could speak of death as "stepping over," thereby camouflaging a hopeless act of self-destruction as a noble and brave act of "revolutionary suicide," and the members accepted his words.

Self-Justification

> Both salvation and punishment for man lie in the fact that if he lives wrongly he can befog himself so as not to see the misery of his position.
> —Tolstoy, "The Kreutzer Sonata"

Analyzing Jonestown in terms of obedience and the power of the situation can help to explain why the people *acted* as they did. Once the Peoples Temple had moved to Jonestown, there was little the members could do other than follow Jim Jones's dictates. They were comforted by an authority of absolute power. They were left with few options, being surrounded by armed guards and by the jungle, having given their passports and various documents and confessions to Jones, and believing that conditions in the outside world were even more threatening. The members' poor diet, heavy workload, lack of sleep, and constant exposure to Jones's diatribes exacerbated the coerciveness of their predicament; tremendous pressures encouraged them to obey.

By the time of the final ritual, opposition or escape had become almost impossible for most of the members. Yet even then, it is doubtful that many *wanted* to resist or to leave. Most had come to believe in Jones—one woman's body was found with a message scribbled on her arm during the final hours: "Jim Jones is the only one" (Cahill, 1979). They seemed to have accepted the necessity, and even the beauty, of dying—just before the ritual began, a guard approached Charles Garry, one of the Temple's hired attorneys, and exclaimed, "It's a great moment... we all die" (Lifton, 1979). A survivor of Jonestown, who happened to be away at the dentist, was interviewed a year following the deaths:

> If I had been there, I would have been the first one to stand in that line and take that poison and I would have been proud to take it. The thing I'm sad about is this; that I missed the ending. [Gallagher, 1979.]

It is this aspect of Jonestown that is perhaps the most troubling. To the end, and even beyond, the vast majority of the Peoples Temple members *believed* in Jim Jones. External forces, in the form of power or persuasion, can exact compliance. But one must examine a different set of processes to account for the members' internalizing those beliefs.

Although Jones's statements were often inconsistent and his methods cruel, most members maintained their faith in his leadership. Once they were isolated at Jonestown, there was little opportunity or motivation to think otherwise—resistance or escape was out of the question. In such a situation, the individual is motivated to rationalize his or her predicament; a person confronted with the inevitable tends to regard it more positively. For example, social psychological research has shown that when children believe that they will be served more of a vegetable they dislike, they will convince themselves that it is not so noxious (Brehm, 1959), and when a person thinks that she will be interacting with someone, she tends to judge a description of that individual more favorably (Darley and Berscheid, 1967).

A member's involvement in the Temple did not begin at Jonestown—it started much earlier, closer to home, and less dramatically. At first, the potential member would attend meetings voluntarily and might put in a few hours each week working for the church. Though the established members would urge the recruit to join, he or she felt free to choose whether to stay or to leave. Upon deciding to join, a member expended more effort and became more committed to the Peoples Temple. In small increments, Jones increased the demands made on the member, and only after a long sequence did he escalate the oppressiveness of his rule and the desperation of his message. Little by little, the individual's alternatives became more limited. Step by step, the person was motivated to rationalize his or her commitment and to justify his or her behavior.

Jeanne Mills, who managed to defect two years before the Temple relocated in Guyana, begins her account, *Six Years With God* (1979), by writing: "Every time I tell someone about the six years we spent as members of the Peoples Temple, I am faced with an unanswerable question: 'If the church was so bad, why did you and your family stay in for so long?'" Several classic studies from social psychological research investigating processes of self-justification and the theory of cognitive dissonance (see Aronson, 1980, chapter 4; Aronson, 1969) can point to explanations for such seemingly irrational behavior.

According to dissonance theory, when a person commits an act or holds a cognition that is psychologically inconsistent with his or her self-concept, the inconsistency arouses an unpleasant state of tension. The individual tries to reduce this "dissonance," usually by altering his or her attitudes to bring them more into line with the previously discrepant action or belief. A number of occurrences in the Peoples Temple can be illuminated by viewing them in light of this process. The horrifying events of Jonestown were not due merely to the threat of force, nor did they erupt instantaneously. That is, it was *not* the case that something "snapped" in people's minds, suddenly causing them to behave in bizarre ways. Rather, as the theory of cognitive dissonance spells out, people seek to *justify* their choices and commitments.

Just as a towering waterfall can begin as a trickle, so too can the impetus for doing extreme or calamitous actions be provided by the consequences of agreeing to do seemingly trivial ones. In the Peoples Temple, the process started with the effects of undergoing a severe initiation to join the church, was reinforced by the tendency to justify one's commitments, and was strengthened by the need to rationalize one's behavior.

Consider the prospective member's initial visit to the People's Temple, for example. When a person undergoes a severe initiation in order to gain entrance into a group, he or she is apt to judge that group as being more attractive, in order to justify expending the effort or enduring the pain. Aronson and Mills (1959) demonstrated that students who suffered greater embarrassment as a prerequisite for being allowed to participate in a discussion group rated its conversation (which actually was quite boring) to be significantly more interesting than did those students who experienced little or no embarrassment in order to be admitted. Not only is there a tendency to justify undergoing the experience by raising one's estimation of the goal—in some circumstances, choosing to experience a hardship can go so far as to affect a person's perception of the discomfort or pain he or she felt. Zimbardo (1969) and his colleagues showed that when subjects volunteered for a procedure that involves their being given electric shocks, those thinking that they had more choice in the matter reported feeling less pain from the shocks. More specifically, those who experienced greater dissonance, having little external justification to account for their choosing to endure the pain, described it as being less intense. This extended beyond their impressions and verbal reports; their performance on a task was hindered less, and they even recorded somewhat lower readings on a physiological instrument measuring galvanic skin responses. Thus the dissonance-reducing process can be double-edged: Under proper guidance, a person who voluntarily experiences a severe initiation not only comes to regard its ends more positively, but may also begin to see the means as less aversive: "We begin to appreciate the long meetings, because we were told that spiritual growth comes from self-sacrifice" (Mills, 1979).

Once involved, a member found ever-increasing portions of his or her time and energy devoted to the Peoples Temple. The services and meetings occupied weekends and several evenings each week. Working on Temple projects and writing the required letters to politicians and the press took much of one's "spare" time. Expected monetary contributions changed from "voluntary" donations (though they were recorded) to the required contribution of a quarter of one's income. Eventually, a member was supposed to sign over all personal property, savings, social security checks, and the like to the Peoples Temple. Before entering the meeting room for each service, a member stopped at a table and wrote self-incriminating letters or signed blank documents that were turned over to the church. If anyone objected, the refusal was interpreted as denoting a "lack of faith" in Jones. Finally, members were asked to live at Temple facilities to save money and to be able to work more efficiently, and many of their children were raised under the care of other families. Acceding to each new demand had two repercussions: In practical terms, it enmeshed the person further into the Peoples Temple web and made leaving more difficult; on an attitudinal level, it set the aforementioned processes of self-justification into motion. As Mills (1979) describes:

> We had to face painful reality. Our life savings were gone. Jim had demanded that we sell the life insurance policy and turn the equity over to the church, so that was gone. Our property had all been taken from us. Our dream of going to an overseas mission was gone. We thought that we had alienated our parents when we told them we were leaving the country. Even the children whom we had left in the care of Carol and Bill were openly hostile toward us. Jim had accomplished all this in such a short time! All we had left now was Jim and the Cause, so we decided to buckle under and give our energies to these two.

Ultimately, Jim Jones and the Cause would require the members to give their lives.

What could cause people to kill their children and themselves? From a detached perspective, the image seems unbelievable. In fact, at first glance, so does the idea of so many individuals committing so much of their time, giving all of their money, and even sacrificing the control of their children to the Peoples Temple. Jones took advantage of rationalization processes that allow people to justify their commitments by raising their estimations of the goal and minimizing its costs. Much as he gradually increased his demands, Jones carefully orchestrated the members' exposure to the concept of a "final ritual." He utilized the leverage provided by their previous commitments to push them closer and closer to its enactment. Gaining a "foot in the door" by getting a person to agree to a moderate request makes it more probable that he or she will agree to do a much larger deed later, as social psychologists—and salespeople—have found (Freedman and Fraser, 1966). Doing the initial task causes something that might have seemed unreasonable at first appear less extreme in comparison, and it also motivates a person to make his or her behavior appear more consistent by consenting to the larger request as well.

After indoctrinating the members with the workings of the Peoples Temple itself, Jones began to focus on broader and more basic attitudes. He started by undermining the members' belief that death was to be fought and feared and set the stage by introducing the possibility of a cataclysmic ending for the church. As several accounts corroborate (see Mills, 1979; Lifton, 1979; Cahill, 1979), Jones directed several "fake" suicide drills, first with the elite Planning Commission of the Peoples Temple and later with the general membership. He would give them wine and then announce that it had been poisoned and that they would soon die. These became tests of faith, of the members' willingness to follow Jones even to death. Jones would ask people if they were ready to die and on occasion would have the membership "decide" its own fate by voting whether to carry out his wishes. An ex-member recounted that one time, after a while

> Jones smiled and said, "Well, it was a good lesson. I see you're not dead." He made it sound like we needed the 30 minutes to do very strong, introspective type of thinking. We all felt strongly dedicated, proud of ourselves.... [Jones] taught that it was a privilege to die for what you believed in, which is exactly what I would have been doing. [Winfrey, 1979.]

After the Temple moved to Jonestown, the "White Nights," as the suicide drills were called, occurred repeatedly. An exercise that appears crazy to the observer was a regular, justifiable occurrence for the Peoples Temple participant. The reader might ask whether this caused the members to think that the actual suicides were merely another practice, but there were many indications that they knew that the poison was truly deadly on that final occasion. The Ryan visit had been climatic, there were several new defectors, the cooks—who had been excused from the prior drills in order to prepare the upcoming meal—were included, Jones had been growing increasingly angry, desperate, and unpredictable, and, finally, everyone could see the first babies die. The membership was manipulated, but they were not unaware that this time the ritual was for real.

A dramatic example of the impact of self-justification concerns the physical punishment that was meted out in the Peoples Temple. As discussed earlier, the threat of being beaten or humiliated forced the member to comply with Jones's orders: A person will obey as long as he or she is being threatened and supervised. To affect a person's *attitudes*, however, a mild threat has been demonstrated to be more effective than a severe threat (Aronson and Carlsmith, 1963) and its influence has been shown to be far longer lasting (Freedman, 1965). Under a mild threat, the individual has more difficulty attributing his or her behavior to such a minor external restraint, forcing the person to alter his or her attitudes in order to justify the action. Severe threats elicit compliance, but, imposed from the outside, they usually fail to cause the behavior to be internalized. Quite a different dynamic ensues when it is not so clear that the action is being imposed upon the person. When an individual feels that he or she played an active role in carrying out an action that hurts someone, there comes a motivation to justify one's part in the cruelty by rationalizing it as necessary or by derogating the victim by thinking that the punishment was deserved (Davis and Jones, 1960).

Let's step back for a moment. The processes doing on at Jonestown obviously were not as simple as those in a well-controlled laboratory experiment; several themes were going on simultaneously. For example, Jim Jones had the power to impose any punishments that he wished in the Peoples Temple, and, especially towards the end, brutality and terror at Jonestown were rampant. But Jones carefully controlled how the punishments were carried out. He often called upon the members themselves to agree to the imposition of beatings. They were instructed to testify against fellow members, bigger members told to beat up smaller ones, wives or lovers forced to sexually humiliate their partners, and parents asked to consent to and assist in the beatings of their children (Mills, 1979; Kilduff and Javers, 1978). The punishments grew more and more sadistic, the beatings so severe as to knock the victim unconscious and cause bruises that lasted for weeks. As Donald Lunde, a psychiatrist who has investigated acts of extreme violence, explains:

> Once you've done something that major, it's very hard to admit even to yourself that you've made a mistake, and subconsciously you will go to great lengths to rationalize what you did. It's very tricky defense mechanism exploited to the hilt by the charismatic leader. [*Newsweek*, 1978a.]

A more personal account of the impact of this process is provided by Jeanne Mills. At one meeting, she and her husband were forced to consent to the beating of their daughter as punishment for a very minor transgression. She relates the effect this had on her daughter, the victim, as well as on herself, one of the perpetrators:

> As we drove home, everyone in the car was silent. We were all afraid that our words would be considered treasonous. The only sounds came from Linda, sobbing quietly in the back seat. When we got into our house, Al and I sat down to talk with Linda. She was in too much pain to sit. She stood quietly while we talked with her. "How do you feel about what happened tonight?" Al asked her.
>
> "Father was right to have me whipped," Linda answered. "I've been so rebellious lately, and I've done a lot of things that were wrong.... I'm sure Father knew about those things, and that's why he had me hit so many times."
>
> As we kissed our daughter goodnight, our heads were spinning. It was hard to think clearly when things were so confusing. Linda had been the victim, and yet we were the only people angry about it. She should have been hostile and angry. Instead, she said that Jim had actually helped her. We knew Jim had done a cruel thing, and yet everyone acted as if he were doing a loving thing in whipping our disobedient child. Unlike a cruel person hurting a child, Jim had seemed calm, almost loving, as he observed the beating and counted off the whacks. Our minds were not able to comprehend the atrocity of the situation because none of the feedback we were receiving was accurate. [Mills, 1979.]

The feedback one received from the outside was limited, and the feedback from inside the Temple member was distorted. By justifying the previous actions and commitments, the groundwork for accepting the ultimate commitment was established.

Conclusion

> Only months after we defected from Temple did we realize the full extent of the cocoon in which we'd lived. And only then did we understand the fraud, sadism, and emotional blackmail of the master manipulator.
> —Jeanne Mills, Six Years with God

Immediately following the Jonestown tragedy, there came a proliferation of articles about "cults" and calls for their investigation and control. From Synanon to Transcendental Meditation, groups and practices were examined by the press, which had a difficult time determining what constituted a "cult" or differentiating between those that might be safe and beneficial and those that could be dangerous. The Peoples Temple and the events at Jonestown make such a definition all the more problematic. A few hours before his murder, Congressman Ryan addressed the membership: "I can tell you right now that by the few conversations I've had with some of the folks ... there are some people who believe this is the best thing that ever happened in their whole lives" (Krause, 1978). The acquiescence of so many and the letters they left behind indicate that this feeling was widely shared—or at least expressed—by the members.

Many "untraditional"—to mainstream American culture—groups or practices, such as Eastern religions or meditation techniques, have proven valuable for the people who experience them but may be seen as very strange and frightening to others. How can people determine whether they are being exposed to a potentially useful alternative way of living their lives or if they are being drawn to a dangerous one?

The distinction is a difficult one. Three questions suggested by the previous analysis, however, can provide important clues: Are alternatives being provided or taken away? Is one's access to new and different information being broadened or denied? Finally, does the individual assume personal responsibility and control or is it usurped by the group or by its leader?

The Peoples Temple attracted many of its members because it provided them an alternative way of viewing their lives; it gave many people who were downtrodden a sense of purpose, and even transcendence. But it did so at a cost, forcing them to disown their former friendships and beliefs and teaching them to fear anything outside of the Temple as "the enemy." Following Jones became the *only* alternative.

Indeed, most of the members grew increasingly unaware of the possibility of any other course. Within the Peoples Temple, and especially at Jonestown, Jim Jones controlled the information to which members would be exposed. He effectively stifled any dissent that might arise within the church and instilled a distrust in each member for contradictory messages from outside. After all, what credibility could be carried by information supplied by "the enemy" that was out to destroy the Peoples Temple with "lies"?

Seeing no alternatives and having no information, a member's capacity for dissent or resistance was minimized. Moreover, for most members, part of the Temple's attraction resulted from their willingness to relinquish much of the responsibility and control over their lives. These were primarily the poor, the minorities, the elderly, and the unsuccessful—they were happy to exchange personal autonomy (with its implicit assumption of personal responsibility for their plights) for security, brotherhood, the illusion of miracles, and the promise of salvation. Stanley Cath, a psychiatrist who has studied the conversion techniques used by cults, generalizes: "Converts have to believe only what they are told. They don't have to think, and this relieves tremendous tensions" (*Newsweek*, 1978a). Even Jeanne Mills, one of the better-educated Temple members, commented:

> I was amazed at how little disagreement there was between the members of this church. Before we joined the church, Al and I couldn't even agree on whom to vote for in the presidential election. Now that we all belonged to a group, family arguments were becoming a thing of the past. There was never a question of who was right, because Jim was always right. When our large household met to discuss family problems, we didn't ask for opinions. Instead, we put the question to the children, "What would Jim do?" It took the difficulty out of life. There was a type of "manifest destiny" which said the Cause was right and would succeed. Jim was right and those who agreed with him were right. If you disagreed with Jim, you were wrong. It was as simple as that. [Mills, 1979.]

Though it is unlikely that he had any formal exposure to the social psychological literature, Jim Jones utilized several very powerful and effective techniques for controlling people's behavior and altering their attitudes. Some analyses have compared his tactics to those involved in "brainwashing," for both include the control of communication, the manipulation of guilt, and dispensing power over people's existence (Lifton, 1979), as well as isolation, an exacting regimen, physical pressure, and the use of confessions (Cahill, 1979). But using the term brainwashing makes the process sound too esoteric and unusual. There *were* some unique and scary elements in Jones' personality—paranoia, delusions of grandeur, sadism, and a preoccupation with suicide. Whatever his personal motivation, however, having formulated his plans and fantasies, he took advantage of well-established social psychological tactics to carry them out. The decision to have a community destroy itself was crazy, but those who performed the deed were "normal" people who were subjected to a tremendously impactful situation, the victims of powerful internal forces as well as external pressures.

Postscript

Within a few weeks of the deaths at Jonestown, the bodies had been transported back to the United States, the remnants of the Peoples Temple membership were said to have disbanded, and the spate of stories and books about the suicide/murders had begun to lose the public's attention. Three months afterwards, Michael Prokes, who had escaped from Jonestown because he was assigned to carry away a box of Peoples Temple funds, called a press conference in a California motel room. After claiming that Jones had been misunderstood and demanding the release of a tape recording of the final minutes [quoted earlier], he stepped into the bathroom and shot himself in the head. He left behind a note, saying that if his death inspired another book about Jonestown, it was worthwhile (Newsweek, 1979).

Postscript

Jeanne and Al Mills were among the most vocal of the Peoples Temples critics following their defection, and they topped an alleged "death list" of its enemies. Even after Jonestown, the Mills's had repeatedly expressed fear for their lives. Well over a year after the Peoples Temple deaths, they and their daughter were murdered in their Berkeley home. Their teen-aged son, himself an ex-Peoples Temple member, has testified that he was in another part of the large house at the time. At this writing, no suspect has been charged. There are indications that the Mills's knew their killer—there were no signs of forced entry, and they were shot at close range. Jeanne Mills had been quoted as saying, "It's going to happen. If not today, then tomorrow." On the final tape of Jonestown, Jim Jones had blamed Jeanne Mills by name, and had promised that his followers in San Francisco "will not take our death in vain" (Newsweek, 1980).

References

ARONSON, E. *The social animal* (3rd ed.) San Francisco: W. H. Freeman and Company, 1980.
ARONSON, E. The theory of cognitive dissonance: A current perspective. In L. Berkowitz (ed.), *Advances in experimental social psychology*. Vol. 4. New York: Academic Press, 1969.
ARONSON E., AND CARLSMITH, J. M. Effect of the severity of threat on the devaluation of forbidden behavior. *Journal of Abnormal and Social Psychology*. 1963, 66, 584–588.
ARONSON, E., AND MILLS, J. The effects of severity of initiation on liking for a group. *Journal of Abnormal and Social Psychology*. 1959, 59, 177–181.
ASCH, S. Opinions and social pressure. *Scientific American*, 1955, 193. (Also reprinted in this volume.)
Tape hints early decision by Jones on mass suicide. *Baltimore Sun*. March 15, 1979.
BLAKEY, D. Affidavit: Georgetown, Guyana. May 12, 1978.
BLAKEY, D. Affidavit: San Francisco. June 15, 1978.
BREHM, J. Increasing cognitive dissonance by a *fait-accompli*. *Journal of Abnormal and Social Psychology*, 1959, 58, 379–382.
CAHILL, T. In the valley of the shadow of death. *Rolling Stone*. January 25, 1979.
Committee on Foreign Affairs, U.S. House of Representatives, Report of a staff investigative group. *The assassination of Representative Leo J. Ryan and the Jonestown, Guyana tragedy*. Washington, D.C.: Government Printing Office, May 15, 1979. (Many of the other press reports are reprinted in this volume.)
CRAWFORD, Y. Affidavit: San Francisco. April 10, 1978.
DARLEY, J., AND BERSCHEID, E. Increased liking as a result of the anticipation of personal contact. *Human Relations*, 1967, 20, 29–40.
DAVIS, K., AND JONES, E. Changes in interpersonal perception as a means of reducing cognitive dissonance. *Journal of Abnormal and Social Psychology*, 1960, 61, 402–410.
"Don't be afraid to die" and another victim of Jonestown. *Newsweek*, March 10, 1980.
A fatal prophecy is fulfilled. *Newsweek*, March 10, 1980.
FREEDMAN, J. Long-term behavioral effects of cognitive dissonance. *Journal of Experimental Social Psychology*, 1965, 1, 145–155.
FREEDMAN, J., AND FRASER, S. Compliance without pressure: The foot-in-the-door technique. *Journal of Personality and Social Psychology*, 1966, 4, 195–202.
GALLAGHER, N. Jonestown: The survivors' story. *New York Times Magazine*, November 18, 1979.
KASINDORF, J. Jim Jones: The seduction of San Francisco. *New West*, December 18, 1978.
KILDUFF, M., AND JAVERS, R. *The suicide cult*. New York: Bantam, 1978, and *San Francisco Chronicle*.
KILDUFF, M., AND TRACY, P. Inside Peoples Temple. *New West*, August 1, 1977.
KRAUSE, C. *Guyana massacre*. New York: Berkley, 1978, and *Washington Post*.
LIFTON, R. J. Appeal of the death trip. *New York Times Magazine*, January 7, 1979.
MILGRAM, S. Behavioral study of obedience. *Journal of Abnormal and Social Psychology*, 1963, 67, 371–378. (Also reprinted in E. Aronson (ed.), *Readings about the social animal*.)
MILGRAM, S. Liberating effects of group pressure. *Journal of Personality and Social Psychology*, 1965, 1, 127–134.
MILLS, J. *Six years with God*. New York: A & W Publishers, 1979.
REITERMAN, T. Scared too long. *San Francisco Examiner*, November 13, 1977.
The sounds of death. *Newsweek*, December 18, 1978b.
Special report: The cult of death. *Newsweek*, December 4, 1978a.
TRACY, P. Jim Jones: The making of a madman. *New West*, December 18, 1978.
WINFREY, C. Why 900 died in Guyana. *New York Times Magazine*, February 25, 1979.
YOUNG, S. Report on Jonestown. *The CBS Evening News with Walter Cronkite*. November 16, 1979.
ZIMBARDO, P. *The cognitive control of motivation*. Glenview, Ill.: Scott Foresman, 1969.
ZIMBARDO, P., EBBESON, E., AND MASLACH, C. *Influencing attitudes and changing behavior* (2nd ed.). Reading, Mass.: Addison-Wesley, 1977.

Reciprocation

The Old Give and Take . . . and Take

Robert B. Cialdini

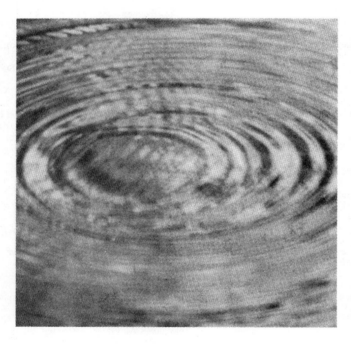

"Pay every debt, as if God wrote the bill."
Ralph Waldo Emerson

A few years ago, a university professor tried a little experiment. He sent Christmas cards to a sample of perfect strangers. Although he expected some reaction, the response he received was amazing—holiday cards addressed to him came pouring back from people who had never met nor heard of him. The great majority of those who returned cards never inquired into the identity of the unknown professor. They received his holiday greeting card, *click*, and *whirr*, they automatically sent cards in return (Kuntz & Woolcott, 1976).

While small in scope, this study shows the action of one of the most potent of the weapons of influence around us—the rule of reciprocation. The rule says that we should try to repay, in kind, what another person has provided us. If a woman does us a favor, we should do her one in return; if a man sends us a birthday present, we should remember his birthday with a gift of our own; if a couple invites us to a party, we should be sure to invite them to one of ours. By virtue of the reciprocity rule, then, we are *obligated* to the future repayment of favors, gifts, invitations, and the like. So typical is it for indebtedness to accompany the receipt of such things that a phrase like "much obliged" has become a synonym for "thank you," not only in the English language but in others as well.

The impressive aspect of reciprocation with its accompanying sense of obligation is its pervasiveness in human culture. It is so widespread that, after intensive study, Alvin Gouldner (1960), along with other sociologists, report that all human societies subscribe to the rule.[1] Within each society it seems pervasive also; it permeates exchanges of every kind. Indeed, it may well be that a developed system of indebtedness flowing from the rule of reciprocation is a unique property of human culture. The noted archaeologist Richard Leakey ascribes

---

[1] Certain societies have formalized the rule into ritual. Consider for example the Vartan Bhanji, an institutionalized custom of gift exchange common to parts of Pakistan and India. In commenting upon the Vartan Bhanji, Gouldner (1960) remarks:

It is . . . notable that the system painstakingly prevents the total elimination of outstanding obligations. Thus, on the occasion of a marriage, departing guests are given gifts of sweets. In weighing them out, the hostess may say, "These five are yours," meaning "These are a repayment for what you formerly gave me," and then she adds an extra measure, saying, "These are mine." On the next occasion, she will receive these back along with an additional measure which she later returns, and so on.

the essence of what makes us human to the reciprocity system. He claims that we are human because our ancestors learned to share food and skills "in an honored network of obligation" (Leakey & Lewin, 1978). Cultural anthropologists Lionel Tiger and Robin Fox (1971) view this "web of indebtedness" as a unique adaptive mechanism of human beings, allowing for the division of labor, the exchange of diverse forms of goods and different services, and the creation of interdependencies that bind individuals together into highly efficient units.

It is a sense of future obligation that is critical to produce social advances of the sort described by Tiger and Fox. A widely shared and strongly held feeling of future obligation made an enormous difference in human social evolution because it meant that one person could give something (for example, food, energy, care) to another with confidence that the gift was not being lost. For the first time in evolutionary history, one individual could give away any of a variety of resources without actually giving them away. The result was the lowering of the natural inhibitions against transactions that must be *begun* by one person's providing personal resources to another. Sophisticated and coordinated systems of aid, gift giving, defense, and trade became possible, bringing immense benefits to the societies that possessed them. With such clearly adaptive consequences for the culture, it is not surprising that the rule for reciprocation is so deeply implanted in us by the process of socialization we all undergo.

I know of no better illustration of the way reciprocal obligations can reach long and powerfully into the future than the perplexing story of $5,000 of relief aid that was exchanged between Mexico and Ethiopia. In 1985, Ethiopia could justly lay claim to the greatest suffering and privation in the world. Its economy was in ruin. Its food supply had been ravaged by years of drought and internal war. Its inhabitants were dying by the thousands from disease and starvation. Under these circumstances, I would not have been surprised to learn of a $5,000 relief donation from Mexico to that wrenchingly needy country. I remember my feeling of amazement, though, when a brief newspaper item I was reading insisted that the aid had gone in the opposite direction. Native officials of the Ethiopian Red Cross had decided to send the money to help the victims of that year's earthquakes in Mexico City.

It is both a personal bane and a professional blessing that whenever I am confused by some aspect of human behavior, I feel driven to investigate further. In this instance, I was able to track down a fuller account of the story. Fortunately, a journalist who had been as bewildered as I by the Ethiopians' actions had asked for an explanation. The answer he received offered eloquent validation of the reciprocity rule: Despite the enormous needs prevailing in Ethiopia, the money was being sent to Mexico because, in 1935, Mexico had sent aid to Ethiopia when it was invaded by Italy ("Ethiopian Red Cross," 1985). So informed, I remained awed, but I was no longer puzzled. The need to reciprocate had transcended great cultural differences, long distances, acute famine, many years, and immediate self-interest. Quite simply, a half-century later, against all countervailing forces, obligation triumphed.

HOW THE RULE WORKS

Make no mistake, human societies derive a truly significant competitive advantage from the reciprocity rule and, consequently, they make sure their members are trained to comply with and believe in it. Each of us has been taught to live up to the rule, and each of us knows the social sanctions and derision applied to anyone who violates it. Because there is a general distaste for those who take and make no effort to give in return, we will often go to great lengths to avoid being considered a moocher, ingrate, or welsher. It is to those lengths that we will often be taken in, in the process, be "taken" by individuals who stand to gain from our indebtedness.

To understand how the rule of reciprocation can be exploited by one who recognizes it as the weapon of influence it certainly is, we might closely examine an experiment conducted by psychologist Dennis Regan (1971). A subject who participated in the study rated, along with another subject, the quality of some paintings as part of an experiment on "art appreciation." The other rater—we can call him Joe—was only posing as a fellow subject and was actually Dr. Regan's assistant. For our purposes, the experiment took place under two different conditions. In some cases, Joe did a small, unsolicited favor for the true subject. During a short rest period, Joe left the room for a couple of minutes and returned with two bottles of Coca-Cola, one for the subject and one for himself, saying "I asked him [the experimenter] if I could get myself a Coke, and he said it was OK, so I bought one for you, too." In other cases, Joe did not provide the subject with a favor; he simply returned from the two-minute break empty-handed. In all other respects, however, Joe behaved identically.

Later on, after the paintings had all been rated and the experimenter had momentarily left the room, Joe asked the subject to do *him* a favor. He indicated that he was selling raffle tickets for a new car and that if he sold the most tickets, he would win a $50 prize. Joe's request was for the subject to buy some raffle tickets at 25 cents apiece: "Any would help, the more the better." The major finding of the study concerns the number of tickets subjects purchased from Joe under the two conditions. Without question, Joe was more successful in selling his raffle tickets to the subjects who had received his earlier favor. Apparently feeling that they owed him something, these subjects bought twice as many tickets as the subjects who had not been given the prior favor. Although the Regan study represents a fairly simple demonstration of the workings of the rule of reciprocation, it illustrates several important characteristics of the rule that, upon further consideration, help us to understand how it may be profitably used.

The Rule Is Overpowering

One of the reasons reciprocation can be used so effectively as a device for gaining another's compliance is its power. The rule possesses awesome strength, often producing a yes response to a request that, except for an existing feeling of indebtedness, would have surely been refused. Some evidence of how the rule's force can overpower the influence of other factors that normally determine compliance with a request can be seen in a second result of the Regan study. Besides his interest in the impact of the reciprocity rule on compliance, Regan was also investigating how liking for a person affects the tendency to comply with that person's request. To measure how liking toward Joe affected the subjects' decisions to buy his raffle tickets, Regan had them fill out several rating scales indicating how much they had liked Joe. He then compared their liking responses with the number of tickets they had purchased from Joe. There was a significant tendency for subjects to buy more raffle tickets from Joe the more they liked him. This alone is hardly a startling finding, since most of us would have guessed that people are more willing to do a favor for someone they like.

The interesting finding of the Regan experiment, however, was that the relationship between liking and compliance was completely wiped out in the condition under which subjects had been given a Coke by Joe. For those who owed him a favor, it made no difference whether they liked him or not; they felt a sense of obligation to repay him, and they did. The subjects who indicated that they disliked Joe bought just as many of his tickets as did those who indicated that they liked him. The rule for reciprocity was so strong that it simply overwhelmed the influence of a factor—liking for the requester—that normally affects the decision to comply.

Think of the implications. People we might ordinarily dislike—unsavory or unwelcome sales operators, disagreeable acquaintances, representatives of strange or unpopular organizations—can greatly increase the chance that we will do what they wish merely by providing us with a small favor prior to their requests. Let's take an example that, by now, many of us have encountered. The Hare Krishna Society is an Eastern religious sect with centuries-old roots traceable to the Indian city of Calcutta. Its spectacular modern-day story occurred in the 1970s when it experienced a remarkable growth, not only in followers, but also in wealth and property. The economic growth was funded through a variety of activities, the principal and still most visible of which is society members' requests for donations from passersby in public places. During the early history of the group in this country, the solicitation for contributions was attempted in a fashion memorable for anyone who saw it. Groups of Krishna devotees—often with shaved heads, and wearing ill-fitting robes, leg wrappings, beads, and bells—would canvass a city street, chanting and bobbing in unison while begging for funds.

Although highly effective as an attention-getting technique, this practice did not work especially well for fund raising. The average American considered the Krishnas weird, to say the least, and was reluctant to provide money to support them. It quickly became clear to the society that it had a considerable public-relations problem. The people being asked for contributions did not like the way the members looked, dressed, or acted. Had the society been an ordinary commercial organization, the solution would have been simple—change the things the public does not like. The Krishnas are a religious organization, however, and the way members look, dress, and act is partially tied to religious factors. Since religious factors are typically resistant to change because of worldly considerations, the Krishna leadership was faced with a real dilemma. On the one hand were beliefs, modes of dress, and hairstyles that had religious significance. On the other hand, threatening the organization's financial welfare, were the less-than-positive feelings of the American public toward these things. What's a sect to do?

The Krishnas' resolution was brilliant. They switched to a fund-raising tactic that made it unnecessary for their targets to have positive feelings toward the fund-raisers. They began to employ a donation-request procedure that engaged the rule for reciprocation, which, as demonstrated by the Regan study, was strong enough to overcome dislike for the requester. The new strategy still involved the solicitation of contributions in public places with much pedestrian traffic (airports are a favorite), but, before a donation was requested, the target person was given a "gift"—a book (usually the *Bhagavad Gita*), the *Back to Godhead* magazine of the society, or, in the most cost-effective version, a flower. The unsuspecting passersby who suddenly found flowers pressed into their hands or pinned to their jackets were under no circumstances allowed to give them back, even if they asserted that they did not want them. "No, it is our gift to you," said the solicitor, refusing to take it back. Only after the Krishna member had thus brought the force of the reciprocation rule to bear on the situation was the target asked to provide a contribution to the society. This benefactor-before-beggar strategy has been wildly successful for the Hare Krishna Society, producing large-scale economic gains and funding, the ownership of temples, businesses, houses, and property in 321 centers in the United States and abroad.

As an aside, it is instructive that the reciprocation rule has begun to outlive its usefulness for the Krishnas, not because the rule itself is any less potent societally, but because we have found ways to prevent the Krishnas from using it on us. After once falling victim to their tactic, many travelers are now alert to the presence of robed Krishna society solicitors in airports and train stations, adjusting their paths to avoid an encounter and preparing beforehand to ward off a solicitor's "gift." Although the society has tried to counter this increased vigilance by instructing members to be dressed and groomed in modern styles to avoid immediate recognition when soliciting (some actually carry flight bags or suitcases), even disguise has not worked especially well for the Krishnas. Too many individuals now know better than to accept unrequested offerings in public places such as airports.

As a result, the Krishnas have experienced a severe financial reversal over the past 10 years. In North America alone, nearly 30 percent of their temples have been closed for economic reasons, and the number of devotees staffing the remaining temples has plummeted from a high of 5,000 to an estimated 800. The Krishnas are a resilient group, though. Officials admit that the organization is struggling to maintain its long-standing presence in North America, but they report that it is thriving in the newly opened "markets" of Eastern Europe—where, apparently, people haven't yet caught on to the Krishnas' strategic benevolence.

It is a testament to the societal value of reciprocation that even those of us who know what the Krishnas are up to have chosen to avoid them or to deflect their flowers rather than to withstand the force of their gift giving directly by taking the flower and walking away with it. The reciprocation rule that empowers their tactic is too strong—and socially beneficial—for us to want to challenge head-on.

Politics Politics is another arena in which the power of the reciprocity rule shows itself. Reciprocation tactics appear at every level:

- At the top, elected officials engage in "log-rolling" and the exchange of favors that makes politics the place of strange bedfellows, indeed. The out-of-character vote of one of our elected representatives on a bill or measure can often be understood as a favor returned to the bill's sponsor. Political analysts were amazed at Lyndon Johnson's success in getting so many of his programs through Congress during his early administration. Even congress-members who were thought to be strongly opposed to the proposals were voting for them. Close examination by political scientists has found the cause to be not so much Johnson's political savvy as the large score of favors he had been able to provide to other legislators during his many years of power in the House and Senate. As President, he was able to produce a truly remarkable amount of legislation in a short time by calling in those favors. It is interesting that this same process may account for the problems Jimmy Carter had in getting his programs through Congress during his early administration, despite heavy Democratic majorities in both the House and Senate. Carter came to the presidency from outside the Capitol Hill establishment. He campaigned on his outside-Washington identity, saying that he was indebted to no one. Much of his legislative difficulty upon arriving may be traced to the fact that no one there was indebted to *him*.

- At another level, we can see the recognized strength of the reciprocity rule in the desire of corporations and individuals to provide judicial and legislative officials with gifts and favors and in the series of legal restrictions against such gifts and favors. Even with legitimate political contributions, the stockpiling of obligations often underlies the stated purpose of supporting a favorite candidate. One look at the lists of companies and organizations that contribute to the campaigns of *both* major candidates in important elections gives evidence of such motives. A skeptic, requiring direct evidence of the *quid pro quo* expected by political contributors, might look to the remarkably bald-faced admission by Charles H. Keating, Jr., who was later convicted on multiple counts of fraud in this country's Savings & Loan disaster. Addressing the question of whether a connection existed between the $1.3 million he had contributed to the campaigns of five U.S. senators and their subsequent actions on his behalf against federal regulators, he asserted, "I want to say in the most forceful way I can: I certainly hope so."

- At the grass-roots level, local political organizations have learned that a principal way to keep their candidates in office is to make sure they provide a wide range of little favors to the voters. The "ward heelers" of many cities still operate effectively in this fashion. But ordinary citizens are not alone in trading political support for small personal favors. During the 1992 presidential primary campaign, actress Sally Kellerman was asked why she was lending her name and efforts to the candidacy of Democratic hopeful, Jerry Brown. Her reply: "Twenty years ago, I asked ten friends to help me move. He was the only one who showed up."

The Not-So-Free Sample Of course, the power of reciprocity can be found in the merchandising field as well. Although the number of examples is large, let's examine a pair of familiar ones. As a marketing technique, the free sample has a long and effective history. In most instances, a small amount of the relevant product is given to potential customers to see if they like it. Certainly this is a legitimate desire of the manufacturer—to expose the public to the qualities of the product. The beauty of the free sample, however, is that it is also a gift and, as such, can engage the reciprocity rule. In true jujitsu fashion, a promoter who provides free samples can release the natural indebting force inherent in a gift, while innocently appearing to have only the intention to inform.

A favorite place for free samples is the supermarket, where customers are frequently given small amounts of a certain product to try. Many people find it difficult to accept samples from the always smiling attendant, return only the toothpicks or cups, and walk away. Instead, they buy some of the product, even if they might not have liked it very much. A highly effective variation on this marketing procedure is illustrated in the case, cited by Vance Packard in *The Hidden Persuaders* (1957), of the Indiana supermarket operator who sold an astounding 1,000 pounds of cheese in a few hours one day by putting out the cheese and inviting customers to cut off slivers for themselves as free samples.

A different version of the free-sample tactic is used by the Amway Corporation, a rapid-growth company that manufactures and distributes household and personal-care products in a vast national network of door-to-door neighborhood sales. The company, which has grown from a basement-run operation a few years ago to a $1.5 billion yearly sales business, makes use of the free sample in a device called the BUG. The BUG consists of a collection of Amway products—bottles of furniture polish, detergent, or shampoo, spray containers of deodorizers, insect killers, or window cleaners—carried to a customer's home in a specially designed tray or just a polyethylene bag. The confidential Amway

Career Manual then instructs the salesperson to leave the BUG with the customer "for 24, 48, or 72 hours, at no cost or obligation to her. Just tell her you would like her to try the products.... That's an offer no one can refuse." At the end of the trial period, the Amway representative is to return and pick up orders for the products the customer wishes to purchase. Since few customers use up the entire contents of even one of the product containers in such a short time, the salesperson may then take the remaining product portions in the BUG to the next potential customer down the line or across the street and start the process again. Many Amway representatives have several BUGS circulating in their districts at one time.

Of course, by now you and I know that the customer who has accepted and used the BUG products has been trapped by the reciprocity rule. Many such customers yield to a sense of obligation to order the products that they have tried and partially consumed—and, of course, by now the Amway Corporation knows that to be the case. Even in a company with as excellent a growth record as Amway, the BUG device has created a big stir. Reports by state distributors to the parent company record a remarkable effect:

> Unbelievable! We've never seen such excitement. Product is moving at an unbelievable rate, and we've only just begun.... Local distributors took the BUGS, and we've had an unbelievable increase in sales [from Illinois distributor]. The most fantastic retail idea we've ever had!... On the average, customers purchased about half the total amount of the BUG when it is picked up.... In one word, tremendous! We've never seen a response within our entire organization like this [from Massachusetts distributor].

The Amway distributors appear to be bewildered—happily so, but nonetheless bewildered—by the startling power of the BUG. Of course, by now you and I should not be.

The reciprocity rule governs many situations of a purely interpersonal nature where neither money nor commercial exchange is at issue. Perhaps my favorite illustration of the enormous force available from the reciprocation weapon of influence comes from such a situation. The European scientist Eibl-Eibesfeldt (1975) provides the account of a German soldier during World War I whose job was to capture enemy soldiers for interrogation. Because of the nature of the trench warfare at that time, it was extremely difficult for armies to cross the no-man's-land between opposing front lines, but it was not so difficult for a single soldier to crawl across and slip into an enemy trench position. The armies of the Great War had experts who regularly did so to capture enemy soldiers, who would then be brought back for questioning. The German expert had often successfully completed such missions in the past and was sent on another. Once again, he skillfully negotiated the area between fronts and surprised a lone enemy soldier in his trench. The unsuspecting soldier, who had been eating at the time, was easily disarmed. The frightened captive, with only a piece of bread in his hand, then performed what may have been the most important act of his life. He gave his enemy some of the bread. So affected was the German by this gift that he could not complete his mission. He turned from his benefactor and recrossed the no-man's-land empty-handed to face the wrath of his superiors.

An equally compelling point regarding the power of reciprocity comes from an account of a woman who saved her own life, not by *giving* a gift as did the captured soldier, but by *refusing* a gift and the powerful obligations that went with it. In November 1978 Jim Jones the leader of Jonestown, Guyana, called for the mass suicide of all residents, most of whom compliantly drank and died from a vat of poison-laced Kool-Aid. Diane Louie, a resident, however, rejected Jones's command and made her way out of Jonestown and into the jungle. She attributes her willingness to do so to her earlier refusal to accept special favors from him when she was in need. She turned down his offer of special food while she was ill, because "I knew once he gave me those privileges, he'd have me. I didn't want to owe him nothin'" (Anderson & Zimbardo, 1984)....

SUSPECT CONFESSIONS

He's made mincemeat of false memories. But the social psychologist Richard Ofshe has a more pressing question: Why do innocent people admit to crimes they didn't commit?

Richard Jerome

Richard Jerome is a senior writer at People *magazine.*

THROUGH A THICKENING FOG, RICHARD J. OFSHE WINDS his white BMW homeward into the Oakland hills, leaving behind the University of California at Berkeley, where he is a professor of social psychology. In florid tones refined by 30 years at the lectern, Ofshe is expounding on his latest area of interest, the ways in which police interrogations can elicit false confessions. Specifically, he is bemoaning the case of Jessie Lloyd Misskelley Jr., a teen-ager from a squalid Arkansas trailer park who confessed—falsely, Ofshe maintains—to taking part in the ghastly murder of three 8-year-old boys. In spite of Ofshe's voluminous expert testimony on his behalf, Misskelley, who has an I.Q. in the 70's, was sentenced to life plus 40 years in prison.

"It was like walking straight into 'Deliverance,'" Ofshe says, casually veering around another hairpin turn. "The trial was a travesty. The conduct of the judge was outrageous."

At 54, Ofshe has acquired a muted celebrity for his work on extreme influence tactics and thought control. He shared in the 1979 Pulitzer Prize in public service after assisting The Point Reyes (Calif.) Light in its exposé of Synanon, a Bay Area drug rehabilitation group that evolved into an armed cult. More recently, Ofshe has been an aggressive and influential debunker of "recovered memory," the theory whereby long-repressed traumas are retrieved by patients undergoing what Ofshe calls exceedingly manipulative psychotherapy. As such, Ofshe is a vivid figure in "Remembering Satan," Lawrence Wright's book about the case of Paul Ingram, a former Olympia, Wash., sheriff's deputy now serving 20 years in prison primarily because he became convinced that the accusations of one of his daughters, who claimed that he had indulged in a 17-year binge of satanism, incest and infanticide, were true. Ofshe, a champion of Ingram, dissects the affair in his recent book, "Making Monsters: False Memories, Psychotherapy and Sexual Hysteria," written with Ethan Watters.

But for the most part, Ofshe has set aside violent cults and overzealous shrinks and is fixated on the third of his bêtes noires: false confessions. According to Ofshe and a considerable body of literature, modern interrogation tactics are so subtly powerful that police can—entirely unwittingly—coerce innocent suspects into admitting to the most heinous crimes. Sometimes, Ofshe says, a suspect admits guilt simply to escape the stress of the interrogation. More rarely, a suspect comes to believe that he actually committed the crime in question, though he has no memory of it.

For Ofshe, exorcising both kinds of false confession from the American justice system has become an almost obsessive quest. All told, he has consulted or testified in more than 80 criminal cases involving suspects from whom, he concluded, confessions were coerced; in most of these cases, the physical evidence strongly suggested innocence. Although he makes money at it overall—$40,000 in 1993—he sometimes works pro bono. With dark, disdaining eyes set against a shock of gray curls and a swirling beard, Ofshe looks vaguely sinister—a wily Renaissance pol, perhaps, or Claudius in a road company of Hamlet. Confession, he points out, is the anchor of a trial in which there is no hard evidence. "And false confession," he says, "ranks third after perjury and eyewitness error as a cause of wrongful convictions in American homicide cases."

His numbers are based on several studies, most recently work by the sociologist Michael L. Radelet of the University of Florida, Hugo Adam Bedau, professor of philosophy at Tufts University, and Constance E. Putnam, a Boston-based writer. In their 1992 book, "In Spite of Innocence," the authors review more than 400 cases in which innocent people were convicted of capital crimes in the United States. Fourteen percent were caused by false confession. "If it happened just one-half of 1 percent of the time," Ofshe says, "it still means that hundreds, or perhaps thousands, of people each year are being unjustly imprisoned. Even if one innocent man or woman is convicted, it's too many. And it's unnecessary because this is a fixable problem" – fixable, he adds, if only police interrogations were electronically recorded, a requirement now only in Alaska and Minnesota.

"Now I don't think for one second," Ofshe stresses, "that the detectives and prosecutors in cases of false confessions want to bring about that result. But because they don't understand the mistake as it is being made, the case moves forward and takes everyone along with it."

THE BMW IS NOW TUCKED SAFELY UNder Ofshe's red Ferrari, which sits on a raised hoist in the garage of his hillside home, a quasi-Mediterranean mix of stone and stucco. Inside, rock music from a new stereo system tumbles down the coiled stairs of a three-and-a-half-story central rotunda, into a cherry-paneled library where Ofshe, propped like a pasha on a brown leather couch, surveys his domain with a reverent sigh: "I never thought I'd ever get to have a house like this."

It mirrors its inhabitant: spare, opulent, imposing yet accessible. One can well appreciate that Ofshe's fondest boyhood memory is of the austere charms of the Frick Collection mansion. His father, a dress designer, moved the family from the Bronx to Queens when Ofshe was a child. Ofshe attended Queens College, then went to graduate school at Stanford. "I honestly can't tell you now what led me to psychology," he says. "I suppose I'm a watcher. I'm comfortable observing people and lecturing at them — but I am absolutely incapable of making small talk, a gift I consider one of the great mysteries of life."

During graduate school, Ofshe was married briefly and then, as he puts it, "got un-married." (He married his present wife, Bonnie Blair, a successful designer of sweaters, in 1981.) Ofshe gravitated toward social psychology; his work on cults grew out of a study of utopian societies he undertook in the early 1970's. One such community was Synanon, begun as a drug treatment center by Charles Dederich. But by 1978, Dederich had accumulated a substantial arsenal, as well as a large cadre of loyal followers. By this time, The Point Reyes Light, a weekly based near Ofshe's summer home, had begun an investigative series on Synanon, on which Ofshe collaborated. As a result of the media exposure, Synanon lost its tax-exempt status and disintegrated. Dederich sued Ofshe three times unsuccessfully for libel, prompting him to retaliate with a malicious prosecution suit. " 'When this is over, I'll be the one driving the red Ferrari,' " Ofshe says he told people at the time. The Ferrari, he now confides, "accounts for a small percentage of my settlement. A very small percentage."

Material success aside, Ofshe seems to revel most in the validation of his work by respected media outlets. It takes little prodding for him to express his glee at Lawrence Wright's description of him as "Zeus-like" in "Remembering Satan" — which first appeared as an article in The New Yorker, a magazine Ofshe clearly reveres. And he is quick to point out that the television movie of Wright's book, currently being filmed, features him as the central character — as played by William Devane.

What saves this self-absorption from being insufferable is Ofshe's interest in helping people he considers innocent. He first focused on police interrogation in 1987, after a phone call from Joseph G. Donahey Jr., a veteran Florida attorney. Donahey was representing Thomas F. Sawyer, a Clearwater golf course groundskeeper who in 1986, after an uncommonly grueling 16-hour interrogation, confessed to the brutal murder of a neighbor; the police convinced Sawyer that he'd lost all memory of the incident during an alcoholic blackout. (Sawyer, against whom there was no physical evidence, had quickly recanted.) "Donahey realized something was terribly wrong with Tom's confession," Ofshe says. "At first I was skeptical. But once I read the transcript of the interrogation, it became obvious what had happened to Tom."

Ofshe spent 300 hours analyzing the Sawyer interrogation — which, by a lucky quirk, was taped in its entirety — and concluded it was "a tour de force of psychological coercion." Sawyer's police interrogators, Peter Fire and John Dean, invited Sawyer to the station house on the premise that he was being asked to "assist" with their investigation. Then, Ofshe says, they flattered him into providing his own hypothetical murder scenario. The detectives then used leading questions to shape the groundskeeper's responses, eventually tossing his answers back as evidence of his guilt. Consider the following dialogue, slightly condensed, on the position of the victim's body:

FIRE: And he would put her in the bed how? Like she's doing what?

SAWYER: Sleeping.
FIRE: O.K. What would you put her on? Her. . . .
SAWYER: On her back.
FIRE: Put her on her back? . . .
SAWYER: I'd put her on her back sleeping.
FIRE: Put her on her back, sleeping?
SAWYER: Don't you sleep on your back?
FIRE: No. . . .
SAWYER: I don't sleep on my side.
FIRE: Well, what other way could you put her?
SAWYER: Face down.
FIRE: O.K. Face down. . . .
SAWYER: I'd put her on her stomach. . . .
FIRE: You hit the nail on the head. You put her on her stomach.

Deception, typically by lying about the presence of witnesses or physical evidence or about polygraph results, is a common interrogation tactic, Ofshe says, and it was used baldly against Sawyer. ("We found a lot of hairs and fibers on her body," Fire insisted at one point. "We have your hair. . . . There's a lot of evidence. There's a lot of evidence. A lot of evidence.")

"If you're dealing with middle-class types," Ofshe says, "or at least middle-class types socialized by my mother, they're hearing: 'It's inevitable that you'll be caught and punished to the max.' I have no interest in stripping police of tactics that make perfect sense — when those tactics are supported by compelling physical evidence. But the same things that can convince a guilty person that he's been caught can convince someone who's innocent that he's caught."

Under this intense barrage, Sawyer, who for hours steadfastly maintained his innocence, exhibited his first trace of self-doubt: "I honestly believe that I didn't do it. . . . I don't remember doing it. If I did, and I don't think I did. . . . You almost got me convinced I did, but. . . . "

"He went from straight denial to 'I couldn't have done something like this,'" Ofshe says. "And finally, when he confessed, it was so beautiful, so perfect in the way he verbalized it: 'I guess all the evidence is in, I guess I must have done it.'"

Strong evidence of a false confession, Ofshe says, is when the narrative is at odds with the known facts of the case or has been clearly fed to the suspect, however inadvertently, by the police themselves. "Sawyer was wrong about almost everything," Ofshe says, "except for several details" — like the position of the victim's body — "that were clearly introduced by Fire and Dean."

Ultimately, Ofshe's testimony helped exonerate Sawyer, whose confession was suppressed in 1989 after the groundskeeper had spent 14 months in jail awaiting trial. Shortly thereafter, Ofshe — by now increasingly sought by desperate defense attorneys — helped free Mark Nunez, Leo Bruce and Dante Parker, who, fingered by a psychiatric patient and subjected to a highly coercive interrogation, had falsely confessed to killing nine people at a Buddhist temple outside Phoenix. In Flagstaff, Ofshe was instrumental in winning the 1988 acquittal of George Abney, a graduate student with a history of depression, who had admitted to the ritualistic murder of a Navajo woman. In the Phoenix case, the real murderer was eventually caught and prosecuted.

"WHAT SOME OF THE PSYCHOLOGISTS SAY IS I put you in a room, you're all emotional and at the end of five or six hours, I've fed you everything," Lieut. Ralph M. Lacer is saying in his Oakland police office, several miles from Ofshe's home. "Well, if I was on the jury, I'd be rolling my eyes saying: 'Who is the dumb [expletive] who thinks this is gonna go over?'"

Fiftyish, ruddy and blond, the bespectacled Lacer was one of the interrogating officers in the high-profile case of Bradley Page, a handsome Berkeley student who had admitted — falsely, so Page and his attorneys maintained — to murdering his girlfriend, Roberta (BiBi) Lee, in a fit of anger in 1984. After two trials, the second of which Ofshe consulted on, Page was convicted of manslaughter. (He was released, after serving part of a six-year sentence, in February.)

Only part of the Page interrogation was recorded. From 11:50 A.M. to 1:10 P.M. on Dec. 10, 1984, Lacer and his partner, Sgt. Jerry Harris, taped Page as he gave them a firm, lucid account of his movements during the time since Lee had disappeared a month before — none of which included bludgeoning her to death. Then the detectives shut off the machine until 7:07 P.M., by which time Page was highly emotional, confessing to murder, albeit in vague, halting language peppered with "might haves," "would haves" and other subjunctive phrases that left Ofshe highly suspicious. Lacer freely acknowledges that Page's admission of guilt, made in the absence of hard evidence, was the heart and soul of the case against him. "If we hadn't gotten the confession," Lacer says, "Brad would've walked."

I raise Ofshe's argument, that taping interrogations in full might resolve any ambiguities.

"First of all, a tape is inhibiting," Lacer counters. "It's hard to get at the truth. And say we go for 10 hours — we have 10 hours of tape that maybe boil down to 15 or 20 minutes of you saying, 'Yes, I killed Johnny Jones.' You bet the public defender's going to have the jury listen to all 10 hours of that tape and by that time the jury won't remember what it's all about."

According to Lacer, the craft of interrogation is learned through experience. "Every day when you stop someone on the street, you're interrogating them," he says. "'Where do you live? Where you headed to?' We definitely try to establish rapport — basically, I want to get you to talk to me. But when we bring a suspect in, we keep the room bare, a table and two or three chairs, a locked door."

I glance around, aware for the first time that the

interview is unfolding in the ideal interrogation setting. I ask Lacer what would happen if a person being questioned invokes his constitutional right of silence or, if he is not under arrest, his right to simply walk out the door.

"Well, that would be the end of the situation," he says. "But many times it won't happen, and here's why: I see you've got a wedding ring on, Rich. Well, say Mrs. Rich ends up dead in the house. We call you down and you say, 'I don't think I want to talk to you guys, I'm out of here.' Well, the thing is, your in-laws find out that you took that route and they know right away who killed your wife.

"Now most of the time, the suspect will set up barriers. Like you got your legs crossed — that's kind of a psychological barrier. And I lean forward, violate your personal space, get closer and closer and pretty soon we're nose to nose." As Lacer edges toward me, his eyes, though still genial, bear into mine.

"Now remember, I'm just talking, not yelling or bullying," he says. "It's not going to help matters if I suddenly say '[Expletive], that's a [expletive] black sweater you have on — I threw away the last black sweater I had like that!'" You can maybe bully a little bit verbally by saying: 'Rich, that last story was [expletive]. Let's not even go into that again.'" Lacer's eyes turn caustic through his aviator glasses.

"Now as far as yelling," he says, chummy again, "about the only time we do it here in Oakland is if someone's talking over you or if they're going off on a tangent, and I'd say, 'Hey Rich, let's get back to the *subject!*'" His voice slices through the claustrophobia of the room — a ferocity all the more unnerving because it booms from Lacer's amiable shell.

"We've been in a room together for a while, Rich," he says, chuckling. "Do you feel like confessing to anything?"

"LACER RATIONALIZES THAT SOMEONE LIKE Bradley Page — or you and I — cannot be made to confess," Ofshe says on the day after my encounter with the Oakland lieutenant. "Because it is in many ways one of the worst professional errors you can make — like a physician amputating the wrong arm."

Prevention, he adds, is surprisingly simple: "Above all, no confession ought be accepted unless it has been corroborated with clear-cut and powerful evidence. And you must never instigate a high-pressure, accusatory interrogation unless you have a good and sound reason to do it." Another safeguard, Ofshe reiterates, is to record interrogations. Early last year, the professor helped win a significant victory in the same Clearwater courthouse where the Sawyer case was heard. Relying substantially on Ofshe's testimony, Judge Claire K. Luten formed a forceful opinion that the confession of Francis Dupont, an alcoholic drifter who had admitted to murdering a friend, was psychologically coerced. Moreover, Luten ruled that the failure to tape the interrogation of Dupont was in direct violation of due process.

"I'd be content to devote myself to that issue until I am too old to work on it," Ofshe says.

In a sense, this is Ofshe's moment, for never has the nation been more attuned to what happens in a courtroom. Yet for the plain citizen — the juror — he is also a problematic figure, a bearded academic speaking in tones of unassailable authority about social psychology, a discipline that resounds with squishy inexactitude. Ofshe's theories about false confession, however well researched, risk being perceived as just another set of legal loopholes. And his "one innocent man or woman" might well be shrugged off — probably not worth the trouble and surely not worth the risk.

For which reason Ofshe emphasizes the most basic preventive to false confession: if you find yourself being questioned about a crime you know you did not commit, resist at all costs the impulse to be helpful, no matter how charming or forbidding the interrogator might be.

"I tell my classes," Ofshe says, "that if they ever find themselves in that situation, remember the four magic words of the criminal justice system: 'I want a lawyer.'"

Social Relationships

Solitude and Affiliation (Articles 21 and 22)
Evolutionary Psychological Perspectives (Articles 23 and 24)
Love and Marriage (Articles 25 and 26)

A young man stands on a narrow suspension bridge that stretches over a river 230 feet below. The bridge is only 5 feet wide, over 400 feet long, and it constantly swings and sways in the wind. Even for someone without a fear of heights, crossing this bridge while looking at the river far below is definitely an arousing experience. In fact, a considerable number of the people who visit this popular tourist spot every year find themselves unable to cross the bridge at all. While standing on the bridge, the young man is approached by an attractive young woman who asks him to participate in a psychology research project she is working on—all he has to do is write a brief imaginative story in response to a picture she gives him. He does so, and when he is finished, the experimenter gives him her phone number in case he wants to learn more about the experiment.

A few miles away, another young man stands on another bridge—but this one is not scary at all. It is solidly built, does not sway and wobble, and stands only 10 feet above a peaceful stream. The same attractive woman approaches this man with the same request, and, again she gives him her phone number when the experiment ends. Who do you think is more likely to call the young woman later? When this experiment was actually carried out, the results were clear—men on the arousing bridge were much more likely than men on the safe bridge to call the female experimenter later on. Not only that, but the stories the men on the arousing bridge wrote were noticeably different; they contained significantly more references to sex. In short, the men on the arousing bridge apparently reacted in a very different way to the young woman—they experienced a greater sense of physical attraction to her, and acted on that attraction later on by calling her up. Even though men on the sturdy bridge met the same young woman, they did not experience the same physical attraction.

This experiment is just one example of some of the work done by psychologists who study social relationships. This area of social psychology turns out to be a very broad one indeed, and a wide variety of topics fall under its umbrella. One research question, for example, that has attracted a lot of attention is this: What are the factors that influence the initial attraction (both romantic and nonromantic) that we feel for another person? Considerable research indicates that being similar to the other person is important, as is the sheer physical attractiveness of that other. Living or working in close proximity to other people also increases the likelihood of attraction to them.

Other researchers have tackled issues such as identifying the processes that are important for maintaining friendships over time. The level of self-disclosure in the relationship seems to be important, as does the general feeling by both participants that what they are receiving from the relationship is roughly equivalent to what their partner is receiving; that is, issues of fairness seem to play a crucial role. Still, other investigators have concerned themselves with the question of long-term romantic relationships: Which factors lead to initial romantic attraction; Which factors contribute to long-term satisfaction; How do couples deal with conflict and disagreements in long-term relationships?

The selections in this unit are divided into three sections. The first subsection addresses the general issue of affiliation—the tendency that humans have to enjoy and seek out social contact. The first selection, "Solitude Provides an Emotional Tune-Up," describes recent research that points up the necessity—even for a sociable species like humans—of spending some time alone. Having at least some time for solitude appears to have a rejuvenating effect on feelings of well-being. The second article in this subsection, "Social Ties Reduce Risk of a Cold," suggests that people who have less variety in their social networks are actually more susceptible to colds than people with many different contacts.

The second subsection focuses on evolutionary psychology and its perspective on male-female relationships. In "The Biology of Beauty," Geoffrey Cowley summarizes the evolutionary perspective on physical attractiveness: what makes men attractive to women, and women attractive to men. The evolutionary view is that physical features serve as indicators of physical and reproductive fitness to potential mates, and that certain features are therefore

UNIT 6

universal indicators of attractiveness. In "Infidelity and the Science of Cheating," Sharon Begley presents the evolutionary perspective on jealousy, which attempts to explain a common finding: that men are typically more upset by a mate's sexual infidelity, while women are more upset by a mate's emotional infidelity.

In the final subsection, two articles address the topic of love and marriage more generally. In the first, "The Lessons of Love," Beth Livermore reviews a number of social psychological approaches to this topic; in addition to evolutionary forces, she also examines evidence for the role of culture in influencing love and the research exploring attachment and emotion. The second article, "Rescuing Marriages before They Begin," focuses explicitly on the inevitable conflict that occurs in marriages. It disucsses several recent approaches that are being taken to helping people learn how to handle such conflict before it begins.

Looking Ahead: Challenge Questions

Do you agree that all people have a need for solitude? What evidence do you see of that? What evidence is not consistent with this view?

What do you think of the evolutionary psychologists' explanation for some of the differences between men and women in the area of sexual behavior? What is their strongest evidence? What is their weakest evidence? Can their findings be explained in any other way?

What is meant by the term "love styles"? What are the six different styles of love, and how do they differ from one another? Can you think of people in your life who illustrate each style?

Is conflict in a marriage always a negative thing? What does the research evidence suggest about the best way to handle conflicts when they arise?

Solitude provides an emotional tune-up

We all need solitude for rejuvenation and contemplation,
but some people have a chronic need to be alone.

By Hugh McIntosh

Conventional wisdom says that successful relationships are key to well-being and that solitude, consequently, may signal abnormality. But solitude seems to have a positive side, too.

For centuries poets, mystics and philosophers have reported the soothing, creative effects of time alone. And in recent years, psychologists have begun to identify healthy people who partake of solitude for rejuvenation, contemplation and other beneficial uses.

The need for solitude has both a state component and a trait component, according to psychologist Peter Suedfeld, PhD, of the University of British Columbia. Suedfeld studies restricted environmental stimulation in lone voyages, polar stations and other solitary situations.

Taking a breather

Everyone experiences states where they need solitude more than at other times, Suedfeld said. In addition, some people seem to have a trait for solitude, chronically wanting or needing it more than others do.

Research related to the state component of solitude suggests that most people have some need of time alone to satisfy any of several psychological needs, including rejuvenation. This need probably results from the cumulative effects of social stimulation over recent days or weeks, Suedfeld said. People with few demands and little social stimulation seem to need less solitude and, in fact, may avoid it. His research has found, however, that those with heavy demands on their attention, social skills or coping mechanisms—professors, business executives, mothers of small children—tend to need more time alone.

"It gives you a chance to restore your coping resources, to rest, relax," he said. It replenishes psychological energy and physical well-being, as measured by reduced stress hormones, improved immune functioning and other physiological changes.

What one does during time alone—walking, meditation, systematic relaxation—seems less important for rejuvenation than simply achieving solitude. Convicts, he noted, sometimes hit a guard or break other rules in order to be put into solitary confinement, where they recoup from the hassle of prison life.

The amount of solitude people need for rejuvenation depends on how long it takes them to recover from the demands of their environment. An hour every few days may be enough to renew some people, although it may not be enough to achieve other benefits of solitude such as creative inspiration, Suedfeld said.

Time alone satisfies at least four other psychological needs, or functions, besides rejuvenation, says Darhl Pedersen of Brigham Young University. His research on privacy suggests that contemplation is the most important need fulfilled by solitude.

"It gives people a chance to contemplate who they are, what their relationships are to other people, and what their goals will be," he said. "It is a kind of settling and self-defining function."

Solitude also fosters creativity in self-actualizing people, he said, giving them a chance to speculate on new concepts without the censorship and evaluation that comes with putting forth ideas in public. History shows, in fact, that people have long used solitude—voluntary or involuntary—for creativity. It appears, though, that creative solitude is not a time of particular happiness, according to psychologist Reed Larson, PhD, of the University of Illinois, whose research focuses on solitude in adolescents. He speculates that creative people are moderately lonely in solitude but feel activated. "They are probably into what they are doing," he said. "They might describe it at least sometimes as enthralling, sometimes as tormenting. But my guess is that they describe time with others as being their happy times."

Two other psychological needs that solitude meets are autonomy—"the chance to do your own thing, to act freely, and be who you are"—as well as "confiding," according to Pedersen. The latter, he said, was a somewhat surprising response from research subjects, who may use the term to describe a prayerful relationship with deity. (Or, he said, subjects may have misunderstood the term "solitude" and assumed a confidante could be included.)

Pedersen's studies have found no gender differences in how often people seek solitude, he said. But they do indicate that women use solitude for contemplation and creativity more than men do. Men, on the other hand, have a stronger preference for isolation, a type of solitude where one geographically removes oneself from others by, for example, going up into the mountains or out for a long drive, rather than retreating to an office or bedroom.

The trait component of solitude suggests that some people have a preference for solitude that is much higher than the periodic need most people have for time alone. Psychologist Jerry Burger, PhD, of Santa Clara University, speculates that only a small percentage of the population, perhaps no more than 10 percent, shows this trait.

Contrary to social stereotypes, "these are folks who are well-adjusted," Burger said. "They're high in a sense of well-being or happiness, contentment with life." They are self-actualized, are good communicators, do well in social situations, and enjoy their friends. In addition, they like solitude, so they arrange time alone on a regular basis. "If they have to go several days without getting their 'fix' . . . they find that they don't feel as good."

This preference for solitude has a developmental aspect to it, appearing more frequently in people who have reached middle age, he said. It seems also to have a cyclical aspect. People need to develop a certain level of well-being in order to appreciate the benefits of solitude, and spending time alone helps to further develop well-being.

Children and adolescents

Solitude appears to have salutary effects at other stages of development, particularly in adolescence. Adolescents report having higher concentration and lower self-consciousness during solitude, Larson said, suggesting a more productive mental state. After they've been alone, adolescents are in better moods than at other times. In addition, data indicate that adolescents who spend intermediate amounts of time alone—20 percent to 35 percent of waking hours—are better adjusted than those who spend more or less time alone.

Adolescents say they're lonely when they're by themselves, Larson said. But he distinguishes between the loneliness of solitude and loneliness relative to other people. "Feeling loneliness in relationship to friends is bad," he said. "But going off by yourself on a retreat or going to your room to be by yourself and feeling a little lonely, that's probably healthy."

In children, solitary play is often considered a sign of shyness. Children, however, play alone for many reasons, says psychologist Robert Coplan, PhD, of Carleton University. For most children, playing alone is the first step up the ladder toward playing with others. "The problem that we worry about is these children who never make it up to the next rung," he said.

In studies of preschoolers, Coplan and Kenneth Rubin, PhD, of the University of Maryland, have observed three different types of children who tend to play by themselves. One type is shy, wanting to interact with others but afraid or anxious about doing so. The second type is probably socially immature, a bit aggressive, active, and noisy, playing alone presumably because no one else wants to play with them. A third type, however, seems to enjoy playing alone in constructive ways, preferring toys, puzzles and other objects to people.

"Kids who play alone in these kinds of constructive ways . . . don't stick out in terms of indices of maladjustment," he said. "They're not more afraid. They're not more immature. Their parents don't rate them as more shy." They do, however, have longer attention spans than other children, and they do not do well with person-oriented tasks, such as playing show-and-tell.

"Right now, I don't think people can tell you for sure what happens to these kids when they grow up," he said. "But I would predict that most of them would become your everyday average kids."

Hugh McIntosh is a freelance writer in Arlington, Va.

Social Ties Reduce Risk of a Cold

By SUSAN GILBERT

BUILDING on a dozen studies correlating friendship and fellowship with health, a new study has found that people with a broad array of social ties are significantly less likely to catch colds than those with sparse social networks.

The incidence of infection among people who knew many different kinds of people was nearly half that among those who were relatively isolated, the researchers reported. The lack of diverse social contacts was the strongest of the risk factors for colds that were examined, including smoking, low vitamin C intake and stress. The study is being published today in The Journal of the American Medical Association.

"I think the interesting things are the size of the effect and the dose response," said Dr. Sheldon Cohen, a psychiatry professor at Carnegie Mellon University in Pittsburgh who was the lead author of the study. "Every increment in the size of the diversity of the network had an effect on the chance of getting a cold." Dr. Cohen published pioneering research in 1991 showing a connection between stress and colds.

Other researchers praised the study. "If you didn't believe that lack of social support can cause you to get sick, here's an experimental study that ought to convince anybody," said Dr. Redford B. Williams,

> One expert is persuaded: A lack of social support can make you sick.

director of the behavioral medicine research center at Duke University Medical Center in Durham, N.C. His research has found that heart disease patients with few social ties are six times as likely to die within six months as those with a lot of relatives, friends and acquaintances.

"It's a nice piece of work because it directly links an illness outcome with personal relationships," said Dr. Janice Kiecolt-Glaser, director of health psychology at the Ohio State University College of Medicine in Columbus. Dr. Kiecolt-Glaser and her husband, Dr. Ronald Glaser, a virologist at Ohio State, have reported that a person's immune response to vaccines increases with the strength of his or her social support.

The new study included 276 healthy adults from 18 to 55 years old. First, they were asked to name the types of relationships in their social circle from a list of 12. The categories included spouse, children, other relatives, neighbors, friends, colleagues at work, members of social or recreational organizations and members of religious groups. Each category was counted if a participant spoke, either in person or on the phone, with someone from it at least once every two weeks.

The researchers also assessed many other characteristics that were known to be associated with the risk of colds, including smoking, drinking, vitamin C intake and levels of certain stress hormones.

Next the volunteers were given nose drops containing one of two cold viruses. They were quarantined in a hotel for five days and allowed to interact, but at a distance of three or more feet so as not to infect one another. Each day, they were tested for signs of the virus in their nasal secretions and observed for cold symptoms like runny nose and congestion.

The people with the most categories of social relationships had the lowest susceptibility to colds, the researchers found. The incidence of colds in the study was 35 percent among the people with six or more types of relationships, 43 percent among those with four to five types and about 62 percent among those with three of fewer. When they did get colds, the people with the greatest diversity of social ties had the mildest symptoms, the report said.

One curious finding was that the total number of people in a person's social world had no bearing on his chance of developing a cold. The key was the variety of people.

More friends also mean more exposure to germs.

Dr. Cohen believes that having a diverse social network is beneficial because it tempers a person's response to stress. For example, he said, someone who has a family as well as friends and acquaintances outside of work is likely to weather job-related stress more easily than someone who cannot escape the pressure by spending time with family and friends, he said.

Dr. Cohen also acknowledged that knowing a lot of people might increase a person's chance of getting sick if those people are prone to colds. For example, many parents find that they get more colds once their children are exposed to roomfuls of classmates with runny noses. "There's probably some trade-off, a cost as well as a benefit," he said.

Dr. David Spiegel, a psychiatrist at the Stanford University School of Medicine who studies the health effects of social support, said that exposure to more germs could stimulate a person's immune system enough to improve its ability to thwart infections in the long run.

Dr. Cohen and his colleagues had set out to identify a biological mechanism related to colds that went up or down depending on the breadth of a person's social contracts, like levels of stress hormones or replication of cold viruses. While they found that these mechanisms were related to a person's chance of becoming infected, they were not related to the size of a person's web of relationships.

Other studies have found an association between social contacts and levels of certain stress hormones and immune system chemicals, and Dr. Cohen said he did not know why he did not.

Dr. Williams said one reason the researchers did not find elevated levels of stress hormones in people with the fewest types of social relationships could be that the measurements were taken while the people were in quarantine rather than in their homes. He said stress hormones were known to go down when people went into the hospital and that being in quarantine might have had the same effect.

Dr. Williams and Dr. Ronald Glaser, the virologist, said they did not think the study's failure to identify a biological mechanism weakened its findings. Dr. Glaser said he agreed with the researchers that social ties could influence a person's resistance to all sorts of diseases and that this correlation might in turn affect a person's longevity.

"That's a fair statement," he said. "But it's also fair to say that more studies need to be done looking at immune response and social support."

Looking good is a universal human obsession. How do we perceive physical beauty, and why do we place so much stock in it? Scientists are now taking those questions seriously, and gaining surprising insights.

THE BIOLOGY OF BEAUTY

By Geoffrey Cowley

WHEN IT COMES TO CHOOSING a mate, a female penguin knows better than to fall for the first creep who pulls up and honks. She holds out for the fittest suitor available—which in Antarctica means one chubby enough to spend several weeks sitting on newly hatched eggs without starving to death. The Asian jungle bird *Gallus gallus* is just as choosy. Males in that species sport gaily colored head combs and feathers, which lose their luster if the bird is invaded by parasites. By favoring males with bright ornaments, a hen improves her odds of securing a mate (and bearing offspring) with strong resistance to disease. For female scorpion flies, beauty is less about size or color than about symmetry. Females favor suitors who have well-matched wings—and with good reason. Studies show they're the most adept at killing prey and at defending their catch from competitors. There's no reason to think that any of these creatures understands its motivations, but there's a clear pattern to their preferences. "Throughout the animal world," says University of New Mexico ecologist Randy Thornhill, "attractiveness certifies biological quality."

Is our corner of the animal world different? That looks count in human affairs is beyond dispute. Studies have shown that people considered attractive fare better with parents and teachers, make more friends and more money, and have better sex with more (and more beautiful) partners. Every year, 400,000 Americans, including 48,000 men, flock to cosmetic surgeons. In other lands, people bedeck themselves with scars, lip plugs or bright feathers. "Every culture is a 'beauty culture'," says Nancy Etcoff, a neuroscientist who is studying human attraction at the MIT Media Lab and writing a book on the subject. "I defy anyone to point to a society, any time in history or any place in the world, that wasn't preoccupied with

23. Biology of Beauty

Beauty isn't all that matters in life; most of us manage to attract mates and bear offspring despite our physical imperfections. And the qualities we find alluring say nothing about people's moral worth. Our weakness for 'biological quality' is the cause of endless pain and injustice.

beauty." The high-minded may dismiss our preening and ogling as distractions from things that matter, but the stakes can be enormous. "Judging beauty involves looking at another person," says University of Texas psychologist Devendra Singh, "and figuring out whether you want your children to carry that person's genes."

It's widely assumed that ideals of beauty vary from era to era and from culture to culture. But a harvest of new research is confounding that idea. Studies have established that people everywhere—regardless of race, class or age—share a sense of what's attractive. And though no one knows just how our minds translate the sight of a face or a body into rapture, new studies suggest that we judge each other by rules we're not even aware of. We may consciously admire Kate Moss's legs or Arnold's biceps, but we're also viscerally attuned to small variations in the size and symmetry of facial bones and the placement of weight on the body.

This isn't to say that our preferences are purely innate—or that beauty is all that matters in life. Most of us manage to find jobs, attract mates and bear offspring despite our physical imperfections. Nor should anyone assume that the new beauty research justifies the biases it illuminates. Our beautylust is often better suited to the Stone Age than to the Information Age; the qualities we find alluring may be powerful emblems of health, fertility and resistance to disease, but they say nothing about people's moral worth. The human weakness for what Thornhill calls "biological quality" causes no end of pain and injustice. Unfortunately, that doesn't make it any less real.

NO ONE SUGGESTS THAT POINTS OF attraction never vary. Rolls of fat can signal high status in a poor society or low status in a rich one, and lip plugs go over better in the Kalahari than they do in Kansas. But local fashions seem to rest on a bedrock of shared preferences. You don't have to be Italian to find Michelangelo's David better looking than, say, Alfonse D'Amato. When British researchers asked women from England, China and India to rate pictures of Greek men, the women responded as if working from the same crib sheet. And when researchers at the University of Louisville showed a diverse collection of faces to whites, Asians and Latinos from 13 countries, the subjects' ethnic background scarcely affected their preferences.

To a skeptic, those findings suggest only that Western movies and magazines have overrun the world. But scientists have found at least one group that hasn't been exposed to this bias. In a series of groundbreaking experiments, psychologist Judith Langlois of the University of Texas, Austin, has shown that even infants share a sense of what's attractive. In the late '80s, Langlois started placing 3- and 6-month-old babies in front of a screen and showing them pairs of facial photographs. Each pair included one considered attractive by adult judges and one considered unattractive. In the first study, she found that the infants gazed significantly longer at "attractive" white female faces than at "unattractive" ones. Since then, she has repeated the drill using white male faces, black female faces, even the faces of other babies, and the same pattern always emerges. "These kids don't read Vogue or watch TV," Langlois says. "They haven't been touched by the media. Yet they make the same judgments as adults."

What, then, is beauty made of? What are the innate rules we follow in sizing each other up? We're obviously wired to find robust health a prettier sight than infirmity. "All animals are attracted to other animals that are healthy, that are clean by their standards and that show signs of competence," says Rutgers University anthropologist Helen Fisher. As far as anyone knows, there isn't a village on earth where skin lesions, head lice and rotting teeth count as beauty aids. But the rules get subtler than that. Like scorpion flies, we love symmetry. And though we generally favor average features over unusual ones, the people we find extremely beautiful share certain exceptional qualities.

WHEN RANDY THORNHILL STARTED measuring the wings of Japanese scorpion flies six years ago, he wasn't much concerned with the orgasms and infidelities of college students. But sometimes one thing leads to another. Biologists have long used bilateral symmetry—the extent to which a creature's right and left sides match—to gauge what's known as developmental stability. Given ideal growing conditions, paired features such as wings, ears, eyes and feet would come out matching perfectly. But pollution, disease and other hazards can disrupt development. As a result, the least resilient individuals tend to be the most lopsided. In chronicling the scorpion flies' daily struggles, Thornhill found that the bugs with the most symmetrical wings fared best in the competition for food and mates. To his amazement, females preferred symmetrical males even when they were hidden from view; evidently, their smells are more attractive. And when researchers started noting similar trends in other species, Thornhill turned his attention to our own.

Working with psychologist Steven Gangestad, he set about measuring the body symmetry of hundreds of college-age men and women. By adding up right-left disparities in seven measurements—the breadth of the feet, ankles, hands, wrists, and elbows, as well as the breadth and length of the ears—the researchers scored each subject's overall body asymmetry. Then they had the person fill out a confidential questionnaire covering everything from temperament to sexual behavior, and set about looking for connections. They weren't disappointed. In a 1994 study, they found that the most symmetrical males had started having sex three to four years earlier than their most lopsided brethren. For both men and women, greater symmetry predicted a larger number of past sex partners.

That was just the beginning. From what they knew about other species, Thornhill and Gangestad predicted that women would be more sexually responsive to symmetrical men, and that men would exploit that advantage. To date, their findings support both suspicions. Last year they surveyed 86 couples and found that women with highly symmetrical partners were more than twice as likely to climax during intercourse (an event that may foster conception by ushering sperm into the uterus) than those with low-symmetry partners. And in separate surveys, Gangestad and Thornhill have found that, compared with regular Joes, extremely symmetrical men are less attentive to their partners and more likely to cheat on them. Women showed no such tendency.

It's hard to imagine that we even notice the differences between people's elbows, let alone stake our love lives on them. No one carries calipers into a singles bar. So why do these measurements predict so much? Because, says Thornhill, people with symmetrical elbows tend to have "a whole suite of attractive features." His findings suggest that besides having attractive (and symmetrical) faces, men with symmetrical bodies are typically larger, more muscular and more athletic than their peers, and more dominant in personality. In a forthcoming study, researchers at the University of Michigan find evidence that facial symmetry is also associated with health. In analyzing diaries kept by 100 students over a two-month period, they found that the least symmetrical had the most physical complaints, from insomnia to nasal congestion, and reported more anger, jealousy and withdrawal. In light of all Thornhill and Gangestad's findings, you can hardly blame them.

IF WE DID GO COURTING WITH calipers, symmetry isn't all we would measure. As we study each other in the street, the office or the gym, our beauty radars pick up a range of signals. Oddly enough, one of the qualities shared by attractive people is their averageness. Researchers discovered more than a century ago that if they superimposed photographs of several faces, the resulting composite was usually better looking than any of the images that went into it. Scientists can now average faces digitally, and it's still one of the surest ways to make them more attractive. From an evolutionary perspective, a preference for extreme normality' makes sense. As Langlois has written, "Individuals with average population characteristics should be less likely to carry harmful genetic mutations."

So far, so good. But here's the catch: while we may find average faces attractive, the faces we find most beautiful are not average. As New Mexico State University psychologist Victor Johnston has shown, they're extreme. To track people's preferences, Johnston uses a computer program called FacePrints. Turn it on, and it generates 30 facial images, all male or all female, which you rate on a 1–9 beauty scale. The program then "breeds" the top-rated face with one of the others to create two digital offspring, which replace the lowest-rated faces in the pool. By rating round after round of new faces, you create an ever more beautiful population. The game ends when you award some visage a perfect 10. (If you have access to the World Wide Web, you can take part in a collective face-breeding experiment by visiting http://www-psych.nmsu.edu/~vic/faceprints/.)

For Johnston, the real fun starts after the judging is finished. By collecting people's ideal faces and comparing them to average faces, he can measure the distance between fantasy and reality. As a rule, he finds that an ideal female has a higher forehead than an average one, as well as fuller lips, a shorter jaw and a smaller chin and nose. Indeed, the ideal 25-year-old woman, as configured by participants in a 1993 study, had a 14-year-old's abundant lips and an 11-year-old's delicate jaw. Because her lower face was so small, she also had relatively prominent eyes and cheekbones.

The participants in that study were all college kids from New Mexico, but researchers have since shown that British and Japanese students express the same bias. And if there are lingering doubts about the depth of that bias, Johnston's latest findings should dispel them. In a forthcoming study, he reports that male volunteers not only consciously prefer women with small lower faces but show marked rises in brain activity when looking at pictures of them. And though Johnston has yet to publish specs on the ideal male, his unpublished findings suggest that a big jaw, a strong chin and an imposing brow are as prized in a man's face as their opposites are in a woman's.

Few of us ever develop the heart-melting proportions of a FacePrints fantasy. And if it's any consolation, beauty is not an all-or-nothing proposition. Madonna became a sex symbol despite her strong nose, and Melanie Griffith's strong jaw hasn't kept her out of the movies. Still, special things have a way of happening to people who approximate the ideal. We pay them huge fees to stand on windblown bluffs and stare into the distance. And past studies have found that square-jawed males not only start having sex earlier than their peers but attain higher rank in the military.

None of this surprises evolutionary psychologists. They note that the facial features we obsess over are precisely the ones that diverge in males and females during puberty, as floods of sex hormones wash us into adulthood. And they reason that hormonal abundance would have been a good clue to mate value in the hunter-gatherer world where our preferences evolved. The tiny jaw that men favor in women is essentially a monument to estrogen—and, obliquely, to fertility. No one claims that jaws reveal a woman's odds of getting pregnant. But like breasts, they imply that she could.

Likewise, the heavy lower face that women favor in men is a visible record of the surge in androgens (testosterone and other male sex hormones) that turns small boys into 200-pound spear-throwers. An oversized jaw is biologically expensive, for the androgens required to produce it tend to compromise the immune system. But from a female's perspective, that should make jaw size all the more revealing. Evolutionists think of androgen-based

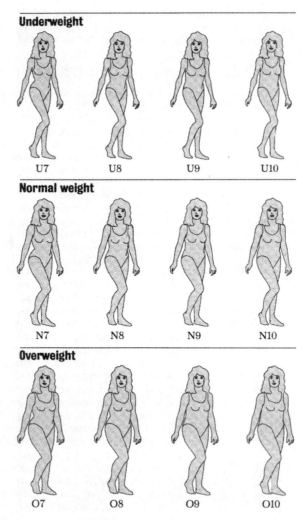

BODY LANGUAGE
When men are asked to rank figures with various weights and waist-hip ratios (0.7 to 1.0), they favor a pronounced hourglass shape. The highest-ranked figures are N7, N8 and U7 (in that order). The lowest ranked is O10.

THE ORDER CHOSEN: (1) N7, (2) N8, (3) U7, (4) U8, (5) N9, (6) N10, (7) O7, (8), U9, (9) O8, (10) U10, (11) O9, (12) O10 SOURCE: DEVENDRA SINGH, UNIVERSITY OF TEXAS AT AUSTIN

features as "honest advertisements" of disease resistance. If a male can afford them without falling sick, the thinking goes, he must have a superior immune system in the first place.

No one has tracked the immune responses of men with different jawlines to see if these predictions bear out (Thornhill has proposed a study that would involve comparing volunteers' responses to a vaccine). Nor is it clear whether penis size figures into these equations. Despite what everyone thinks he knows on the subject, scientists haven't determined that women have consistent preferences one way or the other.

OUR FACES ARE SIGNAtures, but when it comes to raw sex appeal, a nice chin is no match for a perfectly sculpted torso—especially from a man's perspective. Studies from around the world have found that while both sexes value appearance, men place more stock in it than women. And if there are social reasons for that imbalance, there are also biological ones. Just about any male over 14 can produce sperm, but a woman's ability to bear children depends on her age and hormone levels. Female fertility declines by two thirds between the ages of 20 and 44, and it's spent by 54. So while the both sexes may eyeball potential partners, says Donald Symons, an anthropologist at the University of California in Santa Barbara, "a larger proportion of a woman's mate value can be detected from visual cues." Mounting evidence suggests there is no better cue than the relative contours of her waist and hips.

FACIAL FANTASIES

As a rule, average faces are more attractive than unusual ones. But when people are asked to develop ideal faces on a computer, they tend to exaggerate certain qualities.

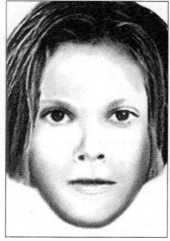 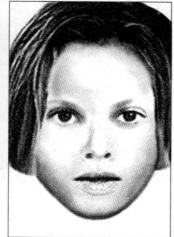

Average proportions
This computer-generated face has the dimensions typical of Caucasian 20-year-olds.

Ideal proportions
Most visions of the perfect female face have small jaws and abnormally lush lips.

SOURCE: VICTOR JOHNSTON, NEW MEXICO STATE UNIVERSITY

and thighs. Those pounds contain roughly the 80,000 calories needed to sustain a pregnancy, and the curves they create provide a gauge of reproductive potential. "You have to get very close to see the details of a woman's face," says Devendra Singh, the University of Texas psychologist. "But you can see the shape of her body from 500 feet, and it says more about mate value."

Almost anything that interferes with fertility—obesity, malnutrition, pregnancy, menopause—changes a woman's shape.

23. Biology of Beauty

this range are healthy and capable of having children, of course. But as researchers in the Netherlands discovered in a 1993 study, even a slight increase in waist size relative to hip size can signal reproductive problems. Among 500 women who were attempting in vitro fertilization, the odds of conceiving during any given cycle declined by 30 percent with every 10 percent increase in WHR. In other words, a woman with a WHR of .9 was nearly a third less likely to get pregnant than one with a WHR of .8, regardless of her age or weight. From an evolutionary perspective, it's hard to imagine men not responding to such a revealing signal. And as Singh has shown repeatedly, they do.

Defining a universal standard of body beauty once seemed a fool's dream; common sense said that if spindly Twiggy and Rubens's girthy Three Graces could all excite admiration, then nearly anyone could. But if our ideals of size change from one time and place to the next, our taste in shapes is amazingly stable. A low waist-hip ratio is one of the few features that a long, lean Barbie doll shares with a plump, primitive fertility icon. And Singh's findings suggest the fashion won't change any time soon. In one study, he compiled the measurements of Playboy centerfolds and Miss America winners from 1923 to 1990. Their bodies got measurably leaner over the decades, yet their waist-hip ratios stayed within the narrow range of .68 to .72. (Even Twiggy was no tube; at the peak of her fame in the 1960s, the British model had a WHR of .73.)

The same pattern holds when Singh generates line drawings of different female fig-

Even infants spend more time gazing at pictures of 'attractive' faces than at 'unattractive' ones. 'These kids don't read Vogue or watch TV, yet they make the same judgments as adults,' says psychologist Judith Langlois.

Before puberty and after menopause, females have essentially the same waistlines as males. But during puberty, while boys are amassing the bone and muscle of paleolithic hunters, a typical girl gains nearly 35 pounds of so-called reproductive fat around the hips

Healthy, fertile women typically have waist-hip ratios of .6 to .8, meaning their waists are 60 to 80 percent the size of their hips, whatever their actual weight. To take one familiar example, a 36-25-36 figure would have a WHR of .7. Many women outside

ures and asks male volunteers to rank them for attractiveness, sexiness, health and fertility. He has surveyed men of various backgrounds, nationalities and ages. And whether the judges are 8-year-olds or 85-year-olds, their runaway favorite is a figure of average weight with a .7 WHR. Small wonder that when women were liberated from corsets and bustles, they took up girdles, wide belts and other waist-reducing contraptions. Last year alone, American women's outlays for shape-enhancing garments topped a half-billion dollars.

TO SOME CRITICS, THE SEARCH FOR a biology of beauty looks like a thinly veiled political program. "It's the fantasy life of American men being translated into genetics," says poet and social critic Katha Pollitt. "You can look at any feature of modern life and make up a story about why it's genetic." In truth, says Northwestern University anthropologist Micaela di Leonardo, attraction is a complicated social phenomenon, not just a hard-wired response. If attraction were governed by the dictates of baby-making, she says, the men of ancient Greece wouldn't have found young boys so alluring, and gay couples wouldn't crowd modern sidewalks. "People make decisions about sexual and marital partners inside complex networks of friends and relatives," she says. "Human beings cannot be reduced to DNA packets."

Homosexuality is hard to explain as a biological adaptation. So is stamp collecting. But no one claims that human beings are mindless automatons, blindly striving to replicate our genes. We pursue countless passions that have no direct bearing on survival. If we're sometimes attracted to people who can't help us reproduce, that doesn't mean human preferences lack any coherent design. A radio used as a doorstop is still a radio. The beauty mavens' mission—and that of evolutionary psychology in general—is not to explain everything people do but to unmask our biases and make sense of them. "Our minds have evolved to generate pleasurable experiences in response to some things while ignoring other things," says Johnston. "That's why sugar tastes sweet, and that's why we find some people more attractive than others."

The new beauty research does have troubling implications. First, it suggests that we're designed to care about looks, even though looks aren't earned and reveal nothing about character. As writer Ken Siman observes in his new book, "The Beauty Trip," "the kind [of beauty] that inspires awe, lust, and increased jeans sales cannot be evenly distributed. In a society where everything is supposed to be within reach, this is painful to face." From acne to birth defects, we wear our imperfections as thorns, for we know the world sees them and takes note.

A second implication is that sexual stereotypes are not strictly artificial. At some level, it seems, women are designed to favor dominant males over meek ones, and men are designed to value women for youthful qualities that time quickly steals. Given the slow pace of evolutionary change, our innate preferences aren't likely to fade in the foreseeable future. And if they exist for what were once good biological reasons, that doesn't make them any less nettlesome. "Men often forgo their health, their safety, their spare time and their family life in order to get rank," says Helen Fisher, the Rutgers anthropologist, "because unconsciously, they know that rank wins women." And all too often, those who can trade cynically on their rank do.

But do we have to indulge every appetite that natural selection has preserved in us? Of course not. "I don't know any scientist who seriously thinks you can look to nature for moral guidance," says Thornhill. Even the fashion magazines would provide a better compass.

With KAREN SPRINGEN

SOCIETY: YOU MUST REMEMBER THIS, A KISS IS BUT A KISS

Infidelity and the Science of Cheating

Why do men find sexual infidelity by their mates so distressing? Why do women find emotional infidelity so threatening? The new view blames it all on our genetic inheritance, a faddish intellectual trend that is likely to gain momentum in the coming years.

BY SHARON BEGLEY

Think of a committed romantic relationship that you have now, or that you had in the past. Now imagine that your spouse, or significant other, becomes interested in someone else. What would distress you more:
- Discovering that he or she has formed a deep emotional attachment to the other, confiding in that person and seeking comfort there rather than from you?
- Discovering that your partner is enjoying daily passionate sex with the other person, trying positions rarely seen outside the Kamasutra?

While this makes for an interesting party game—though we don't advise trying it around the family Christmas table—the question has a more serious purpose. Researchers have been using such "forced choice" experiments to probe one of the more controversial questions in psychology: why do more men than women say sexual betrayal is more upsetting, while more women than men find emotional infidelity more disturbing? Psychologist David Buss of the University of Texas, Austin, first reported this gender gap in 1992. Since then other researchers have repeatedly found the same pattern. But when it comes to explaining *why* men and women differ, the battle rages.

The year now ending brought claims that genes inherited from our parents make us risk takers or neurotic, happy or sad. In the new year, watch out for ever more studies on how genes passed down from Neanderthal days make us what we are. "There is tremendous interest in evolutionary perspectives in psychology," says John Kihlstrom of Yale University, editor of the journal Psychological Science. And not just among scientists. In 1996, magazine articles waxed scholarly on how evolu-

Why do men prefer women in short skirts? At the dawn of humanity women in long skirts tripped, squashing their babies.

tion explains, for instance, Dick Morris's extramarital escapades. Basically, his DNA made him do it.

The debate shapes up like this. Evolutionary psychologists argue that sex differences in jealousy are a legacy of humankind's past, a biological imperative that no amount of reason, no veneer of civilization, can entirely quash. In other words, genes for traits that characterized the earliest humans shape how we think, feel and act, even if we are doing that thinking, feeling and acting in cities rather than in caves. In particular, men fly into a rage over adultery because to do so is hard-wired into their genes (not to mention their jeans). The reason is that a man can never be altogether sure of paternity. If, at the dawn of humanity, a man's partner slept around, he could have wound up inadvertently supporting the child of a rival; he would also have had fewer chances of impregnating her himself. That would have given him a poor chance of transmitting his genes to the next generation. Or, put another way, only men who carried the gene that made them livid over a spouse's roaming managed to leave descendants. Says UT's Buss, "Any man who didn't [do all he could to keep his wife from straying sexually] is not our ancestor."

FOR A WOMAN, THE STAKES WERE DIFFERENT. IF HER partner sired another's child, his infidelity could have been over in minutes. (OK, seconds.) But if he became emotionally involved with another woman, he might have abandoned wife No. 1. That would have made it harder for her to raise children. So women are evolutionarily programmed to become more distressed at emotional infidelity than sexual infidelity.

The journal Psychological Science recently devoted a special section to the controversy. Leading off: a study by Buss, working with colleagues from Germany and the Netherlands, in which 200 German and 207 Dutch adults were asked the standard "which is more upsetting" question. As usual, more men than women in both cultures said that sexual infidelity bothered them more than emotional infidelity. "This sex difference is quite solid," says Buss. "It's been replicated by our critics and in crosscultural studies, giving exactly the results that the evolutionary theory predicts."

Critics of the evolutionary paradigm say it is dangerous to call the jealousy gender gap a product of our genes. "This theory holds profound implications for legal and social policy," says psychologist David DeSteno of Ohio State University. "Men could get away with murder [of a sexually unfaithful spouse] by attributing it to their biology and saying they had no control over themselves." What's more, he argues, the theory is wrong. First, if there are genes for jealousy, they can apparently be influenced by culture. Although in every country more men than women were indeed more upset by sexual infidelity than the emotional variety, the differences between the sexes varied widely. Three times as many American men than women said that sexual treachery upset them more; only 50 percent more German men than women said that. The Dutch fell in between. So the society in which one lives can change beliefs, and thus make the gender gap larger or smaller.

More problematic for evolutionary psychology is another repeated finding. Yes, more men than women find sexual infidelity more disturbing. Something like 45 percent of men and 10 percent of women, or 30 percent of men and 8 percent of women (the numbers depend, says Buss, on how the question is worded), were more upset by the idea of sexual betrayal. But look more closely at the numbers for men. If 45, or 30, percent say that sexual betrayal disturbs them more, that means that most (55 percent, 70 percent) are *not* disturbed more by it. Yet evolutionary theory predicts that, even though men should not be indifferent to emotional infidelity, they should care more about the sexual kind.

Scientists who have been skeptical about the "my genes made me think it" theory have a different explanation for the jealousy gender gap. What triggers jealousy depends not on ancient genes, they argue, but on how you think the opposite gender connects love to sex and sex to love. Or, as psychologists Christine Harris and Nicholas Chistenfeld of the University of California, San Diego, propose, "reasonable differences between the sexes in how they interpret evidence of infidelity" explain the gender gap. In other words, a man thinks that women have sex only when they are in love; if he learns that a woman has had sex with another man, he assumes that she loves him, too. Thus sexual infidelity means emotional infidelity as well. But men believe also that women can be emotionally intimate with another man without leaping into bed with him. A woman's emotional infidelity, then, implies nothing beyond that. By this reasoning, men see sexual betrayal as what Peter Salovey of Yale University and OSU's DeSteno call a "double shot" of infidelity. Sexual infidelity is therefore more threatening than mere emotional infidelity.

A woman, on the other hand, notices that men can have sex without love. Thus a man's sexual betrayal does not necessarily mean that he has fallen in love with someone else. So adultery bothers her less than it does men. But a woman also notices that men do not form emotional attachments easily. When they do, it's a real threat to the relationship. Says DeSteno, "Whichever type of infidelity represents a double shot would bother someone more."

Now scientists are designing experiments to show whether the mind's ability to reason, rather than genes, can explain the jealousy gender gap. The UCSD team asked 137 undergraduates the "which distresses you more" question. As expected, more men than women picked sexual infidelity as more upsetting. But the researchers also found differences in men's and women's beliefs. Women thought that, for men, love implies sex more often than sex implies love. And men said that, for women, sex implies love about as strongly as love implies sex. This difference in assessments of the opposite sex, argue the UCSD psychologists, explains all the gender gap in jealousy. Of course a woman is more bothered by a man's emotional infidelity than by sexual betrayal: a man in love is a man having sex, they figure, but a man having sex is not necessarily a man in love. Now, there's a shock.

OTHER EXPERIMENTS UNDERMINE AS WELL THE "MY genes made me think it" argument. DeSteno and Salovey asked 114 undergraduates, and then 141 adults ages 17 to 70, how likely it is that someone of the opposite sex who is in love will soon be having sex, and how likely that someone of the opposite sex who is having sex is or will be in love. Anyone, man or woman, who believed that love is more likely to mean sex than sex is to mean love was more upset by emotional infidelity than by sexual infidelity. And anyone, man or woman, who believed that someone having sex is someone in love found sexual infidelity more upsetting. These data, says DeSteno, "argue against the evolutionary interpretation. Which infidelity upsets you more seems related to [gender] only because [gender] is correlated with beliefs about whether sex implies love and love implies sex."

Evolutionary psychologists don't buy it. Buss points to studies showing that a woman is at greatest risk of being battered, and even murdered, by her partner when he suspects her of sexual infidelity. "Men's sexual jealousy is an extremely powerful emotion. It makes them go berserk," says Buss. "The 'rational' arguments don't square with [the fact that] jealousy feels 'beyond rationality.' This vague implication that culture and socialization [cause sex differences] is very old-social-science stuff that sophisticated people don't argue anymore. . . . Sometimes I feel that I am amidst members of the Flat Earth Society."

For all the brickbats being hurled, there is some common ground between the opposing camps. Buss and colleagues believe that jealousy, like other emotions sculpted by evolution, is "sensitive to sociocultural conditions." And those who scoff at evolutionary psychology agree that, as DeSteno says, "of course evolution plays a role in human behavior." The real fight centers on whether that role is paramount and direct, or whether biology is so dwarfed by culture and human reason that it adds little to our understanding of behavior. Spinning stories of how Neanderthal genes make us think and act the way we do undeniably makes for a lively parlor game. (Example: men prefer women in short skirts because they learned, millennia ago on the savanna, that women in long skirts tended to trip a lot and squash their babies.) And it is one that will be played often in 1997. If there is a lesson here, it may be this: be wary of single-bullet theories advanced so brilliantly that their dazzle gets in the way of their content.

THE LESSONS OF LOVE

Yes, we've learned a few things. We now know that it is the insecure rather than the confident who fall in love most readily. And men fall faster than women. And who ever said sex had anything to do with it?

Beth Livermore

As winter thaws, so too do icicles on cold hearts. For with spring, the sap rises—and resistance to love wanes. And though the flame will burn more of us than it warms, we will return to the fire—over and over again.

Indeed, love holds central in everybody's everyday. We spend years, sometimes lifetimes pursuing it, preparing for it, longing for it. Some of us even die for love. Still, only poets and songwriters, philosophers and playwrights have traditionally been granted license to sift this hallowed preserve. Until recently. Over the last decade and a half, scientists have finally taken on this most elusive entity. They have begun to parse out the intangibles, the *je ne sais quoi* of love. The word so far is—little we were sure of is proving to be true.

OUT OF THE LAB, INTO THE FIRE

True early greats, like Sigmund Freud and Carl Rogers, acknowledged love as important to the human experience. But not till the 1970s did anyone attempt to define it—and only now is it considered a respectable topic of study.

One reason for this hesitation has been public resistance. "Some people are afraid that if they look too close they will lose the mask," says Arthur Aron, Ph.D., professor of psychology at the University of California, Santa Cruz. "Others believe we know all that we need to know." But mostly, to systematically study love has been thought impossible, and therefore a waste of time and money.

No one did more to propagate this false notion than former United States Senator William Proxmire of Wisconsin, who in 1974 launched a very public campaign against the study of love. As a member of the Senate Finance Committee, he took it upon himself to ferret out waste in government spending. One of the first places he looked was the National Science Foundation, a federal body that both funds research and promotes scientific progress.

Upon inspection, Proxmire found that Ellen Berscheid, Ph.D., a psychologist at the University of Minnesota who had already broken new ground scrutinizing the social power of physical attractiveness, had secured an $84,000 federal grant to study relationships. The proposal mentioned romantic love. Proxmire loudly denounced such work as frivolous—tax dollars ill spent.

The publicity that was given Proxmire's pronouncements not only cast a pall over all behavioral science research, it set off an international firestorm around Berscheid that lasted the next two years. Colleagues were fired. Her office was swamped with hate mail. She even received death threats. But in the long run, the strategy backfired, much to Proxmire's chagrin. It generated increased scientific interest in the study of love, propelling it forward, and identified Berscheid as the keeper of the flame. Scholars and individuals from Alaska to then-darkest Cold War Albania sent her requests for information, along with letters of support.

Berscheid jettisoned her plans for very early retirement, buttoned up the country house, and, as she says, "became a clearinghouse" for North American love research. "It became eminently clear that there were people who really did want to learn more about love. And I had tenure."

PUTTING THE SOCIAL INTO PSYCHOLOGY

This incident was perfectly timed. For during the early 1970s, the field of social psychology was undergoing a revolution of sorts—a revolution that made the study of love newly possible.

For decades behaviorism, the school of psychology founded by John B. Watson, dominated the field. Watson argued that only overt actions capable of direct observation and measurement were worthy of study. However, by the early seventies, dissenters were openly calling this approach far too narrow. It excluded unobservable mental events such as ideas and emotions. Thus rose cognitive science, the study of the mind, or perception, thought, and memory.

Now psychologists were encouraged to ask human subjects what they thought and how they felt about things. Self-report questionnaires emerged as a legitimate research tool. Psychologists were encouraged to escape laboratory confines—to study real people in the real world. Once out there, they discovered that there was plenty to mine.

Throughout the seventies, soaring divorce rates, loneliness, and isolation began to dominate the emotional landscape of America. By the end of that decade, love had become a pathology. No longer was the question "What is love?" thought to be trivial. "People in our culture dissolve unions when love disappears, which has a lasting effect on society," says Berscheid. Besides, "we already understood the mating habits of the stickleback fish." It was time to turn to a new species.

Today there are hundreds of research papers on love. Topics range from romantic ideals to attachment styles of the young and unmarried. "There were maybe a half dozen when I wrote my dissertation on romantic attraction in 1969," reports Aron. These days, a national association and an international society bring "close relationship" researchers close together annually. Together or apart they are busy producing and sharing new theories, new questionnaires to use as research instruments, and new findings. Their unabashed aim: to improve the human condition by helping us to understand, to repair, and to perfect our love relationships.

SO WHAT *IS* LOVE?

"If there is anything that we have learned about love it is its variegated nature," says Clyde Hendrick, Ph.D., of Texas Tech University in Lubbock. "No one volume or theory or research program can capture love and transform it into a controlled bit of knowledge."

Instead, scholars are tackling specific questions about love in the hopes of nailing down a few facets at a time. The expectation is that every finding will be a building block in the base of knowledge, elevating understanding.

Elaine Hatfield, Ph.D., now of the University of Hawaii, has carved out the territory of passionate love. Along with Berscheid, Hatfield was at the University of Minnesota in 1964 when Stanley Schacter, formerly a professor there and still a great presence, proposed a new theory of emotion. It said that any emotional state requires two conditions: both physiological arousal and relevant situational cues. Already studying close relationships, Hatfield and Berscheid were intrigued. Could the theory help to explain the turbulent, all-consuming experience of passionate love?

Hatfield has spent a good chunk of her professional life examining passionate love, "a state of intense longing for union with another." In 1986, along with sociologist Susan Sprecher, she devised the Passionate Love Scale (PLS), a questionnaire that measures thoughts and feelings she previously identified as distinctive of this "emotional" state.

Lovers rate the applicability of a variety of descriptive statements. To be passionately in love is to be preoccupied with thoughts of your partner much of the time. Also, you likely idealize your partner. So those of you who are passionately in love would, for example, give "I yearn to know all about—" a score somewhere between "moderately true" and "definitely true" on the PLS.

True erotic love is intense and involves taking risks. It seems to demand a strong sense of self.

The quiz also asks subjects if they find themselves trying to determine the other's feelings, trying to please their lover, or making up excuses to be close to him or her—all hallmarks of passionate, erotic love. It canvasses for both positive and negative feelings. "Passionate lovers," explains Hatfield, "experience a roller coaster of feelings: euphoria, happiness, calm, tranquility, vulnerability, anxiety, panic, despair."

For a full 10 percent of lovers, previous romantic relationships proved so painful that they hope they will never love again.

Passionate love, she maintains, is kindled by "a sprinkle of hope and a large dollop of loneliness, mourning, jealousy, and terror." It is, in other words, fueled by a juxtaposition of pain and pleasure. According to psychologist Dorothy Tennov, who interviewed some 500 lovers, most of them expect their romantic experiences to be bittersweet. For a full 10 percent of them, previous romantic relationships proved so painful that they hope never to love again.

Contrary to myths that hold women responsible for romance, Hatfield finds that both males and females love with equal passion. But men fall in love faster. They are, thus, more romantic. Women are more apt to mix pragmatic concerns with their passion.

And people of all ages, even four-year-old children, are capable of "falling passionately in love." So are people of any ethnic group and socioeconomic stratum capable of passionate love.

Hatfield's most recent study, of love in three very different cultures, shows that romantic love is not simply a product of the Western mind. It exists among diverse cultures worldwide.

Taken together, Hatfield's findings support the idea that passionate love is an evolutionary adaptation. In this scheme, passionate love works as a bonding mechanism, a necessary kind of interpersonal glue that has existed since the start of the human race. It assures that procreation will take place, that the human species will be perpetuated.

UP FROM THE SWAMP

Recent anthropological work also supports this notion. In 1991, William Jankowiak, Ph.D., of the University of Nevada in Las Vegas, and Edward Fischer, Ph.D., of Tulane University published the first study systematically comparing romantic love across 166 cultures.

They looked at folklore, indigenous advice about love, tales about lovers, love potion recipes—anything related. They found "clear evidence" that romantic love is known in 147, or 89 percent, of cultures. Further, Jankowiak suspects that the lack of proof in the remaining 19 cultures is due more to field workers' oversights than to the absence of romance.

Unless prompted, few anthropologists recognize romantic love in the populations that they study, explains Jankowiak. Mostly because romance takes different shapes in different cultures, they do not know what to look for. They tend to recognize romance only in the form it takes in American culture—a progressive phenomenon leading from flirtation to marriage. Elsewhere, it may be a more fleeting fancy. Still, reports Jankowiak, "when I ask them specific questions about behavior, like 'Did couples run away from camp together?', almost all of them have a positive response."

For all that, there is a sizable claque of scholars who insist that romantic love is a cultural invention of the last 200 years or so. They point out that few cultures outside the West embrace romantic love with the vigor that we do. Fewer still build marriage, traditionally a social and economic institution, on the individualistic pillar of romance.

Romantic love, this thinking holds, consists of a learned set of behaviors; the phenomenon is culturally transmitted from one generation to the next by example, stories, imitation, and direct instruc-

LOVE ME TENDER

How To Make Love to a Man
(what men like, in order of importance)

taking walks together
kissing
candle-lit dinners
cuddling
hugging
flowers
holding hands
making love
love letters
sitting by the fireplace

How To Make Love to a Woman
(what women like, in order of importance)

taking walks together
flowers
kissing
candle-lit dinners
cuddling
declaring "I love you"
love letters
slow dancing
hugging
giving surprise gifts

---

tion. Therefore, it did not rise from the swamps with us, but rather evolved with culture.

THE ANXIOUS ARE ITS PREY

Regardless whether passionate, romantic love is universal or unique to us, there is considerable evidence that what renders people particularly vulnerable to it is anxiety. It whips up the wherewithal to love. And anxiety is not alone; in fact, there are a number of predictable precursors to love.

To test the idea that emotions such as fear, which produces anxiety, can amplify attraction, Santa Cruz's Arthur Aron recorded the responses of two sets of men to an attractive woman. But one group first had to cross a narrow 450-foot-long bridge that swayed in the wind over a 230-foot drop—a pure prescription for anxiety. The other group tromped confidently across a seemingly safe bridge. Both groups encountered Miss Lovely, a decoy, as they stepped back onto terra firm.

Aron's attractive confederate stopped each young man to explain that she was doing a class project and asked if he would complete a questionnaire. Once he finished, she handed him her telephone number, saying that she would be happy to explain her project in greater detail.

Who called? Nine of the 33 men on the suspension bridge telephoned, while only two of the men on the safe bridge called. It is not impossible that the callers simply wanted details on the project, but Aron suspects instead that a combustible mix of excitement and anxiety prompted the men to become interested in their attractive interviewee.

Along similar if less treacherous lines, Aron has most recently looked at eleven possible precursors to love. He compiled the list by conducting a comprehensive literature search for candidate items. If you have a lot in common with or live and work close to someone you find attractive, your chances of falling in love are good, the literature suggests.

Other general factors proposed at one time or another as good predictors include being liked by the other, a partner's positive social status, a partner's ability to fill your needs, your readiness for entering a relationship, your isolation from others, mystery, and exciting surroundings or circumstances. Then there are specific cues, like hair color, eye expression, and face shape.

Love depends as much on the perception of being liked as on the presence of a desirable partner. Love isn't possible without it.

To test the viability and relative importance of these eleven putative factors, Aron asked three different groups of people to give real-life accounts of falling in love. Predictably, desirable characteristics, such as good looks and personality, made the top of the list. But proximity, readiness to develop a relationship, and exciting surroundings and circumstances ranked close behind.

The big surprise: reciprocity. Love is at heart a two-way event. The perception of being liked ranked just as high as the presence of desirable characteristics in the partner. "The combination of the two appears to be very important," says Aron. In fact, love just may not be possible without it.

Sprecher and his colleagues got much the same results in a very recent cross-cultural survey. They and their colleagues interviewed 1,667 men and women in the U.S., Russia, and Japan. They asked the people to think about the last time they had fallen in love or been infatuated. Then they asked about the circumstance that surrounded the love experience.

Surprisingly, the rank ordering of the factors was quite similar in all three cultures. In all three, men and women consider reciprocal liking, personality, and physical appearance to be especially important. A partner's social status and the approval of family and friends are way down the list. The cross-cultural validation of predisposing influences suggests that reciprocal liking, desirable personality and physical features may be universal elements of love, among the *sine qua non* of love, part of its heart and soul.

FRIENDSHIP OVER PASSION

Another tack to the intangible of love is the "prototype" approach. This is the study of our conceptions of love, what we "think" love is.

In 1988, Beverly Fehr, Ph.D., of the University of Winnipeg in Canada conducted a series of six studies designed to determine what "love" and "commitment" have in common. Assorted theories suggested they could be anything from mutually inclusive to completely separate. Fehr asked subjects to list characteristics of love and to list features of commitment. Then she asked them to determine which qualities were central and which more peripheral to each.

People's concepts of the two were to some degree overlapping. Such elements as trust, caring, respect, honesty, devotion, sacrifice, and contentment were deemed attributes of both love and commitment. But such other factors as intimacy, happiness, and a desire to be with the other proved unique to love (while commitment alone demanded perseverance, mutual agreement, obligation, and even a feeling of being trapped).

The findings of Fehr's set of studies, as well as others', defy many expectations. Most subjects said they consider caring, trust, respect, and honesty central to love—while passion-related events like touching, sexual passion, and physical attraction are only peripheral. "They are not very central to our concept of love," Fehr shrugs.

Recently, Fehr explored gender differences in views of love—and found remarkably few. Both men and women put forth friendship as primary to love. Only in a second study, which asked subjects to match their personal ideal of love to various descriptions, did any differences show up. More so than women, men tended to rate erotic, romantic love closer to their personal conception of love.

Both men and women deem romance and passion far less important than support and warm fuzzies . . .

Still, Fehr is fair. On the whole, she says, "the essence, the core meaning of love differs little." Both genders deem romance and passion far less important than support and warm fuzzies. As even Nadine Crenshaw, creator of steamy romance novels, has remarked, "love gets you to the bathroom when you're sick."

LOVE ME TENDER

Since the intangible essence of love cannot be measured directly, many researchers settle for its reflection in what people do. They examine the behavior of lovers.

Clifford Swensen, Ph.D., professor of psychology at Purdue University, pioneered this approach by developing a scale with which to measure lovers' behavior. He produced it from statements people made when asked what they did for, said to, or felt about people they loved . . . and how these people behaved towards them.

Being supportive and providing encouragement are important behaviors to all love relationships—whether with a friend or mate, Swensen and colleagues found. Subjects also gave high ratings to self-disclosure, or talking about personal matters, and a sense of agreement on important topics.

But two categories of behaviors stood out as unique to romantic relationships.

Lovers said that they expressed feelings of love verbally; they talked about how they enjoyed being together, how they missed one another when apart, and other such murmurings. They also showed their affection through physical acts like hugging and kissing.

Elaborating on the verbal and physical demonstrations of love, psychologist Raymond Tucker, Ph.D., of Bowling Green State University in Ohio probed 149 women and 48 men to determine "What constitutes a romantic act?" He asked subjects, average age of 21, to name common examples. There was little disagreement between the genders.

Both men and women most often cited "taking walks" together. For women, "sending or receiving flowers" and "kissing" followed close on its heels, then "candle-lit dinners" and "cuddling." Outright declarations of "I love you came in a distant sixth. (Advisory to men: The florists were right all along. Say it with flowers instead.)

. . . as one romance novelist confides, "love gets you to the bathroom when you're sick."

For men, kissing and "candle-lit dinners" came in second and third. If women preferred demonstrations of love to outright declarations of it, men did even more so; "hearing and saying 'I love you didn't even show up among their top ten preferences. Nor did "slow dancing or giving or receiving surprise gifts," although all three were on the women's top-ten list. Men likewise listed three kinds of activity women didn't even mention: "holding hands," "making love"—and "sitting by the fireplace." For both sexes, love is more tender than most of us imagined.

All in all, says Tucker, lovers consistently engage in a specific array of actions. "I see these items show up over and over and over again." They may very well be the bedrock behaviors of romantic love.

SIX COLORS OF LOVE

That is not to say that once in love we all behave alike. We do not. Each of us has a set of attitudes toward love that colors what we do. While yours need not match your mate's, you best understand your partner's approach. It underlies how your partner is likely to treat you.

There are six basic orientations toward love, Canadian sociologist John Allen Lee first suggested in 1973. They emerged from a series of studies in which subjects matched story cards, which contain statements projecting attitudes, to their own personal relationships. In 1990 Texas Tech's Clyde Hendrick, along with wife/colleague Susan Hendrick, Ph.D., produced a Love Attitude Scale to measure all six styles. You may embody more than one of these styles. You are also likely to change style with time and circumstance.

Both men and women prefer demonstrations of love to outright declarations of it.

You may, for example, have spent your freewheeling college years as an Eros lover, passionate and quick to get involved, setting store on physical attraction and sexual satisfaction. Yet today you may find yourself happy as a Storge lover, valuing friendship-based love, preferring a secure, trusting relationship with a partner of like values.

There are Ludus lovers, game-players who like to have several partners at one time. Their partners may be very different from one another, as Ludus does not act on romantic ideals. Mania-type lovers, by contrast, experience great emotional highs and lows. They are very possessive—and often jealous. They spend a lot of their time doubting their partner's sincerity.

Pragma lovers are, well, pragmatic. They get involved only with the "right" guy or gal—someone who fills their needs or meets other specifications. This group is happy to trade drama and excitement for a partner they can build a life with. In contrast, Agape, or altruistic, lovers form relationships because of what they may be able to give to their partner. Even sex is not an urgent concern of theirs. "Agape functions on a more spiritual level," Hendrick says.

The Hendricks have found some gender difference among love styles. In general, men are more ludic, or game-playing. Women tend to be more storgic,

THE COLORS OF LOVE

How do I love thee? At least six are the ways.

There is no one type of love; there are many equally valid ways of loving. Researchers have consistently identified six attitudes or styles of love that, to one degree or another, encompass our conceptions of love and color our romantic relationships. They reflect both fixed personality traits and more malleable attitudes. Your relative standing on these dimensions may vary over time—being in love NOW will intensify your responses in some dimensions. Nevertheless, studies show that for most people, one dimension of love predominates.

Answering the questions below will help you identify your own love style, one of several important factors contributing to the satisfaction you feel in relationships. You may wish to rate yourself on a separate sheet of paper. There are no right or wrong answers, nor is there any scoring system. The test is designed to help you examine your own feelings and to help you understand your own romantic experiences.

After you take the test, if you are currently in a relationship, you may want to ask your partner to take the test and then compare your responses. Better yet, try to predict your partner's love attitudes before giving the test to him or her.

Studies show that most partners are well-correlated in the areas of love passion and intensity (Eros), companionate or friendship love (Storge), dependency (Mania), and all-giving or selfless love (Agape). If you and your partner aren't a perfect match, don't worry. Knowing your styles can help you manage your relationship.

Directions: Listed below are several statements that reflect different attitudes about love. For each statement, fill in the response on an answer sheet that indicates how much you agree or disagree with that statement. The items refer to a specific love relationship. Whenever possible, answer the questions with your current partner in mind. If you are not currently dating anyone, answer the questions with your most recent partner in mind. If you have never been in love, answer in terms of what you think your responses would most likely be.

FOR EACH STATEMENT:
A = Strongly agree with the statement
B = Moderately agree with the statement
C = Neutral, neither agree nor disagree
D = Moderately disagree with the statement
E = Strongly disagree with the statement

Eros
Measures passionate love as well as intimacy and commitment. It is directly and strongly correlated with satisfaction in a relationship, a major ingredient in relationship success. Eros gives fully, intensely, and takes risks in love; it requires substantial ego strength. Probably reflects secure attachment style.

1. My partner and I were attracted to each other immediately after we first met.
2. My partner and I have the right physical "chemistry" between us.
3. Our lovemaking is very intense and satisfying.
4. I feel that my partner and I were meant for each other.
5. My partner and I became emotionally involved rather quickly.
6. My partner and I really understand each other.
7. My partner fits my ideal standards of physical beauty/handsomeness.

Ludus
Measures love as an interaction game to be played out with diverse partners. Relationships do not have great depth of feeling. Ludus is wary of emotional intensity from others, and has a manipulative or cynical quality to it. Ludus is negatively related to satisfaction in relationships. May reflect avoidant attachment style.

8. I try to keep my partner a little uncertain about my commitment to him/her.
9. I believe that what my partner doesn't know about me won't hurt him/her.
10. I have sometimes had to keep my partner from finding out about other partners.
11. I could get over my affair with my partner pretty easily and quickly.
12. My partner would get upset if he/she knew of some of the things I've done with other people.
13. When my partner gets too dependent on me, I want to back off a little.
14. I enjoy playing the "game of love" with my partner and a number of other partners.

Storge
Reflects an inclination to merge love and friendship. Storgic love is solid, down to earth, presumably enduring. It is evolutionary, not revolutionary, and may take time to develop. It is related to satisfaction in long-term relationships.

15. It is hard for me to say exactly when our friendship turned to love.
16. To be genuine, our love first required caring for a while.
17. I expect to always be friends with my partner.
18. Our love is the best kind because it grew out of a long friendship.
19. Our friendship merged gradually into love over time.
20. Our love is really a deep friendship, not a mysterious, mystical emotion.
21. Our love relationship is the most satisfying because it developed from a good friendship.

Pragma
Reflects logical, "shopping list" love, rational calculation with a focus on desired attributes of a lover. Suited to computer-matched dating. Related to satisfaction in long-term relationships.

22. I considered what my partner was going to become in life before I committed myself to him/her.
23. I tried to plan my life carefully before choosing my partner.
24. In choosing my partner, I believed it was best to love someone with a similar background.
25. A main consideration in choosing my partner was how he/she would reflect on my family.
26. An important factor in choosing my partner was whether or not he/she would be a good parent.
27. One consideration in choosing my partner was how he/she would reflect on my career.
28. Before getting very involved with my partner, I tried to figure out how compatible his/her hereditary background would be with mine in case we ever had children.

Mania
Measures possessive, dependent love. Associated with high emotional expressiveness and disclosure, but low self-esteem; reflects uncertainty of self in the relationship. Negatively associated with relationship satisfaction. May reflect anxious/ambivalent attachment style.

29. When things aren't right with my partner and me, my stomach gets upset.
30. If my partner and I break up, I would get so depressed that I would even think of suicide.
31. Sometimes I get so excited about being in love with my partner that I can't sleep.
32. When my partner doesn't pay attention to me, I feel sick all over.
33. Since I've been in love with my partner, I've had trouble concentrating on anything else.
34. I cannot relax if I suspect that my partner is with someone else.
35. If my partner ignores me for a while, I sometimes do stupid things to try to get his/her attention back.

Agape
Reflects all-giving, selfless, nondemanding love. Associated with altruistic, committed, sexually idealistic love. Like Eros, tends to flare up with "being in love now."

36. I try to always help my partner through difficult times.
37. I would rather suffer myself than let my partner suffer.
38. I cannot be happy unless I place my partner's happiness before my own.
39. I am usually willing to sacrifice my own wishes to let my partner achieve his/hers.
40. Whatever I won is my partner's to use as he/she chooses.
41. When my partner gets angry with me, I still love him/her fully and unconditionally.
42. I would endure all things for the sake of my partner.

Adapted from Hendrick, Love Attitudes Scale

more pragmatic—and more manic. However, men and women seem to be equally passionate and altruistic in their relationships. On the whole, say the Hendricks, the sexes are more similar than different in style.

Personality traits, at least one personality trait, is strongly correlated to love style, the Hendricks have discovered. People with high self-esteem are more apt to endorse eros, but less likely to endorse mania than other groups. "This finding fits with the image of a secure, confident eros lover who moves intensely but with mutuality into a new relationship," they maintain.

When they turned their attention to ongoing relationships, the Hendricks' found that couples who stayed together over the course of their months-long study were more passionate and less game-playing than couples who broke up. "A substantial amount of passionate love" and "a low dose of game-playing" love are key to the development of satisfying relationships—at least among the college kids studied.

YOUR MOTHER MADE YOU DO IT

The love style you embrace, how you treat your partner, may reflect the very first human relationship you ever had—probably with Mom. There is growing evidence supporting "attachment theory," which holds that the rhythms of response by a child's primary care giver affect the development of personality and influence later attachment processes, including adult love relationships.

First put forth by British psychiatrist John Bowlby in the 1960s and elaborated by American psychologist Mary Ainsworth, attachment theory is the culmination of years of painstaking observation of infants and their adult caregivers—and those separated from them—in both natural and experimental situations. Essentially it suggests that there are three major patterns of attachment; they develop within the first year of life and stick with us, all the while reflecting the responsiveness of the caregiver to our needs as helpless infants.

Those whose mothers, or caregivers, were unavailable or unresponsive may grow up to be detached and nonresponsive to others. Their behavior is Avoidant in relationships. A second group takes a more Anxious-Ambivalent approach to relationships, a response set in motion by having mothers they may not have been able to count on—sometimes responsive, other times not. The lucky among us are Secure in attachment, trusting and stable in relationships, probably the result of having had consistently responsive care.

While attachment theory is now driving a great deal of research on children's social, emotional, and cognitive development, University of Denver psychologists Cindy Hazan and Philip Shaver set out not long ago to investigate the possible effect of childhood relationships on adult attachments. First, they developed descriptive statements that reflect each of the three attachment styles. Then they asked people in their community, along with college kids, which statements best describe how they relate to others. They asked, for example, about trust and jealousy, about closeness and desire for reciprocation, about emotional extremes.

The distribution of the three attachment styles has proved to be about the same in grown-ups as in infants, the same among collegians as the fully fledged. More than half of adult respondents call themselves Secure; the rest are split between Avoidant and Ambivalent. Further, their adult attachment patterns predictably reflect the relationship they report with their parents. Secure people generally describe their parents as having been warm and supportive. What's more, these adults predictably differ in success at romantic love. Secure people reported happy, long-lasting relationships. Avoidants rarely found love.

Secure adults are more trusting of their romantic partners and more confident of a partner's love, report Australian psychologists Judith Feeney and Patricia Noller of the University of Queensland. The two surveyed nearly 400 college undergraduates with a questionnaire on family background and love relationships, along with items designed to reveal their personality and related traits.

In contrast to the Secure, Avoidants indicated an aversion to intimacy. The Anxious-Ambivalent participants were characterized by dependency and what Feeney and Noller describe as "a hunger" for commitment. Their approach resembles the Mania style of love. Each of the three groups reported differences in early childhood experience that could account for their adult approach to relationships. Avoidants, for example, were most likely to tell of separations from their mother.

It may be, Hazan and Shaver suggest, that the world's greatest love affairs are conducted by the Ambitious-Ambivalents—people desperately searching for a kind of security they never had.

THE MAGIC NEVER DIES

Not quite two decades into the look at love, it appears as though love will not always mystify us. For already we are beginning to define what we think about it, how it makes us feel, and what we do when we are in love. We now know that it is the insecure, rather than the confident, who fall in love more readily. We know that outside stimuli that alter our emotional state can affect our susceptibility to romance; it is not just the person. We now know that to a certain extent your love style is set by the parenting you received. And, oh yes, men are more quickly romantic than women.

The best news may well be that when it comes to love, men and women are more similar than different. In the face of continuing gender wars, it is comforting to think that men and women share an important, and peaceful, spot of turf. It is also clear that no matter how hard we look at love, we will always be amazed and mesmerized by it.

Rescuing Marriages Before They Begin

By HARA ESTROFF MARANO

CALL it the toilet-seat theory of romance. Whether a man puts the toilet seat down holds a major clue to the success of a marriage: it is a sign that he understands and respects his wife's needs and is open to the kind of giving and taking of influence that leads to long-term marital stability.

Contrary to popular belief, says Dr. John Gottman, a professor of psychology at the University of Washington in Seattle, it is the mundane events of everyday life that build love in marriage. Connecting in the countless "mindless moments" that usually go by unnoticed establishes a positive emotional climate.

That protects partners, helping them to ignore the irritability that typically accompanies a spouse's complaints. In short, it puts a natural cap on the fights that are virtually inevitable in relationships.

With the aid of videotape and sensors that monitor people's bodily responses, Dr. Gottman has spent 25 years scrutinizing what actually goes on in marriages. He has followed 670 couples, from newlyweds to retirees, for up to 14 years. He recently reported his surprising findings at the first conference of the Coalition of Marriage, Family and Couples Education, a newly formed group of counselors and educators.

At the four-day meeting in Arlington, Va., dozens of pioneers in marriage education described new approaches to curtailing family breakdown, not by making divorce more difficult but by making marriage more satisfying for both partners. Only 20 percent of divorces are caused by an affair, Dr. Gottman said; "Most marriages die with a whimper, as people turn away from one another, slowly growing apart."

Diane Sollee, a social worker who is a family therapist, organized the conference after becoming convinced of the limits of therapy for what she sees as normal problems of living. "While the numbers of therapists and access to treatment have increased dramatically in 20 years," she said, "the divorce rate hasn't budged much below 50 percent." The meeting formally recognized a directional shift that has been building largely unnoticed for more than a decade: educating people how to prevent distress long before it starts.

Marriage education not only immunizes couples against disappointment and despair, said Dr. Howard Markman, a psychologist at the University of Denver, it also prevents the development of problems that are costly to children and all of society. Mismanaged conflict, he said, predicts both marital distress and negative physical and mental health effects on children. His studies, conducted at the University of Denver, where he is a professor of psychology, find that marital conflict also leads to decreased work productivity, especially for men.

Contradicting Tolstoy's famous dictum ("Happy families are all alike"), he emphasized that "there are many ways to have a happy marriage, but only a few ways marriages go bad." Having a good relationship is a skill, and the heart of the skill involves ways of speaking, and especially ways of listening to a partner's concerns without counterattacking or defending one's own innocence. "Men have more trouble expressing and hearing negative emotions, and are more reactive to them," Dr. Markman said. "But our studies show that the critical skill in successful relationships is being able to listen to a wife's concerns and complaints about the relationship."

Along with a colleague, Dr. Scott Stanley, Dr. Markman has translated the research into a 12-hour course called PREP, or Prevention and Relationship Enhancement Program. He calls it a Geneva Convention for conflict in marriage. In lectures and coaching sessions, couples learn and practice ground rules for airing complaints so they do not get stuck in the negativity that is so corrosive to love.

In a study in Germany, 64 couples who took PREP are being tracked along with 32 members of a comparison group, 18 who received standard premarital counseling and 14 who received no counseling at all. Five years after the course, given in six weekly sessions of two hours, the PREP couples have a divorce rate of 4 percent. In comparison, 24 percent of the couples in the comparison group have divorced. Those who took PREP also reported half the incidence of physical aggression.

One reason that adults lack necessary relationship skills, said Dr. Sherod Miller, a psychologist in Littleton, Colo., is that their world has turned turbulent. "In my lifetime, couples have gone from taking roles precast by the culture along gender lines" to making roles according to their needs, Dr. Miller said. As a result, everything couples do every day is open to negotiation, especially after the first baby arrives, when marital satisfaction "drops precipitously" for 75 percent of them.

Dr. Miller has developed a Couples Communication course that is taught to mental health professionals around the country. They, in turn, set up private classes for couples in their areas.

Professionals, however, are not the only experts imparting vital information on relationships. Two separate programs are recruiting "marriage mentors," experienced older couples in a community who can be available for general guidance to younger couples and provide a realistic picture of married life. Dr. Leslie Parrott, who is co-director of a marriage mentor program in Seattle, said, "The point of mentoring is not to give answers but to tell your story: this is what works for us, this hasn't." Dr. Parrott and her husband, Dr. Les Parrott, both associate professors of psychology at Seattle Pacific University, are founders of the university's Center for Relationship Development, and established a marriage mentor program five years ago that is now citywide.

In a follow-up study in which they traced 150 of 300 couples mentored in the past five years, the Parrots said they found not a single instance of divorce. Yet another new effort to save marriages early is the community marriage policy. Religious institutions of all denominations in a community sign an agreement to perform weddings only for couples who undergo training in communication and conflict resolution. The goal is to affect as many couples as possible, since 74 percent of marriages are performed by the clergy. So far, 64 cities have instituted a marriage policy. The most recent one was signed last month for Minneapolis-St. Paul.

Learning skills for everyday life can head off divorce.

It is a mistake to confine divorce prevention to the religious realm, Judge James E. Sheridan of Adrian, Mich., told conferees; it is a civic matter. All taxpayers bear the expenses of family breakdown. He has initiated America's first total community marriage policy, involving judges and magistrates as well as members of the clergy. Starting next week, all couples seeking a marriage license in Lenawee County, Mich., will first have to receive marital education by a certified professional. "All I'm asking is that couples be responsible," Judge Sheridan said.

Dr. David H. Olson, a professor of family psychology at the University of Minnesota, has developed a 165-item questionnaire, called Prepare, that partners fill out independently of each other. Extensively refined and tested, the questionnaire inventories attitudes that have been found important in relationships, like "My partner would not make an important decision without consulting me" and "I wish my partner were more willing to share his/her feelings with me." Variations of the questionnaire have been developed for married couples, step-families, and, most recently, high-school students.

In one study, 10 percent of engaged couples given the questionnaire decided against marriage. Their scores proved to be in the same range as those of couples who ultimately divorced, Dr. Olson reported.

To be really effective, education about relationships should begin in high school, Dr. Olson believes. In just the last two years, three programs started independently began offering programs in high schools around the country. All include conflict-resolution and problem-solving skills. One, called Partners, was developed by a divorce lawyer, Lynne Gold-Bikan, during her tenure as head of the family-law division of the American Bar Association.

In the beginning, said Dr. Miller, there was psychoanalysis. Then there was psychotherapy. And now we are entering the era of psychoeducation.

"It is now possible to give people an idea of how things really work in a marriage," said Dr. Gottman, who has created a course for couples: the Marriage Survival Kit. "We can prevent marital meltdown."

For couples who are seeking to avert a meltdown, a nationwide directory of marriage-education courses is accessible on the Internet (www.his.com/~cmfce/).

Prejudice, Discrimination, and Stereotyping

Prejudice (Articles 27 and 28)
Discrimination (Articles 29–31)
Stereotyping (Articles 32 and 33)

In colonial America, relatively few people were allowed to vote. Women could not. Blacks could not. Even white men, if they lacked property, could not. It took many years, the Civil War, and the passage of constitutional amendments for this particular form of discrimination to eventually pass from the scene. Even so, many would argue today that discrimination against women, minorities, and those at the lower end of the economic spectrum continues, although usually in less obvious forms. The tendency for humans to make negative judgments about others on the basis of their membership in some social group, and then to act on those judgments, is a powerful one.

As the title implies, this unit covers three distinct but related topics: prejudice, discrimination, and stereotyping. *Prejudice* refers to the negative attitude that is directed toward some people simply because they are members of some particular social group. Thus, the feelings of distaste that one might experience when encountering a member of some minority group would be an example of prejudice. In such a case, the prejudiced feelings would also probably influence the way in which our hypothetical person evaluated and judged everything that the minority group member did. In contrast, *discrimination* refers to a negative action directed toward the members of some particular social group. That is, while prejudice refers only to negative feelings, discrimination crosses the line into actual behavior. Thus, yelling a racial slur, or failing to hire someone because of her religion, would be examples of discrimination. As you might imagine, however, those who hold prejudiced attitudes are generally more likely to engage in discriminatory behavior as well. The third concept—*stereotyping*—is more cognitive in tone than the other two. Stereotyping refers to the tendency that people have to see all members of a specific social group as being alike—that is, to not recognize the differences that exist and to exaggerate the similarities. Thus, stereotypes per se are distinct from the negative feelings and negative behavior that characterize prejudice and discrimination.

The first unit subsection considers the topic of prejudice, and both articles are concerned with a recent and highly influential approach to studying prejudice. In "Prejudice Is a Habit That Can Be Broken," Beth Azar reports on research suggesting that everyone—prejudiced and nonprejudiced alike—is aware of racial stereotypes and has that knowledge automatically activated by encountering a member of that race. What distinguishes prejudiced and nonprejudiced people is what comes next; prejudiced people largely accept those stereotypes and act on them, while nonprejudiced people consciously inhibit these initial responses and substitute other, more tolerant values. In the second selection, "Breaking the Prejudice Habit," psychologist Patricia Devine takes this argument a bit further and describes some of her own research that supports the idea that nonprejudiced people often find themselves wrestling with conflicting impulses: their immediate prejudiced reaction and their conscious rejection of that response.

The second subsection tackles the issue of discrimination. In "Crimes against Humanity," Ward Churchill makes the case that the actual language used to describe members of social groups can help perpetuate racial and ethnic prejudice. To illustrate, he offers numerous examples of the ways in which Native Americans are routinely demeaned in U.S. society, especially in the area of sports symbolism. The second selection, "Study: Racism Is Health Risk to Black Americans," examines what some of the effects might be on the person who is discriminated against. Recent research suggests that such discrimination might even constitute a health risk to minorities by increasing heart rate and blood pressure. In "Societal Values Dictate Job Paths for Women," Tori DeAngelis describes some work on "social dominance" theory. This theory argues that women are frequently channeled into particular types of jobs because employers believe that such jobs are a good fit with women's stereotypical values. This article summarizes some recent work supporting this view.

The third subsection consists of two articles that address stereotyping. The first, "Minorities' Performance Is Hampered by Stereotypes" describes some research by Claude Steele that indicates that the very *existence* of a negative stereotype about some group can hinder that group's performance. The article also describes some interventions that successfully counteract such "stereotype threat." The final selection, "Who Is a Whiz Kid?" provides

UNIT 7

a first-person account of what it is like to be saddled with *positive* rather than negative stereotypes.

Looking Ahead: Challenge Questions

What kind of evidence supports the view that both prejudiced and nonprejudiced people are familiar with negative racial stereotypes? Do you agree that nonprejudiced people must deliberately and consciously attempt to substitute tolerant values for their own unconscious stereotyped beliefs? Does this research suggest any possible solutions to the problem of prejudice in society?

How much power does the use of racially demeaning language have in perpetuating prejudice and discrimination? What did you find to be the most convincing evidence in the article "Crimes against Humanity"? The least convincing?

Not all discrimination is blatant. What subtle forms of discrimination can you identify in today's society toward women, minorities, or any other group? Is any form of discrimination ever justified?

What are all the ways (positive and negative) that stereotypes can affect the individual who is being stereotyped?

Prejudice Is a Habit That Can Be Broken

Peoples' responses are based on cultural stereotypes, even if they don't believe in those stereotypes.

Beth Azar

Monitor staff

A black youth sits next to you on an empty subway car. An openly gay man interviews with you for a job in your office. A Hispanic woman asks you for directions. How should you react? How *do* you react?

Few people openly admit they should or would react with prejudice to situations like these. And yet, blatant and more subtle forms of prejudice occur every day. People may withhold promotions from minority persons or may be less willing to give directions or the time of day to someone of a different race.

Even people who score low on the Modern Racism Scale—a widely used test of prejudice—tend to show subtle bias when interacting with certain ethnic groups. They may avoid eye contact and physical closeness or act less friendly.

Automatic Prejudice

Some people claim that prejudice hasn't actually declined over the past 20 years, but is just better disguised. Several researchers addressed these problems and potential solutions in symposia on prejudice and stereotyping.

A powerful technique lets researchers "get inside the heads of subjects" and record subtle unconscious or unadmitted biases, said Russell Fazio, PhD, of Indiana University. The technique, called "priming," records people's subconscious reactions to stimuli.

Subjects are primed by a word or picture, then asked to respond to another stimulus—often a word. For example, a prime could be the face of a white person. After researchers show subjects the face, they ask them to perform certain tasks. The subjects may have to judge adjectives as positive or negative or fill in missing letters to form words.

Priming is based on the idea that thinking of a word activates a spot in the brain where the word is stored as well as connections to other words and ideas related to that word.

So after seeing a prime word people access terms or ideas related to the prime faster than terms or ideas unrelated to the prime. For example, if people are primed with "dog" they will be faster at recognizing "cat" than "car." Researchers get this priming effect even if the prime is shown so quickly that the subject doesn't remember seeing it.

Researchers find prejudicial reactions in many people after numerous priming tasks—even people who claim not to be prejudiced. For example, people primed with a photo of an Asian person holding a sign that says "N_P" most often fill in the blank letter with an "i" to spell NIP—a derogatory term for Asians.

In a recent experiment, Fazio and his colleagues briefly presented high-resolution color images of black and white faces, then had subjects identify obviously positive or negative adjectives as positive or negative by pressing one of two buttons. For example, a subject would see "attractive" and would press the "positive" button. The faster the response, the more related the adjective would be to the prime in the subjects' mind.

They found a highly significant interaction between the race of the person in the photo and the speed of subjects' reaction to positive and negative adjectives. When white subjects saw a black face and then a negative adjective, they responded faster than when they saw a white face. The opposite occurred for positive adjectives.

On average, whites displayed negativity toward blacks, and vice versa, said Fazio. However, there were many individual differences, with some white subjects reacting highly negatively toward blacks and others reacting as positively toward blacks as blacks themselves.

They found that the automatic responses in white subjects predicted subtle nonverbal behaviors in a 10-minute, one-on-one interaction with a black experimenter. The experimenter rated subjects on friendliness, paying attention to such nonverbal behaviors as eye contact, personal distance and smiling. People's scores correlated with their scores on the priming task.

These subtle prejudicial responses don't necessarily mean people will act in an openly biased fashion. Fazio and other prejudice researchers have found that some people are motivated

'Powerful' People are More Apt to Stereotype

People stereotype other races and cultures to preserve a sense of self and a feeling of personal power, according to research by Steven Spencer, PhD, and Susan Fiske, PhD.

Spencer, of the State University of New York, Buffalo, conducted a series of studies that put subjects in situations that threatened their self-esteem. In one study, subjects took an intelligence test and received either a positive or negative score manipulated by the experimenter. The experimenters rated the subjects' self-esteem using a standard questionnaire. Then subjects rated the qualifications of a hypothetical Jewish-American woman for a job.

Subjects who thought they'd scored low on the intelligence test more often rated the job candidate negatively. A self-esteem test taken afterward showed significant increases in self-esteem after subjects engaged in stereotyping.

He also found that people were more likely to stereotype in such self-esteem–threatening situations if they scored high on the Modern Racism Scale—a standard questionnaire.

"Stereotyping seems to be automatic for some people when they sense a threat to their self-esteem," said Spencer.

Fiske theorizes that people in positions of power tend to engage in more stereotyping. The powerful—bosses, supervisors, managers—are rarely stereotyped themselves because power demands attention and stereotyping demands that one not pay attention.

Two processes make the powerful prone to stereotyping others, said Fiske, of the University of Massachusetts, Amherst. First, because they're powerful, they stereotype by default—they simply don't pay attention to information that makes people unique. Second, when the powerful must justify decisions they make about other people, they stereotype by design. They don't have time to see people as unique so they hear and see only things that confirm their stereotypes.

To test these theories, Fiske and graduate student Stephanie Goodwin had subjects judge hypothetical job applicants. Half of the subjects were given a lot of power in the decision and half were given little power. They reviewed applications from a Hispanic and a white woman.

They found that subjects with the most decision-making power paid less attention to individualizing information and more attention to stereotype-confirming information. For example, the powerful would ignore personal references about the Hispanic woman's efficiency and pay particular attention to references that implied she was ignorant or unreliable. As power increased, use of stereotyping information increased, said Fiske.

The researchers conducted a second study examining whether a dominant personality had any effect on stereotyping. All the subjects had equal power but the researchers found that people with dominant personalities ignored individualizing information and paid particular attention to stereotyping information, just as the powerful subjects had in the previous study.

Fiske imagines the powerful driving around in a fog and tuned into one radio station—the one that confirms their stereotypes.

—Beth Azar

---

to control overt prejudice depending on the situation. For example, people will temper their answers to the Modern Racism Scale to look less prejudice if the interviewer is black.

There seem to be three types of people: those who are openly prejudiced and show it in their overt and covert actions; those who believe they are not prejudiced and try to act that way, but show some covert signs of bias; and those who believe they are not prejudiced and whose covert actions show no signs of bias.

Not Just Attitude

Patricia Devine, PhD, believes that breaking down prejudice is a process. Like every bad habit, it goes away in stages. Devine is professor of psychology at the University of Wisconsin, Madison. She believes people's responses are based on cultural stereotypes, even if they don't believe in those stereotypes. Low-prejudice people are especially vulnerable to conflict between their beliefs and unintentional responses, said Devine. She asked high- and low-prejudice people how they thought they should respond in interactions with people of different races or sexual orientation.

She then gave them a set of hypothetical interactions and asked them how they would respond in certain situations. She asked, for example, if they would feel uncomfortable being interviewed by a gay man, a black man or a woman. As expected, low-prejudice people thought they should, and would, respond with less prejudice than high-prejudice people did.

However, many low-prejudice people admitted they would respond with more prejudice than they thought they should. When asked how subjects felt immediately after they answered the questions, low-prejudice people who saw a discrepancy between their beliefs and their actions felt guilty, annoyed, and frustrated and were critical of themselves.

The bigger the discrepancy between beliefs and actions, the more people engaged in guilt and other self-directed negative responses. She takes this as evidence that many people who claim to be unprejudiced truly don't want to be.

To test whether self-directed negative responses can help people overcome automatic prejudiced responses, she tested people's responses to racial jokes. She had subjects listen to racial jokes and had those who laughed compare their response to their beliefs about prejudice. The low-prejudice people felt guilty and, as a result, found a second set of jokes less amusing.

"The comparison activates a self-regulatory process," said Devine. "If people don't recognize the discrepancy, however, they won't feel guilt and this process won't activate." Her work shows that even people with a nonprejudice attitude often fail to bring their behaviors in line. "Prejudice appears to be a habit that can be broken," said Devine. "We need to teach people to become skilled rather than try to change their attitudes."

Breaking the Prejudice Habit

Patricia G. Devine, PhD,
University of Wisconsin, Madison

Patricia G. Devine, PhD, is Professor of Psychology at the University of Wisconsin, Madison. Before becoming Professor, she was a Visiting Fellow at Yale University and an Associate Professor at Wisconsin.

Dr. Devine received the Gordon Allport Intergroup Relations Prize from the Society for the Psychological Study of Social Issues in 1990 and the APA Distinguished Scientific Award for Early Career Contribution to Psychology in 1994. She is the author or coauthor of several journal articles and is the coeditor of *Social Cognition: Impact on Social Psychology* (Academic Press, 1994). Her research interests include prejudice and intergroup relations, stereotyping, dissonance, and resistance to persuasion. Dr. Devine received her PhD in Social Psychology from Ohio State University in 1986.

Legal scholars, politicians, legislators, social scientists, and lay people alike have puzzled over the paradox of racism in a nation founded on the fundamental principle of human equality. Legislators responded with landmark legal decisions (e.g., Supreme Court ruling on school desegregation and the Civil Rights laws) that made overt discrimination based on race illegal. In the wake of the legislative changes, social scientists examined the extent to which shifts in whites' attitudes kept pace with the legal changes. The literature, however, reveals conflicting findings. Whereas overt expressions of prejudice on surveys declined (i.e., verbal reports), more subtle indicators (i.e., nonverbal measures) continue to reveal prejudice even among those who say they renounced prejudice. A central challenge presented to contemporary prejudice researchers is to explain the disparity between verbal reports and the more subtle measures.

Some reject the optimistic conclusion suggested by survey research and argue that prejudice in America is not declining; it is only changing form—becoming more subtle and disguised. By this argument, most (if not all) Americans are assumed to be racist, with only the *type* of racism differing between people. Such conclusions are based on the belief that *any* response that results in differential treatment between groups is taken as evidence of prejudice. However, this definition fails to consider *intent* or motive and is based on the assumption that nonthoughtful (e.g., nonverbal) responses are, by definition, more trustworthy than thoughtful responses. Indeed, nonverbal measures are assumed to be good indicators of prejudice precisely because they do not typically involve careful thought and people do not control them in the same way that they can control their verbally reported attitudes.

Rather than dismiss either response as necessarily untrustworthy, my colleagues and I have tried to understand the origin of both thoughtful and nonthoughtful responses. By directly addressing the disparity between thoughtful and nonthoughtful responses, our approach offers a more optimistic analysis regarding prospects for prejudice reduction than the extant formulations. To foreshadow, our program of research has been devoted to understanding (a) how and why those who truly renounce prejudice may continue to experience prejudice-like thoughts and feelings and (b) the nature of the rather formidable challenges and obstacles that must be overcome before one can succeed in reducing the disparity between thoughtful and nonthoughtful responses.

Automatic and Controlled Processes in Prejudice

The distinction between automatic and controlled cognitive processes has been central to our analysis in prejudice reduction. Automatic processes occur unintentionally, spontaneously, and unconsciously. We have evidence that both low- and high-prejudiced people are vulnerable to automatic stereotype activation. Once the stereotype is well-learned, its influence is hard to avoid because it so easily comes to mind. Controlled processes, in contrast, are under the intentional control of the individual. An important aspect of such processes is that their initiation and use requires time and sufficient cognitive *capacity*. Nonprejudiced responses require inhibiting the spontaneously activated stereotypes and deliberately activating personal beliefs to serve as the basis for responses. Without sufficient time or cognitive capacity, responses may well be stereotype-based and, therefore, appear prejudiced.

The important implication of the automatic/controlled process distinction is that if one looks only at nonthoughtful, automatic responses, one may well conclude that all white Americans are prejudiced. We have found important differences between low- and high-prejudiced people based on the personal beliefs that each hold, despite similar knowledge of and vulnerability to the activation of cultural stereotypes. Furthermore, low-prejudiced people have established and internalized nonprejudiced personal standards for how to treat members of stereotyped groups. When given sufficient time, low-prejudiced people censor responses based on the stereotype and, instead, respond based on their beliefs. High-prejudiced people, in contrast, do not reject the stereotype and are not personally motivated to overcome its effect on their behavior.

A strength of this approach is that it delineates the role of both thoughtful and nonthoughtful processes in response to stereotyped group members. Eliminating prejudice requires overcoming a lifetime of socialization experiences, which, unfortunately, promote prejudice. We have likened reducing prejudice to the breaking of a habit in that people must first make a decision to eliminate the habit and then *learn* to inhibit the habitual (prejudiced) responses. Thus, the change from being prejudiced to nonprejudiced is not viewed as an all or none event, but as a process during which the low-prejudiced person is especially vulnerable to conflict between his or her enduring negative responses and endorsed nonprejudiced beliefs. For those who renounce prejudice, overcoming the "prejudice habit" presents a formidable task that is likely to entail a great deal of internal conflict over a protracted period of time.

Prejudice With and Without Compunction

In subsequent work, we examined the nature and consequences of the internal conflict associated with prejudice reduction. Specifically, we have focused on the challenges faced by those individuals who have internalized nonprejudiced personal standards and are trying to control their prejudiced responses, but sometimes fail. We have shown that people high and low in prejudice (as assessed by a self-report technique) have qualitatively different affective reactions to the conflict between their verbal reports concerning how they *should* respond in situations involving contact with members of stereotyped groups and how they say they actually *would* respond. Low-prejudiced people, for example, believe that they should not feel uncomfortable sitting next to an African American on a bus. High-prejudiced people disagree, indicating that it's acceptable to feel uncomfortable in this situation. When actual responses violate personal standards, low-prejudiced people experience guilt or "prejudice with compunction," but high-prejudiced individuals do not. For low-prejudiced people, the coexistence of such conflicting reactions threatens their nonprejudiced self-concepts. Moreover, these guilt feelings play a functional role in helping people to "break the prejudice habit." That is, violations combined with guilt have been shown to help low-prejudiced people to use controlled processes to inhibit the prejudiced responses and to replace them with responses that are based on their personal beliefs.

Interpersonal Dynamics of Intergroup Contact

Until recently, our research has focused rather exclusively on the nature of internal conflict associated with prejudice reduction efforts. However, many of the challenges associated with prejudice reduction are played out in the interpersonal arena, and we believe it's important to explore the relevance of our work to issues of intergroup tension. Thus, one of our current lines of research is devoted to exploring the nature of the challenges created by the intergroup contact when people's standards are "put on the line."

In interpersonal intergroup contact situations, we have found that although low-prejudiced people are highly motivated to respond without prejudice, there are few guidelines for "how to do the intergroup thing well." As a result, many experience doubt and uncertainty about how to express their nonprejudiced attitudes in intergroup situations. Thus, for low-prejudiced people, their high motivation to respond without prejudice may actually interfere with their efforts to convey accurately their nonprejudiced intentions. Under these circumstances, they become socially anxious; this anxiety disrupts the typically smooth and coordinated aspects of social interaction. Their interaction styles become awkward and strained resulting in nonverbal behaviors such as decreased eye contact and awkward speech patterns. These are exactly the types of subtle responses that have typically been interpreted as signs of prejudice or antipathy. Indeed, it is not possible to distinguish between the type of tension that arises out of antipathy toward the group or social anxiety based on these signs alone.

We argue that it may be important to acknowledge that there are qualitatively distinct forms of intergroup tension experienced by majority group members, which are systematically related to their self-reported level of prejudice. For some, the tension can arise out of antipathy, as was always thought in the prejudice literature, but for others, the tension arises out of anxiety over trying to do the intergroup thing well. Functionally then, we have different starting points for trying to reduce intergroup tension. Strategies for attempting to reduce intergroup tension differ when the problem is conceived as one of improving skills rather than one of changing negative attitudes.

Conclusion

To sum up, although it is not easy and clearly requires effort, time, and practice, prejudice appears to be a habit that can be broken. In contrast to the prevailing, pessimistic opinion that little progress is being made toward the alleviation of prejudice, our program of research suggests that many people appear to be embroiled in the difficult or arduous process of overcoming their prejudices. During this process, low-prejudiced people are confronted with rather formidable challenges from within, as people battle their spontaneous reactions, and from the interpersonal settings in which people's standards are put on the line. We are sanguine that by developing a realistic analysis of the practical challenges faced by those who renounce prejudice, we may be able to identify strategies that may facilitate their prejudice reduction efforts.

It is important to recognize that we are not claiming to have solved the problem of intergroup prejudice, nor are we suggesting that prejudice has disappeared. The past several years have witnessed a disturbing increase in the incidence of hate crimes against minorities. And a sizable proportion of white Americans continue to embrace old-fashioned forms of bigotry. Nevertheless, we hope that by developing an understanding of the challenges associated with breaking the prejudice habit, we may gain insight into the reasons low-prejudiced people establish and internalize nonprejudiced standards. Armed with this knowledge, we may be able to encourage high-prejudiced people to renounce prejudice. And when they do, we will be in a better position to understand their challenges and, perhaps, to assist them in their efforts,

Crimes Against Humanity

If nifty little "pep" gestures like the "Indian Chant" and the "Tomahawk Chop" are just good clean fun, then let's spread the fun around, shall we?

Ward Churchill

During the past couple of seasons, there has been an increasing wave of controversy regarding the names of professional sports teams like the Atlanta "Braves," Cleveland "Indians," Washington "Redskins," and Kansas City "Chiefs." The issue extends to the names of college teams like Florida State University "Seminoles," University of Illinois "Fighting Illini," and so on, right on down to high school outfits like the Lamar (Colorado) "Savages." Also involved have been team adoption of "mascots," replete with feathers, buckskins, beads, spears and "warpaint" (some fans have opted to adorn themselves in the same fashion), and nifty little "pep" gestures like the "Indian Chant" and "Tomahawk Chop."

A substantial number of American Indians have protested that use of native names, images and symbols as sports team mascots and the like is, by definition, a virulently racist practice. Given the historical relationship between Indians and non-Indians during what has been called the "Conquest of America," American Indian Movement leader (and American Indian Anti-Defamation Council founder) Russell Means has compared the practice to contemporary Germans naming their soccer teams the "Jews," "Hebrews," and "Yids," while adorning their uniforms with grotesque caricatures of Jewish faces taken from the Nazis' anti-Semitic propaganda of the 1930s. Numerous demonstrations have occurred in conjunction with games—most notably during the November 15, 1992 match-up between the Chiefs and Redskins in Kansas City—by angry Indians and their supporters.

In response, a number of players—especially African Americans and other minority athletes—have been trotted out by professional team owners like Ted Turner, as well as university and public school officials, to announce that they mean not to insult but to honor native people. They have been joined by the television networks and most major newspapers, all of which have editorialized that Indian discomfort with the situation is "no big deal," insisting that the whole thing is just "good, clean fun." The country needs more such fun, they've argued, and "a few disgruntled Native Americans" have no right to undermine the nation's enjoyment of its leisure time by complaining. This is especially the case, some have argued, "in hard times like these." It has even been contended that Indian outrage at being systematically degraded—rather than the degradation itself—creates "a serious barrier to the sort of intergroup communication so necessary in a multicultural society such as ours."

Okay, let's communicate. We are frankly dubious that those advancing such positions really believe their own rhetoric, but, just for the sake of argument, let's accept the premise that they are sincere. If what they say is true, then isn't it time we spread such "inoffensiveness" and "good cheer" around among *all* groups so that *everybody* can participate *equally* in fostering the round of national laughs they call for? Sure it is—the country can't have too much fun or "intergroup involvement—so the more, the merrier. Simple consistency demands that anyone who thinks the Tomahawk Chop is a swell pastime must be just as hearty in their endorsement of the following ideas—by the logic used to defend the defamation of American Indians—should help us all really start yukking it up.

First, as a counterpart to the Redskins, we need an NFL team called "Niggers" to honor Afro-Americans. Halftime festivities for fans might include a simulated stewing of the opposing coach in a large pot while players and cheerleaders dance around it, garbed in leopard skins and wearing fake bones in their noses. This concept obviously goes along with the kind of gaiety attending the Chop, but also with the actions of the Kansas City Chiefs, whose team members—prominently including black team members—lately appeared on a poster looking "fierce" and "savage" by way of wearing Indian regalia. Just a bit of harmless "morale boosting," says the Chiefs' front office. You bet.

So that the newly-formed Niggers sports club won't end up too out of sync while expressing the "spirit" and "identity" of Afro-Americans in the above fashion, a baseball franchise—let's call this one the "Sambos"—should be formed. How about a basketball team called the "Spearchuckers?" A hockey team called the "Jungle Bunnies?" Maybe the "essence" of these teams could be depicted by images of tiny black faces adorned with huge pairs of lips. The players could appear on TV every week or so gnawing on chicken legs and spitting watermelon seeds at one another. Catchy, eh? Well, there's "nothing to be upset about," according to those who love wearing "war bonnets" to the Super Bowl or having "Chief Illiniwik" dance around the sports arenas of Urbana, Illinois.

And why stop there? There are plenty of other groups to include. "Hispanics?" They can be "represented" by the Galveston "Greasers" and San Diego "Spics," at least until the Wisconsin "Wetbacks" and Baltimore "Beaners" get off the ground. Asian Americans? How about the "Slopes," "Dinks," "Gooks," and "Zipperheads?" Owners of the latter teams might get their logo ideas from editorial page cartoons printed in the nation's newspapers during World War II: slant-eyes, buck teeth, big glasses, but nothing racially insulting or derogatory, according to the editors and artists involved at the time. Indeed, this Second World War-vintage stuff can be seen as just another barrel of laughs, at least by what current editors say are their "local standards" concerning American Indians.

Let's see. Who's been left out? Teams like the Kansas City "Kikes," Hanover "Honkies," San Leandro "Shylocks," Daytona "Dagos," and Pittsburgh "Polacks" will fill a certain social void among white folk.

Cleveland "Indians"

Have a religious belief? Let's all go for the gusto and gear up the Milwaukee "Mackerel Snappers" and Hollywood "Holy Rollers." The Fighting Irish of Notre Dame can be rechristened the "Drunken Irish" or "Papist Pigs." Issues of gender and sexual preference can be addressed through creation of teams like the St. Louis "Sluts," Boston "Bimbos," Detroit "Dykes," and the Fresno "Fags." How about the Gainesville "Gimps" and Richmond "Retards," so the physically and mentally impaired won't be excluded from our fun and games?

Now, don't go getting "overly sensitive" out there. None of this is demeaning or insulting, at least not when it's being done to Indians. Just ask the folks who are doing it, or their apologists like Andy Rooney in the national media. They'll tell you—as in fact they *have* been telling you—that there's been no harm done, regardless of what their victims think, feel, or say. The situation is exactly the same as when those with precisely the same mentality used to insist that Step 'n' Fetchit was okay, or Rochester on the Jack Benny Show, or Amos and Andy, Charlie Chan, the Frito Bandito, or any of the other cutsey symbols making up the lexicon of American racism. Have we communicated yet?

Let's get just a little bit real here. The notion of "fun" embodied in rituals like the Tomahawk Chop must be understood for what it is. There's not a single non-Indian example used above which can be considered socially acceptable in even the most marginal sense. The reasons are obvious enough. So why is it different where American Indians are concerned? One can only conclude that, in contrast to the other groups at issue, Indians are (falsely) perceived as being too few, and therefore too weak, to defend themselves effectively against racist and otherwise offensive behavior.

Fortunately, there are some glimmers of hope. A few teams and their fans have gotten the message and have responded appropriately. Stanford University, which opted to drop the name "Indians" from Stanford, has experienced no resulting drop-off in attendance. Meanwhile, the local newspaper in Portland, Oregon recently decided its long-standing editorial policy prohibiting use of racial epithets should include derogatory team names. The Redskins, for instance, are now referred to as "the Washington team," and will continue to be described in this way until the franchise adopts an inoffensive moniker (newspaper sales in Portland have suffered no decline as a result).

Such examples are to be applauded and encouraged. They stand as figurative beacons in the night, proving beyond all doubt that it is quite possible to indulge in the pleasure of athletics without accepting blatant racism into the bargain.

Yuma "Indians"

Nuremberg Precedents

On October 16, 1946, a man named Julius Streicher mounted the steps of a gallows. Moments later he was dead, the sentence of an international tribunal composed of representatives of the United States, France, Great Britain, and the Soviet Union having been imposed. Streicher's body was then cremated, and—so horrendous were his crimes thought to have been—his ashes dumped into an unspecified German river so that "no one should ever know a particular place to go for reasons of mourning his memory."

Julius Streicher had been convicted at Nuremberg, Germany of what were termed "Crimes Against Humanity." The lead prosecutor in his case—Justice Robert Jackson of the United States Supreme Court—had not argued that the defendant had killed anyone, nor that he had personally committed any especially violent act. Nor was it contended that Streicher had held any particularly important position in the German government during the period in which the so-called Third Reich had exterminated some 6,000,000 Jews, as well as several million Gypsies, Poles, Slavs, homosexuals, and other untermenschen (subhumans).

The sole offense for which the accused was ordered put to death was in having served as publisher/editor of a Bavarian tabloid entitled *Der Sturmer* during the early-to-mid 1930s, years before the Nazi genocide actually began. In this capacity, he had penned a long series of virulently anti-Semitic editorials and "news" stories, usually accompanied by cartoons and other images graphically depicting Jews in extraordinarily derogatory fashion. This, the prosecution asserted, had done much to "dehumanize" the targets of his distortion in the mind of the German public. In turn, such dehumanization had made it possible—or at least easier—for average Germans to later indulge in the outright liquidation of Jewish "vermin." The tribunal agreed, holding that Streicher was therefore complicit in genocide and deserving of death by hanging.

During his remarks to the Nuremberg tribunal, Justice Jackson observed that, in implementing its sentences, the participating powers were morally and legally binding themselves to adhere forever after to the same standards of conduct that were being applied to Streicher and the other Nazi leaders. In the alternative, he said, the victorious allies would have committed "pure murder" at Nuremberg—no different in substance from that carried out by those they presumed to judge—rather than establishing the "permanent benchmark for justice" which was intended.

Yet in the United States of Robert Jackson, the indigenous American Indian population had already been reduced, in a process which is ongoing to this day, from perhaps 12.5 million in the year 1500 to fewer than 250,000 by the beginning of the 20th century. This was accomplished, according to official sources, "largely through the cruelty of [EuroAmerican] settlers," and an informal but clear governmental policy which had made it an articulated goal to "exterminate these red vermin," or at least whole segments of them.

Bounties had been placed on the scalps of Indians—any Indians—in places as diverse as Georgia, Kentucky, Texas, the Dakotas, Oregon, and California, and had been maintained until resident Indian populations were decimated or disappeared altogether. Entire peoples such as the Cherokee had been reduced to half their size through a policy of forced removal from their homelands east of the Mississippi River to what were then considered less preferable areas in the West.

Others, such as the Navajo, suffered the same fate while under military guard for years on end. The

United States Army had also perpetrated a long series of wholesale massacres of Indians at places like Horseshoe Bend, Bear River, Sand Creek, the Washita River, the Marias River, Camp Robinson, and Wounded Knee.

Through it all, hundreds of popular novels—each competing with the next to make Indians appear more grotesque, menacing, and inhuman—were sold in the tens of millions of copies in the U.S. Plainly, the Euro-American public was being conditioned to see Indians in such a way as to allow their eradication to continue. And continue it did until the Manifest Destiny of the U.S.—a direct precursor to what Hitler would subsequently call Lebensraumpolitik (the politics of living space)—was consummated.

By 1900, the national project of "clearing" Native Americans from their land and replacing them with "superior" Anglo-American settlers was complete; the indigenous population had been reduced by as much as 98 percent while approximately 97.5 percent of their original territory had "passed" to the invaders. The survivors had been concentrated, out of sight and mind of the public, on scattered "reservations," all of them under the self-assigned "plenary" (full) power of the federal government. There was, of course, no Nuremberg-style tribunal passing judgment on those who had fostered such circumstances in North America. No U.S. official or private citizen was ever imprisoned—never mind hanged—for implementing or propagandizing what had been done. Nor had the process of genocide afflicting Indians been completed. Instead, it merely changed form.

Between the 1880s and the 1980s, nearly half of all Native American children were coercively transferred from their own families, communities, and cultures to those of the conquering society. This was done through compulsory attendance at remote boarding schools, often hundreds of miles from their homes, where native children were kept for years on end while being systematically "deculturated" (indoctrinated to think and act in the manner of Euro Americans rather than as Indians). It was also accomplished through a pervasive foster home and adoption program—including "blind" adoptions, where children would be permanently denied information as to who they were/are and where they'd come from—placing native youths in non-Indian homes.

Westminster "Warriors"

The express purpose of all this was to facilitate a U.S. governmental policy to bring about the "assimilation" (dissolution) of indigenous societies. In other words, Indian cultures as such were to be caused to disappear. Such policy objectives are directly contrary to the United Nations 1948 Convention on Punishment and Prevention of the Crime of Genocide, an element of international law arising from the Nuremberg proceedings. The forced "transfer of the children" of a targeted "racial, ethnical, or religious group" is explicitly prohibited as a genocidal activity under the Convention's second article.

Article II of the Genocide Convention also expressly prohibits involuntary sterilization as a means of "preventing births among" a targeted population. Yet, in 1975, it was conceded by the U.S. government that its Indian Health Service (IHS) then a subpart of the Bureau of Indian Affairs (BIA), was even then conducting a secret program of involuntary sterilization that had affected approximately 40 percent of all Indian women. The program was allegedly discontinued, and the IHS was transferred to the Public Health Service, but no one was punished. In 1990, it came out that the IHS was inoculating Inuit children in Alaska with Hepatitis-B vaccine. The vaccine had already been banned by the World Health Organization as having a demonstrated correlation with the HIV-Syndrome which is itself correlated to AIDS. As this is written, a "field test" of Hepatitis-A vaccine, also HIV-correlated, is being conducted on Indian reservations in the northern plains region.

The Genocide Convention makes it a "crime against humanity" to create conditions leading to the destruction of an identifiable human group, as such. Yet the BIA has utilized the government's plenary prerogatives to negotiate mineral leases "on behalf of" Indian peoples paying a fraction of standard royalty rates. The result has been "super profits" for a number of preferred U.S. corporations. Meanwhile, Indians, whose reservations ironically turned out to be in some of the most mineral-rich areas of North America, which makes us, the nominally wealthiest segment of the continent's population, live in dire poverty.

By the government's own data in the mid-1980s, Indians received the lowest annual and lifetime per capita incomes of any aggregate population group in the United States. Concomitantly, we suffer the highest rate of infant mortality, death by exposure and malnutrition, disease, and the like. Under such circumstances, alcoholism and other escapist forms of substance abuse are endemic in the Indian community, a situation which leads both to a general physical debilitation of the population and a catastrophic accident rate. Teen suicide among Indians is several times the national average.

The average life expectancy of a reservation-based Native American man is barely 45 years; women can expect to live less than three years longer.

Such itemizations could be continued at great length, including matters like the radioactive contamination of large portions of contemporary Indian Country, the forced relocation of traditional Navajos, and so on. But the point should be made: Genocide, as defined in international law, is a continuing fact of day-to-day life (and death) for North America's native peoples. Yet there has been—and is—only the barest flicker of public concern about, or even consciousness of, this reality. Absent any serious expression of public outrage, no one is punished and the process continues.

A salient reason for public acquiescence before the ongoing holocaust in Native North America has been a continuation of the popular legacy, often through more effective media. Since 1925, Hollywood has released more than 2,000 films, many of them rerun frequently on television, portraying Indians as strange, perverted, ridiculous, and often dangerous things of the past. Moreover, we are habitually presented to mass audiences one-dimensionally, devoid of recognizable human motivations and emotions; Indians thus serve as props, little more. We have thus been thoroughly and systematically dehumanized.

Nor is this the extent of it. Everywhere, we are used as logos, as mascots, as jokes: "Big Chief writing tablets, "Red Man" chewing tobacco, "Winnebago" campers, "Navajo and "Cherokee" and "Pontiac" and "Cadillac" pickups and automobiles. There are the Cleveland "Indians," the Kansas City "Chiefs," the Atlanta "Braves" and the Washington "Redskins" professional sports teams—not to mention those in thousands of colleges, high schools, and elementary schools across the country—each with their own degrading caricatures and parodies of Indians and/or things Indian. Pop fiction continues in the same vein, including an unending stream of New Age manuals purporting to expose the inner works of indigenous spirituality in everything from pseudo-philosophical to do-it-yourself styles. Blond yuppies from Beverly Hills amble about the country claiming to be reincarnated 17th century Cheyenne Ushamans ready to perform previously secret ceremonies.

Lamar High School "Home of the Savages"

In effect, a concerted, sustained, and in some ways accelerating effort has gone into making Indians unreal. It is thus of obvious importance that the American public begin to think about the implications of such things the next time they witness a gaggle of face-painted and war-bonneted buffoons doing the "Tomahawk Chop" at a baseball or football game. It is necessary that they think about the implications of the grade-school teacher adorning their child in turkey feathers to commemorate Thanksgiving. Think about the significance of John Wayne or Charleton Heston killing a dozen "savages" with a single bullet the next time a western comes on TV. Think about why Land-o-Lakes finds it appropriate to market its butter with the stereotyped image of an "Indian princess" on the wrapper. Think about what it means when non-Indian academics profess—as they often do—to "know more about Indians than Indians do themselves." Think about the significance of charlatans like Carlos Castaneda and Jamake Highwater and Mary Summer Rain and Lynn Andrews churning out "Indian" bestsellers, one after the other, while Indians typically can't get into print.

Think about the real situation of American Indians. Think about Julius Streicher. Remember Justice Jackson's admonition. Understand that the treatment of Indians in American popular culture is not "cute" or "amusing" or just "good, clean fun."

Know that it causes real pain and real suffering to real people. Know that it threatens our very survival. And know that this is just as much a crime against humanity as anything the Nazis ever did. It is likely that the indigenous people of the United States will never demand that those guilty of such criminal activity be punished for their deeds. But the least we have the right to expect—indeed, to demand—is that such practices finally be brought to a halt.

HEALTH & MEDICINE

Study: Racism is health risk to black Americans

■ The research suggests face-to-face racism may be a factor in high rates of hypertension and heart disease among blacks.

By SUE LANDRY

Times Staff Writer

Warning: Racism can be dangerous to your health.

That's what a Duke University researcher found when she set up confrontations between black people and white people.

Faced with racist provocation, the heart rate and blood pressure of African-American volunteers shot up and stayed elevated after the debate ended.

The study represents the first time a researcher has directly measured the potential health effects of face-to-face racism. The research supports previous theories that chronic racism might be one factor contributing to higher rates of hypertension and heart disease among African-Americans.

"It is well-documented that racism has negative social, economic and political consequences on African-Americans, but the direct effects of racism on physical and emotional health have only begun to be explored," said Duke psychologist Maya McNeilly, whose study was published in the July issue of the *International Journal of Behavioral Medicine*.

Measuring the health effects of racism could help boost societal change, McNeilly said. But it also can help identify methods of coping that help individuals combat the negative effects of racism.

In the past, researchers have tried to determine whether racism affects health by having volunteers view videos of racially charged incidents or by asking volunteers to imagine a racially charged experience. In those studies, volunteers view videos of racially charged incidents or by asking volunteers to imagine a racially charged experience. In those studies, volunteers exhibited a slight increase in blood pressure and heart rate.

McNeilly wanted to investigate a more realistic situation.

In her study, 30 African-American women participated in two debates with a white person. One debate was about a racial topic while the other debates were about controversial, but non-racial, topics. A second African-American sat nearby, in some cases offering supportive comments and gestures, and, in others, sitting quietly.

During each debate, researchers measured the heart rate and blood pressure of the black participants. They also were rated on emotions such as anger, resentment, cynicism and anxiety.

"We thought that this interactive confrontation with provocation would be a lot more lifelike," McNeilly said. "We did, in fact, find that the increases (in blood pressure and heart rate) were much greater."

Participants exhibited blood pressure as much as 40-percent higher during the racial debates than during the non-racial debates. Heart rates among participants were as much as 61-percent higher during the racist confrontations.

Emotions ran at least twice as high, and, in some cases, as much as seven-times higher during the racial confrontations.

The emotions reported by participants could have as significant an effect on health as blood pressure and heart rate. Emotions such as anger and resentment can cause the body to release increased amounts of hormones such as adrenaline and cortisol, which also can damage the heart.

While a single incident of stress wouldn't cause much damage, the physical effects can take a serious toll if the stress is chronic.

During the debates in which the black participant received support from another black person, the participant reported less anger. But the social support didn't change the effect on blood pressure and heart rate.

McNeilly plans to further investigate factors that might buffer the negative effects of racism. Preliminary results of another study indicate that black people who feel hopeless and powerless in the face of racism have higher blood pressures than those who don't have those feelings.

A psychologist at Florida A & M University, John Chambers, has found evidence that African-Americans with a strong sense of identity and a strong awareness of their culture are less likely to have high blood pressure.

McNeilly's studies on racism build on a large body of research at Duke on the effects of mental stress on physical health. That research has documented that family and work-related stress can increase the risk of heart disease by releasing stress hormones and raising blood pressure and heart rate.

Identifying racism as another stress factor with health effects is important because hypertension strikes African-Americans ages 25 to 44 at 20 times the rate it affects Caucasians of the same age. Researchers hypothesize that other factors include genetics, diet and exercise.

McNeilly said her study opens the door to further research. She plans to study the effects of gender discrimination, discrimination within the same race, and the effects of racism on other ethnic groups.

"It has opened up a host of areas that really are in desperate need of exploration," McNeilly said. "There has not been a single study that has looked at the effects of gender discrimination on the heart and blood vessels."

Societal values dictate job paths for women

Why are many jobs still segregated by gender? People's values may provide one answer.

By Tori DeAngelis

Monitor staff

Cultures have traditionally divided the tasks of their group by gender, with women performing some roles and men others. But those duties vary from society to society. In some early tribes, for instance, women built the houses, while men helped rear the children, says Stanford University professor Felicia Pratto, PhD.

Today, gender divisions still pervade the workplace, with women taking on the bulk of "pink-collar" jobs like secretary and men most of the "blue-color" ones such as construction worker. These divisions are based on our society's power structure, with employers undermining women for having values that challenge a male-dominated system, Pratto contends. In particular, Pratto says that managers make hiring decisions on the belief that women hold values that seek to fix injustices in an unfair system. And they hire men in certain jobs based on the view that men have values that aim to perpetuate the system. The findings differ from previous research in showing that employers don't just show bias based on gender, but also on their perceptions of women's values, Pratto says.

Pratto is one of several psychologists studying the gender gap in the workplace. She and others have found that while women have made great professional strides and are no longer barred from any career, employers still use subtle tactics to keep women from gaining equal treatment with men.

31. Societal Values Dictate Job Paths

> "Social ideologies do not merely reflect a kernel of truth about group differences. They [also] justify and perpetuate the social systems of inequality of which they are part."
>
> *Felicia Pratto, PhD*
> *Stanford University*

New York University psychologist Madeleine Heilman, PhD, for example, has found that some employers can't see past women's gender—that even when women posses traditionally "masculine" leadership traits such as decisiveness and strength, employers don't think women are capable of holding leadership positions.

"They see management jobs as requiring male qualities and they see women as not having those qualities," Heilman says.

Similarly, other psychologists have found that people automatically rate a wide range of jobs as "masculine."

Social dominance

In her work, Pratto applies the "social dominance" theory to mangers' perceptions of job candidates' value systems. The theory maintains that one group in a society shapes the direction of values in the entire system. Roles that serve the interests of elite groups are called *hierarchy-enhancing* roles, and those that serve oppressed groups are *hierarchy-attenuating* ones, the theory maintains.

Jobs can be rated in ways that reflect one dimension or the other: Corporate managers, for instance, reflect hierarchy-enhancing values, while civil-rights advocates reflect hierarchy-attenuating ideals. Hierarchy-attenuating jobs tend to be lower-paid than hierarchy-enhancing jobs, and more women are likely to be interested in those jobs than men, given their place in the power structure. But that is of course not always the case, says Pratto.

Testing the idea

In two recent studies examining how this theory may apply at work, Pratto and colleagues Jim Sidanius, PhD, and Bret Siers, PhD, of the University of California, Los Angeles, tested whether "employers" were more likely to hire men for jobs that maintain the status quo (hierarchy-enhancing jobs) and to hire women for jobs that seek to right systemic wrongs or to care for marginalized members of society (hierarchy-attenuating ones). The studies were reported in the January *Journal of Personality and Social Psychology* (Vol. 72, No. 1, p. 37–53).

The team found that employers did have biased perceptions of men's and women's values and acted on those biases, even when they received equivalent information about the job seekers.

In both studies, Pratto used the same paradigm, first with 86 college students, then with 104 business people commuting to work on a train. Participants were given four résumés, each of which reflected a prototypical male "enhancer," a prototypical female "enhancer," a prototypical male "attenuator" and a prototypical female "attenuator." They were asked to place applicants into five positions, each with different levels of hirerarchy-attenuating or enhancing features.

In both studies, participants hired far more women than men into hierarchy-attenuating jobs and far more men than women into hierarchy-enhancing positions, the team found.

"The gender stereotype bias ... was not simply to hire one gender preferentially, but rather to channel men into hierarchy-enhancing jobs and women into hierarchy-attenuating jobs," Pratto concluded.

The findings illuminate the importance of viewing workplace issues not just psychologically, but also sociologically and culturally, Pratto believes.

"Stereotypes and other social ideologies do not merely reflect a kernel of truth about group differences," says Pratto. "They [also] justify and perpetuate the social systems of inequality of which they are part."

Minorities' perfomance is hampered by stereotypes

Women and ethnic minorities may fall short of their potential when they feel judged based on negative stereotypes.

By Tori DeAngelis

Monitor staff

What makes a woman who is gifted in math or science drop out of graduate school, or an African-American who had intended to get a doctoral degree leave college in his sophomore year?

According to current theories, the reasons range from sociocultural to genetic—from the effects of poverty to faulty genes.

Through studies on women and minorities, Stanford University professor Claude Steele, PhD, has inserted a fresh viewpoint into the discussion. In a Master Lecture at APA's 1996 Annual Convention, Steele presented a social psychology theory on minority performance that demonstrates an interface between social events and one's internal interpretation of those events.

Stereotype threat

The theory holds that a source of achievement problems for women in math and blacks more generally in school is what he calls "stereotype threat." For women, the stereotype is that they have limited ability in math and science compared to men; for blacks, it's that they're short on academic ability compared to whites. The fear of being judged by and perhaps conforming to the negative stereotype causes them to effectively "freeze up" and perform worse in the area than they otherwise would.

While stereotype threats affect everyone, they gain more power when they threaten a domain one is heavily invested in, according to Steele. The stereotype that women can never reach the heights of math performance that men can, for example, poses a strong threat to women who heavily identify with the math field. Because the stereotype for women holds that they are *limited* and not *lacking* in math ability, the threat is particularly unnerving because a woman never knows when she'll hit her peak performance, he added.

The theory also accounts for efforts to distance one's self from stereotype threats. If people decide they're not heavily invested in a domain—sometimes because the stereotype threat is too great—they may disavow a domain entirely. Steele believes this is the process by which many African-American youngsters leave school early, and why many women avoid quantitative fields.

Testing the theory

Steele's first experiments to test the theory, done with Steven Spencer, PhD, looked at top-level female math students at the University of Michigan. Here, the team examined the possibility that women for whom math performance is extremely important will be negatively affected by the stereotype that women don't perform as well as men in *high-level* math skills.

The team had male and female math students with equally strong academic records take a math test far above their knowledge level. (The participants weren't told anything about possible stereotypes because Steele believes that the stereotype will activate automatically.) A control group took an English test, where the stereotype for women didn't apply. If the women did worse than men on the difficult math test, Steele reasoned, it

> "The findings show that something as minimal as getting rid of stereotype threat can have a dramatic effect on minority students' grades."
>
> *Claude Steele, PhD*
> *Stanford University*

would be a first step in showing that a stereotype can adversely affect performance. (The finding, however, could also show that women simply perform worse on difficult math tests than men, he noted.)

In fact, the women's test scores were four times lower than men on the math test; they performed equally well on the English test.

The next experiments tested whether women would perform better on an easy math exam compared to a difficult one, to continue to test the notion that it is the higher-level math areas that pose a stereotype challenge to women. As expected, the women did better than the men on the easy test, but much worse on the harder exam.

Until this point in his studies, an outside observer wouldn't find the data surprising, Steele noted: Similar findings have been used to support the contention that genes influence performance and ability, he said.

So for the next set of studies, Steele looked at whether stereotype threat, not ability, affects performance. Again, ace math students took a difficult math test, but this time the women were told they were taking a test on which men and women are known to perform equally well.

"The women's performances went up rather dramatically," Steele said. The results suggest that stereotype threat is to blame, because the equal-performance factor was the only variable to change.

Studies on blacks

Steele and colleague Joshua Aaronson, PhD, have found similar results studying the academic ability of African-Americans. Here, they tested the stereotype that blacks have less academic ability than whites: Steele's theory holds that bright African-American college students in particular would be highly threatened by that stereotype.

In one study, black and white students received a difficult verbal test. Participants in one condition were told the test diagnosed verbal ability; in the other, they were told that the test was a problem-solving procedure. As posited, the blacks did worse in the ability condition, but performed as well as whites in the problem-solving condition.

Steele also examined whether race-based stereotypes interfered with blacks' performance. Again using both ability and "problem-solving" conditions, Steele gave white and African-American students an 80-item, word-completion task. The task has test-takers fill in a third word after two initial words, writing down whatever word comes to mind that is related to the first two words. Ten items could be completed using words based on race issues or stereotypes: "Face" and "rice," for instance, could be completed with "race," while "late" and "lace" could be finished with "lazy."

Black students in the ability group ended items with race-based words much more often than any other participants, indicating that for African-Americans, merely sitting down to take a difficult ability test is enough to activate racial stereotypes in their thinking.

In related studies, blacks in the "ability" condition reported less of a preference for items associated with African-American culture, such as basketball and hip-hop music.

These data highlight the situational nature of stereotype threat, he believes. Past researchers have interpreted minority people's efforts to distance themselves from their group as proof that they internalize negative stereotypes. "But this evidence suggests that distancing is a more situational tactic to avoid being seen stereotypically," he said.

Interventions

For the last five years, Steele has been testing his theory in the field, to see if removing stereotype threats might help African-American students improve their academic performance and integrate more fully into campus life.

He has set up a dormitory-based program at the University of Michigan that is the antithesis of so-called "remedial" programs for ethnic minorities. He recruits a group of students representing the racial and ethnic mix on campus to live in a dorm together and take part in the program during their freshman year.

All of the students join in a workshop that challenges their academic abilities and pushes them to go beyond the curriculum. The purpose is to challenge the stereotype that minorities need extra academic help.

All participants also meet informally each week to discuss the value of diversity and communication. The meeting encourages them to air thoughts and feelings about personal, social and political events. Steele believes the set-up "tells minority students and women they have a legitimate point of view." It also helps to defeat academic-ability stereotypes for blacks, for example, by showing them they're not the only ones to panic over midterms.

The program is helping to close the gap between black students' achievement test scores and their grades, Steele said. As his theory predicts, black students with higher grades and better academic performance benefit the most: They're most likely to be affected by stereotype threats because they're most invested in the academic domain.

For students who enter the program with weaker achievement test scores, the paradigm has been less effective, he admitted. "The findings show that something as minimal as getting rid of stereotype threat can have a dramatic effect on minority students' grades," Steele said. "But for students from any group who aren't well-prepared, more attention may be needed."

MY TURN

WHO IS A WHIZ KID?

Because my sons are Asian-American, people jump to conclusions about their academic gifts

BY TED GUP

Shortly after joining a national magazine some years ago as a writer, I found myself watching in horror as the week's cover story was prepared. The story was about "Asian-American whiz kids," and it featured a series of six student portraits, each face radiating with an intellectual brilliance. Being new to the enterprise, I was at first tentative in my criticism, cautioning that such a story was inherently biased and fueled racial and ethnic stereotypes. My criticism was dismissed. "This is something good we are saying about them," one top editor remarked. I reduced my criticism to writing. "What," I asked, "would be the response if the cover were about 'Jewish whiz kids'? Would anyone really dare to produce such an obviously offensive story?" My memo was ignored. Not long after, the cover appeared on the nation's newsstands, and the criticism began to fly. The editors were taken aback.

As a former Fulbright Scholar to China I have long taken a strong interest in the portrayal of Asian-Americans. But my interest went well beyond the academic. Even as the cover was being prepared, I was waiting to adopt my first son from Korea. His name was to be David. He was 5 months old when he arrived. That did not stop even some otherwise sophisticated friends from volunteering that he would no doubt be a good student. Probably a mathematician, they opined, with a tone that uncomfortably straddled jest and prediction. I tried to take it all with good humor, this idea that a 5-month-old who could not yet sit up, speak a word or control his bowels was already destined for academic greatness. Even his major seemed foreordained.

Many Asian-Americans seem to walk an uneasy line between taking pride in their remarkable achievements and needing to shake off stereotypes. The jokes abound. There is the apocryphal parent who asks "Where is the other point?" when his or her child scores a 99 on a test. Another familiar refrain has the young Asian-American student enumerating his or her hobbies: "studying, studying and more studying."

Several months after David arrived he and I entered a small mom-and-pop convenience store in our neighborhood. The owners were Korean. I noticed that the husband, standing behind the cash register, was eying my son. "Is he Korean?" he asked. "Yes," I nodded. He reached out for him and took him into his arms. "He'll be good in math," declared the man. "My God," I muttered. Not him, too!

It was preposterous. It was funny. And it was unnerving. Embedded in such elevated expectations were real threats to my son. Suppose, I wondered, he should turn out to be only a mediocre student, or, worse yet, not a student at all. I resented the stereotypes and saw them for what they were, the other side of the coin of racism. It is easy to delude one's self into thinking it harmless to offer racial compliments, but that is an inherent contradiction in terms. Such sweeping decriptives, be they negative or positive, deny the one thing most precious to all peoples—individuality. These stereotypes are pernicious for two reasons. First, such attributes are relative and tend to pit one race against another. Witness the seething enmity in many inner cities between Korean store owners and their African-American patrons. Stereotypes that hint at superiority in one race implicitly suggest inferiority in another. They are ultimately divisive, and in their most virulent form, even deadly. Who can forget the costs of the Aryan myth?

Such stereotypes also place a crushing burden on Asian-Americans. Few would deny that disproportionate numbers of Asian surnames appear each year among the winners of the Westinghouse science prizes or in the ranks of National Merit Scholars. But it might be a reflection of parental influences, personal commitment and cultural predilections, not genetic predisposition. A decade ago, as a Fulbright Lecturer in Beijing, I saw firsthand the staggering hours my Chinese students devoted to their studies. Were my students in the United States to invest similar time in their books I would have every reason to expect similar results.

I have often been told that Koreans are the "Jews of Asia," a reference to both their reported skills in business and their inherent intelligence. As a Jew, I cannot help but wince at such descriptions. I remember being one of the very few of my faith in a Midwest boarding school. There were many presumptions weighing on me, most of them grounded in my religion. My own classroom performance almost singlehandedly disabused my teachers of the myth that Jews were academically gifted. I barely made it through. Whether it was a lack of intelligence or simple rebellion against expectation, I do not know. I do know that more than once the fact that I was Jewish was raised as evidence that I could and should be doing better. Expectations based on race, be they raised or lowered, are no less galling.

David is now in the first grade. He is already taking math with the second graders and asking me about square roots and percentiles. I think back to the Korean merchant who took him in his arms and pronounced him a math whiz. Was he right? Do Asian-Americans have it easier, endowed with some special strand of DNA? The answer is a resounding no. Especially in our house. My son David has learning disabilities to overcome and what progress he has made is individual in the purest and most heroic sense. No one can or should take that away from him, suggesting he is just another wunderkind belonging to a favored race.

A year after my first son arrived, we adopted his brother from Korea. His name is Matthew. Let it be known that Matthew couldn't care less about math. He's a bug man. Slugs and earthworms. I suspect he will never be featured on any cover stories about Asian-American whiz kids, but I will continue to resist anything and anyone who attempts to dictate either his interests or his abilities based on race or place of birth. Bugs are fine by me and should be more than fine by him.

GUP, *a writer, lives in Chevy Chase, Md.*

Aggression

Biological Factors (Articles 34 and 35)
Psychological Factors (Articles 36 and 37)
Mass Media Effects (Articles 38 and 39)

The evidence that human beings are capable of great violence is all around us—all you have to do is read a newspaper or watch the evening news. Every day people are shot, stabbed, beaten, or otherwise treated in a violent manner by friends, family, or strangers. People are attacked for the color of their skin, their political ideas, their membership in a rival gang, or just because they were in the wrong place at the wrong time. Nations war against other nations, and, in civil conflicts, nations war against themselves. Faced with millions and millions of victims, it is hard to disagree with the conclusion that the capacity for aggression is fundamental to human nature.

Of course, it may depend on what you mean by aggression. As it turns out, coming up with one clear definition of aggression has been very difficult. For example, does aggression require a clear intention to harm? That is, must I *intend* to hurt you in order for my behavior to be called aggressive? Must aggression be physical in nature, or can my verbal attacks on you also be labeled aggressive? Does aggression have to be directed toward a human being? What about violence toward animals or, even, inanimate objects, such as when I become angry during a round of golf and bend my putter around a tree? Even after decades of research on this topic, social psychologists still disagree on what exactly defines an aggressive act.

Although social psychology does not completely ignore the role of biological factors in aggression (and two of the selections in this unit in fact address this topic), its usual focus is on identifying the environmental factors that influence aggressive behavior. One approach to understanding a form of aggression known as *hostile aggression* (aggression carried out for its own sake) has been to identify situational factors that cause unpleasant emotional states, which might then cause aggressive actions. For example, the failure to reach an important goal might lead to the unpleasant feeling of frustration, and these feelings can then trigger aggression. Hot and uncomfortable environments might also contribute to unpleasant emotional states, and thus contribute to heightened aggression.

In contrast to hostile aggression, which is carried out for its own sake, *instrumental aggression* is carried out in order to attain some other goal or objective. This form of aggression is often explained in terms of social learning theory, which holds that people can learn to carry out aggressive actions when they observe others doing so and when those others are rewarded for their actions. Thus, this theory contends that people frequently learn to use aggression as a tool for getting something they want. One place where such behaviors can be learned, of course, is the mass media, and many studies (and congressional hearings) have been carried out to determine the role of television and other media in teaching violence to children.

The selections in this unit are divided into three subsections. The first subsection focuses on biological factors in aggression, an approach that has only recently become more common in the social psychological literature. In "The Biology of Violence," Robert Wright offers a thoughtful analysis of some controversies in this area. Drawing upon both evolutionary psychology and biological research on serotonin levels, Wright offers the interesting idea that environment and biology work together to help produce aggression; the environmental conditions of those low in social status may influence their serotonin levels, which may then influence violence. In the second article, "Damaged," Malcolm Gladwell describes the work of Dorothy Lewis and Jonathan Pincus that suggests that one factor contributing to the most violent aggression is brain damage in the aggressor. Their examination of violent criminals frequently reveals the kind of physical trauma and abuse at early ages that may lead to substantial brain damage.

The second subsection deals with more psychological factors influencing aggression. "Car Wars: Taming Drivers' Aggression" examines the increasing levels of aggressive behavior that occur on streets and highways by those driving automobiles. It appears that increasing levels of negative response and stress among drivers may contribute to this, along with the feelings of anonymity that people expeience when driving. The second selection,

UNIT 8

"Gunslinging in America," examines the difficulty of answering what appears to be a simple question: Does having a gun in the household increase or decrease the likelihood of gun-related aggression? While the presence of a gun might be thought to act as a cognitive cue for aggression (i.e., the weapons effect), interpreting the research results is difficult.

The final subsection deals with the issue of violence in mass media. "Televised Violence and Kids: A Public Health Problem?" provides an overview of some of the most famous and influential research in this area: a longitudinal study that found evidence that childhood viewing of television violence produced heightened aggression in adulthood. The last selection, "Menace to Society," examines the same issue in a broader way, by taking a more critical look at some of the research: It concludes that the issue is more complicated than it first appears.

Looking Ahead: Challenge Questions

What is the evidence that genetic factors can influence the aggressive behaviors of individuals? What is the evidence that biological factors can play such a role? What is the difference between genetic and biological influences on aggression? Are biological and environmental explanations of aggression mutually exclusive?

What factors seem to be most important in fueling the aggressive behavior of motorists? Have you ever experienced aggressive behavior while driving? What seemed to be the most likely cause?

In your opinion, what is the likely effect on aggressive behavior of owning a gun? On what do you base your opinion? How would you respond to someone with the opposite view? How could you resolve this conflict?

Do you think that seeing violence on television causes children to become more violent? Have *you* been made more violent by your television viewing? How might society use the results of social psychological research to reduce aggression in our culture? Is there any danger in using psychological research for such a purpose?

BRAVE NEW WORLD DEPT.

THE BIOLOGY OF VIOLENCE

Is inner-city violence a response to the social ravages of poverty, or a biochemical syndrome that may be remedied with drugs? Fallout from that debate derailed the Bush Administration's Violence Initiative, but a school of new Darwinians is proposing an answer that will unsettle both sides.

ROBERT WRIGHT

Frederick Goodwin has learned a lot during a lifetime of studying human behavior, but no lesson is more memorable than the one driven home to him over the past three years: becoming known as someone who compares inner-city teen-agers to monkeys is not a ticket to smooth sailing in American public life. As of early 1992, Goodwin's career had followed a steady upward course. He had been the first scientist to demonstrate clinically the antidepressant effects of lithium, and had become known as a leading, if not the leading, expert on manic-depressive illness. He had risen to become head of the Alcohol, Drug Abuse and Mental Health Administration, the top position for a psychiatrist in the federal government, and was poised to be the point man in a policy that the Bush Administration was proudly unveiling: the Federal Violence Initiative. The idea was to treat violence as a public-health problem—to identify violently inclined youth and provide therapy early, before they had killed. The initiative had the strong support of the Secretary of Health and Human Services, Louis Sullivan, and Goodwin planned to make it his organization's main focus.

Then, in early 1992, while discussing the initiative before the National Mental Health Advisory Council, Goodwin made his fateful remarks. Speaking impromptu—and after a wholly sleepless night, he later said—he got off onto an extended riff about monkeys. In some monkey populations, he said, males kill other males and then, with the competition thus muted, proceed to copulate prolifically with females. These "hyperaggressive" males, he said, seem to be also "hypersexual." By a train of logic that was not entirely clear, he then arrived at the suggestion that "maybe it isn't just a careless use of the word when people call certain areas of certain cities jungles." Goodwin elaborated a bit on his obscure transition from monkeys to underclass males, but no matter; these few fragments are what came to form the standard paraphrase of his remarks. As the Los Angeles *Times* put it, Goodwin "made comparisons between inner-city youths and violent, oversexed monkeys who live in the wild."

As if a few seemingly racist quotes weren't enough of a public-relations bonanza for opponents of the Violence Initiative, Goodwin also injected what some took to be Hitlerian overtones. He talked about "genetic factors" inclining human beings toward violence, and suggested that one way to spot especially troublesome kids might be to look for "biological markers" of violent disposition. Within months, the Violence Initiative was abandoned, amid charges of racism. And Goodwin, facing the same charges, was reassigned to head the National Institute of Mental Health—not a huge demotion, but a conspicuous slap on the wrist. Finally, last year, he left that job for a position in academe after intermittent coolness from the Clinton Administration. Though no Clinton official ever told him he was a political liability, Goodwin found himself no longer invited to meetings he had once attended—meetings on violence, for example.

Goodwin is a victim of a vestigial feature of the American liberal mind: its undiscerning fear of the words "genetic" and "biological," and its wholesale hostility to Darwinian explanations of behavior. It turns out, believe it or not, that comparing violent inner-city males to monkeys isn't necessarily racist, or even necessarily right wing. On the contrary, a truly state-of-the-art comprehension of the comparison yields what is in many ways an archetypally liberal view of the "root causes" of urban violence. This comprehension comes via a young, hybrid academic discipline known as evolutionary psychology. Goodwin himself actually has little familiarity with the field, and doesn't realize how far to the left one can be dragged by a modern Darwinian view of the human mind. But he's closer to realizing it than the people whose outrage has altered his career.

As it happens, the nominally dead Federal Violence Initiative isn't really dead. Indeed, one of the few things Goodwin and his critics agree on is that its "life" and "death" have always been largely a question of labelling. Goodwin, who recently broke a thirty-month silence on the controversy, makes the point while dismissing the sinister aims attributed to the program. "They've made it sound like a cohesive new program that had some uniform direction to it and was directed by one person—namely, me," he told me. "The word 'initiative,' in bureaucratese, is simply a way of pulling stuff together to argue for budgets. In effect, that's what this was—a budget-formulation document, at Sullivan's request." Goodwin's critics look at the other side of the coin: just as the bulk of the Violence Initiative predated the name itself, the bulk of it survived the name's deletion. Thus the war against the violence initiative—lower case—must go on.

THE person who was most responsible for turning Goodwin's monkey remarks into a life-changing and policy-influencing event is a psychiatrist named Peter Breggin, the founder and executive director of the Center for the Study of Psychiatry, in Bethesda, Maryland, just outside Washington. The center doubles as Breggin's home, and the center's research director, Ginger Ross Breggin, doubles as Breggin's wife. (Goodwin says of Peter Breggin, in reference to the center's lack of distinct physical existence, "People who don't know any better think he's a legitimate person.") Both Breggins take some credit for Goodwin's recent departure from government. "We've been all over the man for three years," Ginger Breggin observes.

Goodwin and Peter Breggin interned together at SUNY Upstate Medical Center in the nineteen-sixties. Both took a course taught by Thomas Szasz, the author of "The Myth of Mental Illness," which held that much of psychiatry is merely an oppressive tool by which the powers that be label inconvenient behavior "deviant." Szasz had formed his world view back when the most common form of oppression was locking people up, and Breggin, since founding his center, in 1971, has carried this view into the age of psychopharmacology. He fought lithium, Goodwin's initial claim to fame. He fought the monoamine-oxidase inhibitors, a somewhat crude generation of antidepressants, and now he fights a younger, less crude generation of them. "Talking Back to Prozac," written in collaboration with his wife and published last June, is among the anti-psychopharmacology books he has recently churned out. So is "The War Against Children," published last fall, in which the Breggins attack Goodwin, the Violence Initiative, and also the drug Ritalin. In Breggin's view, giving Ritalin to "hyperactive" children is a way of regimenting spirited kids rather than according them the attention they need—just as giving "anti-aggression" drugs to inner-city kids would be an excuse for continued neglect. And Breggin is convinced that such drugs will be used in precisely this fashion if the Goodwins of the world get their way. This is the hidden agenda of the Violence Initiative, he says. And Goodwin concedes that pharmacological therapy was a likely outcome of the initiative.

Breggin's all-embracing opposition to psychopharmacology has earned him a reputation among psychiatrists as a "flat-earther." Some, indeed, go further in their disparagement, and Breggin is aware of this. "I am not a kook," he will tell a reporter whether or not the reporter has asked. People try to discredit him, Breggin says, because he is a threat to their interests—to the money made by drug companies, which insidiously bias research toward chemical therapy, and to the power of Goodwin and other "biological psychiatrists," who earn their status by "medicalizing" everything they see. "How is it that some spiritually passionate people become labeled schizophrenic and find themselves being treated as mental patients?" he asks in a 1991 book, "Toxic Psychiatry."

Breggin says he is struck by the parallels between the Violence Initiative and Nazi Germany: "the medicalization of social issues, the declaration that the victim of oppression, in this case the Jew, is in fact a genetically and biologically defective person, the mobilization of the state for eugenic purposes and biological purposes, the heavy use of psychiatry in the development of social-control programs." This is the sort of view that encouraged some members of the Congressional Black Caucus to demand that Goodwin be disciplined; it also helped get Breggin on Black Entertainment Television, and led to such headlines in black newspapers as "PLOT TO SEDATE BLACK YOUTH."

Breggin's scenario, the question of its truth aside, did have the rhetorical virtue of simple narrative form. ("He made a nice story of it," Goodwin says, in a tone not wholly devoid of admiration.) There has lately been much interest in, and much federally funded research into, the role that the neurotransmitter serotonin plays in violence. On average, people with low serotonin levels are more inclined toward impulsive violence than people with normal levels. Since Goodwin was a co-author of the first paper noting the correlation between serotonin and violence, he would seem to have a natural interest in this issue. And, since the "serotonin-reuptake inhibitors," such as Eli Lilly's Prozac, raise serotonin levels, there would seem to exist a large financial incentive to identify low serotonin as the source of urban ills. Hence, from Breggin's vantage point it all fell into place—a confluence of corporate and personal interests that helped make serotonin the most talked-about biochemical in federal violence research. But, Breggin says, we mustn't lose sight of its larger significance: serotonin is "just a code word for biological approaches."

IT was in the late seventies that Goodwin and several colleagues stumbled on the connection between serotonin and violence, while studying servicemen who were being observed for possible psychiatric discharge. Since then, low serotonin has been found in other violent populations, such as children who torture animals, children who are unusually hostile toward their mothers, and people who score high for aggression on standardized tests. Lowering people's serotonin levels in a laboratory setting made them more inclined to give a person electrical shocks (or, at least, what experimenters deceived them into thinking were electrical shocks).

It isn't clear whether serotonin influences aggression per se or simply impulse control, since low serotonin correlates also with impulsive arson and with attempted suicide. But serotonin level does seem to be a rough predictor of misbehavior—a biological marker. In a study of twenty-nine children with "disruptive behavior disorders," serotonin level helped predict future aggression. And in a National Institutes of Health study of fifty-eight violent offenders and impulsive arsonists serotonin level, together with another biochemical index, predicted with eighty-four-per-cent accuracy whether they would commit crimes after leaving prison.

It doesn't take an overactive imagination to envision parole boards screening prisoners for biological markers before deciding their fate—just as Goodwin had suggested that using biological markers might help determine which children need antiviolence therapy. These are the kinds of scenarios that make Breggin worry about a world in which the government labels some people genetically deficient and treats them accordingly. In reply, Goodwin stresses that a "biological" marker needn't be a "genetic" one. Though N.I.H. studies suggest that some people's genes are conducive to low serotonin, environmental influences can also lower serotonin, and federal researchers are studying these. Thus a "biological" marker may be an "environmental" marker, not a "genetic" one. To this Breggin replies, "It's not what they believe, it's not in a million years what they really believe." This attempt to cast biological research as research into environment "shows their desperation, because this was never their argument until they got attacked," he says. "It's a political move."

In truth, federal researchers, including Goodwin, were looking into "environmental influences" on biochemistry well before being attacked by Breggin. Still, they do often employ a narrower notion of the term's meaning that Breggin would like. When Goodwin talks about such influences, he doesn't dwell on the sort of social forces that interest Breggin, such as poverty and bad schools. He says, for example, that he has looked into "data on head injuries, victims of abuse, poor prenatal nutrition, higher levels of lead," and so on.

In other words, he is inclined to view violence as an illness, whether it is the product of aberrant genes or of pathological—deeply unnatural—circumstances, or both. This is not surprising, given his line of work: he is a psychiatrist, a doctor; his job is to cure people, and people without pathologies don't need curing. "Once I learned that seventy-nine per cent of repeated violent offenses were by seven per cent of youth, it began to look to me like a clinical population, a population that had something wrong with it that resulted in this behavior," he says. Other federal researchers on violence tend to take the same approach. After all, most of them work at one of the National Institutes of Health, whether the National Institute of Mental Health, the National Institute on Alcohol Abuse and Alcoholism, or some other affiliate. For the Violence Initiative to be successful in the pragmatic aims that Goodwin acknowledges—as a way "to argue for budgets" for the Department of Health and Human Services—it pretty much had to define violence as a pathology, characteristic of inner-city kids who have something "wrong" with them.

Breggin would rather depict violence as the not very surprising reaction of normal people to oppressive circumstances. A big problem with biological views of behavior generally, he says, is that they so often bolster the medical notions of "deviance" and "pathology"—and thus divert attention from the need to change social conditions.

But "biological" views don't have to be "medical" views. This is where the field of evolutionary psychology enters the picture, and modern Darwinian thought begins to diverge from Goodwin's sketchier and more dated ideas about human evolution. Evolutionary psychologists share Goodwin's conviction that genes, neurotransmitters such as serotonin, and biology more generally are a valid route to explaining human behavior; and they share his belief in the relevance of studying nonhuman primates. Yet they are much more open than he is to the Bregginesque view that inner-city violence is a "natural" reaction to a particular social environment.

To most N.I.H. researchers, evolutionary psychology is terra incognita. Goodwin, for one, professes only vague awareness of the field. But the field offers something that should intrigue him: a theory about what serotonin is, in the deepest sense—why natural selection designed it to do the things it does. This theory would explain, for example, the effect that Prozac has on people. More to the point, this theory would explain the link that Goodwin himself discovered between low serotonin and violence.

THE two acknowledged experts on human violence within evolutionary psychology are Martin Daly and Margo Wilson, of McMaster University, in Ontario. Their 1988 book, "Homicide," barely known outside Darwinian-social-science circles, is considered a classic within them. Listening to Margo Wilson talk about urban crime is like entering a time warp and finding yourself chatting with Huey Newton or Jane Fonda in 1969. "First of all, what's a crime?" she asks. It all depends on "who are the rule-makers, who's in power. We call it theft when somebody comes into your house and steals something, but we don't call it theft when we get ripped off by political agendas or big-business practices." And as for gang violence: "It's a coalition of males who are mutually supporting each other to serve their interests against some other coalition. How is that different from some international war?"

To hear this sort of flaming liberal rhetoric from a confirmed Darwinian should surprise not just Peter Breggin but anyone familiar with intellectual history. For much of this century, many people who took a Darwinian view of human behavior embraced the notorious ideology of social Darwinism. They emphatically did not view social deviance as some arbitrary and self-serving designation made by the ruling class; more likely, crime was a sign of "unfitness," of an innate inability to thrive legitimately. The "unfit" were best left to languish in jail, where they could not reproduce. And "unfit" would-be immigrants—those from, say, Eastern Europe, who were congenitally ill equipped to enrich American society—were best kept out of the country.

What permits Margo Wilson to sound a quite different theme is two distinguishing features of evolutionary psychology. First, evolutionary psychologists are not much interested in genetic differences, whether among individuals or among groups. The object of study is, rather, "species-typical mental adaptations"—also known as "human nature." A basic tenet of evolutionary psychologists is that there *is* such a thing as human nature—that people everywhere have fundamentally the same minds.

A second tenet of evolutionary psychologists is respect for the power of environment. The human mind, they say, has been designed to adjust to social circumstances. The vital difference between this and earlier forms of environmental determinism is the word "designed." Evolutionary psychologists believe that the developmental programs that convert social experience into personality were created by natural selection, which is to say that those programs lie in our genes. Thus, to think clearly about the influence of environment we must think about what sorts of influences would have been favored by natural selection.

If, for example, early social rejection makes people enduringly insecure, then we should ask whether this pattern of development might have had a genetic payoff during evolution. Maybe people who faced such rejection saw their chances of survival and reproduction plummet unless they became more socially vigilant—neurotically attentive to nourishing their social ties. Thus genes that responded to rejection by instilling this neurotic vigilance, this insecurity, would have flourished. And eventually those genes could have spread through the species, becoming part of human nature.

These two themes—universal human nature and the power of environment—are related. It is belief in the power of environment—of family milieu, cultural milieu, social happenstance—that allows evolutionary psychologists to see great variation in human behavior, from person to person or from group to group, without reflexively concluding that the explanation lies in genetic variation. The explanation lies in the genes, to be sure. Where else could a program for psychological development ultimately reside? But it doesn't necessarily lie in differences among different people's genes.

This is the perspective that Martin Daly and Margo Wilson bring to the subject of violence. They think about genes in order to understand the role of environment. And one result of this outlook is agreement with Peter Breggin that inner-city violence shouldn't be labelled a "pathology." In a paper published last year Daly and Wilson wrote, "Violence is abhorrent. . . . Violence is so aversive that merely witnessing an instance can be literally sickening. . . ." There is thus "but a short leap to the metaphorical characterization of violence itself as a sort of 'sickness' or 'dysfunction.'" But, they insisted, this leap is ill advised. Violence is eminently functional—something that people are designed to do.

Especially men. From an evolutionary point of view, the leading cause of violence is maleness. "Men have evolved the morphological, physiological and psychological means to be effective users of violence," Daly and Wilson wrote. The reason, according to modern evolutionary thought, is simple. Because a female can reproduce only once a year, whereas a male can reproduce many times a year, females are the scarcer sexual resource. During evolution, males have competed over this resource, with the winners impregnating more than their share of women and the losers impregnating few or none. As always with natural selection, we're left with the genes of the winners—in this case, genes inclining males toward fierce combat. One reflection of this history is that men are larger and stronger than women. Such "sexual dimorphism" is seen in many species, and biologists consider it a rough index of the intensity of male sexual competition.

To say that during evolution men have fought over women isn't to say that they've always fought directly over women, with the winner of a bout walking over and claiming his nubile trophy. Rather, human beings are somewhat like our nearest relatives, the chimpanzees: males compete for status, and status brings access to females. Hence skills conducive to successful status competition would have a "selective advantage"—would be favored by natural selection. As Daly and Wilson have put it, "if status has persistently contributed to reproductive success, and a capacity for controlled violence has regularly contributed to status, then the selective advantage of violent skills cannot be gainsaid."

It's easy to find anecdotal evidence that status has indeed tended to boost the reproductive success of males. (It was Henry Kissinger who said that power is an aphrodisiac, and Representative Pat Schroeder who observed that a middle-aged congresswoman doesn't exert the same animal magnetism on the opposite sex that a middle-aged congressman does.) But more telling is evidence drawn from hunter-gatherer societies, the closest thing to real-life examples of the pre-agrarian social context for which the human mind was designed. Among the Ache of Paraguay, high-status men have more extramarital affairs and more illegitimate children than low-status men. Among the Aka Pygmies of central Africa, an informal leader known as a *kombeti* gets more wives and offspring than the average Aka. And so on. The Aka, the Ache, and Henry Kissinger all demonstrate that violence against other men is hardly the only means by which male status is sought. Being a good hunter is a primary route to status among the Ache, and being a wily social manipulator helps in all societies (even, it turns out, in chimp societies, where males climb the status ladder by forging "political" coalitions). Still, in all human societies questions of relative male status are sometimes settled through fighting. This form of settlement is, of course, more prevalent in some arenas than others—more in a bikers' bar than in the Russian Tea Room, more in the inner city than on the Upper East Side. But, as Daly and Wilson note, one theme holds true everywhere: men compete for status through the means locally available. If men in the Russian Tea Room don't assault one another, that's because assault isn't the route to status in the Russian Tea Room.

According to Daly and Wilson, a failure to see the importance of such circumstances is what leads well-heeled people to express patronizing shock that "trivial" arguments in barrooms and ghettos escalate to murder. In "Homicide" they wrote, "An implicit contrast is drawn between the foolishness of violent men and the more rational motives that move sensible people like ourselves. The combatants are in effect denigrated as creatures of some lower order of mental functioning, evidently governed by immediate stimuli rather than by foresightful contemplation." In truth, Daly and Wilson say, such combatants are typical of our species, as it has been observed around the world: "In most social milieus, a man's reputation depends in part upon the maintenance of a credible threat of violence." This fact is "obscured in modern mass society because the state has assumed a monopoly on the legitimate use of force. But wherever that monopoly is relaxed—whether in an entire society or in a neglected underclass—then the utility of that credible threat becomes apparent." In such an environment, "a seemingly minor affront is not merely a 'stimulus' to action, isolated in time and space. It must be understood within a larger social context of reputations, face, relative social status, and enduring relationships. Men are known by their fellows as . . . people whose word means action and people who are full of hot air."

That a basic purpose of violence is display—to convince peers that you will defend your status—helps explain an otherwise puzzling fact. As Daly and Wilson note, when men kill men whom they know, there is usually an audience. This doesn't seem to make sense—why murder someone in the presence of witnesses?—except in terms of evolutionary psychology. Violence is in large part a performance.

Thus the dismay often inspired by reports that a black teen-ager killed because he had been "dissed" is naïve. Nothing was more vital to the reproductive success of our male ancestors than respect, so there is nothing that the male mind will more feverishly seek to neutralize than disrespect. All men spend much of their lives doing exactly this; most are just lucky enough to live in a place where guns won't help them do it. These days, well-educated men do their status maintenance the way Goodwin and Breggin do it, by verbally defending their honor and verbally assailing the honor of their enemies. But back when duelling was in vogue even the most polished of men might occasionally try to kill one another.

THIS view from evolutionary psychology in some ways jibes with a rarely quoted point that Goodwin made during his rambling remarks on monkeys: that inner-city violence may be caused by a "loss of structure in society"; in an environment where violence is deemed legitimate, the male inclination for violence may reassert itself. Of monkeys, Goodwin had said, "that is the natural way of it for males, to knock each other off," and the implicit comparison was supposed to be with all human males, not just black ones; his point was that many black males now live in neighborhoods where social restraints have dissolved. This is the sense in which Goodwin says he meant to compare the inner cities to jungles, and the transcript of his remarks bears him out. His poor choice of imagery still haunts him. "If I had said that in the Wild West, where there was no structure, there was a hell of a lot of violence, no one would have noticed."

There is a crucial difference between this emphasis on social milieu as rendered by Goodwin and as rendered by evolutionary psychologists; namely, they don't abandon it when they start thinking about the interface between biology and environment. Whereas pondering this interface steers Goodwin's thoughts toward "pathology"—the biological effects of malnutrition, or brain damage due to child abuse—evolutionary psychologists try to figure out how normal, everyday experience affects the biochemistry of violence.

Consider serotonin. In particular, consider an extensive study of serotonin in monkeys done by Michael McGuire, an evolutionary psychologist, and his colleagues at U.C.L.A. Vervet monkeys have a clear male social hierarchy: low-status males defer to high-status males over access to limited resources, including females. McGuire found that the highest-ranking monkeys in the male social hierarchy have the highest serotonin levels. What's more, the lower-ranking males tend to be more impulsively violent. Other studies have linked low serotonin to violence in monkeys even more directly.

At first glance, such findings might appear to be what Peter Breggin, and many liberals, would consider their worst nightmare. If this biochemical analogy between monkeys and human beings is indeed valid, the lesson would seem to be this: some individuals are born to be society's leaders, some are born to be its hoodlums; the chairman of I.B.M. was born with high serotonin, the urban gang member was born with low serotonin. And what if it turns out that blacks on average have less serotonin than whites do?

There certainly is evidence that some sort of analogy between the social lives of monkeys and human beings is in order. McGuire has found that officers of college fraternities have higher serotonin levels than the average frat-house resident, and that college athletes perceived as team leaders have higher levels than their average teammate. But grasping the import of the analogy requires delving into the details of McGuire's monkey research.

When McGuire examines a dominant male monkey before he becomes a dominant—before he climbs the social hierarchy by winning some key fights with other males—serotonin level is often unexceptional. It rises during his ascent, apparently in response to sometimes inconspicuous social cues. Indeed, his serotonin may begin to creep upward before he physically challenges any higher-ranking males; the initial rise may be caused by favorable attention from females (who play a larger role in shaping the male social hierarchy than was once appreciated). When, on the other hand, a dominant male suffers a loss of status, his serotonin level drops.

What's going on here? There is no way to look inside a monkey's mind and see how serotonin makes him feel. But there is evidence that in human beings high serotonin levels bring high self-esteem. Raising self-esteem is one effect of Prozac and other serotonin boosters, such as Zoloft. And, indeed, high-ranking monkeys—or, to take a species more closely related to us, high-ranking chimpanzees—tend to behave the way people with high self-esteem behave: with calm self-assurance; assertively, yes, but seldom violently. (This subtle distinction, as Peter Kramer notes in "Listening to Prozac," is also seen in human beings. Prozac may make them more socially assertive, but less irritable, less prone to spontaneous outbursts.) To be sure, an alpha-male chimp may periodically exhibit aggression—or, really, a kind of ritual mock-aggression—to remind everyone that he's the boss, but most alphas tend not to be as fidgety and perturbable as some lower-ranking apes, except when leadership is being contested.

All this suggests a hypothesis. Maybe one function of serotonin—in human and non-human primates—is to regulate self-esteem in accordance with social feedback; and maybe one function of self-esteem is, in turn to help primates negotiate social hierarchies, climbing as high on the ladder as circumstance permits. Self-esteem (read serotonin) keeps rising as long as one encounters social success, and each step in this elevation inclines one to raise one's social sights a little higher. Variable self-esteem, then, is evolution's way of preparing us to reach and maintain whatever level of social status is realistic, given our various attributes (social skills, talent, etc.) and our milieu. High serotonin, in this view, isn't nature's way of destining people from birth for high status; it is nature's way of equipping any of us for high status should we find ourselves possessing it. The flip side of this hypothesis is that low self-esteem (and low serotonin) is evolution's way of equipping us for low status should our situation not be conducive to elevation.

This *doesn't* mean what an earlier generation of evolutionists would have thought: that Mother Nature wants people with low status to endure their fate patiently for "the greater good." Just the opposite. A founding insight of evolutionary psychology is that natural selection rarely designs things for the "good of the group." Any psychological inclinations that offer a way to cope with low status provide just that—a way to cope, a way to make the best of a bad situation. The purpose of low self-esteem isn't to bring submission for the sake of social order; more likely, its purpose is to discourage people from conspicuously challenging higher-status people who are, by virtue of their status, in a position to punish such insolence.

AND what about the antisocial tendencies, the impulsive behavior linked with low serotonin in both human beings and monkeys? How does evolutionary psychology explain them? This is where the demise of "good of the group" logic opens the way for especially intriguing theories. In particular: primates may be designed to respond to low status by "breaking the rules" when they can get away with it. The established social order isn't working in their favor, so they circumvent its strictures at every opportunity. Similarly, inner-city thugs may be functioning as "designed": their minds absorb environmental input reflecting their low socioeconomic standing and the absence of "legitimate" routes to social elevation, and incline their behavior in the appropriately criminal direction.

The trouble with breaking rules, of course, is the risk of getting caught and punished. But, as Daly and Wilson note by quoting Bob Dylan, "When you ain't got nothin', you got nothin' to lose." In the environment of our evolution, low status often signified that a male had had little or no reproductive success to date; for such a male, taking risks to raise status could make sense in Darwinian terms. In hunter-gatherer societies, Daly and Wilson write, "competition can sometimes be fiercest near the bottom of the scale, where the man on track for total [reproductive] failure has nothing to lose by the most dangerous competitive tactics, and may therefore throw caution to the winds." Even as low self-esteem keeps him from challenging dominant males, he may behave recklessly toward those closer to him on the social ladder. Thus may the biochemistry of low status, along with the attendant states of mind, encourage impulsive risk-taking.

This theory, at any rate, would help make sense of some long-unexplained data. Psychologists found several decades ago that artificially lowering people's self-esteem—by giving them false reports about scores on a personality test—makes them more likely to cheat in a subsequent game of cards. Such risky rule-breaking is just the sort of behavior that makes more sense for a low-status animal than for a high-status animal.

To say that serotonin level is heavily influenced by social experience isn't to say that a person's genetic idiosyncrasies aren't significant. But it is to say that they are at best half the story. There are not yet any definitive studies on the "heritability" of serotonin level—the amount of the variation among people that is explained by genetic difference. But the one study that has been done suggests that less than half the variation in the population studied came from genetic differences, and the rest from differences in environment. And even this estimate of heritability is probably misleadingly high. Presumably, self-esteem correlates with many other personal attributes, such as physique or facial attractiveness. Impressive people, after all, inspire the sort of feedback that raises self-esteem and serotonin. Since these attributes are themselves quite heritable—traceable largely to a person's distinctive genes—some of the "heritability" estimate for serotonin may reflect genes not for high serotonin per se but for good looks, great body, and so on. (The technical term for this oblique genetic effect is "reactive heritability.")

At least some of the variation in serotonin level is grounded more directly in genetic difference. N.I.H. researchers have identified a human gene that helps convert tryptophan, an amino acid found in some grains and fruits, into serotonin, and they have found a version of the gene that yields low serotonin levels. Still, there is no reason to believe that different ethnic groups have different genetic endowments for serotonin. Indeed, even if it turned out that American blacks on average had lower serotonin than whites, there would be no cause to implicate genes. One would expect groups that find themselves shunted toward the bottom of the socioeconomic hierarchy to have low serotonin. That may be nature's way of preparing them to take risks and to evade the rules of the powers that be.

This Darwinian theory integrating serotonin, status, and impulsive violence remains meagrely tested and is no doubt oversimplified. One complicating factor is modern life. People in contemporary America are part of various social hierarchies. An inner-city gang leader may get great, serotonin-boosting respect ("juice," as the suggestive street slang calls it) from fellow gang members while also getting serotonin-sapping signs of disrespect when he walks into a tony jewelry store, or even when he turns on the TV and sees that wealthy, high-status males tend to bear no physical or cultural resemblance to him. The human mind was designed for a less ambiguous setting—a hunter-gatherer society, in which a young man's social reference points stay fairly constant from day to day. We don't yet know how the mind responds to a world of wildly clashing status cues.

Another hidden complexity in this Darwinian theory lies in the fact that serotonin does lots of things besides mediate self-esteem and impulsive aggression. Precisely what it does depends on the part of the brain it is affecting and the levels of other neurotransmitters. Over-all serotonin level is hardly the subtlest imaginable chemical index of a human being's mental state. Still, though we don't yet fathom the entire biochemistry of things like self-esteem, impulsiveness, and violence, there is little doubt among evolutionary psychologists that the subject is fathomable—and that it will get fathomed much faster if biomedical researchers, at N.I.H. and elsewhere, start thinking in Darwinian terms.

IF evolutionary psychologists are right in even the broad contours of their outlook, then there is good news and bad news for both Frederick Goodwin and Peter Breggin. For Goodwin, the good news is that his infamous remarks were essentially on target: he was right to compare violent inner-city males—or any other violent human males—to nonhuman primates (though he exaggerated the incidence of actual murder among such primates). The bad news is that his Violence Initiative, in failing to pursue that insight, in clinging to the view of violence as pathology, was doomed to miss a large part of the picture; the bulk of inner-city violence will probably never be explained by reference to head injuries, poor nutrition, prenatal exposure to drugs, and bad genes. If violence is a public-health problem, it is so mainly in the sense that getting killed is bad for your health.

Evolutionary psychology depicts all kinds of things often thought to be "pathological" as "natural": unyielding hatred, mild depression, a tendency of men to treat women as their personal property. Some Darwinians even think that rape may in some sense be a "natural" response to certain circumstances. Of course, to call these things "natural" isn't to call them beyond self-control, or beyond the influence of punishment. And it certainly isn't to call them good. If anything, evolutionary psychology might be invoked on behalf of the doctrine of Original Sin: we are in some respects born bad, and redemption entails struggle against our nature.

Many people, including many social scientists and biomedical researchers, seem to have trouble with the idea of a conflict between nature and morality. "I think this is a source of resistance to evolutionary ways of thinking," says John Tooby, a professor at the University of California at Santa Barbara, who along with his wife, Leda Cosmides, laid down some of the founding doctrines of evolutionary psychology. "There's a strong tendency to want to return to the romantic notion that the natural is the good." Indeed, "one modern basis for establishing morals is to try to ground them in the notion of sickness. Anything people don't like, they accuse the person doing it of being sick."

Thomas Szasz couldn't have said it better. Herein lies evolutionary psychology's good news for Peter Breggin: yes, it is indeed misleading to call most violence a pathology, a disorder. The bad news for Breggin is that, even though the causes of violence are broadly environmental, as he insists, they are nonetheless biological, because environmental forces are mediated biologically—in this case by, among other things, serotonin. Thus, a scientist can be a "biological determinist" or a "biological reductionist" without being a genetic determinist. He or she can say—as Daly and Wilson and Tooby and Cosmides do—that human behavior is driven by biological forces impinging on the brain, yet can view those forces largely as a reflection of a person's distinctive environment.

This confronts Breggin with a major rhetorical complication. Much of his success in arousing opposition to the Violence Initiative lay in conveniently conflating the terms "biological" and "genetic." He does this habitually. In suggesting that the initiative grew out of Goodwin's long-standing designs, Breggin says he has Baltimore *Evening Sun* articles from 1984 in which "Goodwin is talking about crime and violence being genetic and biological." In truth, these articles show Goodwin saying nothing about genes—only that violence has some biological correlates and might respond to pharmacological treatment. In Breggin's mind, "genetic" and "biological" are joined at the waist.

That these terms are not, in fact, inseparable—that something utterly biological, like serotonin level, may differ between two people because of environmental, not genetic, differences—poses a second problem for Breggin. The best way to illuminate the environmental forces he stresses may be to study the biological underpinnings of behavior, and that is a prospect he loathes. If serotonin is one chemical that converts poverty and disrespect into impulsiveness or aggression or low self-esteem, then it, along with other chemicals, may be a handy index of all these things—something whose level can be monitored more precisely than the things themselves. (Studies finding that blacks on average don't suffer from low self-esteem are based on asking black people and white people how they feel about themselves—a dubious approach, since expressions of humility seem to be more highly valued in white suburban culture than in black urban culture.)

That Breggin may be wrong in the way he thinks about biology and behavior doesn't mean that the unsettling scenarios he envisions are far-fetched. The government may well try to use biochemical "markers" to select violently inclined kids for therapy, or to screen prisoners for parole. (Then again, if these chemicals aren't simple "genetic markers," but rather are summaries of the way genes and environment have together molded a person's state of mind, how are they different from a standard psychological evaluation, which summarizes the same thing?) There may also be attempts to treat violently inclined teenagers with serotonin-boosting drugs, as Breggin fears. And, though some teenagers might thus be helped into the mainstream economy, these drugs could also become a palliative, a way to keep the inner city tranquil without improving it. The brave new world of biochemical diagnosis and therapy is coming; and, for all the insight evolutionary psychology brings, it won't magically answer the difficult questions that will arise.

The point to bear in mind is simply that less eerie, more traditionally liberal prescriptions for urban violence continue to make sense after we've looked at black teen-agers as animals—which, after all, is what human beings are. The view from evolutionary psychology suggests that one way to reduce black violence would be to make the inner cities places where young men have nonviolent routes to social status and the means and motivation to follow them. Better-paying jobs, and better public schools, for example, wouldn't hurt. Oddly enough, thinking about genes from a Darwinian standpoint suggests that inner-city teen-agers are victims of their environment.

CRIME AND SCIENCE

DAMAGED

Why do some people turn into violent criminals?
New evidence suggests that it may all be in the brain.

BY MALCOLM GLADWELL

On the morning of November 18, 1996, Joseph Paul Franklin was led into Division 15 of the St. Louis County Courthouse, in Clayton, Missouri. He was wearing a pair of black high-top sneakers, an orange jumpsuit with short sleeves that showed off his prison biceps, and a pair of thick black-rimmed glasses. There were two guards behind him, two guards in front of him, and four more guards stationed around the courtroom, and as he walked into the room—or, rather, shuffled, since his feet were manacled—Franklin turned to one of them and said "Wassup?" in a loud, Southern-accented voice. Then he sat down between his attorneys and stared straight ahead at the judge, completely still except for his left leg, which bounced up and down in an unceasing nervous motion.

Joseph Franklin takes credit for shooting and paralyzing Larry Flynt, the publisher of *Hustler*, outside a Lawrenceville, Georgia, courthouse in March of 1978, apparently because Flynt had printed photographs of a racially mixed couple. Two years later, he says, he gunned down the civil-rights leader Vernon Jordan outside a Marriott in Fort Wayne, Indiana, tearing a hole in Jordan's back the size of a fist. In the same period in the late seventies, as part of what he later described as a "mission" to rid America of blacks and Jews and of whites who like blacks and Jews, Franklin says that he robbed several banks, bombed a synagogue in Tennessee, killed two black men jogging with white women in Utah, shot a black man and a white woman coming out of a Pizza Hut in a suburb of Chattanooga, Tennessee, and on and on—a violent spree that may have spanned ten states and claimed close to twenty lives, and, following Franklin's arrest, in 1980, earned him six consecutive life sentences.

Two years ago, while Franklin was imprisoned in Marion Federal Penitentiary, in Illinois, he confessed to another crime. He was the one, he said, who had hidden in the bushes outside a synagogue in suburban St. Louis in the fall of 1977 and opened fire on a group of worshippers, killing forty-two-year-old Gerald Gordon. After the confession, the State of Missouri indicted him on one count of capital murder and two counts of assault. He was moved from Marion to the St. Louis County jail, and from there, on a sunny November morning last year, he was brought before Judge Robert Campbell, of the St. Louis County Circuit Court, so that it could be determined whether he was fit to stand trial—whether, in other words, embarking on a campaign to rid America of Jews and blacks was an act of evil or an act of illness.

The prosecution went first. On a television set at one side of the courtroom, two videotapes were shown—one of an interview with Franklin by a local news crew and the other of Franklin's formal confession to the police. In both, he seems lucid and calm, patiently retracing how he planned and executed his attack on the synagogue. He explains that he bought the gun in a suburb of Dallas, answering a classified ad, so the purchase couldn't be traced. He drove to the St. Louis area and registered at a Holiday Inn. He looked through the Yellow Pages to find the names of synagogues. He filed the serial number off his rifle and bought a guitar case to carry the rifle in. He bought a bicycle. He scouted out a spot near his chosen synagogue from which he could shoot without being seen. He parked his car in a nearby parking lot and rode his bicycle to the synagogue. He lay in wait in the bushes for several hours, until congregants started to emerge. He fired five shots. He rode the bicycle back to the parking lot, climbed into his car, pulled out of the lot, checked his police scanner to see if he was being chased, then drove south, down I-55, back home toward Memphis.

In the interview with the news crew, Franklin answered every question, soberly and directly. He talked about his tattoos ("This one is the Grim Reaper. I got it in Dallas") and his heroes ("One person I like is Howard Stern. I like his honesty"), and he respectfully disagreed with the media's description of racially motivated crimes as "hate crimes," since, he said, "every murder is committed out of hate." In his confession to the police, after he detailed every step of the synagogue attack, Franklin was asked if there was anything he'd like to say. He stared thoughtfully over the top of his glasses. There was a long silence. "I can't think of anything," he answered. Then he was asked if he felt any remorse. There was another silence. "I can't say that I do," he said. He paused again, then added, "The only thing I'm sorry about is that it's not legal."

"What's not legal?"

Franklin answered as if he'd just been asked the time of day: "Killing Jews."

After a break for lunch, the defense called Dorothy Otnow Lewis, a psychiatrist at New York's Bellevue Hospital and a professor at New York University School of Medicine. Over the past twenty years, Lewis has examined, by her own rough estimate, somewhere between a hundred and fifty and two hundred murderers. She was the defense's only expert witness in the trial of Arthur Shawcross, the Rochester serial killer who strangled eleven prostitutes in the late eighties. She examined Joel Rifkin, the Long Island serial killer, and Mark David Chapman, who shot John Lennon—both for the defense. Once, in a Florida prison, she sat for hours talking with Ted Bundy. It was the day before his execution, and when they had finished Bundy bent down and kissed her cheek. "Bundy thought I was the only person who didn't *want* something from him," Lewis says. Frequently, Lewis works with Jonathan Pincus, a neurologist at Georgetown University. Lewis does the psychiatric examination; Pincus does the neurological examination. But Franklin put his foot down. He could tolerate being examined by a Jewish woman, evidently, but not by a Jewish man. Lewis testified alone.

Lewis is a petite woman in her late fifties, with short dark hair and large, liquid brown eyes. She was wearing a green blazer and a black skirt with a gold necklace, and she was so dwarfed by the witness stand that from the back of the courtroom only her head was visible. Under direct examination she said that she had spoken with Franklin twice—once for six hours and once for less than half an hour—and had concluded that he was a paranoid schizophrenic: a psychotic whose thinking was delusional and confused, a man wholly unfit to stand trial at this time. She talked of brutal physical abuse he had suffered as a child. She mentioned scars on his scalp from blows Franklin had told her were inflicted by his mother. She talked about his obsessive desire to be castrated, his grandiosity, his belief that he may have been Jewish in an earlier life, his other bizarre statements and beliefs. At times, Lewis seemed nervous, her voice barely audible, but perhaps that was because Franklin was staring at her unblinkingly, his leg bouncing faster and faster under the table. After an hour, Lewis stepped down. She paused in front of Franklin and, ever the psychiatrist, suggested that when everything was over they should *talk*. Then she walked slowly through the courtroom, past the defense table and the guards, and out the door.

Later that day, on the plane home to New York City, Lewis worried aloud that she hadn't got her point across. Franklin, at least as he sat there in the courtroom, didn't *seem* insane. The following day, Franklin took the stand himself for two hours, during which he did his own psychiatric diagnosis, confessing to a few "minor neuroses," but not to being "stark raving mad," as he put it. Of the insanity defense, he told the court, "I think it is hogwash, to tell you the truth. I knew exactly what I was doing." During his testimony, Franklin called Lewis "a well-intentioned lady" who "seems to embellish her statements somewhat." Lewis seemed to sense that that was the impression she'd left: that she was overreaching, that she was some kind of caricature—liberal Jewish New York psychiatrist comes to Middle America to tell the locals to feel *sorry* for a murderer. Sure enough, a week later the Judge rejected Lewis's arguments and held Franklin competent to stand trial. But, flying back to New York, Lewis insisted that she wasn't making an ideological point of Franklin; rather, she was saying that she didn't feel that Franklin's brain worked the way brains are supposed to work—that he had identifiable biological and psychiatric problems that diminished his responsibility for his actions. "I just don't believe people are born evil," she said. "To my mind, that is mindless. Forensic psychiatrists tend to buy into the notion of evil. I felt that that's no explanation. The deed itself is bizarre, grotesque. But it's not evil. To my mind, evil bespeaks conscious control over something. Serial murderers are not in that category. They are driven by forces beyond their control."

The plane was in the air now. By some happy set of circumstances, Lewis had been bumped up to first class. She was sipping champagne. Her shoes were off. "You know, when I was leaving our last interview, he sniffed me right here," she said, and she touched the back of her neck and flared her nostrils in mimicry of Franklin's gesture. "He'd said to his attorney, 'You know, if you weren't here, I'd make a play for her.'" She had talked for six hours to this guy who hated Jews so much that he hid in the bushes and shot at them with a rifle, and he had come on to her, just like that. She shivered at the memory: "He said he wanted some *pussy*."

WHEN Dorothy Lewis graduated from Yale School of Medicine, in 1963, neurology, the study of the brain and the rest of the nervous system, and psychiatry, the study of behavior and personality, were entirely separate fields. This was still the Freudian era. Little attempt was made to search for organic causes of criminality. When, after medical school, she began working with juvenile delinquents in New Haven, the theory was that these boys were robust, healthy. According to the prevailing wisdom, a delinquent was simply an ordinary kid who had been led astray by a troubled home life—by parents who were too irresponsible or too addled by drugs and alcohol to provide proper discipline. Lewis came from the archetypal do-gooding background—reared on Central Park West; schooled at Ethical Culture; a socialist mother who as a child had once introduced Eugene V. Debs at a political rally; father in the garment business; heated dinner-table conversations about the Rosenbergs—and she accepted this dogma. Criminals were just like us, only they had been given bad ideas about how to behave. The trouble was that when she began working with delinquents they didn't seem like that at all. They didn't lack for discipline. If anything, she felt, they were being disciplined too much. And these teen-agers weren't robust and rowdy; on the contrary, they seemed to be damaged and impaired. "I was studying for my boards in psychiatry, and in order to do a good job you wanted to do a careful medical history and a careful mental-status exam," she says. "I discovered that many of these kids had had serious accidents, injuries, or illnesses that seemed to have affected the central nervous system and that hadn't been identified previously."

In 1976, she was given a grant by the State of Connecticut to study a group of nearly a hundred juvenile delinquents. She immediately went to see Pincus, then a young professor of neurology at Yale. They had worked together once before. "Dorothy came along and said she wanted to do this project with me," Pincus says. "She wanted to look at violence. She had this hunch that there was something physically wrong with these kids. I said, 'That's ridiculous. Everyone knows violence has nothing to do with neurology.'" At that point, Pincus recalls, he went to his bookshelf and began reading out loud from what was then the definitive work in the field: "Criminality and Psychiatric Disorders," by Samuel Guze, the chairman of the psychiatry department of Washington University, in St. Louis. "Sociopathy, alcoholism, and drug dependence are the psychiatric disorders characteristically associated with serious crime," he read. "Schizophrenia, primary affective disorders, anxiety neurosis, obsessional neurosis, phobic neurosis, and"—and there he paused—"brain syndromes are not." But Lewis would have none of it. "She said, 'We should do it anyway.' I said, 'I don't have the time.' She said, 'Jonathan, I can *pay* you.' So I would go up on Sunday, and I would examine three or four youths, just give them a standard neurological examination." But, after seeing the kids for himself, Pincus, too, became convinced that the prevailing wisdom about juvenile delinquents—and, by extension, about adult criminals—was wrong, and that Lewis was right. "Almost *all* the violent ones were damaged," Pincus recalls, shaking his head.

Over the past twenty years, Lewis and Pincus have testified for the defense in more than a dozen criminal cases, most of them death-penalty appeals. Together, they have published a series of groundbreaking studies on murderers and delinquents, painstakingly outlining the medical and psychiatric histories of the very violent; one of their studies has been cited twice in United States Supreme Court opinions. Of the two, Pincus is more conservative. He doesn't have doubts about evil the way Lewis does, and sharply disagrees with her on some of the implications of their work. On the core conclusions, however, they are in agreement. They believe that the most vicious criminals are, overwhelmingly, people with some combination of abusive childhoods, brain injuries, and psychotic symptoms (in particular, paranoia), and that while each of these problems individually has no connection to criminality (most people who have been abused or have brain injuries or psychotic symptoms never end up harming anyone else), somehow these factors together create such terrifying synergy as to impede these individuals' ability to play by the rules of society.

Trying to determine the causes of human behavior is, of course, a notoriously tricky process. Lewis and Pincus haven't done the kind of huge, population-wide studies that could definitively answer just how predictive of criminality these factors are. Their findings are, however, sufficiently tantalizing that their ideas have steadily gained ground in recent years. Other researchers have now done some larger studies supporting their ideas. Meanwhile, a wave of new findings in the fields of experimental psychiatry and neurology has begun to explain why it is that brain dysfunction and child abuse can have such dire effects. The virtue of this theory is that it sidesteps all the topics that so cripple contemporary discussions of violence—genetics, biological determinism, and, of course, race. In a sense, it's a return to the old liberal idea that environment counts, and that it is possible to do something significant about crime by changing the material conditions of people's lives. Only, this time the maddening imprecision of the old idea (what, exactly, was it about bad housing, say, that supposedly led to violent crime?) has been left behind. Lewis and Pincus and other neurologists and psychiatrists working in the field of criminal behavior think they are beginning to understand what it is that helps to turn some people into violent criminals—right down to which functions of the brain are damaged by abuse and injury. That's what Lewis means when she says she doesn't think that people are intrinsically evil. She thinks that some criminals simply suffer from a dysfunction of the brain, the way cardiac patients suffer from a dysfunction of the heart, and this is the central and in some ways disquieting thing about her. When she talks about criminals as victims, she doesn't use the word in the standard liberal metaphorical sense. She means it literally.

Lewis works out of a tiny set of windowless offices on the twenty-first floor of the new wing of Bellevue Hospital, in Manhattan's East Twenties. The offices are decorated in institutional colors—gray carpeting and bright-orange trim—and since they're next to the children's psychiatric ward you can sometimes hear children crying out. Lewis's desk is stacked high with boxes of medical and court records from cases she has worked on, and also with dozens of videotapes of interviews with murderers which she has conducted over the years. She talks about some of her old cases—especially some of her death-row patients—as if they had just happened, going over and over details, sometimes worrying about whether she made the absolutely correct diagnosis. The fact that everyone else has long since given up on these people seems to be just what continues to attract her. Years ago, when she was in college, Lewis found herself sitting next to the Harvard theologian Paul Tillich on the train from New York to Boston. "When you read about witches being burned at the stake," Tillich asked her, in the midst of a long and wide-ranging conversation, "do you identify with the witch or with the people looking on?" Tillich said he himself identified with the crowd. Not Lewis. She identified with the witch.

In her offices, Lewis has tapes of her interviews with Shawcross, the serial killer, and also tapes of Shawcross being interviewed by Park Elliott Dietz, the psychiatrist who testified for the prosecution in that case. Dietz is calm, in control, and has a slightly bored air, as if he had heard everything before. By contrast, Lewis, in her interviews, has a kind of innocence about her. She seems completely caught up in what is happening, and at one point, when Shawcross makes some particularly outrageous comment on what he did to one of the prostitutes he murdered, she looks back at the camera wide-eyed, as if to say "Wow!" When Dietz was on the stand, his notes were beside him in one of those rolling evidence carts, where everything is labelled and items are distinguished by color-coded dividers, so that he had the entire case at his fingertips. When Lewis testified, she kept a big stack of untidy notes on her lap and fussed through them after she was asked a question. She is like that in everyday life as well—a little distracted and spacey, wrapped up in the task at hand. It makes her so approachable and so unthreatening that it's no wonder she gets hardened criminals to tell her their secrets. It's another way of identifying with the witch. Once, while talking with Bundy, Lewis looked up after several hours and found that she had been so engrossed in their conversation that she hadn't noticed that everyone outside the soundproof glass of the interview booth—the guard, the prison officials at their desks—had left for lunch. She and Bundy were utterly alone. Terrified, Lewis stayed glued to her seat, her eyes never leaving his. "I didn't bat an eyelash," she recalls. Another time, after Lewis had interviewed a murderer in a Tennessee prison, she returned to her hotel room to find out that there had been a riot in the prison while she was there.

THE human brain comprises, in the simplest terms, four interrelated regions, stacked up in ascending order of complexity. At the bottom is the brain stem, which governs the most basic and primitive functions—breathing, blood pressure, and body temperature. Above that is the diencephalon, the seat of sleep and appetite. Then comes the limbic region, the seat of sexual behavior and instinctual emotions. And on top, covering the entire outside of the brain in a thick carpet of gray matter, is the cortex, the seat of both concrete and abstract thought. It is the function of the cortex—and, in particular, those parts of the cortex beneath the forehead, known as the frontal lobes—to modify the impulses that surge up from within the brain, to provide judgment, to organize behavior and decision-making, to learn and adhere to rules of everyday life. It is the dominance of the cortex and the frontal lobes, in other words, that is responsible for making us human; and the central argument of the school to which Lewis and Pincus belong is that what largely distinguishes many violent criminals from the rest of us is that something has happened inside their brains to throw the functioning of the cortex and the frontal lobes out of whack. "We are a highly socialized animal. We can sit in theatres with strangers and not fight with each other," Stuart Yudofsky, the chairman of psychiatry at Baylor College of Medicine, in Houston, told me. "Many other mammals could never crowd that closely together. Our cortex helps us figure out when we are and are not in danger. Our memory tells us what we should be frightened of and angry with and what we shouldn't. But if there are problems there—if it's impaired—one can understand how that would lead to confusion, to problems with disinhibition, to violence." One of the most important things that Lewis and Pincus have to do, then, when they evaluate a murderer is check for signs of frontal-lobe impairment. This, the neurological exam, is Pincus's task.

Pincus begins by taking a medical history: he asks about car accidents and falls from trees and sports injuries and physical abuse and problems at birth and any blows to the head of a kind that might have caused damage to the frontal lobes. He asks about headaches, tests for reflexes and sensorimotor functions, and compares people's right and left sides and observes gait. "I measure the head circumference—if it's more than two standard deviations below the normal brain circumference, there may be some degree of mental retardation, and, if it's more than two standard deviations above, there may be hydrocephalus," Pincus told me. "I also check gross motor coördination. I ask people to spread their fingers and hold their hands apart and look for choreiform movements—discontinuous little jerky movements of the fingers and arms." We were in Pincus's cluttered office at Georgetown University Medical Center, in Washington, D.C., and Pincus, properly professorial in a gray Glen-plaid suit, held out his hand to demonstrate. "Then I ask them to skip, to hop," he went on, and he hopped up and down in a small space on the floor between papers and books.

Pincus stands just over six feet, has the long-limbed grace of an athlete, and plays the part of neurologist to perfection: calm, in command, with a distinguished sprinkle of white hair. At the same time, he has a look of mischief in his eyes, a streak of irreverence that allows him to jump up and down in his office before a total stranger. It's an odd combination, like Walter Matthau playing Sigmund Freud.

"Then I check for mixed dominance, to see if the person is, say, right-eyed, left-footed," he said. "If he is, it might mean that his central nervous system hasn't differentiated the way it should." He was sitting back down now. "No one of these by itself means he is damaged. But they can tell us something in aggregate."

At this point, Pincus held up a finger forty-five degrees to my left and moved it slowly to the right. "Now we're checking for frontal functions," he said. "A person should be able to look at the examiner's finger and follow it smoothly with his eyes. If he can only follow it jerkily, the frontal eye fields are not working properly. Then there's upward gaze." He asked me to direct my eyes to the ceiling. "The eye should go up five millimetres and a person should also be able to direct his gaze laterally and maintain it for twenty seconds. If he can't, that's motor impersistence." Ideally, Pincus will attempt to amplify his results with neuropsychological testing, an EEG (an electroencephalogram, which measures electrical patterns in the brain), and an M.R.I. scan (that's magnetic resonance imaging), to see if he can spot scarring or lesions in any of the frontal regions which might contribute to impairment.

Pincus is also interested in measuring judgment. But since there is no objective standard for judgment, he tries to pick up evidence of an inability to cope with complexity, a lack of connection between experience and decision-making which is characteristic of cortical dysfunction. Now he walked behind me, reached over the top of my head, and tapped the bridge of my nose in a steady rhythm. I blinked once, then stopped. That, he told me, was normal.

"When you tap somebody on the bridge of the nose, it's reasonable for a person to blink a couple of times, because there is a threat from the outside," Pincus said. "When it's clear there is no threat, the subject should be able to accommodate that. But, if the subject blinks more than three times, that's 'insufficiency of suppression,' which may reflect frontal-lobe dysfunction. The inability to accommodate means you can't adapt to a new situation. There's a certain rigidity there."

Arthur Shawcross, who had a cyst pressing on one temporal lobe and scarring in both frontal lobes (probably from, among other things, being hit on the head with a sledgehammer and with a discus, and falling on his head from the top of a forty-foot ladder), used to walk in absolutely straight lines, splashing through puddles instead of walking around them, and he would tear his pants on a barbed-wire fence instead of using a gate a few feet away. That's the kind of behavior Pincus tries to correlate with abnormalities on the neurological examination. "In the Wisconsin Card Sorting Test, the psychologist shows the subject four playing cards—three red ones, one black one—and asks which doesn't fit," Pincus said. "Then he shows the subject, say, the four of diamonds, the four of clubs, the four of hearts, and the three of diamonds. Somebody with frontal-lobe damage who correctly picked out the black one the first time—say, the four of clubs—is going to pick the four of clubs the second time. But the rules have changed. It's now a three we're after.

We're going by numbers now, not color. It's that kind of change that people with frontal-lobe damage can't make. They can't change the rules. They get stuck in a pattern. They keep using rules that are demonstrably wrong. Then there's the word-fluency test. I ask them to name in one minute as many different words as they can think of which begin with the letter 'f.' Normal is fourteen, plus or minus five. Anyone who names fewer than nine is abnormal."

This is not an intelligence test. People with frontal-lobe damage might do just as well as anyone else if they were asked, say, to list the products they might buy in a supermarket. "Under those rules, most people can think of at least sixteen products in a minute and rattle them off," Pincus said. But that's a structured test, involving familiar objects, and it's a test with rules. The thing that people with frontal-lobe damage can't do is cope with situations where there are no rules, where they have to improvise, where they need to make unfamiliar associations. "Very often, they get stuck on one word—they'll say 'four,' 'fourteen,' 'forty-four,'" Pincus said. "They'll use the same word again and again—'farm' and then 'farming.' Or, as one fellow in a prison once said to me, '——,' '——,' '——.' They don't have the ability to come up with something else."

What's at stake, fundamentally, with frontal-lobe damage is the question of inhibition. A normal person is able to ignore the tapping after one or two taps, the same way he can ignore being jostled in a crowded bar. A normal person can screen out and dismiss irrelevant aspects of the environment. But if you can't ignore the tapping, if you can't screen out every environmental annoyance and stimulus, then you probably can't ignore being jostled in a bar, either. It's living life with a hair trigger.

A recent study of two hundred and seventy-nine veterans who suffered penetrating head injuries in Vietnam showed that those with frontal-lobe damage were anywhere from two to six times as violent and aggressive as veterans who had not suffered such injuries. This kind of aggression is what is known as neurological, or organic, rage. Unlike normal anger, it's not calibrated by the magnitude of the original insult. It's explosive and uncontrollable, the anger of someone who no longer has the mental equipment to moderate primal feelings of fear and aggression.

"There is a reactivity to it, in which a modest amount of stimulation results in a severe overreaction," Stuart Yudofsky told me. "Notice that reactivity implies that, for the most part, this behavior is not premeditated. The person is rarely violent and frightening all the time. There are often brief episodes of violence punctuating stretches when the person does not behave violently at all. There is also not any gain associated with organic violence. The person isn't using the violence to manipulate someone else or get something for himself. The act of violence does just the opposite. It is usually something that causes loss for the individual. He feels that it is out of his control and unlike himself. He doesn't blame other people for it. He often says, 'I hate myself for acting this way.' The first person with organic aggression I ever treated was a man who had been inflating a truck tire when the tire literally exploded and the rim was driven into his prefrontal cortex. He became extraordinarily aggressive. It was totally uncharacteristic: he had been a religious person with strong values. But now he would not only be physically violent—he would curse. When he came to our unit, a nurse offered him some orange juice. He was calm at that moment. But then he realized that the orange juice was warm, and in one quick motion he threw it back at her, knocking her glasses off and injuring her cornea. When we asked him why, he said, 'The orange juice was warm.' But he also said, 'I don't know what got into me.' It wasn't premeditated. It was something that accelerated quickly. He went from zero to a hundred in a millisecond." At that point, I asked Yudofsky an obvious question. Suppose you had a person from a difficult and disadvantaged background, who had spent much of his life on the football field, getting his head pounded by the helmets of opposing players. Suppose he was involved in a tempestuous on-again, off-again relationship with his ex-wife. Could a vicious attack on her and another man fall into the category of neurological rage? "You're not the first person to ask that question," Yudofsky replied dryly, declining to comment further.

Pincus has found that when he examines murderers neurological problems of this kind come up with a frequency far above what would be expected in the general population. For example, Lewis and Pincus published a study of fifteen death-row inmates randomly referred to them for examination; they were able to verify forty-eight separate incidents of significant head injury. Here are the injuries suffered by just the first three murderers examined:

1. three years: beaten almost to death by father (multiple facial scars)
early childhood: thrown into sink onto head (palpable scar)
late adolescence: one episode of loss of consciousness while boxing
2. childhood: beaten in head with two-by-fours by parents
childhood: fell into pit, unconscious for several hours
seventeen years: car accident with injury to right eye
eighteen years: fell from roof apparently because of a blackout
3. six years: glass bottle deliberately dropped onto head from tree (palpable scar on top of cranium)
eight years: hit by car
nine years: fell from platform, received head injury
fourteen years: jumped from moving car, hit head.

Dorothy Lewis's task is harder than Jonathan Pincus's. He administers relatively straightforward tests of neurological function. But she is interested in the psychiatric picture, which means getting a murderer to talk about his family, his feelings and behavior, and, perhaps most important, his childhood. It is like a normal therapy session, except that Lewis doesn't have weeks in which to establish intimacy. She may have only a session or two. On one occasion, when she was visiting a notorious serial killer at San Quentin, she got lucky. "By chance, one of the lawyers had sent me some clippings from the newspaper, where I read that when he was caught he had been carrying some Wagner records," she told me. "For some reason, that stuck in my mind. The first time I went to see him, I started to approach him and he pointed at me and said, 'What's happening on June 18th?' And I said, 'That's the first night PBS is broadcasting "Der Ring des Nibelungen."' You know, we'd studied Wagner at Ethical Culture. Granted, it was a lucky guess. But I showed him some respect, and you can imagine the rapport that engendered."

Lewis says that even after talking for hours with someone guilty of horrendous crimes she never gets nightmares. She seems to be able to separate her everyday life from the task at hand—to draw a curtain between her home and her work. Once, I visited Lewis at her home: she and her husband, Mel, who is a professor of psychiatry at Yale, live in New Haven. The two dote on each other ("When I met Mel, I knew within a week that this was the man I wanted to marry," she says, flushing, "and I've never forgiven him, because it took him two weeks to ask me"), and as soon as I walked in they insisted on giving me a detailed tour of their house, picking up each memento, pointing out their children's works of art, and retelling the stories behind thirty years of anniversaries and birthdays: sometimes they told their stories in alternating sentences, and sometimes they told a story twice, first from Dorothy's perspective and then from Mel's. All in all, it was a full hour of domestic vaudeville. Then Dorothy sat on her couch, with her cat, Ptolemy, on her lap, and began to talk about serial killers, making a seamless transition from the sentimental to the unspeakable.

At the heart of Lewis's work with murderers is the search for evidence of childhood abuse. She looks for scars. She combs through old medical records for reports of suspicious injuries. She tries to talk to as many family members and friends as possible. She does all this because, of course, child abuse has devastating psychological consequences for children and the adults they become. But there is the more important reason—the one at the heart of the new theory of violence—which is that finding evidence of prolonged child abuse is a key to understanding criminal behavior because abuse also appears to change the anatomy of the brain.

When a child is born, the parts of his brain that govern basic physiological processes—that keep him breathing and keep his heart beating—are fully intact. But a newborn can't walk, can't crawl, can't speak, can't reason or do much of anything besides sleep and eat, because the higher regions of his brain—the cortex, in particular—aren't developed yet. In the course of childhood, neurons in the cortex begin to organize themselves—to differentiate and make connections—and that maturation process is in large part responsive to what happens in the child's environment. Bruce Perry, a psychiatrist at Baylor College of Medicine, has done brain scans of children who have been severely neglected, and has found that their cortical and subcortical areas never developed properly, and that, as a result, those regions were roughly twenty or thirty per cent smaller than normal. This kind of underdevelopment doesn't affect just intelligence; it affects emotional health. "There are parts of the brain that are involved in attachment behavior—the connectedness of one individual to another—and in order for that to be expressed we have to have a certain nature of experience and have that experience at the right time," Perry told me. "If early in life you are not touched and held and given all the somatosensory stimuli that are associated with what we call love, that part of the brain is not organized in the same way."

According to Perry, the section of the brain involved in attachment—which he places just below the cortex, in the limbic region—would look different in someone abused or neglected. The wiring wouldn't be as dense or as complex. "Such a person is literally lacking some brain organization that would allow him to actually make strong connections to other human beings. Remember the orphans in Romania? They're a classic example of children who, by virtue of not being touched and held and having their eyes gazed into, didn't get the somatosensory bath. It doesn't matter how much you love them after age two—they've missed that critical window."

In a well-known paper in the field of child abuse, Mary Main, a psychologist at Berkeley, and Carol George, now at Mills College, studied a group of twenty disadvantaged toddlers, half of whom had been subjected to serious physical abuse and half of whom had not. Main and George were interested in how the toddlers responded to a classmate in distress. What they found was that almost all the nonabused children responded to a crying or otherwise distressed peer with concern or sadness or, alternatively, showed interest and made some attempt to provide comfort. But not one of the abused toddlers showed any concern. At the most, they showed interest. The majority of them either grew distressed and fearful themselves or lashed out with threats, anger, and physical assaults. Here is the study's description of Martin, an abused boy of two and a half, who—emotionally retarded in the way that Perry describes—seemed incapable of normal interaction with another human being:

Martin . . . tried to take the hand of the crying other child, and when she resisted, he slapped her on the arm with his open hand. He then turned away from her to look at the ground and began vocalizing very strongly. "Cut it out! CUT IT OUT!," each time saying it a little faster and louder. He patted her, but when she became disturbed by his patting, he retreated "hissing at her and baring his teeth." He then began patting her on the back again, his patting became beating, and he continued beating her despite her screams.

Abuse also disrupts the brain's stress-response system, with profound results. When something traumatic happens—a car accident, a fight, a piece of shocking news—the brain responds by releasing several waves of hormones, the last of which is cortisol. The problem is that cortisol can be toxic. If someone is exposed to too much stress over too long a time, one theory is that all that cortisol begins to eat away at the organ of the brain known as the hippocampus, which serves as the brain's archivist: the hippocampus organizes and shapes memories and puts them in context, placing them in space and time and tying together visual memory with sound and smell. J. Douglas Bremner, a psychiatrist at Yale, has measured the damage that cortisol apparently does to the hippocampus by taking M.R.I. scans of the brains of adults who suffered severe sexual or physical abuse as children and comparing them with the brains of healthy adults. An M.R.I. scan is a picture of a cross-section of the brain—as if someone's head had been cut into thin slices like a tomato, and then each slice had been photographed—and in the horizontal section taken by Bremner the normal hippocampus is visible as two identical golf-ball-size organs, one on the left and one on the right, and each roughly even with the ear. In child-abuse survivors, Bremner found, the golf ball on the left is on average twelve per cent smaller than that of a healthy adult, and the theory is that it was shrunk by cortisol. Lewis says that she has examined murderers with dozens of scars on their backs, and that they have no idea how the scars got there. They can't remember their abuse, and if you look at Bremner's scans that memory loss begins to make sense: the archivist in their brain has been crippled.

Abuse also seems to affect the relationship between the left hemisphere of the brain, which plays a large role in logic and language, and the right hemisphere, which is thought to play a large role in creativity and depression. Martin Teicher, a professor of psychiatry at Harvard and McLean Hospital, recently gave EEGs to a hundred and fifteen children who had been admitted to a psychiatric facility, some of whom had a documented history of abuse. Not only did the rate of abnormal EEGs among the abused turn out to be twice that of the nonabused but all those abnormal brain scans turned out to be a result of problems on the left side of the brain. Something in the brain's stress response, Teicher theorized, was interfering with the balanced development of the brain's hemispheres.

Then Teicher did M.R.I.s of the brains of a subset of the abused children, looking at what is known as the corpus callosum. This is the fibre tract—the information superhighway—that connects the right and the left hemispheres. Sure enough, he found that parts of the corpus callosum of the abused kids were smaller than they were in the nonabused children. Teicher speculated that these abnormalities were a result of something wrong with the sheathing—the fatty substance, known as myelin, that coats the nerve cells of the corpus callosum. In a healthy person, the myelin helps the neuronal signals move quickly and efficiently. In the abused kids, the myelin seemed to have been eaten away, perhaps by the same excess cortisol that is thought to attack the hippocampus.

Taken together, these changes in brain hardware are more than simple handicaps. They are, in both subtle and fundamental ways, corrosive of self. Richard McNally, a professor of psychology at Harvard, has done memory studies with victims of serious trauma, and he has discovered that people with post-traumatic-stress disorder, or P.T.S.D., show marked impairment in recalling specific autobiographical memories. A healthy trauma survivor, asked to name an instance when he exhibited kindness, says, "Last Friday, I helped a neighbor plow out his driveway." But a trauma survivor with P.T.S.D. can only say something like "I was kind to people when I was in high school." This is what seems to happen when your hippocampus shrinks: you can't find your memories. "The ability to solve problems in the here and now depends on one's ability to access specific autobiographical memories in which one has encountered similar problems in the past," McNally says. "It depends on knowing what worked and what didn't." With that ability impaired, abuse survivors cannot find coherence in their lives. Their sense of identity breaks down.

It is a very short walk from this kind of psychological picture to a diagnosis often associated with child abuse; namely, dissociative identity disorder, or D.I.D. Victims of child abuse are thought sometimes to dissociate, as a way of coping with their pain, of distancing themselves from their environment, of getting away from the danger they faced. It's the kind of disconnection that would make sense if a victim's memories were floating around without context and identification, his left and right hemispheres separated and unequal, and his sense of self fragmented and elusive. It's also a short walk from here to understanding how someone with such neurological problems could become dangerous. Teicher argues that in some of his EEG and M.R.I. analyses of the imbalance between the left and the right hemispheres he is describing the neurological basis for the polarization so often observed in psychiatrically disturbed patients—the mood swings, the sharply contrasting temperaments. Instead of having two integrated hemispheres, these patients have brains that are, in some sense, divided down the middle. "What you get is a kind of erraticness," says Frank Putnam, who heads the Unit on Developmental Traumatology at the National Institute of Mental Health, in Maryland. "These kinds of people can be very different in one situation compared with another. There is the sense that they don't have a larger moral compass."

Several years ago, Lewis and Pincus worked together on an appeal for David Wilson, a young black man on death row in Louisiana. Wilson had been found guilty of murdering a motorist, Stephen Stinson, who had stopped to help when the car Wilson was in ran out of gas on I-10 outside New Orleans; and the case looked, from all accounts, almost impossible to appeal. Wilson had Stinson's blood on his clothes, in his pocket he had a shotgun shell of the same type and gauge as the one found in the gun at the murder scene, and the prosecution had an eyewitness to the whole shooting. At the trial, Wilson denied that the bloody clothes were his, denied that he had shot Stinson, denied that a tape-recorded statement the prosecution had played for the jury was of his voice, and claimed he had slept through the entire incident. It took the jury thirty-five minutes to convict him of first-degree murder and sixty-five minutes more, in the sentencing phase, to send him to the electric chair.

But when Lewis and Pincus examined him they became convinced that his story was actually much more complicated. In talking to Wilson's immediate family and other relatives, they gathered evidence that he had never been quite normal—that his personality had always seemed fractured and polarized. His mother recalled episodes from a very early age during which he would become "glassy-eyed" and seem to be someone else entirely. "David had, like, two personalities," his mother said. At times, he would wander off and be found, later, miles away, she recalled. He would have violent episodes during which he would attack his siblings' property, and subsequently deny that he had done anything untoward at all. Friends would say that they had seen someone who looked just like Wilson at a bar, but weren't sure that it had been Wilson, because he'd been acting altogether differently. On other occasions, Wilson would find things in his pockets and have no idea how they got there. He sometimes said he was born in 1955 and at other times said 1948.

What he had, in other words, were the classic symptoms of dissociation, and when Lewis and Pincus dug deeper into his history they began to understand why. Wilson's medical records detailed a seemingly endless list of hospitalizations for accidents, falls, periods of unconsciousness, and "sunstroke," dating from the time Wilson was two through his teens—the paper trail of a childhood marked by extraordinary trauma and violence. In his report to Wilson's attorneys, based on his examination of Wilson, Pincus wrote that there had been "many guns" in the home and that Wilson was often shot at as a child. He was also beaten "with a bull whip, 2x4's, a hose, pipes, a tree approximately 4 inches in diameter, wire, a piece of steel and belt buckles . . . on his back, legs, abdomen and face," until "he couldn't walk." Sometimes, when the beatings became especially intense, Wilson would have to "escape from the house and live in the fields for as long as two weeks." A kindly relative would leave food surreptitiously for him. The report goes on:

> As a result of his beatings David was ashamed to go to school lest he be seen with welts. He would "lie down in the cold sand in a hut" near his home to recuperate for several days rather than go to school.

At the hearing, Lewis argued that when Wilson said he had no memory of shooting Stinson he was actually telling the truth. The years of abuse had hurt his ability to retrieve memories.

Lewis also argued that Wilson had a violent side that he was, quite literally, unaware of; that he had the classic personality polarization of the severely abused who develop dissociative identity disorder. Lewis has videotapes of her sessions with Wilson: he is a handsome man with long fine black hair, sharply defined high cheekbones, and large, soft eyes. In the videotapes, he looks gentle. "During the hearing," Lewis recalls, "I was testifying, and I looked down at the defense table and David wasn't there. You know, David is a sweetie. He has a softness and a lovable quality. Instead, seated in his place there was this glowering kind of character, and I interrupted myself. I said, 'Excuse me, Your Honor, I just wanted to call to your attention that that is not David.' Everyone just looked." In the end, the judge vacated Wilson's death sentence.

Lewis talks a great deal about the Wilson case. It is one of the few instances in which she and Pincus succeeded in saving a defendant from the death penalty, and when she talks about what happened she almost always uses one of her favorite words—"poignant," spoken with a special emphasis, with a hesitation just before and just afterward. "In the course of evaluating someone, I always look for scars," Lewis told me. We were sitting in her Bellevue offices, watching the video of her examination of Wilson, and she was remembering the *poignant* moment she first met him. "Since I was working with a male psychologist, I said to him, 'Would you be good enough to go into the bathroom and look at David's back?' So he did that, and then he came back out and said, 'Dorothy! You must come and see this.' David had scars all over his back and chest. Burn marks. Beatings. I've seen a lot. But that was really grotesque."

ABUSE, in and of itself, does not necessarily result in violence, any more than neurological impairment or psychosis does. Lewis and Pincus argue, however, that if you mix these conditions together they become dangerous, that they have a kind of pathological synergy, that, like the ingredients of a bomb, they are troublesome individually but explosive in combination.

Several years ago, Lewis and some colleagues did a followup study of ninety-five male juveniles she and Pincus had first worked with in the late nineteen-seventies, in Connecticut. She broke the subjects into several groups: Group 1 consisted of those who did not have psychiatric or neurological vulnerabilities or an abusive childhood; Group 2 consisted of those with vulnerabilities but no abuse at home; Group 3 consisted of those with abuse but no vulnerabilities; yet another group consisted of those with abuse and extensive vulnerabilities. Seven years later, as adults, those in Group 1 had been arrested for an average of just over two criminal offenses, none of which were violent, so the result was essentially no jail time. Group 2, the psychiatrically or neurologically impaired kids, had been convicted of an average of almost ten offenses, two of which were violent, the result being just under a year of jail time. Group 3, the abused kids, had 11.9 offenses, 1.9 of them violent, the result being five hundred and sixty-two days in jail. But the group of children who had the most vulnerabilities and abuse were in another league entirely. In the intervening seven years, they had been arrested for, on average, 16.8 crimes, 5.4 of which were violent, the result being a thousand two hundred and fourteen days in prison.

In another study on this topic, a University of Southern California psychologist named Adrian Raine looked at four thousand two hundred and sixty-nine male children born and living in Denmark, and classified them according to two variables. The first was whether there were complications at birth—which correlates, loosely, with neurological impairment. The second was whether the child had been rejected by the mother (whether the child was unplanned, unwanted, and so forth)—which correlates, loosely, with abuse and neglect. Looking back eighteen years later, Raine found that those children who had not been rejected and had had no birth complications had roughly the same chance of becoming criminally violent as those with only one of the risk factors—around three per cent. For the children with both complications and rejection, however, the risk of violence tripled: in fact, the children with both problems accounted for eighteen per cent of all the violent crimes, even though they made up only 4.5 per cent of the group.

There is in these statistics a powerful and practical suggestion for how to prevent crime. In the current ideological climate, liberals argue that fighting crime requires fighting poverty, and conservatives argue that fighting crime requires ever more police and prisons; both of these things may be true, but both are also daunting. The studies suggest that there may be instances in which more modest interventions can bring large dividends. Criminal behavior that is associated with specific neurological problems is behavior that can, potentially, be diagnosed and treated like any other illness. Already, for example, researchers have found drugs that can mimic the cortical function of moderating violent behavior. The work is preliminary but promising. "We are on the cusp of a revolution in treating these conditions," Stuart Yudofsky told me. "We can use anticonvulsants, antidepressants, antihypertensive medications. There are medications out there that are F.D.A.-approved for other conditions which have profound effects on mitigating aggression." At the prevention end, as well, there's a strong argument for establishing aggressive child-abuse-prevention programs. Since 1992, for example, the National Committee to Prevent Child Abuse, a not-for-profit advocacy group based in Chicago, has been successfully promoting a program called Healthy Families America, which, working with hospitals, prenatal clinics, and physicians, identifies mothers in stressful and potentially abusive situations either before they give birth or immediately afterward, and then provides them with weekly home visits, counselling, and support for as long as five years. The main thing holding back nationwide adoption of programs like this is money: Healthy Families America costs up to two thousand dollars per family per year, but if we view it as a crime-prevention measure that's not a large sum.

These ideas, however, force a change in the way we think about criminality. Advances in the understanding of human behavior are necessarily corrosive of the idea of free will. That much is to be expected, and it is why courts have competency hearings, and legal scholars endlessly debate the definition and the use of the insanity defense. But the new research takes us one step further. If the patient of Yudofsky's who lashed out at his nurse because his orange juice was warm had, in the process, accidentally killed her, could we really hold him criminally responsible? Yudofsky says that that scenario is no different from one involving a man who is driving a car, has a heart attack, and kills a pedestrian. "Would you put *him* in jail?" he asks. Or consider Joseph Paul Franklin. By all accounts, he suffered through a brutal childhood on a par with that of David Wilson. What if he has a lesion on one of his frontal lobes, an atrophied hippocampus, a damaged and immature corpus callosum, a maldeveloped left hemisphere, a lack of synaptic complexity in the precortical limbic area, a profound left-right hemisphere split? What if in his remorselessness he was just the grownup version of the little boy Martin, whose ability to understand and relate to others was so retarded that he kept on hitting and hitting, even after the screams began? What if a history of abuse had turned a tendency toward schizophrenia—recall Franklin's colorful delusions—from a manageable impairment into the engine of murderousness? Such a person might still be sane, according to the strict legal definition. But that kind of medical diagnosis suggests, at the very least, that his ability to live by the rules of civilized society, and to understand and act on the distinctions between right and wrong, is quite different from that of someone who had a normal childhood and a normal brain.

What is implied by these questions is a far broader debate over competency and responsibility—an attempt to make medical considerations far more central to the administration of justice, so that we don't bring in doctors only when the accused seems really crazy but, rather, bring in doctors all the time, to add their expertise to the determination of responsibility.

One of the state-of-the-art diagnostic tools in neurology and psychiatry is the PET scan, a computerized X-ray that tracks the movement and rate of the body's metabolism. When you sing, for instance, the neurons in the specific regions that govern singing will start to fire. Blood will flow toward those regions, and if you take a PET scan at that moment the specific areas responsible for singing will light up on the PET computer monitor. Bremner, at Yale, has done PET scans of Vietnam War veterans suffering from post-traumatic-stress disorder. As he scanned the vets, he showed them a set of slides of Vietnam battle scenes accompanied by an appropriate soundtrack of guns and helicopters. Then he did the same thing with vets who were not suffering from P.T.S.D. Bremner printed out the results of the comparison for me, and they are fascinating. The pictures are color-coded. Blue shows the parts of the brain that were being used identically in the two groups of veterans, and most of each picture is blue. A few parts are light blue or green, signifying that the P.T.S.D. vets were using those regions a little less than the healthy vets were. The key color, however, is white. White shows brain areas that the healthy vets were using as they watched the slide show and the unhealthy vets were hardly using at all; in Bremner's computer printout, there is a huge white blob in the front of every non-P.T.S.D. scan.

"That's the orbitofrontal region," Bremner told me. "It's responsible for the extinction of fear." The orbitofrontal region is the part of your brain that evaluates the primal feelings of fear and anxiety which come up from the brain's deeper recesses. It's the part that tells you that you're in a hospital watching a slide show of the Vietnam War, not in Vietnam living through the real thing. The vets with P.T.S.D. weren't using that part of their brain. That's why every time a truck backfires or they see a war picture in a magazine they are forced to relive their wartime experiences: they can't tell the difference.

It doesn't take much imagination to see that this technique might someday be used to evaluate criminals—to help decide whether to grant parole, for example, or to find out whether some kind of medical treatment might aid reëntry into normal society. We appear to be creating a brand-new criminal paradigm: the research suggests that instead of thinking about and categorizing criminals merely by their acts—murder, rape, armed robbery, and so on—we ought to categorize criminals also according to their disabilities, so that a murderer with profound neurological damage and a history of vicious childhood abuse is thought of differently from a murderer with no brain damage and mild child abuse, who is, in turn, thought of differently from a murderer with no identifiable impairment at all. This is a more flexible view. It can be argued that it is a more sophisticated view. But even those engaged in such research—for example, Pincus—confess to discomfort at its implications, since something is undoubtedly lost in the translation. The moral force of the old standard, after all, lay in its inflexibility. Murder was murder, and the allowances made for aggravated circumstances were kept to a minimum. Is a moral standard still a moral standard when it is freighted with exceptions and exemptions and physiological equivocation?

When Lewis went to see Bundy, in Florida, on the day before his execution, she asked him why he had invited her—out of a great many people lining up outside his door—to see him. He answered, "Because everyone else wants to know what I did. You are the only one who wants to know why I did it." It's impossible to be sure what the supremely manipulative Bundy meant by this: whether he genuinely appreciated Lewis, or whether he simply regarded her as his last conquest. What is clear is that, over the four or five times they met in Bundy's last years, the two reached a curious understanding: he was now part of her scientific enterprise.

"I wasn't writing a book about him," Lewis recalls. "That he knew. The context in which he had first seen me was a scientific study, and this convinced him that I wasn't using him. In the last meeting, as I recall, he said that he wanted any material that I found out about him to be used to understand what causes people to be violent. We even discussed whether he would allow his brain to be studied. It was not an easy thing to talk about with him, let me tell you." At times, Lewis says, Bundy was manic, "high as a kite." On one occasion, he detailed to her just how he had killed a woman, and, on another occasion, he stared at her and stated flatly, "The man sitting across from you did not commit any murders." But she says that at the end she sensed a certain breakthrough. "The day before he was executed, he asked me to turn off the tape recorder. He said he wanted to tell me things that he didn't want recorded, so I didn't record them. It was very confidential." To this day, Lewis has never told anyone what Bundy said. There is something almost admirable about this. But there is also something strange about extending the physician-patient privilege to a killer like Bundy—about turning the murderer so completely into a patient. It is not that the premise is false, that murderers can't also be patients. It's just that once you make that leap—once you turn the criminal into an object of medical scrutiny—the crime itself inevitably becomes pushed aside and normalized. The difference between a crime of evil and a crime of illness is the difference between a sin and a symptom. And symptoms don't intrude in the relationship between the murderer and the rest of us: they don't force us to stop and observe the distinctions between right and wrong, between the speakable and the unspeakable, the way sins do. It was at the end of that final conversation that Bundy reached down and kissed Lewis on the cheek. But that was not all that happened. Lewis then reached up, put her arms around him, and kissed him back.

Car wars: taming drivers' aggression

Cars and roads are designed to be safer than ever. So why are drivers so nervous and irritable?

By Scott Sleek

Monitor staff

When it comes to patience, kindness and caution, American motorists are running on empty.

At least that's the perception of the public and the media. News accounts of dramatic traffic fatalities and highway violence, not to mention Americans' simmering aggravation with clogged highways, have left people fearing a new rampant safety hazard—aggressive driving. Our roadways are now viewed as a lethal mixture of insolence, impatience and hostility.

And that combination sometimes results in bizarre deaths. In April, three people in Washington, D.C., were killed after two drivers—in an anger-laced race—skipped a median and plowed into oncoming traffic. And last year in Detroit, a woman plunged to her death from a bridge while trying to escape an enraged motorist who was chasing her for rear-ending his car.

Even the most even-tempered Americans can admit to occasionally shouting or honking at other aggravating motorists—the elderly man who drives only 45 mph in the passing lane, the teen-ager who brashly weaves through traffic on the freeway, or the anxious executive who plows through a stop sign.

Have we become a society of road warriors?

A small contingent of psychologists is studying that question, and reaching mixed conclusions. Some say people are no more aggressive (although perhaps more complacent) on the highway than they were 20 years ago. But others believe that increasingly crowded highways and busier schedules have made drivers more frantic and hostile, and call for widespread psychoeducational efforts—anger-management techniques, for instance—to restore civility and safety to the road.

A Hawaii psychology professor has even created an undergraduate course on what he calls traffic psychology, which aims to help people become kinder, gentler motorists.

Hostility or complacency?

The study of aggressive driving dates back to at least the late 1960s, when British researchers concluded that motorists who demonstrated high aggression levels were accident-prone. In a questionnaire, a small percentage of the participants stated, "At times, I felt I could gladly kill another driver." Subsequent studies have also linked aggression with accident liability.

Many people apparently fear that those driving sentiments have risen in the last 30 years. Surveys by the American Automobile Association in the Washington, D.C. area indicate that many people regard aggressive driving as more of a threat on the roads than drunk driving.

But what is aggressive driving? Highway safety experts have come to develop a definition that is far narrower than the public's. Researchers view it only as *hostile* actions, such as forcing another motorist off the road, shouting obscenities at a passing driver or, in extreme cases, shooting at another car—as motorists did in the late 1980s in California.

Laypeople tend to define the behavior as simple *risk-taking,* in the form of speeding, tailgating, weaving dangerously through traffic and ignoring stop signs and red lights. That type of conduct is a far more prevalent problem than the more belligerent highway behavior, and results in far more injuries and deaths, safety experts say.

"If we define aggressive driving as risk-taking, and not just hostile action, then 'we's the enemy,'" said Mike Smith, a researcher at the National Highway Traffic Safety Administration. "The human being is such that he's always testing the envelope. In some ways, we're all juvenile delinquents at heart."

That inherent vehicular rebellion makes dangerous driving difficult to quantify, Smith added.

"Years ago, we tried to find 'the bad driver,'" he said. "What we found is we couldn't identify him. In other types of behaviors, the deviants are more easily spotted. But because of the sheer number of drivers out there, and the fact that we're *all* bending the rules a bit, it's hard to measure bad drivers."

Traffic fatality rates, however, are easily measured, and statistics show that highway deaths have declined substantially over the last 30 years. Traffic fatalities and injuries are still considered a major public health problem: More than 40,000 people die each year in roadway crashes.

But the annual fatality rate today averages about 1.8 deaths per 100 million miles traveled, compared to 5.5 deaths per 100 [million] miles traveled in 1966, according to governmental measures. Experts attribute that drop to the rising use of seat belts, child restraints and motorcycle helmets; tougher penalties for drunk driving; and new vehicle safety features, such as airbags and antilock brakes.

The need for speed

But while cars have become safer, drivers have become more distressed—in part because they can't drive fast enough. Psychologists agree that swelling congestion on the highways is creating more aggravation that may presage pugnacity among motorists.

Urbanization, dual-income families and workplace downsizing have left more people living in crowded communities, faced with more to do and less time to do it, said E. Scott Geller, PhD, a psychology professor at Virginia Polytechnic Institute and State University and a senior partner in a consulting group called Safety Performance Solutions. People thus feel rushed everywhere, and their stress is particularly noticeable when they drive, Geller said.

Other psychologists regard social ills such as family discord, job dissatisfaction and even physical illness as a possible *result* of driving distress.

In his studies of Southern California drivers, Raymond Novaco, PhD, a psychology professor at the University of California, Irvine, found that people report more overall stress the longer and farther they drive to work. And studies indicate that traffic jams and other driving stressors can affect mood, health, work attendance, job stability and life satisfaction, he said.

People who have long commutes to work, for example, are found to have higher blood pressure than those who commute shorter distances. And people who have more roads to travel to get to their jobs call in sick more often than those who drive on fewer roads, Novaco added.

The frustration and stress resulting from traffic conditions don't automatically generate aggressive actions, but they do increase the risk for such behavior, researchers say.

Some believe traffic-induced aggression stems in part from territorial defensiveness. They describe the car as an extension of personal space. People become contentious when someone encroaches on that private territory, such as bumping their car from behind, he said.

"To some people, their car is their moving castle," said Smith. "They look at it as their private sanctum. And when someone interferes with that, it can lead to inappropriate behavior."

The normal inhibitions against nasty behavior erode in the anonymity of modern highways, Novaco adds. In the confines of their cars, people feel they can be discourteous without accountability: Chances are you'll never again see the truck driver whom you just cut off in traffic.

Research psychologists believe they've demonstrated that the cloak of anonymity indeed spawns more antagonistic driving.

Researchers at Maryland's Towson State University, for example, reached such a conclusion by measuring people's use of their car horns. In the study, a confederate driver looked for convertibles or jeeps approaching a stoplight, and pulled in front of them before they reached the signal. When the light turned green, the confederate driver remained idle and recorded the subject's reaction, particularly their use of the car horn. Subjects driving their vehicles with the tops up began honking their horns sooner, and kept at it longer, than those with their tops down.

"It appears that an enclosed automobile may provide the occupant with a sense of anonymity which, in turn, serves to facilitate aggressive behavior," the researchers wrote in a 1955 article in the *Journal of Social Behavior and Personality*.

Blaming the other guy

Psychologists have developed several ideas for promoting safer, more relaxed driving behavior. But they also believe that the biggest task in generating safer highways is convincing people to scrutinize their own conduct rather than blaming other drivers. In a variety of surveys, most people who were questioned rated the safety of their own driving as better than the average motorist's—a self-image that experts believe is inflated.

"Admonitions to people to drive safely are likely to have little effect," IIHS psychologists wrote last year in the *Journal of Safety Research*. "It seems likely that people will view these messages as applying to others."

The public furor over aggressive driving reflects that tendency to blame others instead of being more cautious ourselves, Lund said. None of us sees ourselves as one of the proverbial "nuts behind the wheel," he said.

GUNSLINGING IN AMERICA

Does a gun make you safer or increase your likelihood of violent death? A slew of recent studies have claimed to answer this question once and for all. But all they may actually prove is how difficult it is to say anything about violence and human behavior. **By Fred Guterl**

SAM WALKER WAS NOT YOUR AVERAGE AMERICAN GUN owner. For one thing, he had no interest whatsoever in hunting. And whereas the average gun owner owns at least three guns, Walker owned only one, a .38-caliber revolver, which friends persuaded him to buy for the sole purpose of protecting himself and his family in their suburban Houston home. Walker didn't even particularly like guns. He still hadn't gotten around to acquainting himself with his new weapon when his burglar alarm went off one weekday morning last December. Notified by his security company of the intrusion, Walker rushed home from work, quietly entered the house, took the gun out from the spot where he had left it for safekeeping, and, hearing a noise, moved stealthily up the stairs and opened a closet door. He saw a movement, a figure, and in a split second fired. The smoothly oiled gun worked perfectly, and Walker's aim was true. A body fell to the floor. It was his 16-year-old daughter. She had cut school that day and had hidden in the closet to avoid her father. It wound up costing her her life.

If Walker's tragic story argues against the benefits to be gained by gun ownership, consider an incident that happened a month later, across the country in New York City. One weekday morning in January, in front of a Brooklyn government building in broad daylight, Eric Immesberger stopped to give a man directions. Suddenly a second man came out from behind a pillar and knocked Immesberger to the ground. The two men then demanded his wallet and started beating him. Now, it just so happens that Immesberger is an investigator for the Brooklyn district attorney, and, more to the point, he was armed with a 9-millimeter semiautomatic handgun. He managed to pull his weapon and shoot one of the robbers in the chest. The other fled. Immesberger was later treated at a hospital for a broken nose.

Which case better represents the reality of owning a gun? It depends, of course, on whom you ask. But one point is indisputable: murder is committed more frequently in the United States than just about anywhere else in the developed world, and guns are its chief instrument. For African American males between the ages of 14 and 25, guns are the leading cause of death. And despite the recent downward blip in the numbers, crimes in the United States are far more likely to lead to death than they are in any other developed country. Every two and a half years, guns kill as many Americans as died in the Vietnam War. The litany of statistics is as deadening as it is depressing. Although few people would argue that cleansing the population of all guns wouldn't go a long way to trimming the firearms fatality rate, the country's 230 million guns, shielded by the Second Amendment, seem likely to remain in circulation for a long time.

Lacking a consensus on gun control, lawmakers have in recent years at least tried to put fewer guns in the hands of criminals and more in the hands of law-abiding citizens. The Brady Bill, for instance, seeks to curtail the proliferation of handguns, the weapons of choice for both crime and self-defense, by imposing background checks and a waiting period on new purchases. At the same time, the states are passing laws making it easy for residents to carry concealed handguns. But is arming the citizenry a good way to offset the risk of crime?

In the last decade researchers have focused unprecedented attention on the problem, and authors of some of the more dramatic studies have managed to amass impressively large stacks of press clippings. But science has not been especially helpful here. So far, nobody has been able to marshal convincing evidence for either side of the debate. "The first point that's obvious in any scientific reading of the field is the extreme paucity of data," says Franklin Zimring, a professor of law at the University of California at Berkeley. "What we have is critically flawed—on both sides." Indeed, the scientific literature on the subject seems to teach very little, except for the tedious fact that it is difficult to say anything rigorously scientific about human behavior—particularly aggression.

WHAT'S OBVIOUS BY NOW TO MOST SCIENTISTS is that assessing the risk of owning a gun is nothing like assessing the risk of smoking cigarettes was 30 or 40 years ago. Back then medical researchers convinced themselves quickly of the cause-and-effect relationship between cigarettes and cancer. Although they had no direct, mechanistic proof, the epidemiological evidence proved the case far beyond any reasonable doubt. With guns, such a link has proved elusive, to say the least. Researchers think that about half of American households possess guns, they're fairly sure that about two-thirds of these households have handguns, and they believe the proportion of handguns, within the total number of guns of all types, is rising. Their reasoning rests partly on the assumption that most guns bought these days are intended for self-defense; because of their small size, handguns are the overwhelming choice for this purpose. They also assume that the relative number of handguns owned will be reflected in the relative number of firearms deaths caused by handguns—about 60 percent.

Given the magnitude of the violence and the prevalence of the weapons, it is surprising that science has come to the issue of risk only recently. Criminologists have spent several decades exploring the impact of guns on crime and the behavior of criminals, but they have neglected the question of individual risk. When the medical profession got interested in guns in the early 1980s, it made them a public health issue, looking at the risk to the public at large. Emergency room doctors see the associated hazards every day, in the children who die or are wounded by playing with guns, in the successful and unsuccessful teenage suicides, and in countless other gun-related accidents such as Walker's, in which the gun itself functions properly in only a narrow mechanical sense and the risk is more clearly seen in retrospect. And this public health perspective spurred renewed interest in studies that test to what degree the presence of guns increases the likelihood of death to their owners. But this approach, of course, focused on gun ownership as a societal issue; it did not assume the point of view of the individual. Doing so would have treated a gun as a consumer product, like a power drill or a lawn mower or a food processor, that carries with it a certain risk of accidental injury or death that must be weighed against its benefits.

Many of these public health studies attracted a great deal of publicity because they seemed to settle the question of risk once and for all. Arthur Kellermann, an emergency room doctor, is perhaps the most prolific and visible of the medical researchers who have tried to quantify the risk of owning a gun. Although he is a southerner who was raised with guns and who likes target shooting, he has nonetheless become a major source of bumper-sticker statistics for gun-control advocates. He insists that he has proved not only that a gun is a poor deterrent to residential crime but that having one actually increases the chance that somebody in your home will be shot and killed. In particular, his studies conclude that gun-owning households, when compared with gunless ones, are almost three times as likely to be the scene of a homicide and almost five times as likely to be the scene of a suicide. "If having a gun in the home was a good deterrent," Kellermann says, "then we should have seen few guns in the homes of murder victims. But we found the opposite."

Kellermann's work has drawn fire from researchers who suspect that his passion for the issue has blinded him to ambiguities in his data. "Kellermann has decided that guns are bad, and he's out to prove it," says Yale sociologist Albert Reiss. Although in general criminologists don't object to Kellermann's research methods, they part company in their interpretation of his results. His evidence, say critics, is so riddled with uncertainties as to preclude any definitive interpretation.

UPON CLOSE INSPECTION, KELLERMANN'S RESULTS are much more modest than his dramatic conclusions would indicate. He chose to study guns in the home not only because lots of people buy them for self-defense and keep them in a drawer beside their beds but also because *home* is a well-defined place that simplifies the task of collecting data. Police homicide records specifically include the location of each incident and the weapon used, and it was a straightforward matter for Kellermann to follow up each case by interviewing surviving family members and friends. The problem was in coming up with a suitable control group against which to draw comparisons. Ideally, you want to pair each victim with a control that differs from the victim only in that one was shot and the other wasn't. Kellermann devised a clever methodology for doing so. For each victim, he randomly selected one neighbor after another until he found someone who was the same age, sex, and race. Eventually he assembled "matched pairs" for 388 homicide victims.

When he compared the victims with the control group, however, he found that many more factors differentiated the two groups than their victim status. It turned out that the households in which homicides took place were more likely to contain a family member who abused alcohol or drugs and had a history of domestic violence—these factors contributed to the likelihood of homicide independent of the existence of guns. Kellermann took pains to compensate for these other factors using standard statistical techniques of epidemiology. In essence, he tried to estimate how much each factor, such as alcohol abuse, might have influenced the homicide rate among victims in his study, and then he adjusted his figures accordingly.

What neither Kellermann nor his critics can know for certain is whether this statistical juggling actually uncovers any underlying trends or whether something else is going on that Kellermann hasn't accounted for. Kellermann himself admits the possibility of some kind of "psychological confounding"—that some intangible factor such as aggression, rather than merely the presence of guns, is influencing the results. Critics also

37. Gunslinging in America

> **THE RESULTS OF ONE SURVEY, TO FIND OUT HOW OFTEN GUNS ARE USED IN SELF-DEFENSE, DEPICT THE COUNTRY'S GUN OWNERS AS HOLDING BACK A TIDAL WAVE OF VIOLENCE AND CRIME.**

point out that the victims in Kellermann's study may have gotten guns because they felt themselves to be threatened in some way, which means they might have suffered higher homicide rates even if they hadn't bothered to arm themselves. "Kellermann has shown that homicide victims are more likely to keep a gun at home, but criminologists have known that for years," says Gary Kleck, of Florida State University in Tallahassee.

Kellermann's even more dramatic figures on suicide in the home are especially problematic, mainly because Kellermann relies on the numbers without offering an explanation. "There's no theory to account for his conclusion," says Zimring. Suicide is also thought to be prone to substitution—that is, although guns are the preferred instrument of suicide in the United States, a person bent on suicide can easily find a substitute if need be. Since Kellermann's study focuses on suicides in the home, it doesn't account for the victim, who lacking a gun, decides instead to jump off a bridge.

Regardless of their personal feelings on guns, criminologists, who tend to look at violence through the lens of police statistics and surveys, are usually more open than doctors to the possibility that a gun can now and then deter a crime. Trouble is, social scientists are poorly equipped to measure events that do not occur—crimes that are averted because the would-be victim had a gun. As a result, criminologists have resorted to surveys to get at this phenomenon. Most recently, Kleck conducted a survey to find out how often gun owners actually use their guns in self-defense. His controversial results depict the country's gun owners as holding back a tidal wave of violence and crime. He estimates that 2.5 million times each year, somebody somewhere in America uses a gun in self-defense. This figure has become a mantra of the National Rifle Association (with whom Kleck has no affiliation).

Most other criminologists are critical of Kleck's methods, and almost all of them are incredulous at the results. A big complaint is that he leaves it to his survey respondents to define a "defensive gun use," so he may have captured incidents that most people would consider trivial. "An awful lot of what some people would call self-defense is, like, somebody asks you for a quarter and you tell them to get lost, but as you walk away you keep your hand on your gun," says Philip Cook, a Duke University economist. In addition, many incidents that people report as self-defense may in fact be assault, in which the respondent takes a more active role than he admits. "In many instances, we may only be talking to one side of an argument," says Zimring.

What this criticism comes down to is that Kleck, like Kellermann and all the other researchers in this field, is guilty of failing to explain what happens when people carry guns, and how possessing one affects their interactions with criminals. As Reiss puts it, "We know very little about how motivation enters into an action." Zimring likens efforts to understand the deterrent effect of guns to "dancing with clouds." Kleck himself admits that "the better the research, the more it tends to support the null hypothesis—that gun ownership and control laws have no net effect on violence."

Even when a seemingly perfect opportunity for a real-life experiment presents itself, as it did recently to criminologist David McDowall, the null hypothesis is often all that a criminologist is left with. Several years ago, Florida, Mississippi, and Oregon adopted "shall issue" laws requiring the states to issue a license to almost anybody who wants to carry a concealed handgun. McDowall saw that the effect of these laws would give him a laboratory in which to test the arms-race hypothesis: he could find out whether criminals, knowing their victims are more likely to be armed with handguns, are more likely to use guns themselves. He could also find out whether citizens, when armed, can deter crime.

After the new laws were passed, permits to carry concealed handguns rose enormously—in Florida the number of licenses soared from 17,000 before the law was passed in 1987 to 141,000 seven years later. After studying five cities, McDowall found that the rate of firearms homicides increased overall by 26 percent. Although this would seem to support the arms-race hypothesis, the results were inconsistent. Whereas McDowall had expected the effects of the liberalized laws to be greatest in Miami, the biggest city in the study and the one with the highest crime rate, the rise in homicides there was too small to be statistically significant. However, McDowall believes his evidence is strong enough to show that armed citizens do not decrease the number of firearms-related deaths.

DESPITE THE FRUSTRATING LACK OF CLARITY, researchers are universally optimistic that, with time and the accretion of data, insight into the mechanism of violence will come, and with it, a greater consensus on the real risks of guns. For the time being, however, there will remain very little one researcher can say about risk that another researcher cannot refute. Most favor restricting the availability of guns by mandating background checks and waiting periods, which serve to some degree to keep guns out of the hands of "hotheads" and criminals. There is also a consensus that higher homicide rates have everything to do with the preponderance of guns—an obvious inference when considering, say, crime statistics of London and New York. These two cities have similar crime rates, but the homicide rate from burglaries and robberies in gun-rich New York is vastly higher—54 times higher in 1992, according to Zimring. "America doesn't have a crime problem," he says, "it has a lethal violence problem. It's that thin layer of lethal crime that Americans are afraid of."

Given that purging guns from the population is problematic, would the world be safer if each law-abiding citizen carried a gun? Alessandro Veralli hesitates before answering this question. For most of his adult life, he has carried a concealed handgun almost everywhere he goes, whether it's out to the movies with his wife or to the local hardware store on a Saturday afternoon. Yet Veralli, a Master Firearms Instructor for the New York City Police Department and an NRA life member, admits that as a civilian he has had very little opportunity to use his gun. If he ever found himself a customer at a liquor store that was being held up, in most cases his training and common sense would tell him to lie low rather than start a shoot-out. If he was out with his wife and a thief demanded his wallet, he would probably hand it over. "In a robbery, there's not much you can do except maybe shoot at the guy as he's walking away," he says. "But what if he shoots back? I'd be putting my wife in danger, and for what?" He carries a gun for the hypothetical extreme case when having it might mean the difference between life and death. "Personally I'd hate to get into a bad situation and think that I might have been able to do something if I had had a gun," he says.

But should other citizens carry guns? "I'm tempted to say yes," he says, but then he demurs. "Maybe it makes sense in other parts of the country where they have more space. New York, though, is too crowded. There's something about all these people being confined in a small space. People can fly off the handle over little things. I don't think I'd want to see each and every one of them carrying a gun."

Televised Violence and Kids: A Public Health Problem?

When Leonard Eron surveyed every 8-year-old child in Columbia County, New York, in 1960, he found something he wasn't looking for: an astonishing, and unmistakable, correlation between the amount of violence the youngsters saw on television and the aggressiveness of their behavior.

More than three decades and two follow-up studies later, after several related research projects and countless hearings and conferences, the work of Eron and his ISR colleague, L. Rowell Huesmann, has become an "overnight sensation." As leading researchers on the effects of media violence on the young, they have been making the rounds of TV talk and news programs and radio call-in shows, while fielding almost daily calls from reporters.

Their message is ultimately a simple one: Aggression is a learned behavior, it is learned at an early age, and media violence is one of its teachers. But because it is a learned behavior, there is hope that it can be unlearned, or never taught in the first place.

Both Eron and Huesmann are professors of psychology at the University of Michigan and research scientists at ISR's Research Center for Group Dynamics. Huesmann is also a professor of communication and acting chair of the Department of Communication. Their talents and interests have complemented each other since they met at Yale in the early 1970s. Eron's research interest is aggression, while Huesmann, who minored in mathematics as a U-M undergraduate in the early '60s, brings his prowess in data analysis and expertise in cognitive mechanisms and development to the team.

"I wanted to measure child-rearing practices as they related to aggression" in the 1960 survey, says Eron. "The parents knew what the study was about and, in the interviews, we were asking sensitive questions about how parents punished their children, what their disagreements were, and so forth. So we wanted to buffer those with what we called 'Ladies' Home Journal' questions — Had they read Dr. Spock? How often did their child watch TV? What were his or her favorite shows?

"But the computer was unaware of our humor and analyzed those TV programs," he adds. "And, lo and behold, the more aggressive that kids were in school, the higher the violence content of the shows they watched."

But that still left the chicken-and-egg ambiguity. Did watching violent TV make kids more aggressive, or did more aggressive kids watch violent TV? That's where time, and Huesmann, came in. In 1970, the U.S. Surgeon General formed a committee on television and social behavior, and asked Eron to re-survey as many of the Columbia County kids as he could find. Eron, in turn, sought the services of Huesmann, then an assistant professor at Yale.

"How can they say their programs have no effect on behavior when they're in the business of selling ads?"

—Leonard Eron

"The analysis of long-term data on children's behavior required some sophisticated mathematical and statistical analysis," says Huesmann, "and that was the area in which I was trained."

The project also struck another responsive chord, he says: "The models that had been advanced to explain the long-terms effects of television violence were lacking an explanation of how the effects of watching television violence could last way into adulthood."

So it was back to the Hudson Valley of upstate New York in 1971. They found about 500 of the now 19-year-olds from the original sample of 875 youngsters. The results were just as powerful, if not more so.

"The correlation between violence-viewing at age 8 and how aggressive the individual was at 19 was higher than the correlation between watching violence at age 8 and behaving aggressively at age 8," says Eron. "There was no correlation between violence-viewing at age 19 and aggressiveness at 19. It seems there was a cumulative effect going on here."

Its persistence was documented once more in 1981, when 400 of the subjects were surveyed again, along with 80 of their offspring. The 30-year-old men who had been the most aggressive when they were 8 had more arrests for drunk

---

"The evidence is overwhelming. The strength of the relationship is the same as cigarettes causing lung cancer. Is there any doubt about that?"

—Leonard Eron

---

driving, more arrests for violent crime, were more abusive to their spouses . . . and had more aggressive children. And of the 600 subjects whose criminal justice records were reviewed, those who watched more violence on TV when they were 8 had been arrested more often for violent crimes, and self-reported more fights when consuming alcohol.

In other words, their viewing choices and behavior as 8-year-olds were better predictors of their behavior at age 30 than either what they watched on TV or how aggressively they behaved later in life.

"Children learn programs for how to behave that I call scripts," says Huesmann. "In a new social situation, how do you know how to behave? You search for scripts to follow. Where is a likely place for those scripts to come from? From what you've observed others doing in life, films, TV. So, as a child, you see a Dirty Harry movie, where the heroic policeman is shooting people right and left. Even years later, the right kind of scene can trigger that script and suggest a way to behave that follows it. Our studies have come up with a lot of evidence that suggests that's very possible. Moreover, we find that watching TV violence affects the viewer's beliefs and attitudes about how people are going to behave."

The longitudinal data were so compelling that the 1993 report of the American Psychological Association's Commission on Violence and Youth, which Eron chaired, stated unequivocally that there is "absolutely no doubt that higher levels of viewing violence on television are correlated with increased acceptance of aggressive attitudes and increased aggressive behavior."

"The evidence is overwhelming," says Eron. "The strength of the relationship is the same as cigarettes causing lung cancer. Is there any doubt about that?"

Only among those who profit from tobacco, just as TV and movie industry executives have generated most of the criticism of the ISR colleagues' work. While the media in general were fascinated by the damning data, especially after the APA report was released last August, the visual media in particular were equally eager to defend themselves and defuse the evidence.

This is not a message the industry wants to hear. Its position is that the off-on switch is the ultimate defense, and parents wield it. Eron says that's unrealistic.

"Parents can't do it all by themselves, especially in these days of single-parent families and two parents working," he says. "They can't be with their children all the time."

If the industry can't or won't regulate itself, should the government intervene? It's an obvious question to ask and a difficult one to answer, especially for believers in the First Amendment.

"The scientific evidence clearly shows that long-term exposure to TV violence makes kids behave more aggressively," says Huesmann, "but it doesn't show the same effect on adults. What you watch now won't have nearly the effect of what you saw when you were 8. What we're talking about is regulating what kids see, not adults, and there are reasonable precedents for this — alcohol and tobacco regulations, for example."

"What we're talking about is regulating what kids see, not adults, and there are reasonable precedents for this—alcohol and tobacco regulations, for example."

—L. Rowell Huesmann

In their view, watching TV violence is every bit as dangerous to kids as smoking and drinking. They see it as a matter of public health, not free speech. And they are grimly amused by the industry's protestations of exculpability. "How can they say their programs have no effect on behavior when they're in the business of selling ads?" Eron asks.

Then there are those who wonder how it is that Detroit and Windsor, Ontario, which face each other across the Detroit River and receive the same TV signals, have such disparate crime rates. "If we said TV violence is the only cause, then they'd have an argument," says Eron. "But we don't say that."

They are, in fact, well aware that any number of psychological, physiological and macro-social factors are simmering in the stew of violence. "TV is really a minor part of our research," says Eron, "although it's gotten the most play. We're interested in how children learn aggression. Violence on TV is only one cause, but it's a cause we can do something about."

Two projects they are currently involved in show signs of making progress toward that end. Huesmann is directing the second phase of a study begun in 1977 that looks, he says, at "whether the effects of media violence generalize across different countries and cultures."

Researchers are collecting longitudinal data on subjects in Poland, Australia, Finland and Israel, as well as the United States. Meanwhile, Eron, Huesmann and three researchers at the University of Illinois (where Huesmann spent 20 years before returning to U-M in 1992) are conducting an ambitious study of inner-city schools "in which we are trying to change the whole school atmosphere," says Eron.

In the former study, almost 2,000 children were interviewed and tested in either first or third grade and for two consecutive years thereafter. "In all countries, the children who watched more violence were the more aggressive," says Huesmann. "This was a study showing that this was a real effect across countries and not a special, one-time study of Columbia County."

The only exceptions were found in Australia and Israel. In Australia, there was a correlation between watching violence and behaving aggressively, but it was not as persistent as in other countries. In Israel, the correlation was stronger for city-raised children than for those growing up in kibbutzes. Huesmann suspects that the communal nature of the kibbutz, with its attendant reinforcement of pro-social behaviors, neutralized the effect of televised violence. And Australia? "We have no good explanation," he says.

"As a child, you see a Dirty Harry movie, where the heroic policeman is shooting people right and left. Even years later, the right kind of scene can trigger that script and suggest a way to behave that follows it."

—L. Rowell Huesmann

Perhaps the second phase, revisiting subjects who are now in their early 20s, will provide one. Interviewing is almost complete in the United States and Finland and began in Poland this winter as one of the collaborative projects between ISR and ISS [Institute for Social Studies], its Polish sibling. Work will begin in Israel near the end of 1994.

The project in Illinois attempts to measure the relative influence of multiple contexts, including schools, peers, families, and neighborhoods, and the cost-effectiveness of targeting each. "This is a public health model," says Eron, "from primary prevention to tertiary prevention."

Both teachers and students will be taught techniques for handling aggression and solving problems. Youngsters who are believed to be at high risk for becoming aggressive will also be seen in groups of six by research staffers. And half of those youngsters will receive family therapy as well, what Eron calls "an increased dosage" of treatment.

"We don't think just working with kids in the schools will help much," Eron says. "Studies show kids change attitudes, but there's no data to show they change behavior. In this program, we're trying to change the whole school atmosphere. We're also trying to see what the cost-effectiveness is. Is it enough to have a school program? Or do you always have to do family therapy, which is the most costly? Does it really add to the effectiveness of the treatment?"

The problem clearly isn't simple, but some of the data are nonetheless clear. "Over the years, Rowell and I have testified at many congressional hearings," says Eron, "and now it's having an effect. The public sentiment is there's too much of this stuff, and we've got the data to show it. I think we are having an impact, finally."

Eron himself estimates that TV is only responsible for perhaps 10% of the violent behavior in this country. "But," he says, "if we could reduce violence by 10%, that would be a great achievement."

MENACE TO SOCIETY

WORRIED ABOUT MEDIA VIOLENCE? CARTOONS MAY BE THE REAL CULPRITS

JOHN DAVIDSON

JOHN DAVIDSON *is a writer living in Austin, Texas.*

WITH THREE-QUARTERS OF AMERICANS surveyed convinced that movies, television and music spur young people to violence, and politicians on the left and right blasting the entertainment industry for irresponsibility, the debate over violence in popular culture is likely to be a key issue in the presidential campaign.

Republican presidential front-runner Bob Dole, conservative guru William Bennett, black activist C. DeLores Tucker and liberal Democrat Sen. Paul Simon all have attacked portrayals of violence, treating the link between art and reality as gospel truth. They've found support for their claims from the American Psychological Association and the American Psychiatric Association, which have both issued reports stating that television violence causes aggression.

And a new controversy surrounding video games has been sparked by Lt. Col. Dave Grossman, a psychologist and Army Ranger. In his book *On Killing*, he claims that these games function like firing ranges, using the same type of conditioning employed to overcome soldiers' built-in inhibition to killing in the Vietnam War.

The research, however, is less clear. Most experts who have studied the issue believe there is *some* link—indirect, perhaps—between seeing violence and commiting it, but there is no agreement on how strong that link is or how to measure it. What's more, even those who argue most persuasively that there is a case to be made for connecting violence and culture agree that the biggest problem may not be teenagers seeing *Natural Born Killers* or listening to the Geto Boys but small children watching Saturday morning cartoons.

FOR THE LAST 40 YEARS, SOCIAL SCIENTISTS have attempted to measure how media violence affects people, with the bulk of the research focused on television. One of the most influential studies was directed by George Gerbner. Beginning in 1967, Gerbner, who at that time was dean of the Annenberg School for Communication at the University of Pennsylvania, and his colleagues created a violence index that is still used to measure the percentage of network programs that have violence, the number of violent acts, the percentage of characters involved in violence and the percentage involved in killing. Their index doesn't reflect the increased amount of violent material made available through cable television and VCRs. (That count, according to the National Coalition on Television Violence, is that children in homes with cable TV and/or a VCR will see about 32,000 murders and 40,000 attempted murders by the time they're 18.)

Gerbner's group concluded that television acts as an electronic melting pot, which creates a national culture. Part of that culture is "the mean-world syndrome," which leads people to believe that they are more likely to be victims of violence than they are in reality. "People who watch the most television are usually the ones who have fewer options, less money and less education," says Nancy Signorielli, a professor of communication at the University of Delaware who worked on the Gerbner study. "Their views of the world reflect what they see on television, and they overestimate their chances of being involved in violence." Like the man in Louisiana who in 1992 shot and killed a Japanese exchange student looking for a Halloween party, people overreact to perceived threats and act violently.

Remarkably, Gerbner found that the indexes have remained relatively constant during the past two decades. Nonetheless, he's been accused of exaggerating the amount of violence by not taking context into consideration. A poke in the eye, as far as he's concerned, is basically a poke in the eye; his group counts *The Three Stooges* and Road Runner cartoons as violent programming.

A landmark study funded by the four major networks in response to congressional pressure and released this past fall attempted to correct that deficiency and qualify different types of violence by looking at time slot, parental advisory, duration, explicitness, relation to the story and consequences. Researchers at the Center for Communication Policy at the University of California at Los Angeles confirmed that context is crucial. In other words, a TV program that shows kids beating up a fellow student with impunity could have a more harmful effect than one that shows a couple of murderers who end up in jail. Even Signorielli acknowledges that context is important: "What we have in the U.S. is happy violence. In Japan, violence is much more graphic and much more realistic," she says. "There, television violence may actually work as a deterrent. But here, if someone's shot we don't see the wound. There's not much bleeding on U.S. television."

Leonard Eron, a research scientist at the University of Michigan, has taken another approach. He began by studying how aggression develops in children, never considering television to be important. "I thought television was just another version of the sort of things children were exposed to in the past—fairy tales, stories and movies," says Eron. "But television is different, if in no other way than [that programs are] repeated over and over again."

Eron and his colleagues tested 875 third-graders in New York's Columbia County and interviewed about 80 percent of their parents. To relieve tension in the interviews, Eron threw in a question about television viewing. What surprised him was the correlation between aggression and viewing habits. Children whose parents said they watched a lot of violent television turned out to be aggressive in school, and 10 years later, in the first of the follow-up studies, Eron discovered that what a child watched at 8 years old was "one of the best predictors" of adult aggression—more important than the parents' child-rearing habits or socioeconomic factors. "I could compare children over time," says Eron. "At 8, if the less aggressive of two children was watching more television violence, at 18, he would be the more aggressive of the two."

Eron's findings correspond with what psychologists believe about child development: Children are most vulnerable to television from ages 2 to about 8, when they become more capable of distinguishing what they see on the screen from reality. The conclusions also conform to what we know about the development of a child's moral sense: It is developed by age 9 at the latest.

Just how children learn from the media is the subject of competing theories. According to the simplest, the viewing of aggressive material triggers aggressive thoughts that influence subsequent actions. Kids imitate what they see, just as adults emulate styles of dress and behavior observed in movies and TV shows.

The theory is fine as far as it goes but doesn't take into account the child's expectations and comprehension—nor does it explain the cumulative effects of watching violence. Educators theorize that a child's response depends upon five variables: the child's intellectual achievement, social popularity, identification with television characters, belief in the realism of the violence and the amount of fantasizing about aggression. If a child identifies with the characters, for instance, then he tends to internalize "scripts" for future aggressive behavior. As a child becomes more aggressive, he becomes less popular and more troublesome in school. The more trouble he has with teachers and friends, the more likely it is he will turn to aggressive television for affirmation, thus establishing a vicious cycle.

What turned out to be the most startling result of Eron's study, however, was that a child's viewing beyond the age of 8 seems to have virtually *no* effect on his level of aggression: Once an 8-year-old's level of aggression is established, it tends to remain stable. If this is true, then most of the attacks on media are far off base. Children under the age of 8 are exposed to feature films but even with VCRs and cable, Hollywood movies are not staples in children's media diets in the same way that *Mighty Morphin Power Rangers* or *Teenage Mutant Ninja Turtles* are. In fact, the UCLA study singled out seven Saturday morning network shows including *Power Rangers* and *Ninja Turtles* for containing "sinister combat violence" or "violence for the sake of violence." The report warned that "the dark overtones and unrelenting combat in these shows constitute a fairly recent trend, which appears to be on the rise."

OF COURSE, ERON'S WORK IS THE SUBJECT of controversy. There are experts who warn against linking culture and violence at all. Jonathan Freedman, a psychology professor at the University of Toronto, says that after thoroughly reviewing all of the existing studies on television and violence, he had to conclude that there was no convincing evidence that the media have an influence on real violence. "You always hear that there are 3,000 studies that prove

sion was measured by showing children a balloon and asking if it would be fun to break it. In others, children were given plastic Bobo dolls that are designed to be hit. Freedman says that most experimenters get positive results because violent programs are simply more arousing than neutral programs and because children respond in the way they think the researchers expect them to. "All that these experiments show is potential effect," says Freedman. "But what is the real effect? In lab experiments they expose children to one kind of media, but in the real world no one watches just violence. You watch lots of different kinds of television. There's lots of different mediating stimuli."

Freedman finds the field studies equally disappointing. He thinks that Eron and his colleagues are true believers because they've devoted their careers to and built their reputations on the damaging effects of television violence. "Most people don't have the statistical and methodological expertise to read and evaluate the studies," Freedman explains. "Since [these study] committees all base their conclusions on the words of these few experts, naturally . . . they all conclude that television violence is harmful.

"People say that children are more aggressive," Freedman continues. "More aggressive than when? Not more than 1880. Somalia and

---

WHAT A CHILD SEES IN FILMS OR ON TELEVISION AFTER AGE 8 MAY HAVE NO EFFECT ON HIS LEVEL OF AGGRESSION.

---

that television contributes to violence," says Freedman, "but that's absolutely false. There are maybe 200 pertinent studies, and almost no one has read the literature. It sounds plausible that television causes violence, and everyone takes the word of the so-called experts. I was amazed at how different the studies were from what was being said about them."

Of those 200 studies, Freedman says, about 160 are lab studies, which he dismisses as "not totally irrelevant but not very meaningful." In typical lab studies, subjects are shown violent films, and then an attempt is made to measure their response. In one study, increased aggres-

Bosnia are worse than here, and Somalia doesn't have television."

The research on video games and rap music is even more inconclusive. A 1993 study of 357 seventh- and eighth-graders, for instance, found that 32 percent said fantasy violence was their favorite game category, while 17 percent chose human violence. But the study is small and doesn't draw conclusions between the games and aggression. As for rap, Peter Christiansen, a professor of communication at Lewis and Clark College, in Portland, Ore., says, "Seventy-six percent of rap is purchased by middle-class kids. For them, rap is a kind of cultural tourism.... They aren't turned on by the explicit lyrics."

Poverty, the easy accessibility of guns, domestic abuse, social instability and the like may all contribute more than the media do to the level of violence. Even researchers like Signorielli warn against drawing cause-and-effect conclusions. "You can't just blame TV for the problems of society," she says, "Television contributes to children's aggressiveness, but it's only one of the factors."

UNFORTUNATELY, THE POLITICAL DEBATE tends to ignore the nuances and uncertainties contained in the research. In reaction to the wave of political pressure, Time Warner sold its interest in Interscope, which distributed some of rap's most inflammatory artists, and Time Warner Chairman Gerald Levin agreed to develop standards for the distribution and labeling of potentially objectionable music. Meanwhile, Jack Valenti, the president of the Motion Picture Association of America, has commented that the entertainment industry "must . . . act as if TV is indeed a factor in anti-social behavior," adding that the industry "has to be more responsible." Valenti, however, still questions the link between media and violence. A sociopath could be triggered by reading a Bible verse as easily as by watching a film. As Valenti says, "We can't create movies that are safe for deviants. Anything can set them off. We can't function at their level."

Fortunately, even the most fervent critics, like William Bennett, still shy away from advocating legislative remedies; Bennett declares he hopes to "shame" the industry into taking a more responsible stand. Meanwhile, the Democrats are still pushing for a federal law that will create a ratings system for all programs and require new TVs to have a V chip, which gives parents the power to shut off certain pornographic or violent channels.

With the presidential race heating up, however, the rhetorical battle isn't likely to cool down any time soon. Dole is demanding in his campaign ads that "Hollywood stop corrupting our children." He has said on the Senate floor: "Those who continue to deny that cultural messages can and do bore deep into the hearts and minds of our young people are deceiving themselves and ignoring reality."

Yet if Saturday morning cartoons are more a problem than Hollywood blockbusters or rap music, who's ignoring reality?

Helping

Early in the semester, you volunteer to participate in a psychology experiment being conducted at your school. When you arrive at the appointed time and place you are greeted by the experimenter, who explains that the research project requires you to complete a series of questionnaires measuring different aspects of your personality. The experimenter gives you the questionnaires and then returns to his office for the 30 minutes it will take you to complete them. After 5 minutes or so, you hear a loud crash in the hallway, and then you hear what sounds like a person groaning softly. What do you do?

UNIT 9

Most of us have a very clear idea about what we would do—we would leave the room, look for the person who apparently fell, and try to help him or her. And sure enough, that is what happens when research like this is conducted . . . some of the time. When students are alone in the room when the crash occurs, they are quite likely to help, just as we might expect. When several students are in the room together, however, they are less likely to help; in fact, the *more* people in the room, the *less* helping occurs. Thus, there is something about being in a group of people that makes us less likely to respond to the needs of another during an emergency. Strange.

Strange it may be, but research like this is one example of the kind of work that is done by social psychologists who study helping behavior. This particular kind of experiment is an attempt to understand a phenomenon known as "bystander intervention"—when bystanders actively get involved during an emergency to try to help the victim. Research has consistently demonstrated that having a large number of bystanders can actually reduce the amount of aid that is given, in part because each person takes less and less responsibility for helping the victim.

Other approaches to helping have tried to uncover the different kinds of motivations that lead people to help. Some people seem to help, for example, because they have a strong sense of obligation to care for others who are in need; this sense of obligation is often created early in life. Sometimes people help in order to reduce the level of arousing distress they feel when they see a victim; thus, helping the other person actually serves to help oneself as well. Helping that also provides a benefit to the helper is usually termed "egoistic" helping. There is also evidence that sometimes people help simply for the goal of easing another's burden, and they are not doing so to achieve personal gain. Helping of this kind is usually referred to as "altruistic" helping, because its ultimate goal is to benefit another.

The first selection in this unit, "The Roots of Good and Evil," examines the behavior of some of our closest biological relatives—chimpanzees—to determine whether some of the helping we offer to each other might have its roots in our evolutionary heritage. As in human society, chimpanzee communities also develop norms of behavior that protect the general good and punish those who violate the rules.

In "Volunteerism and Society's Response to the HIV Epidemic," psychologists Mark Snyder and Allen Omoto focus on a particular form of helping: volunteerism. Each year millions of people donate their time and energy to their communities in some way, and, in this selection, the authors consider the various motives that can lead people to volunteer and the motives that can lead them to continue volunteering over the long haul.

"Cities with Heart" approaches the question of helping in an interesting way: by surreptitiously studying the helping behavior of people living in 36 different U.S. cities to see if they differed in their willingness to help a stranger. In general, people in the largest cities helped the least, and this article considers some of the possible reasons for this, including stress levels and feelings of community.

Finally, in "Cause of Death: Uncertain(ty)," Robert Cialdini discusses the theory mentioned at the beginning of this unit's overview—the bystander intervention model. He describes the model itself, what led to its initial formulation, and how it has been tested. He also provides some very specific, practical advice about how to ensure that you can get help during an emergency.

Looking Ahead: Challenge Questions

What kind of evidence is there for the notion that our concepts of helping and cooperation spring from our evolutionary history? How valid, do you think, is a comparison of human and chimpanzee behavior?

What kind of motivations lead people to volunteer their time and energy to help others? Would you call these motivations "egoistic" or "altruistic"? What factors seem to be especially important in determining whether people continue their volunteering or not?

Do you agree with Robert Levine's findings regarding the relationship between city size and helpfulness? Why do you think that citizens of smaller towns were more helpful? Would similar results have been obtained if the helping opportunity was a true emergency, as in the bystander intervention research?

The Roots of Good and Evil

What can chimps tell us about our moral nature?

GEOFFREY COWLEY

It's a lazy afternoon in Lawrenceville, Ga., and everything should be going Jimoh's way. As the top-ranking male in a group of 20 chimpanzees maintained by the Yerkes Primate Research Center, this muscular, black-haired 29-year-old is every female's favorite escort. And today Peony, one of his own favorites, has a red swelling on her rump, signaling a period of sexual readiness. As the rest of the group lounges, Jimoh sidles up to her, sporting an erection, and the two are briefly united. But when a pair of youngsters sense they're missing out on some fun, they bound over to throw dirt and pound on the amorous couple. Jimoh could throttle the punks, but the alpha male withdraws with a look of calm resignation and waits for a more auspicious moment to mate. "He has to be very tolerant of the juveniles," explains primatologist Frans de Waal. "He can't afford to alienate their moms."

Shifting view: Can't afford to alienate their moms? Until recently, no serious scientist would have uttered such a thought. As everyone knew, humans were cultural animals, born and raised to restrain themselves. Other primates were just plain animals. But the conventional view—both of them and of us—is shifting. A growing number of researchers are studying human and animal social conventions just as they would diets or mating patterns—not as fixed ideals but as biological adaptations. And their findings suggest that the roots of morality are far older than we are. As de Waal shows in his new book, "Good Natured" *(296 pages. Harvard University Press. $24.95),* we're much like other primates when it comes to sharing resources, settling differences and enforcing order. Unfortunately, as other scholars are discovering, the ethical impulses we share with our furry cousins can undermine our best efforts to create a stable community.

De Waal has spent two decades toppling misconceptions about chimpanzee society. He has shown, for example, that males achieve dominance not through sheer force but through shrewd politics. In his new book, he builds on that insight, arguing that the hierarchy is a "mutual contract" between leaders and subordinates. De Waal recounts how Jimoh once caught Socko, an adolescent male, mating with a female he had been pursuing himself. "He chased him all around the enclosure—Socko screaming and defecating in fear." But when the females in the group joined in an angry howl of protest, Jimoh called off the attack and walked away with a nervous grin. "One never hears [such a protest] when a mother punishes her own offspring, or when an adult male controls a tiff among juveniles," de Waal writes. "Thinking in terms of rules and violations may help us [understand it]."

It may also help us understand the chimps' food-sharing rituals. Visit the lush, 117-acre Yerkes field station on an August afternoon and you'll find de Waal's research assistant Mike Seres clipping fresh shoots of bush clover, honeysuckle, sweet gum and muscadine. When he tosses the bundles into the chimps' compound, the rules of rank are briefly suspended. Within minutes, the chimps who haven't secured their own branches gather around someone who has. Despite an occasional skirmish, everyone ends up with something to chew on. De Waal has found that physical attacks increase ninefold when branches are tossed into a pen—but not for the reason you'd expect. The chimps use violence not to secure food but, more often, to rebuff food seekers who have previously failed to share. The implicit moral rule: "Those who seek favors must grant them."

As moral actions go, punishing ill deeds is pretty rudimentary. But chimps sometimes rise above side-taking to exhibit what de Waal calls "community concern." A creature that can survive only in a group is right to perceive social disarray as a threat to its own well-being. And as de Waal recounts from experience, chimps are exceedingly sensitive to disharmony among their group mates. High-ranking males often act as beat cops, quelling disputes before they escalate into riots. Females practice a sort of diplomacy, drawing angry rivals together and encouraging them to reconcile. And when rivals embrace, signaling an end to their hostilities, the entire colony may erupt in joyous pandemonium.

Seeds of civilization: Chimps may not think consciously about harmony; they pursue it as instinctively as they do sex. But de Waal sees in their communal spirit the seeds of civilization. "Human morality can be looked at as community concern made explicit," he writes. "Our ancestors began to understand how to preserve peace and order—hence how to keep their group united against external threats.... They came to judge behavior that systematically undermined the social fabric as wrong, and behavior that made a community worthwhile to live in as right."

Alas, that's not to say that charity comes naturally to us and cruelty doesn't. Social impulses may flourish when they're useful to individuals, but you can count on them to wither when they're not. Mutualism is the rule among groups of Olympic marmots, furry rodents that eke out their living in the rocky meadows of the Olympic Mountains. The woodchuck, a related species found in lush lowland forests, is less dependent on

40. Roots of Good and Evil

its neighbors—and it treats them accordingly. It's the same for chimps and humans. "Different environments require different degrees of moral solidarity," says John Tooby, an anthropologist at the University of California, Santa Barbara. "We tend to be convivial when it pays."

When it doesn't pay, ruthlessness is often the rule. The famed Jane Goodall observed male chimps in Africa patrolling the borders of their territories, mounting gang attacks on members of neighboring groups. "Males race forward and jointly attack mother-infant pair," reads one of her team's field notes. "Mother loses half an ear.... Infant alive and calling for four minutes while being eaten." To anyone who follows the news, that death-squad dynamic should sound chillingly familiar.

If we're quick to deny outsiders any moral consideration, we're even quicker to cheat on our comrades when we think we can get away with it. The chimps at Yerkes may understand rank and reciprocity, but they'll gladly slip out of sight to cop some illicit sex, or feign illness to avoid sharing a choice piece of food. If you think humans are different, consider that a 1994 poll found one American in four would steal $10 million if he knew he wouldn't get caught. Freeloading is hard to get away with in a small group; as de Waal has found in his food-provisioning experiments, cheaters are easily identified, and no one forgets who they are. Throughout vast stretches of evolutionary history, our own ancestors lived in groups of less than 100, where face-to-face accountability would have been the norm. But with the advent of agriculture 10,000 years ago, populations exploded. For the first time, groups of primates had to codify social norms and create governments and religions to administer them.

Not suprisingly, these brave new institutions have turned out to be as troublesome as they are necessary. As our collective efforts make life more comfortable, each of us ends up with more to lose, and the case for self-sacrifice starts to ring hollow. As Dartmouth political scientist Roger Masters observes in his new book, "Machiavelli, Leonardo, and the Science of Power" *(384 pages. Notre Dame Press. $32.95)*, "the very success of [civic] institutions re-creates the pressures that made [them] necessary in the first place." It's comforting to know that notions of right and wrong are part of our animal heritage. But it's not at all clear that our innate moral sense is up to the challenges we've created.

Volunteerism and Society's Response to the HIV Epidemic

Mark Snyder and Allen M. Omoto

Mark Snyder is Professor of Psychology at the University of Minnesota. **Allen M. Omoto** is Assistant Professor of Psychology at the University of Kansas. Address correspondence to Mark Snyder, Department of Psychology, University of Minnesota, 75 East River Road, Minneapolis, MN 55455-0344, or Allen M. Omoto, Department of Psychology, 426 Fraser Hall, University of Kansas, Lawrence, KS 66045-2160.

In 1981, the Centers for Disease Control reported the first case of what would come to be known as AIDS. Now, barely a decade later, there are over 200,000 confirmed cases of AIDS in the United States and an estimated 1.5 million Americans infected with HIV (the virus that causes AIDS). The World Health Organization projects that, by the year 2000, 30 to 40 million adults and children worldwide will have been infected with HIV, and most of them are expected to develop AIDS.[1] Clearly, with neither a vaccine nor a cure in sight, the full impact of AIDS, as devastating and profound as the epidemic has been, has yet to be felt, and will surely touch all of our lives.

Society has responded to the HIV epidemic on a number of fronts, including at least three for which the skills and expertise of psychologists, as scientists and practitioners, can be tapped: (a) providing psychological services for persons living with AIDS (PWAs), (b) developing behavior change campaigns to reduce the likelihood of HIV transmission, and (c) implementing public education programs to address matters of prejudice and discrimination associated with AIDS and PWAs.[2] In our research, we are examining a remarkable social phenomenon born of the HIV epidemic—AIDS volunteerism and its implications for each of these fronts.

A critical component of society's response has been the development of community-based grass-roots organizations of volunteers involved in caring for PWAs and in educating the public about HIV, AIDS, and PWAs. Volunteers fill many roles; some provide emotional and social support as "buddies" to PWAs, whereas others help PWAs with their household chores or transportation needs. Volunteers also staff information, counseling, and referral hotlines; make educational presentations; raise funds; and engage in social, legal, and political advocacy. In the United States, AIDS volunteer programs have emerged in every state, in cities large and small, and in rural areas as well. AIDS volunteerism is a compelling testimonial to human kindness and to the power of communities of "ordinary people" to unite and organize in response to extraordinary events.[3]

As remarkable as AIDS volunteerism is, it actually is part of a pervasive social phenomenon in American society. A recent Gallup Poll estimated that, in 1989, 98.4 million American adults engaged in some form of volunteerism, with 25.6 million giving 5 or more hours per week to volunteer work—volunteer services worth some $170 billion.[4] In addition to working on HIV-related issues, volunteers provide companionship to the elderly, health care to the sick, tutoring to the illiterate, counseling to the troubled, food to the hungry, and shelter to the homeless.

Although the study of helping has long been a mainstay of research in the psychological sciences, volunteerism is a form of prosocial action about which there is little systematic literature.[5] Volunteerism is, however, marked by several distinctive features. Volunteers typically seek out their opportunities to help, often deliberate long and hard about the form and the extent of their involvements, and may carefully consider how different volunteer opportunities fit with their own needs, goals, and motivations. Many forms of volunteerism also entail commitments to ongoing helping relationships that have considerable duration and require sizable personal costs in time, energy, and expense.

We view AIDS volunteerism not only as an intriguing social phenomenon, but also as paradigmatic of sustained and potentially costly helping behavior. In one survey,[6] we found that AIDS volunteers overwhelmingly had actively sought out their volunteer opportunities (over 80% indicated that they had approached their AIDS organizations on their own initiative). Moreover, their involvement represented a substantial and recurring time commitment (on average, 4 hr per week) that extended over a considerable length of time (1½ years on average, and often spanning several years). Finally, these volunteers were giving of themselves in trying and stressful circumstances (spending time with PWAs and confronting the tragic realities of serious illness and death) and doing so at some personal cost (with many reporting feeling stigmatized as a result of their AIDS work).

THREE STAGES OF THE VOLUNTEER PROCESS

In our research, we are seeking to understand the social and psychological aspects of volunteerism. Our research is grounded in a three-stage conceptual model of the *volunteer process,* a model that specifies psychological and behavioral features associated with each stage and speaks to activity at three levels of analysis: the individual volunteer, the organizational context, and the broader social system.[7]

The first stage of the volunteer process involves *antecedents* of volunteerism and addresses the questions "who volunteers?" and "why do they volunteer?" In the case of AIDS, considerations at the antecedents stage focus on the attitudes, values, and motivations that dispose people to serve as AIDS volunteers, as well as the needs and goals that AIDS volunteer work may fulfill for individuals.

The second stage concerns *experiences* of volunteers and the dynamics of the helping relationships that develop between volunteers and the people with whom they work. In the specific case of AIDS, it is important to recognize that these relationships are carried out against the stressful backdrop of chronic illness and even death. Of additional concern are the effects of AIDS volunteers on the general treatment and coping processes of PWAs, as well as changes that occur in volunteers themselves.

The third stage focuses on *consequences* of volunteerism and is concerned with how volunteer work affects volunteers, members of their social networks, and society at large. For AIDS volunteers, it is possible that their work has not only beneficial effects on personal attitudes, knowledge, and behaviors, but also negative consequences of stigmatization and social censure. When it comes to societal issues, moreover, AIDS volunteerism may possess the potential for encouraging social change as volunteers transmit their new attitudes and behavior to their friends and associates and, by extension, to the broader social system.

BASIC RESEARCH AND PRACTICAL PROBLEMS

In our research, we are engaged in a coordinated program of cross-sectional and longitudinal field studies coupled with experiments conducted in the laboratory and sampling from diverse populations of volunteers and nonvolunteers. Thus, we have conducted a national survey of currently active AIDS volunteers, querying them about their motivations for volunteering, their experiences, and the consequences of their involvement in AIDS volunteerism, thereby generating cross-sectional data relevant to the three stages of the volunteer process. In an extended longitudinal study, we are also tracking new volunteers over the course of their service providing emotional support and living assistance to PWAs; in this long-term study, we are examining the same people at all stages of the volunteer process. Finally, we are conducting laboratory experiments and field intervention studies, each relevant to one or more stages of the volunteer process.

At each stage of our conceptual model, relevant psychological theories and the evidence of basic research are helping us to frame research questions, the answers to which, we hope, will have implications for addressing practical issues related to volunteerism, as well as for building bridges between basic research and practical application. To illustrate the ways in which our research builds these bridges, let us examine two important practical matters that are rooted in different stages of the volunteer process and the theoretically informed answers to them derived from our program of research. Specifically, we examine issues of volunteer recruitment and retention.

The Recruitment of Volunteers

Recruitment is one of the key concerns at the antecedents stage. There are many formidable barriers that can keep prospective volunteers from getting involved; in the case of AIDS, not only are there limits of time and energy but also, for many people, fear of AIDS and death and concerns about stigmatization. What, then, motivates people to volunteer to staff an AIDS hotline or to be buddies for PWAs?

Guided by a functionally oriented theory of motivation (which proposes that apparently similar acts of volunteerism may reflect markedly different underlying motivations), we have been examining the motivations of AIDS volunteers. We have utilized exploratory and confirmatory factor analytic techniques in developing and validating a self-report inventory to assess five primary motivations for AIDS volunteerism, each one reliably measured by five different items.[8] The first set of motivations involves personal *values* (e.g., "because of my humanitarian obligation to help others"). The second set invokes considerations related to *understanding* (e.g., "to learn about how people cope with AIDS"). The third set taps *community concern* and reflects people's sense of obligation to or concern about a community or social grouping (e.g., "because of my concern and worry about the gay community"). The fourth set concerns *personal development* and centers on issues of personal growth (e.g., "to challenge myself and test my skills"). The fifth category assesses *esteem enhancement* and includes considerations about current voids or deficits in one's life (e.g., "to feel better about myself").[9]

The development of this motivational inventory has made possible a more thorough analysis of the psychology of AIDS volunteerism. This work has revealed that, despite what appears to be a commonality of purpose in being a volunteer, there is striking individual-to-individual variability in the motivations that are most and least important. An appreciation of different motivations, moreover, has great practical import for volunteer recruitment. Because volunteering serves different psychological functions for different people, volunteer organizations would be well advised to tailor their recruitment messages to particular motivations of selected sets of potential volunteers. In recruiting volunteers who would be motivated by esteem enhancement, for instance, recruitment appeals could stress how AIDS volunteerism provides many opportunities for people to work through personal fears, anxieties, and doubts rather than, say, stressing humanitarian obligations and images of kindness (which could be used to appeal to prospective volunteers motivated by value-based concerns).

The Retention of Volunteers

Why do some volunteers continue to donate their time and services, and why do others stop? A persistent frustration in volunteer programs is the high rate of attrition (i.e., dropout) of volunteers. As difficult as it may be to recruit volunteers, it is sometimes even more difficult to ensure their continued service. Considerations of the experiences and consequences stages of the volunteer process may shed light on matters of attrition and longevity of service because the experiences associated with volunteer work and the consequences that result from it likely influence volunteers' effectiveness, their satisfaction, and the length of time they ultimately remain active. To examine some of these possibilities, we recontacted one set of AIDS volunteers a year after they had told us about their work. At that time, approximately one half of the original sample was still active with their AIDS organizations, and we proceeded to ask both quitters and stayers about their experiences as volunteers and the consequences of their work.[8]

We found no differences between the quitters and stayers in reported satisfaction with their service and commitment to the purposes of their AIDS organizations. Where quitters and stayers differed, however, was in their perceptions of the costs of their volunteer work. Despite having engaged in satisfying and rewarding volunteer work, quitters more than stayers said they felt that volunteering had taken up too much time and—an important point—caused them to feel embarrassed, uncomfortable, or stigmatized. The negative consequences and not the rewards of the work, then, distinguished quitters from volunteers who continued to serve.

Bringing our analysis full circle, we also found that initial motivations for volunteering were related to attrition and length of service. To the extent that people espoused esteem enhancement or personal development reasons for their work (rather than community concern, values, or understanding), they were likely to still be active volunteers at our 1-year follow-up; moreover, esteem enhancement and understanding motivations proved valuable as predictors of the total length of service of these volunteers. Thus, volunteer attrition seemed not to be associated with the relatively "self-less" or other-focused motivations, as one might expect, but with more "selfish" desires of feeling good about oneself and acquiring knowledge and skills. Good, and perhaps romanticized, intentions related to humanitarian concern simply may not be strong enough to sustain volunteers faced with the tough realities and personal costs of working with PWAs. Therefore, volunteer organizations, in combating attrition, may want to remind volunteers of the personal rewards of their work rather than underscoring how volunteer efforts benefit clients and society. Similarly, volunteers may be better prepared for their work by having the potential costs of volunteerism made explicit to them at the outset; in this way, volunteers could be "prepared for the worst" and thereby "inoculated" against the negative impact of the personal costs of their service.

CONCLUSIONS

To conclude, let us explicitly address a recurring theme in our research—the relation between basic research and practical problems. Our research is simultaneously basic and applied. As much as it informs applied concerns with the current and potential roles of volunteerism in society's response to AIDS, our work also speaks directly to theoretical concerns about the nature of helping relationships and, more generally, the dynamics of individual and collective action in response to societal needs. With a dual focus on applied and theoretical concerns, our program of research embodies the essential components of *action research,* in which basic and applied research mutually inform and enrich one another and, under optimal circumstances, basic research is advanced and effective social action is undertaken.[10]

It is said that a society is judged by how it responds in times of need. Clearly, the age of AIDS is a time of the greatest need. The HIV epidemic represents not only a medical crisis, but also a broader set of challenges to individuals and to society. Among these challenges are those to researchers in the social and behavioral sciences. By all accounts, the number of AIDS cases will only increase in the years ahead, and, as medical advances extend the life expectancy of PWAs, more and more people will be living with AIDS and living *longer* with AIDS. As the HIV epidemic continues and intensifies, so too will the importance of contributions of theory-based research relevant to all facets of AIDS. Ultimately, when the history of the HIV epidemic is written, we hope that the psychological sciences will have proven themselves integral to society's collective response to AIDS.

Acknowledgments—This research and the preparation of this manuscript have been supported by grants from the American Foundation for AIDS Research (No. 000741-5 and 000961-7) and from the National Institute of Mental Health (No. 1 RO1 MH47673) to Mark Snyder and Allen M. Omoto. We thank the volunteers and staff of the Minnesota AIDS Project (Minneapolis, MN) and the Good Samaritan Project (Kansas City, MO) for their cooperation and participation in this research.

Notes

1. AIDS spreading faster than thought, *The Kansas City Star*, p. A-3 (February 12, 1992).
2. G.M. Herek and E.K. Glunt, An epidemic of stigma: Public reaction to AIDS, *American Psychologist, 43,* 886–891 (1988); S.F. Morin, AIDS: The challenge to psychology, *American Psychologist, 43,* 838–842 (1988).
3. P.S. Arno, The nonprofit sector's response to the AIDS epidemic: Community-based services in San Francisco, *American Journal of Public Health, 76,* 1325–1330 (1988); S.M. Chambré, The volunteer response to the AIDS epidemic in New York City: Implications for research on voluntarism, *Nonprofit and Voluntary Sector Quarterly, 20,* 267–287 (1991); J.A. Dumont, Volunteer visitors for patients with AIDS, *The Journal of Volunteer Administration, 8,* 3–8 (1989); P.M. Kayal, Gay AIDS voluntarism as political activity, *Nonprofit and Voluntary Sector Quarterly, 20,* 289–331 (1991); S.C. Ouellette Kobasa, AIDS and volunteer associations: Perspectives on social and individual change, *The Milbank Quarterly, 68* (S2), 280–294 (1990); D. Lopez and G.S. Getzel, Strategies for volunteers caring for persons with AIDS, *Social Casework, 68,* 47–53 (1987).
4. Independent Sector, *Giving and Volunteering in the United States* (Gallup Organization for Independent Sector, Washington, DC, 1990).
5. For perspectives on the literature on volunteerism, see S.M. Chambré, Kindling points of light: Volunteering as public policy, *Nonprofit and Voluntary Sector Quarterly, 18,* 249–268 (1989); E.G. Clary and M. Snyder, A functional analysis of altruism and prosocial behavior: The case of volunteerism, *Review of Personality and Social Psychology, 12,* 119–148 (1991); J. Van Til, *Mapping the Third Sector: Voluntarism in a Changing Social Economy* (Foundation Center, New York, 1988).
6. A.M. Omoto, M. Snyder, and J.P. Berghuis, The psychology of volunteerism: A conceptual analysis and a program of action research, in *The Social Psychology of HIV Infection,* J.B. Pryor and G.D. Reeder, Eds. (Erlbaum, Hillsdale, NJ, 1992).
7. A.M. Omoto and M. Snyder, Basic research in action: Volunteerism and society's response to AIDS, *Personality and Social Psychology Bulletin, 16,* 152–165 (1990); Omoto, Snyder, and Berghuis, note 6.
8. M. Snyder and A.M. Omoto, Who helps and why? The psychology of AIDS volunteerism, in *Helping and Being Helped: Naturalistic Studies,* S. Spacapan and S. Oskamp, Eds. (Sage, Newbury Park, CA, 1991); M. Snyder and A.M. Omoto, AIDS volunteers: Who volunteers and why do they volunteer? in *Leadership and Management,* V.A. Hodgkinson and R.D. Sumariwalla, Eds. (Independent Sector, Washington, DC, 1991).
9. Similar sets of motivations have also emerged from other attempts to measure the motives of AIDS volunteers. See, e.g., M.J. Williams, Gay men as "buddies" to persons living with AIDS and ARC, *Smith College Studies in Social Work, 59,* 38–52 (1988); L.M. Wong, S.C. Ouellette Kobasa, J.B. Cassel, and L.P. Platt, *A new scale identifies 6 motives for AIDS volunteers,* poster presented at the annual meeting of the American Psychological Society, Washington, DC (June 1991). On the motivations served by volunteerism in general, see E.G. Clary, M. Snyder, and R.D. Ridge, Volunteers' motivations: A functional strategy for the recruitment, placement, and retention of volunteers, *Nonprofit Management and Leadership* (in press).
10. K. Lewin, *Field Theory in Social Science* (Harper, New York, 1951; original work published 1944); Omoto and Snyder, note 7.

Recommended Reading

Omoto, A.M., Snyder, M., and Berghuis, J.P. (1992). The psychology of volunteerism: A conceptual analysis and a program of action research. In *The Social Psychology of HIV Infection,* J.B. Pryor and G.D. Reeder, Eds. (Erlbaum, Hillsdale, NJ).

Snyder, M., and Omoto, A.M. (1991). Who helps and why? The psychology of AIDS volunteerism. In *Helping and Being Helped: Naturalistic Studies,* S. Spacapan and S. Oskamp, Eds. (Sage, Newbury Park, CA).

Cities With Heart

Article 42

by Robert V. Levine

> **SUMMARY**
>
> Researchers dropped pens, feigned injuries, and begged for change in 36 cities to find out where people are most helpful to strangers. Rochester, New York, is the kindest city surveyed, while New York City ranks last. The unkindest cities are likely to be polluted and have high population density. The kindest cities have a tradition of helping: Rochester also finished first in a similar survey taken 53 years ago.

Thomas Wolfe once wrote that city people "have no manners, no courtesy, no consideration for the rights of others, and no humanity." Here in post-Rodney King America, most of us would agree that urban residents see more than their share of human nature's nastier side. Ample evidence demonstrates that the rates of crime and violence rise with population density.

But what of the benevolent side of city people? While growing up in New York City, I was taught that big cities simply have more of everything, both good and bad. Of course, there were more criminals. But I was assured that beneath the seemingly harsh exteriors, you would find as many compassionate hearts as in any small town.

Over the past two years, my research group—students Todd Martinez, Gary Brase, Kerry Sorenson, and other volunteers—spent much of their summer vacations traveling nationwide conducting these experiments. We compared the frequency of helpful acts in various places to answer two basic questions. First, how does overall helping compare from one city and region to another? Second, which

Robert V. Levine is professor and chair of the psychology department at California State University, Fresno.

42. Cities with Heart

Helping Behavior

Disregard for strangers seems to increase with population density and environmental stress.

(36 cities ranked by overall score for helping behavior, and population density rank, environmental stress rank, and pace of life rank)

overall helping rank		lowest population density	least environmental stress	fastest pace of life
1	Rochester, NY	Bakersfield, CA	East Lansing, MI	Boston, MA
2	East Lansing, MI	Fresno, CA	Indianapolis, IN	Buffalo, NY
3	Nashville, TN	Santa Barbara, CA	Worcester, MA	New York, NY
4	Memphis, TN	Shreveport, LA	Atlanta, GA	Salt Lake City, UT
5	Houston, TX	Chattanooga, TN	Buffalo, NY	Columbus, OH
6	Chattanooga, TN	Knoxville, TN	Memphis, TN	Worcester, MA
7	Knoxville, TN	Nashville, TN	San Francisco, CA	Providence, RI
8	Canton, OH	East Lansing, MI	Shreveport, LA	Springfield, MA
9	Kansas City, MO	Sacramento, CA	Springfield, MA	Rochester, NY
10	Indianapolis, IN	Kansas City, MO	Boston, MA	Kansas City, MO
11	St. Louis, MO	Rochester, NY	Kansas City, MO	St. Louis, MO
12	Louisville, KY	Columbus, OH	Nashville, TN	Houston, TX
13	Columbus, OH	Canton, OH	Providence, RI	Paterson, NJ
14	Detroit, MI	Indianapolis, IN	Rochester, NY	Bakersfield, CA
15	Santa Barbara, CA	Louisville, KY	Chicago, IL	Atlanta, GA
16	Dallas, TX	Memphis, TN	Louisville, KY	Detroit, MI
17	Worcester, MA	St. Louis, MO	Paterson, NJ	Youngstown, OH
18	Springfield, MA	Worcester, MA	Chattanooga, TN	Indianapolis, IN
19	San Diego, CA	Youngstown, OH	Columbus, OH	Chicago, IL
20	San Jose, CA	Springfield, MA	Dallas, TX	Philadelphia, PA
21	Atlanta, GA	Atlanta, GA	Knoxville, TN	Louisville, KY
22	Bakersfield, CA	Dallas, TX	Salt Lake City, UT	Canton, OH
23	Buffalo, NY	San Diego, CA	Detroit, MI	Knoxville, TN
24	Salt Lake City, UT	Houston, TX	Houston, TX	San Francisco, CA
25	Boston, MA	Salt Lake City, UT	Los Angeles, CA	Chattanooga, TN
26	Shreveport, LA	Buffalo, NY	Philadelphia, PA	Dallas, TX
27	Providence, RI	Providence, RI	San Jose, CA	Nashville, TN
28	Philadelphia, PA	Detroit, MI	Bakersfield, CA	San Diego, CA
29	Youngstown, OH	San Jose, CA	Fresno, CA	East Lansing, MI
30	Chicago, IL	Philadelphia, PA	New York, NY	Fresno, CA
31	San Francisco, CA	Boston, MA	Sacramento, CA	Memphis, TN
32	Sacramento, CA	San Francisco, CA	San Diego, CA	San Jose, CA
33	Fresno, CA	Los Angeles, CA	St. Louis, MO	Shreveport, LA
34	Los Angeles, CA	Paterson, NJ	Santa Barbara, CA*	Sacramento, CA
35	Paterson, NJ	Chicago, IL	Canton, OH*	Los Angeles, CA
36	New York, NY	New York, NY	Youngstown, OH*	Santa Barbara, CA*

Note: See Behind the Numbers for explanation of overall helping score. Boxes denote ties.
* data not available
Source: Environmental stress rank is based on Zero Population Growth, Environmental Stress Index, 1991; and author's research

characteristics of communities best predict how helpful residents are toward strangers?

WHERE DO PEOPLE HELP?

The team conducted six different experiments in 36 cities of various sizes in all four regions of the country:

Dropped a Pen. Walking at a moderate pace, the researcher approached a solitary pedestrian passing in the opposite direction. When 15 to 20 feet away, the researcher reached into his pocket, "accidentally" dropped his pen behind him, and continued walking. Helping was scored on

> **Researchers dressed in dark glasses and carried white canes to act the role of blind persons.**

a five-point scale, ranging from no help offered to picking up the pen and running back to hand it to the researcher.

Helping a Blind Person Across the Street. Researchers dressed in dark glasses and carrying white canes acted the role of blind persons needing help crossing the street. Just before the light turned green, they stepped up to the corner, held out their cane, and waited for help. A trial was terminated after 60 seconds or when the light turned red, whichever came first. Helping was measured on a two-point scale: helped or did not help.

A Hurt Leg. Walking with a heavy limp and wearing a large, clearly visible leg brace, researchers "accidentally" dropped and then unsuccessfully struggled to reach down for a pile of magazines as they came within 20 feet of a passing pedestrian. Helping was scored on a three-point scale ranging from no help to picking up the magazines and asking to be of further assistance.

Change for a Quarter. With a quarter in full view, researchers approached pedestrians passing in the opposite direction and asked politely if they could make change. Responses were scored on a four-point scale ranging from totally ignoring

Towns With Pity

Rochester places first in only one measure of helping behavior, but it ranks first overall.

(36 cities ranked by overall score for helping behavior, and ranks for individual tests of helping behavior, 1992)

	overall helping rank	dropped pen	hurt leg	make change	blind person	lost letter	United Way
1	Rochester, NY	Springfield, MA	Chattanooga, TN	Louisville, KY	Kansas City, MO	San Diego, CA	Rochester, NY
2	East Lansing, MI	Santa Barbara, CA	Fresno, CA	Houston, TX	Knoxville, TN	Detroit, MI	Chattanooga, TN
3	Nashville, TN	East Lansing, MI	Nashville, TN	Knoxville, TN	Rochester, NY	East Lansing, MI	Columbus, OH
4	Memphis, TN	Louisville, KY	Sacramento, CA	Canton, OH	Bakersfield, CA	Indianapolis, IN	Indianapolis, IN
5	Houston, TX	San Francisco, CA	Shreveport, LA	Detroit, MI	Dallas, TX	Worcester, MA	St. Louis, MO
6	Chattanooga, TN	Memphis, TN	Memphis, TN	East Lansing, MI	Nashville, TN	Knoxville, TN	Kansas City, MO
7	Knoxville, TN	Dallas, TX	San Diego, CA	Boston, MA	Chicago, IL	Canton, OH	Philadelphia, PA
8	Canton, OH	Houston, TX	Providence, RI	Nashville, TN	Columbus, OH	Columbus, OH	Dallas, TX
9	Kansas City, MO	Salt Lake City, UT	San Jose, CA	Worcester, MA	East Lansing, MI	San Francisco, CA	Nashville, TN
10	Indianapolis, IN	Bakersfield, CA	Canton, OH	Santa Barbara, CA	Indianapolis, IN	San Jose, CA	Boston, MA
11	St. Louis, MO	Detroit, MI	Kansas City, MO	Buffalo, NY	St. Louis, MO	Chattanooga, TN	Springfield, MA
12	Louisville, KY	Canton, OH	Atlanta, GA	Kansas City, MO	Memphis, TN	Rochester, NY	Canton, OH
13	Columbus, OH	Knoxville, TN	Houston, TX	Rochester, NY	Buffalo, NY	Salt Lake City, UT	Atlanta, GA
14	Detroit, MI	Nashville, TN	Paterson, NJ	San Jose, CA	Houston, TX	St. Louis, MO	Worcester, MA
15	Santa Barbara, CA	St. Louis, MO	St. Louis, MO	Indianapolis, IN	Atlanta, GA	Los Angeles, CA	Louisville, KY
16	Dallas, TX	Indianapolis, IN	Bakersfield, CA	Chattanooga, TN	New York, NY	Louisville, KY	Memphis, TN
17	Worcester, MA	San Diego, CA	Youngstown, OH	Memphis, TN	Santa Barbara, CA	Memphis, TN	Buffalo, NY
18	Springfield, MA	Worcester, MA	Rochester, NY	Bakersfield, CA	Louisville, KY	Santa Barbara, CA	Detroit, MI
19	San Diego, CA	Atlanta, GA	Santa Barbara, CA	Salt Lake City, UT	Canton, OH	Youngstown, OH	Houston, TX
20	San Jose, CA	Rochester, NY	Detroit, MI	Columbus, OH	Philadelphia, PA	Houston, TX	Knoxville, TN
21	Atlanta, GA	Fresno, CA	East Lansing, MI	Springfield, IL	Shreveport, LA	Sacramento, CA	San Jose, CA
22	Bakersfield, CA	Paterson, NJ	Salt Lake City, UT	St. Louis, MO	Providence, RI	Buffalo, NY	East Lansing, MI
23	Buffalo, NY	Kansas City, MO	Dallas, TX	Fresno, CA	Detroit, MI	Dallas, TX	Chicago, IL
24	Salt Lake City, UT	Los Angeles, CA	Springfield, IL	Shreveport, LA	Los Angeles, CA	Kansas City, MO	San Francisco, CA
25	Boston, MA	Sacramento, CA	Boston, MA	Youngstown, OH	San Jose, CA	Nashville, TN	Providence, RI
26	Shreveport, LA	Shreveport, LA	Worcester, MA	Dallas, TX	Worcester, MA	New York, NY	Santa Barbara, CA
27	Providence, RI	Chattanooga, TN	Chicago, IL	Los Angeles, CA	Chattanooga, TN	Springfield, IL	Youngstown, OH
28	Philadelphia, PA	Columbus, OH	Indianapolis, IN	Philadelphia, PA	San Francisco, CA	Philadelphia, PA	San Diego, CA
29	Youngstown, OH	Boston, MA	Columbus, OH	Atlanta, GA	Youngstown, OH	Chicago, IL	New York, NY
30	Chicago, IL	Philadelphia, PA	Knoxville, TN	San Diego, CA	Boston, MA	Providence, RI	Los Angeles, CA
31	San Francisco, CA	Providence, RI	Buffalo, NY	Chicago, IL	Fresno, CA	Atlanta, GA	Sacramento, CA
32	Sacramento, CA	San Jose, CA	Louisville, KY	Providence, RI	Paterson, NJ	Boston, MA	Salt Lake City, UT
33	Fresno, CA	Youngstown, OH	Philadelphia, PA	San Francisco, CA	Sacramento, CA	Paterson, NJ	Shreveport, LA
34	Los Angeles, CA	Buffalo, NY	San Francisco, CA	Sacramento, CA	San Diego, CA	Shreveport, LA	Paterson, NJ
35	Paterson, NJ	New York, NY	New York, NY	New York, NY	Springfield, MA	Bakersfield, CA	Bakersfield, CA
36	New York, NY	Chicago, IL	Los Angeles, CA	Paterson, NJ	Salt Lake City, UT	Fresno, CA	Fresno, CA

Note: See text for explanation of individual helping tests. Boxes denote ties. See Behind the Numbers for explanation of overall helping score.

Source: 1990 per capita contributions to the United Way campaigns in each city; and author's research

42. Cities with Heart

the request to stopping to check for change.

Lost Letter. A neat handwritten note reading, "I found this next to your car," was placed on a stamped envelope addressed to the researcher's home. The envelope was then left on the windshield of a randomly selected car parked at a meter in a main shopping area. The response rate was measured by the share of letters that later arrived because people were helpful enough to mail them.

United Way Contributions. As a general measure of charitable contributions, we looked at 1990 per capita contributions to United Way campaigns in each city.

The researchers conducted the experiments in downtown areas on clear summer days during primary business hours, targeting a relatively equal number of able-bodied men and women pedestrians. They conducted 379 trials of the blind-person episode; approached approximately 700 people in each of the dropped-pen, hurt-leg, and asking-for-change episodes; and left a total of 1,032 "lost" letters.

NEW YORK, NEW YORK

New York State is home to both the most and least helpful of the 36 cities. Rochester ranks first, closely followed by a group of small and medium-sized cities in the South and Midwest. New York City ranks last.

Generally speaking, the study did not find much difference from city to city. At the extremes, however, the differences are dramatic. In the dropped-pen situation, a stranger would have lost more than three times as many pens in Chicago as in Springfield, Massachusetts. Nearly 80 percent of passersby checked their pockets for change in first-place Louisville, compared with 11 percent in last-place Paterson, New Jersey. Fresno came in dead last on two measures, returning only half (53 percent) as many letters as did San Diego (100 percent). Also, Fresno's per capita contribution to United Way is less than one-tenth that of front-runner Rochester.

Why are people so much less helpful in some places than in others? Studies have shown that urban dwellers are more likely than rural people to do each other harm. Our results indicate that they are also less likely to do them good. This unwillingness to help increases with the degree of "cityness." In other words, density drives strangers apart.

"Cities give not the human senses room enough," wrote Ralph Waldo Emerson. Urban theorists have long argued that crowding brings out our worst nature, and these data support that notion. Places with lower population densities are far more likely to offer help, particularly in situations that call for face-to-face, spontaneous responses such as a dropped pen, a hurt leg, or the need for change. Research shows that squeezing many people into a small space leads to feelings of alienation,

> **Nearly 80 percent offered to make change in Louisville, Kentucky; only 11 percent did in Paterson, New Jersey.**

anonymity, and social isolation. At the same time, feelings of guilt, shame, and social commitment tend to decline. Ultimately, people feel less responsible for their behavior toward others—especially strangers.

Population density has direct psychological effects on people. It also leads to stressful conditions that can take a toll on helping behavior. For example, people are less helpful in cities that have higher costs of living. These high costs are, in turn, related to population density, because the laws of supply and demand drive up the prices of land and other resources when they are limited.

High concentrations of people also produce stress on the environment. We compared our findings with Zero Population Growth's Environmental Stress Index, which rates the environmental quality of cities. As predicted, people were less helpful in environmentally stressed-out cities.

Stressful situations and their consequent behaviors ultimately sustain one another. Violent crime results from stressful conditions but is itself a source of urban stress. Ultimately, inaction becomes the norm. Big cities see more of the worst and less of the best of human nature.

One characteristic that does not affect helping behavior is the general pace of life. In a previous study of the same cities, we looked at four indicators of the pace of life: walking speed, work speed, speaking speed, and clock and watch accuracy. Since helping people essentially demands a sacrifice of time, people who live in cities where time is at a premium would presumably be less helpful.

Yet there is no consistent relationship between a city's pace of life and its helpfulness. Some cities fit the expected pattern. New York, for example, has the third-fastest pace of life and is the least helpful place. But Rochester has the ninth-fastest pace, and its people are most helpful. Laid-back Los Angeles, the slowest city, is also one of the least helpful, ranking 34th.

Todd Martinez, who gathered data in both New York City and (pre-Rodney King situation) Los Angeles, was acutely aware of the differences between the two cities. "I hated doing L.A. People looked at me but just didn't seem to want to bother," he says. "For a few trials, I was acting the hurt-leg episode on a narrow sidewalk with just enough space for a person to squeeze by. After I dropped my magazines, one man walked up very close to me, checked out the situation, and then sidestepped around me without a word.

"Los Angeles was the only city that I worked where I found myself getting frustrated and angry when people didn't help. In New York, for some reason, I never took it personally. People looked like they were too busy to help. It was as if they saw me, but didn't really notice me or anything else around them."

To real-life strangers in need, of course, thoughts are less important than actions. The bottom line is that a stranger's prospects are just as bleak in New York as in Los Angeles. People either find the time to help or they don't.

ROCHESTER'S SECOND WIN

More than 50 years ago, sociologist Robert Angell combined a series of statistics from the 1940 census to assess the 'moral integration' of 43 U.S. cities. Angell measured the degree to which citizens were willing to sacrifice their own private interests for the public good ("Welfare Effort Index") and the frequency with which people violated one another's person and property ("Crime Index"). Angell's methods are not comparable with the current study, but to our astonishment, Rochester also ranked number one on Angell's moral integration index in 1940.

Harry Reis, a psychology professor at the University of Rochester who grew up in New York City, is "not the least bit surprised" by the performance of his adopted home. "I like to describe Rochester as a nice place to live—in both the best and the mildest sense of the word," he says. "It's very traditional and not always very innovative. But it's a town where the social fabric hasn't deteriorated as much as in other places. Unlike New York City, people here don't laugh when you speak of ideals like 'family values.' They take their norms of social responsibility seriously."

> While growing up in New York City, I was taught by loving, caring people to ignore the cries of strangers.

Even when people do help in New York City, their altruism sometimes takes a hard edge. On the lost-letter measure, many of the envelopes we received from people had been opened. In almost all cases, the finder had resealed the envelope or mailed the letter in a new one. Sometimes they even attached notes, usually apologizing for opening the letter. Only from New York City, however, did we receive an envelope with its entire side ripped and left open. On the back of the letter, the "helper" had scribbled, in Spanish, a very nasty accusation about the researcher's mother. Below that, he or she added in straightforward English: "F— you." It is fascinating to imagine this angry New Yorker, perhaps cursing while walking to the mailbox, yet feeling compelled by the norm of social responsibility to assist a stranger. Ironically, this rudely returned letter added to New York's helpfulness score.

While growing up in New York City, I was taught by loving, caring people to ignore the cries of strangers. I learned to walk around people stretched unconscious on sidewalks, because I was told that they just need to "sleep it off." I learned to ignore screams from fighting couples: "they don't want your help." And I was warned to disregard the ramblings of mentally disturbed street people because "you never know how they'll react." The ultimate message: "Don't get involved."

Do our data prove that urbanites are less caring people? Perhaps not. For one thing, no comparable data from small towns exist to show that people there are more helpful than are urbanites. Furthermore, city dwellers we talked with claimed over and over that they care deeply about the needs of strangers, but that the realities of city living prohibit them from reaching out. Many are simply afraid to make contact with strangers. Some are concerned that others might not want unsolicited help. They claim that the stranger might be afraid of outside contact or, in some cases, that it would be patronizing or insulting to offer them help. People speak with nostalgia about the past, when they thought nothing of picking up hitchhikers or arranging a square meal for a hungry stranger. Many express frustration—even anger—that life today deprives them of the satisfaction of feeling like good Samaritans.

To some degree, these may be the rationalizations of unwilling helpers trying to preserve a benevolent self-image. But the evidence, in fact, indicates that helping is affected less by people's inherent nature than by the environment. Studies reveal that seemingly minor changes in a situation can drastically affect helping behavior. In particular, the size of the place where one was raised has less to do with how helpful one is than does the size of one's current home. In other words, small-town natives and urbanites are both less likely to offer help in urban areas.

The future of urban helping may not be as bleak as it seems. Just as the environment can inhibit helping behavior, researchers are currently exploring ways to modify the environment to encourage it. Experiments have found that increasing the level of personal responsibility people feel in a situation increases the likelihood they will help. It also helps to make people feel guilty when they don't help others.

A little more than a century ago, John Habberton wrote: "Nowhere in the world are there more charitable hearts with plenty of money behind them than in large cities, yet nowhere else is there more suffering." The current status of helping activity in our cities is dismal. But helping, like language and other human skills, is a learned behavior.

Research indicates that children who are exposed to altruistic models on television tend to follow suit. Just think how much good it could do them to see positive role models in real life.

Behind the Numbers Three large, medium, and smaller cities were sampled in each of the four census-defined regions of the U.S. (Northeast, North Central, South, and West). Travel distance within each region was a factor in selection of cities. The data for the five experiments were collected in two or more locations, in downtown areas during main business hours, on clear days during the summer months of 1990 and 1991. For the three measures that required approaching pedestrians, only individuals walking alone were selected. Children apparently under 17 years old, handicapped, very old people, and people with heavy packages were excluded. For the purposes of analysis, each of the 36 cities was treated as a single subject. For each city, the six measures of helping were converted to standardized scores, to which the value "10" was added to eliminate negative values. These adjusted standardized scores were then averaged to produce the overall helping score.

CAUSE OF DEATH: UNCERTAIN(TY)

By Robert B. Cialdini

All the weapons of influence discussed in this book* work better under some conditions than under others. If we are to defend ourselves adequately against any such weapon, it is vital that we know its optimal operating conditions in order to recognize when we are most vulnerable to its influence. We have already had a hint of one time when the principle of social proof worked best—with the Chicago believers. It was a sense of shaken confidence that triggered their craving for converts. In general, *when we are unsure of ourselves, when the situation is unclear or ambiguous, when uncertainty reigns, we are most likely to look to and accept the actions of others as correct* (Tesser, Campbell, & Mickler, 1983).

In the process of examining the reactions of other people to resolve our uncertainty, however, we are likely to overlook a subtle, but important fact: Those people are probably examining the social evidence, too. Especially in an ambiguous situation, the tendency for everyone to be looking to see what everyone else is doing can lead to a fascinating phenomenon called pluralistic ignorance. A thorough understanding of the pluralistic ignorance phenomenon helps explain a regular occurrence in our country that has been termed both a riddle and a national disgrace: the failure of entire groups of bystanders to aid victims in agonizing need of help.

The classic example of such bystander inaction and the one that has produced the most debate in journalistic, political, and scientific circles began as an ordinary homicide case in New York City's borough of Queens. A woman in her late twenties, Catherine Genovese, was killed in a late-night attack on her street as she returned from work. Murder is never an act to be passed off lightly, but in a city the size and tenor of New York, the Genovese incident warranted no more space than a fraction of a column in the *New York Times*. Catherine Genovese's story would have died with her on that day in March 1964 if it hadn't been for a mistake.

The metropolitan editor of the *Times*, A. M. Rosenthal, happened to be having lunch with the city police commissioner a week later. Rosenthal asked the commissioner about a different Queens-based homicide and the commissioner, thinking he was being questioned about the Genovese case, revealed something staggering that had been uncovered by the police investigation. It was something that left everyone who heard it, the commissioner included, aghast and grasping for explanations. Catherine Genovese had not experienced a quick, muffled death. It had been a long, loud, tortured, *public* event. Her assailant had chased and attacked her in the street three times over a period of 35 minutes before his knife finally silenced her cries for help. Incredibly, 38 of her neighbors watched from the safety of their apartment windows without so much as lifting a finger to call the police.

Rosenthal, a former Pulitzer Prize-winning reporter, knew a story when he heard one. On the day of his lunch with the commissioner, he assigned a reporter to investigate the "bystander angle" of the Genovese incident. Within a week, the *Times* published a long, front-page article that was to create a swirl of controversy and speculation. The initial paragraphs of that report provided the tone and focus of the story:

> For more than half an hour 38 respectable, law-abiding citizens in Queens watched a killer stalk and stab a woman in three separate attacks in Kew Gardens.
>
> Twice the sound of their voices and the sudden glow of their bedroom lights interrupted him and frightened him off. Each time he returned, sought her out, and stabbed her again. Not one person telephoned the police during the assault; one witness called after the woman was dead.
>
> That was two weeks ago today. But Assistant Chief Inspector Frederick M. Lussen, in charge of the borough's detectives and a vet-

*From *Influence: Science and Practice, 3/e*, edited by Robert B. Cialdini, chapter 4, pp. 106–114. © 1993 by HarperCollins College Publishers. Reprinted by permission of Addison Wesley Educational Publishers, Inc.

eran of 25 years of homicide investigations, is still shocked.

He can give a matter-of-fact recitation of many murders. But the Kew Gardens slaying baffles him—not because it is a murder; but because "good people" failed to call the police. (Ganzberg, 1964)

As with Assistant Chief Inspector Lussen, shock and bafflement were the standard reactions of almost everyone who learned the story's details. The shock struck first, leaving the police, the newspeople, and the reading public stunned. The bafflement followed quickly. How could 38 "good people" fail to act under those circumstances? No one could understand it. Even the murder witnesses themselves were bewildered. "I don't know," they answered one after another. "I just don't know." A few offered weak reasons for their inaction. For example, two or three people explained that they were "afraid" or "did not want to get involved." These reasons, however, do not stand up to close scrutiny: A simple anonymous call to the police could have saved Catherine Genovese without threatening the witnesses' future safety or free time. No, it wasn't the observers' fear or reluctance to complicate their lives that explained their lack of action; something else was going on there that even they could not fathom.

Confusion, though, does not make for good news copy. So the press as well as the other media—several papers, TV stations, and magazines that were pursuing follow-up stories—emphasized the only explanation available at the time: The witnesses, no different from the rest of us, hadn't cared enough to get involved. Americans were becoming a nation of selfish, insensitive people. The rigors of modern life, especially city life, were hardening them. They were becoming "The Cold Society," unfeeling and indifferent to the plight of their fellow citizens.

In support of this interpretation, news stories began appearing regularly in which various kinds of public apathy were detailed. Also supporting such an interpretation were the remarks of a range of armchair social commentators, who, as a breed, seem never to admit to bafflement when speaking to the press. They, too, saw the Genovese case as having large-scale social significance. All used the word apathy, which, it is interesting to note, had been in the headline of the *Time[s]*'s front-page story, although they accounted for the apathy differently. One attributed it to the effects of TV violence, another to repressed aggressiveness, but most implicated the "depersonalization" of urban life with its "megalopolitan societies" and its "alienation of the individual from the group." Even Rosenthal, the newsman who first broke the story and who ultimately made it the subject of a book, subscribed to the city-caused apathy theory.

> Nobody can say why the 38 did not lift the phone while Miss Genovese was being attacked, since they cannot say themselves. It can be assumed, however, that their apathy was indeed one of the big-city variety. It is almost a matter of psychological survival, if one is surrounded and pressed by millions of people, to prevent them from constantly impinging on you, and the only way to do this is to ignore them as often as possible. Indifference to one's neighbor and his troubles is a conditioned reflex in life in New York as it is in other big cities. (A. M. Rosenthal, 1964)

As the Genovese story grew—aside from Rosenthal's book, it became the focus of numerous newspaper and magazine pieces, several television news documentaries, and an off-Broadway play—it attracted the professional attention of a pair of New York-based psychology professors, Bibb Latané and John Darley. They examined the reports of the Genovese incident and, on the basis of their knowledge of social psychology, hit on what had seemed like the most unlikely explanation of all—the fact that 38 witnesses were present. Previous accounts of the story had invariably emphasized that no action was taken, even *though* 38 individuals had looked on. Latané and Darley suggested that no one had helped precisely because there were so many observers.

The psychologists speculated that, for at least two reasons, a bystander to an emergency will be unlikely to help when there are a number of other bystanders present. The first reason is fairly straightforward. *With several potential helpers around, the personal responsibility of each individual is reduced:* "Perhaps someone else will give or call for aid, perhaps someone else already has." So with everyone thinking that someone else will help or has helped, no one does. The second reason is the more psychologically intriguing one; it is founded on the principle of social proof and involves the pluralistic ignorance effect. Very often an emergency is not obviously an emergency. Is the man lying in the alley a heart-attack victim or a drunk sleeping one off? Is the commotion next door an assault requiring the police or an especially loud marital spat where intervention would be inappropriate and unwelcome? What is going on? In times of such uncertainty, the natural tendency is to look around at the actions of others for clues. We can learn, from the way the other witnesses are reacting, whether the event is or is not an emergency.

What is easy to forget, though, is that everybody else observing the event is likely to be looking for social evidence, too. Because we all prefer to appear poised and unflustered among others, we are likely to search for that evidence placidly, with brief, camouflaged glances at those around us. Therefore everyone is likely to see everyone else looking unruffled and failing to act. As a result, and by the principle of social proof, the event will be roundly interpreted as a nonemergency. This, according to Latané and Darley (1968b) is the state of pluralistic ignorance "in which each person decided that since nobody is concerned, nothing is wrong. Meanwhile, the danger may be mounting to the point where a single individual, uninfluenced by the seeming calm of others, *would* react."[1]

A Scientific Approach

The fascinating upshot of Latané and Darley's reasoning is that, for an emergency victim, the idea of "safety in numbers" may often be completely wrong. It might be that someone in need of emergency aid would have a better chance of survival if a single bystander, rather than a crowd, were present. To test this unusual thesis, Darley, Latané, their students, and colleagues performed a systematic and impressive program of research that produced a clear set of findings (for a review, see Latané & Nida, 1981). Their basic procedure was to stage emergency events that were observed by a single individual or by a group of people. They then recorded the number of times the emergency victim received help under those circumstances. In their first experiment (Darley & Latané, 1968), a New York college student who appeared to be having an epileptic seizure received help 85 percent of the time when there was a single bystander present but only 31 percent of time with five bystanders present. With almost all the single bystanders helping, it becomes difficult to argue that ours is "The Cold Society" where no one cares for suffering others. Obviously it was something about the presence of other bystanders that reduced helping to shameful levels.

Other studies have examined the importance of social proof in causing widespread witness "apathy." They have done so by planting within a group of witnesses to a possible emergency people who are rehearsed to act as if no emergency were occurring. For instance, in another New York-based experiment (Latané & Darley, 1968a), 75 percent of lone individuals who observed smoke seeping from under a door reported the leak; however, when similar leaks were observed by three-person groups, the smoke was reported only 38 percent of the time. The smallest number of bystanders took action, though, when the three-person groups included two individuals who had been coached to ignore the smoke; under those conditions, the leaks were reported only 10 percent of time. In a similar study conducted in Toronto (A. S. Ross, 1971), single bystanders provided emergency aid 90 percent of the time, whereas such aid occurred in only 16 percent of the cases when a bystander was in the presence of two passive bystanders.

After more than a decade of such research, social scientists now have a good idea of when bystanders will offer emergency aid. First, and contrary to the view that we have become a society of callous, uncaring people, once witnesses are convinced that an emergency situation exists, aid is very likely. Under these conditions, the number of bystanders who either intervene themselves or summon help is quite comforting. For example, in four separate experiments done in Florida (R. D. Clark & Word, 1972, 1974), accident scenes involving a maintenance man were staged. When it was clear that the man was hurt and required assistance, he was helped 100 percent of the time in two of the experiments. In the other two experiments, where helping involved contact with potentially dangerous electric wires, the victim still received bystander aid in 90 percent of the instances. In addition, these extremely high levels of assistance occurred whether the witnesses observed the event singly or in groups.

---

[1] The potentially tragic consequences of the pluralistic ignorance phenomenon are starkly illustrated in a UPI news release from Chicago:

A university coed was beaten and strangled in daylight hours near one of the most popular tourist attractions in the city, police said Saturday.
The nude body of Lee Alexis Wilson, 23, was found Friday in dense shubbery alongside the wall of the Art Institute by a 12-year-old boy playing in the bushes.
Police theorized she may have been sitting or standing by a fountain in the Art Institute's south plaza when she was attacked. The assailant apparently then dragged her into the bushes. She apparently was sexually assaulted, police said.
Police said thousands of persons must have passed the site and one man told them he heard a scream about 2 P.M. but did not investigate because no one else seemed to be paying attention.

The situation becomes very different when, as in many cases, bystanders cannot be sure that the event they are witnessing is an emergency. Then a victim is much more likely to be helped by a lone bystander than by a group, especially if the people in the group are strangers to one another (Latané & Rodin, 1969). It seems that the pluralistic ignorance effect is strongest among strangers: Because we like to look graceful and sophisticated in public and because we are unfamiliar with the reactions of those we do not know, we are unlikely to give off or correctly read expressions of concern when in a group of strangers. Therefore, a possible emergency is viewed as a nonemergency and a victim suffers.

A close look at this set of research findings reveals an enlightening pattern. All the conditions that decrease an emergency victim's chances for bystander aid exist normally and innocently in the city, in contrast to rural areas:

1. Cities are more clamorous, distracting, rapidly changing places where it is difficult to be certain of the nature of the events one encounters.
2. Urban environments are more populous; consequently, people are more likely to be with others when witnessing a potential emergency situation.
3. City dwellers know a much smaller percentage of fellow residents than do people who live in small towns; therefore, city dwellers are more likely to find themselves in a group of strangers when observing an emergency.

These three natural characteristics of urban environments—their confusion, their populousness, and their low levels of acquaintanceship—fit in very well with the factors shown by research to decrease bystander aid. Without ever having to resort to such sinister concepts as "urban depersonalization" and "megalopolitan alienation," then, we can explain why so many instances of bystander inaction occur in our cities.

Devictiming Yourself

Explaining the dangers of modern urban life in less ominous terms does not dispel them. Furthermore, as the world's populations move increasingly to the cities—half of all humanity will be city dwellers within a decade (Newland, 1980)—there will be a growing need to reduce those dangers. Fortunately, our newfound understanding of the bystander "apathy" process offers real hope. Armed with this scientific knowledge, an emergency victim can increase enormously the chances of receiving aid from others. The key is the realization that groups of bystanders fail to help because the bystanders are unsure rather than unkind. They don't help because they are unsure an emergency actually exists and whether they are responsible for taking action. When they are sure of their responsibilities for intervening in a clear emergency, people are exceedingly responsive!

Once it is understood that the enemy is the simple state of uncertainty, it becomes possible for emergency victims to reduce this uncertainty, thereby protecting themselves. Imagine, for example, you are spending a summer afternoon at a music concert in a park. As the concert ends and people begin leaving, you notice a slight numbness in one arm but dismiss it as nothing to be alarmed about. Yet, while moving with the crowd to the distant parking areas, you feel the numbness spreading down to your hand and up one side of your face. Feeling disoriented, you decide to sit against a tree for a moment to rest. Soon you realize that something is drastically wrong. Sitting down has not helped; in fact, the control and coordination of your muscles has worsened, and you are starting to have difficulty moving your mouth and tongue to speak. You try to get up but can't. A terrifying thought rushes to mind: "Oh, God, I'm having a stroke!" Groups of people are passing by and most are paying no attention. The few who notice the odd way you are slumped against the tree or the strange look on your face check the social evidence around them and, seeing that no one else is reacting with concern, walk on convinced that nothing is wrong.

Were you to find yourself in such a predicament, what could you do to overcome the odds against receiving help? Because your physical abilities would be deteriorating, time would be crucial. If, before you could summon aid, you lost your speech or mobility or consciousness, your chances for assistance and for recovery would plunge drastically. It would be essential to try to request help quickly. What would be the most effective form of that request? Moans, groans, or outcries probably would not do. They might bring you some attention, but they would not provide enough information to assure passersby that a true emergency existed.

If mere outcries are unlikely to produce help from the passing crowd, perhaps you should be more specific. Indeed, you need to do more than try to gain attention; you should call out clearly your need for assistance. You must not allow bystanders to define your situation as a nonemergency. Use the word "Help" to show your need for emergency aid, and don't worry about being wrong. Embarrassment is a villain to be crushed. If you think you are having a stroke, you cannot afford to be worried about the possibility of overestimating your problem. The difference is that between a moment of embarrassment and possible death or lifelong paralysis.

Even a resounding call for help is not your most effective tactic. Although it may reduce bystanders' doubts that a real emergency exists, it will not remove several other important uncertainties within each onlooker's mind: What kind of aid is required? Should I be the one to provide the aid, or should someone more qualified do it? Has someone else already gone to get professional help, or is it my responsibility? While the bystanders stand gawking at you and grappling with these questions, time vital to your survival could be slipping away.

Clearly, then, as a victim you must do more than alert bystanders to your need for emergency assistance; you must also remove their uncertainties about how that assistance should be provided and who should provide it. What would be the most efficient and reliable way to do so?

Many Are Called But Only One Should Be Chosen

Based on the research findings we have seen, my advice would be to isolate one individual from the crowd: Stare, speak, and point directly at that person and no one else: "You, sir, in the blue jacket, I need help. Call an ambulance." With that one utterance you would dispel all the uncertainties that might prevent or delay help. With that one statement you will have put the man in the blue jacket in the role of "rescuer." He should now understand that emergency aid is needed; he should understand that he, not someone else, is responsible for providing the aid; and, finally, he should understand exactly how to provide it. All the scientific evidence indicates that the result should be quick, effective assistance.

In general, then, your best strategy when in need of emergency help is to reduce the uncertainties of those around you concerning your condition and their responsibilities. Be as precise as possible about your need for aid. Do not allow bystanders to come to their own conclusions because, especially in a crowd, the principle of social proof and the consequent pluralistic ignorance effect might well cause them to view your situation as a nonemergency. Of all the techniques in this book designed to produce compliance with a request, this one is the most important to remember. After all, the failure of your request for emergency aid could mean your life.

Not long ago, I received some firsthand evidence proving this point. I was involved in a rather serious automobile collision. Both I and the other driver were plainly hurt: He was slumped, unconscious, over his steering wheel while I managed to stagger, bloody, from behind mine. The accident had occurred in the center of an intersection in full view of several individuals stopped in their cars at the traffic light. As I knelt in the road beside my car door, trying to clear my head, the light changed. The waiting cars began to roll slowly through the intersection; their drivers gawked but did not stop.

I remember thinking, "Oh no, it's happening just like the research says. They're all passing by!" I consider it fortunate that, as a social psychologist, I knew enough about the bystander studies to have that particular thought. By thinking of my predicament in terms of the research findings, I knew exactly what to do. Pulling myself up so I could be seen clearly, I pointed at the driver of one car: "Call the police." To a second and a third driver, pointing directly each time: "Pull over; we need help." The responses of these people were instantaneous. They summoned a police car and ambulance immediately, they used their handkerchiefs to blot the blood from my face, they put a jacket under my head, they volunteered to serve as witnesses to the accident, and one person even offered to ride with me to the hospital.

Not only was this help rapid and solicitous, it was infectious. After drivers entering the intersection from the other direction saw cars stopping for me, they stopped and began tending to the other victim. The principle of social proof was working for us now. The trick had been to get the ball rolling in the direction of aid. Once that was accomplished, I was able to relax and let the bystanders' genuine concern and social proof's natural momentum do the rest. . . .

Group Processes

In 1961 President John F. Kennedy and a group of his senior advisers held a series of secret meetings to plan a dramatic military action. The plan under consideration was an invasion of Cuba, and the goal was to overthrow the Communist regime of Fidel Castro. This was not to be a massive invasion, however, utilizing the United States' heavy superiority in numbers and technology; such a move would be too provocative. Instead, the plan called for the United States to secretly train and equip a relatively small force of anti-Castro Cubans—exiles driven from their homeland because of Castro's rise to power. This small force of about 1,400 men would begin the invasion by landing at the Bahia de Cochinos, or the Bay of Pigs. Seizing control of radio stations, they would broadcast news of Cuba's liberation and would then sweep across the country picking up support from the Cuban people until they would constitute a force so compelling that Castro could not endure.

They never had a chance. Supplies that were supposed to sustain the invaders failed to arrive; the tiny invading force was completely overwhelmed by the larger, better-trained Cuban military; and the anticipated uprising by the Cuban people never happened. Within three days the entire force had been captured or killed. Instead of a dramatic military success, the United States, and President Kennedy, suffered a humiliating political defeat in the eyes of the world; in fact, the phrase "Bay of Pigs" has come to signify any plan or action that comes to a disastrous end. In the aftermath of this debacle, moreover, it seemed painfully obvious that the plan was doomed from the start. The nagging question, then, was how could some of the smartest people in the country come to agree on a plan that in retrospect seemed to have no chance at all of succeeding? How could the group go so wrong?

That question is one of the many that social psychology has asked about groups and the processes that occur when people meet in groups. In fact, a very interesting line of research into how groups can reach such bad decisions—a phenomenon known as "groupthink"—was directly inspired by the Bay of Pigs fiasco. According to this approach, highly cohesive groups frequently develop a mind-set characterized by secretiveness, overconfidence, and illusions of invulnerability; this in turn can lead them into decisions that overlook what should be obvious flaws. Other approaches to group decision making have focused on another common phenomenon—the fact that when groups have to choose a course of action, they often make a choice that is more extreme than the decision that each individual would make alone. That is, one effect of group discussion is to polarize the attitudes of the group members.

In addition to the issue of how groups make decisions, another topic of interest has been the impact that groups can have on the *behavior* of the individuals who make up the group. For example, it frequently happens that individuals work faster and more productively when in the presence of others than they do when they are alone—at least if the task they are working on is relatively simple, or if it is a task with which they have had a lot of practice. In contrast, on a new task, or one that is very complex, the presence of other people can hurt performance. Researchers who study this phenomenon, called *social facilitation*, have identified a variety of possible explanations for its occurrence.

The selections in this unit represent several different approaches to the study of group processes. The first selection addresses the issue of group decision making. In "Group Decision Fiascoes Continue: Space Shuttle *Challenger* and a Revised Groupthink Framework," the authors use the decision to launch the ill-fated space shuttle *Challenger* as an example of groupthink. They trace how some of the cognitive biases that characterize groupthink were present during the discussions.

In the second selection, "What Messages Are behind Today's Cults?" Philip Zimbardo examines the appeal of cults from a social psychological perspective, asking the

UNIT 10

question: Why are cults so appealing to perfectly normal people? He concludes that cults not only employ traditional social psychological methods of compliance, but they also provide a sense of community for many people.

In the third selection, "The Heavy Burden of Black Conformity," Bill Maxwell gives a vivid example of one power of the group that can be painful for its members—the power to enforce conformity. Maxwell describes the pressure he feels from what he calls the "Soul Patrol"—fellow African Americans who discourage any attempts to criticize their own ethnic group.

Finally, in "Group Processes in the Resolution of International Conflicts: Experiences from the Israeli-Palestinian Case," Herbert Kelman describes his ongoing project designed to help foster greater cooperation between Israelis and Palestinians in the Middle East. By using insights gained from social psychology, Kelman has created interactive problem-solving workshops, which help foster greater understanding and cooperation between these two traditionally antagonistic groups.

Looking Ahead: Challenge Questions

What are the most important characteristics of a group experiencing groupthink? How do those characteristics ultimately influence the decisions reached by the group? Other than the Bay of Pigs and *Challenger* disasters, can you think of any well-known group decisions that might be examples of groupthink? Can you think of any examples from groups in your own life?

After reading Philip Zimbardo's article, can you ever imagine joining a group that some might see as a cult? Even if your answer is "no," what features of such a group do you think might be attractive?

Have you ever experienced conformity pressures from a group to which you belonged? How did it feel? How did you respond to that pressure?

How successful do you think problem-solving groups like those in the Herbert Kelman article will be in reducing group tensions? On what do you base your answer? Can you think of any other techniques that could be helpful?

Group Decision Fiascoes Continue: Space Shuttle Challenger and a Revised Groupthink Framework

Gregory Moorhead, Richard Ference and Chris P. Neck

In this article, the authors review the events surrounding the tragic decision to launch the space shuttle Challenger. Moorhead and his colleagues assert that the decision-making process demonstrates *groupthink*, a phenomenon wherein cohesive groups become so concerned with their own process that they lose sight of the true requirements of their task. The authors review the events in light of this concept, suggesting that the groupthink concept needs to be expanded to consider time pressures, which were surely present in the Challenger situation, as well as the kind of leadership patterns that exist in a group.

In 1972, a new dimension was added to our understanding of group decision making with the proposal of the groupthink hypothesis by Janis (1972). Janis coined the term "groupthink" to refer to "a mode of thinking that people engage in when they are deeply involved in a cohesive in-group, when the members' striving for unanimity override their motivation to realistically appraise alternative courses of action" (Janis, 1972, p. 8). The hypothesis was supported by his hindsight analysis of several political-military fiascoes and successes that are differentiated by the occurrence or non-occurrence of antecedent conditions, groupthink symptoms, and decision making defects.

In a subsequent volume, Janis further explicates the theory and adds an analysis of the Watergate transcripts and various published memoirs and accounts of principals involved, concluding that the Watergate cover-up decision also was a result of groupthink (Janis, 1983). Both volumes propose prescriptions for preventing the occurrence of groupthink, many of which have appeared in popular press, in books on executive decision making, and in management textbooks. Multiple advocacy decision-making procedures have been adopted at the executive levels in many organizations, including the executive branch of the government. One would think that by 1986, 13 years after the publication of a popular book, that its prescriptions might be well ingrained in our management and decision-making styles. Unfortunately, it has not happened.

On January 28, 1986, the space shuttle Challenger was launched from Kennedy Space Center. The temperature that morning was in the mid-20's, well below the previous low temperatures at which the shuttle engines had been tested. Seventy-three seconds after launch, the Challenger exploded, killing all seven astronauts aboard, and becoming the worst disaster in space flight history. The catastrophe shocked the nation, crippled the American space program, and is destined to be remembered as the most tragic national event since the assassination of John F. Kennedy in 1963.

The Presidential Commission that investigated the accident pointed to a flawed decision-making process as a primary contributory cause. The decision was made the night before the launch in the Level I Flight Readiness Review meeting. Due to the work of the Presidential Commission, information concerning that meeting is available for analysis as a group decision possibly susceptible to groupthink.

In this paper, we report the results of our analysis of the Level I Flight Readiness Review meeting as a decision-making situation that displays evidence of groupthink. We review the antecedent conditions, the groupthink symptoms, and the possible decision-making defects, as suggested by Janis (1983). In addition, we take the next and more important step by going beyond the development of another example of groupthink to make recommendations for renewed inquiry into group decision-making processes.

THEORY AND EVIDENCE

The meeting(s) took place throughout the day and evening from 12:36 pm (EST), January 27, 1986 following the decision to not launch the Challenger due to high crosswinds at the launch site. Discussions continued through about 12:00 midnight (EST) via teleconferencing and Telefax systems connecting the Kennedy Space Center in Florida, Morton Thiokol (MTI) in Utah, Johnson Space Center in Houston, and the Marshall Space Flight Center. The Level I Flight Readiness Review is the highest level of review prior to launch. It comprises the highest level of management at the three space centers and at MTI, the private supplier of the solid rocket booster engines.

To briefly state the situation, the MTI engineers recommended not to launch if temperatures of the O-ring seals on the rocket were below 53 degrees Fahrenheit, which was the lowest temperature of any previous flight. Laurence B. Mulloy, manager of the Solid Rocket Booster Project at Marshall Space Flight Center, states:

> The bottom line of that, though, initially was that Thiokol engineering, Bob Lund, who is the Vice President and Director of Engineering, who is here today, recommended that 51-L [the Challenger] not be launched if the O-ring temperatures predicted at launch time would be lower than any previous launch, and that was 53 degrees. (*Report of the Presidential Commission on the Space Shuttle Accident*, 1986, p. 91–92).

This recommendation was made at 8:45 pm, January 27, 1986 (*Report of the Presidential Commission on the Space Shuttle Accident*, 1986). Through the ensuing discussions the decision to launch was made.

Antecedent Conditions

The three primary antecedent conditions for the development of groupthink are: a highly cohesive group, leader preference for a certain decision, and insulation of the group from qualified outside opinions. These conditions existed in this situation.

Cohesive Group. The people who made the decision to launch had worked together for many years. They were familiar with each other and had grown through the ranks of the space program. A high degree of *esprit de corps* existed between the members.

Leader Preference. Two top level managers actively promoted their pro-launch opinions in the face of opposition. The commission report states that several managers at space centers and MTI pushed for launch, regardless of the low temperatures.

Insulation from Experts. MTI engineers made their recommendations relatively early in the evening. The top level decision-making group knew of their objections but did not meet with them directly to review their data and concerns. As Roger Boisjoly, a Thiokol engineer, states in his remarks to the Presidential Commission:

> and the bottom line was that the engineering people would not recommend a launch below 53 degrees Fahrenheit.... From this point on, management formulated the points to base their decision on. There was never one comment in favor, as I have said, of launching by any engineer or other nonmanagement person.... I was not even asked to participate in giving any input to the final decision charts (*Report of the Presidential Commission on the Space Shuttle Accident*, 1986, p. 91–92).

This testimonial indicates that the top decision-making team was insulated from the engineers who possessed the expertise regarding the functioning of the equipment.

Janis identified eight symptoms of groupthink. They are presented here along with evidence from the *Report of the Presidential Commission on the Space Shuttle Accident* (1986).

Invulnerability. When groupthink occurs, most or all of the members of the decision-making group have an illusion of invulnerability that reassures them in the face of obvious dangers. This illusion leads the group to become overly optimistic and willing to take extraordinary risks. It may also cause them to ignore clear warnings of danger.

The solid rocket joint problem that destroyed Challenger was discussed often at flight readiness review meetings prior to flight. However, Commission member Richard Feynman concluded from the testimony that a mentality of overconfidence existed due to the extraordinary record of success of space flights. Every time we send one up it is successful. Involved members may seem to think that on the next one we can lower our standards or take more risks because it always works (*Time*, 1986).

The invulnerability illusion may have built up over time as a result of NASA's own spectacular history. NASA had not lost an astronaut since 1967 when a flash fire in the capsule of Apollo 1 killed three. Since that time NASA had a string of 55 successful missions. They had put a man on the moon, built and launched Skylab and the shuttle, and retrieved defective satellites from orbit. In the minds of most Americans and apparently their own, they could do no wrong.

Rationalization. Victims of groupthink collectively construct rationalizations that discount warnings and other forms of negative feedback. If these signals were taken seriously when presented, the group members would be forced to reconsider their assumptions each time they re-commit themselves to their past decisions.

In the Level I flight readiness meeting when the Challenger was given final launch approval, MTI engineers presented evidence that the joint would fail. Their argument was based on the fact that in the coldest previous launch (air temperature 30 degrees) the joint in question experienced serious erosion and that no data existed as to how the joint would perform at colder temperatures. Flight center officials put forth numerous technical rationalizations faulting MTI's analysis. One of these rationalizations was that the engineer's data were inconclusive. As Mr. Boisjoly emphasized to the Commission:

> I was asked, yes, at that point in time I was asked to quantify my concerns, and I said I couldn't. I couldn't quantify it. I had no data to quantify it, but I did say I knew that it was away from goodness in the current data base. Someone on the net commented that we had soot blow-by on SRM-22 [Flight 61-A, October, 1985] which was launched at 75 degrees. I don't remember who made the comment, but that is where the first comment came in about the disparity between my conclusion and the observed data because SRM-22 [Flight 61-A, October 1985] had blow-by at essentially a room temperature launch. I then said that SRM-15 [Flight 51-C, January, 1985] had much more blow-by indication and that it was indeed telling us that lower temperature was a factor. I was asked again for data to support my claim, and I said I have none other than what is being presented (*Report of the Presidential Commission on the Space Shuttle Accident*, 1986, p. 89).

Discussions became twisted (compared to previous meetings) and no one detected it. Under normal conditions, MTI would have to prove the shuttle boosters readiness for launch, instead they found themselves being forced to prove that the boosters were unsafe. Boisjoly's testimony supports this description of the discussion:

> This was a meeting where the determination was to launch, and it was up to us to prove beyond a shadow of a doubt that it was not safe to do so. This is in total reverse to what the position usually is in a preflight conversation or a flight readiness review. It is usually exactly the opposite of that. (*Report of the Presidential Commission on the Space Shuttle Accident*, 1986, p. 93).

Morality. Group members often believe, without question, in the inherent morality of their position. They tend to ignore the ethical or moral consequences of their decision.

In the Challenger case, this point was raised by a very high level MTI manager, Allan J. McDonald, who tried to stop the launch and said that he would not want to have to defend the decision to launch. He stated to the Commission:

> I made the statement that if we're wrong and something goes wrong on this flight, I wouldn't want to have to be the person to stand up in front of board in inquiry and say that I went ahead and told them to go ahead and fly this thing outside what the motor was qualified to. (*Report of the Presidential Commission on the Space Shuttle Accident*, 1986, p. 95).

Some members did not hear this statement because it occurred during a break. Three top officials who did hear it ignored it.

Stereotyped Views of Others. Victims of groupthink often have a stereotyped view of the opposition of anyone with a competing opinion. They feel that the opposition is too stupid or too weak to understand or deal effectively with the problem.

Two of the top three NASA officials responsible for the launch displayed this attitude. They felt that they completely understood the nature of the joint problem and never seriously considered the objections raised by the MTI engineers. In fact they denigrated and badgered the opposition and their information and opinions.

Pressure on Dissent. Group members often apply direct pressure to anyone who questions the validity of these arguments supporting a decision or position favored by the majority. These same two officials pressured MTI to change its position after MTI originally recommended that the launch not take place. These two officials pressured MTI personnel to prove that it was not safe to launch, rather than to prove the opposite. As mentioned earlier, this was a total reversal of normal preflight procedures. It was this pressure that top MTI management was responding to when they overruled their engineering staff and recommended launch. As the Commission report states:

> At approximately 11 p.m. Eastern Standard Time, the Thiokol/NASA teleconference resumed, the Thiokol management stating that they had reassessed the problem, that the temperature effects were a concern, but that the data was admittedly inconclusive (p. 96).

This seems to indicate the NASA's pressure on these Thiokol officials forced them to change their recommendation from delay to execution of the launch.

Self-Censorship. Group members tend to censor themselves when they have opinions or ideas that deviate from the apparent group consensus. Janis feels that this reflects each member's inclination to minimize to himself or herself the importance of his or her own doubts and counter-arguments.

The most obvious evidence of self-censorship occurred when a vice president of MTI, who had previously presented information against launch, bowed to pressure from NASA and accepted their rationalizations for launch. He then wrote these up and presented them to NASA as the reasons that MTI had changed its recommendation to launch.

Illusion of Unanimity. Group members falling victim to groupthink share an illusion of unanimity concerning judgments made by members speaking in favor of the majority view. This symptom is caused in part by the preceding one and is aided by the false assumption that any participant who remains silent is in agreement with the majority opinion. The group leader and other members support each other by playing up points of convergence in their thinking at the expense of fully exploring points of divergence that might reveal unsettling problems.

No participant from NASA ever openly agreed with or even took sides with MTI in the discussion. The silence from NASA was probably amplified by the fact that the meeting was a teleconference linking the participants at three different locations. Obviously, body language which might have been evidenced by dissenters was not visible to others who might also have held a dissenting opinion. Thus, silence meant agreement.

Mindguarding. Certain group members assume the role of guarding the minds of others in the group. They attempt to shield the group from adverse information that might destroy the majority view of the facts regarding the appropriateness of the decision.

The top management at Marshall knew that the rocket casings had been ordered redesigned to correct a flaw 5 months previous to this launch. This information and other technical details concerning the history of the joint problem was withheld at the meeting.

Decision-Making Defects

The result of the antecedent conditions and the symptoms of groupthink is a defective decision-making process. Janis discusses several defects in decision making that can result.

Few Alternatives. The group considers only a few alternatives, often only two. No initial survey of all possible alternatives occurs. The Flight Readiness Review team had a launch/no-launch decision to make. These were the only two alternatives considered. Other possible alternatives might have been to delay the launch for further testing, or to delay until the temperatures reached an appropriate level.

No Re-Examination of Alternatives. The group fails to re-examine alternatives that may have been initially discarded based on early unfavorable information. Top NASA officials spent time and effort defending and strengthening their position, rather than examining the MTI position.

Rejecting Expert Opinions. Members make little or no attempt to seek outside experts opinions. NASA did not seek out other experts who might have some expertise in this area. They assumed that they had all the information.

Rejecting Negative Information. Members tend to focus on supportive information and ignore any data or information that might cast a negative light on their preferred alternative. MTI representatives repeatedly tried to point out errors in the rationale the NASA officials were using to justify the launch. Even after the decision was made, the argument continued until a NASA official told the MTI representative that it was no longer his concern.

No Contingency Plans. Members spend little time discussing the possible consequences of the decision and, therefore, fail to develop contingency plans. There is no documented evidence in the Rogers Commission Report of any discussion of the possible consequences of an incorrect decision.

The major categories and key elements of the groupthink hypothesis have been presented (albeit somewhat briefly) along with evidence from the discussions prior to the launching of the Challenger, as reported in the President's Commission to investigate the accident. The antecedent conditions were present in the decision-making group, even though the group was in several physical locations. The leaders had a preferred solution and engaged in behaviors designed to promote it rather than critically appraise alternatives. These behaviors were evidence of most of the symptoms leading to a defective decision-making process.

DISCUSSION

This situation provides another example of decision making in which the group fell victim to the groupthink syndrome, as have so many previous groups. It illustrates the situation characteristics, the symptoms of group think, and decision-making defects as described by Janis. This situation, however, also illustrates several other aspects of situations that are critical to the development of groupthink that need to be included in a revised formulation of the groupthink model. First, the element of time in influencing the development of groupthink has not received adequate attention. In the decision to launch the space shuttle Challenger, time was a crucial part of the decision-making process. The launch had been delayed once, and the window for another launch was fast closing. The leaders of the decision team were concerned about public and congressional perceptions of the entire space shuttle program and its continued funding and may have felt that further delays of the launch could seriously impact future funding. With the space

Figure 1 Revised groupthink framework

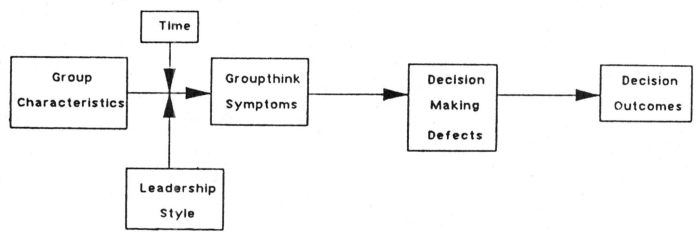

window fast closing, the decision team was faced with a launch now or seriously damage the program decision. One top level manager's response to Thiokol's initial recommendation to postpone the launch indicates the presence of time pressure:

> With this LCC (Launch Commit Criteria), i.e., do not launch with a temperature greater [sic] than 53 degrees, we may not be able to launch until next April. We need to consider this carefully before we jump to any conclusions. (*Report of the Presidential Commission on the Space Shuttle Accident*, 1986, p. 96).

Time pressure could have played a role in the group choosing to agree and to self-censor their comments. We propose that in certain situations when there is pressure to make a decision quickly, the elements may combine to foster the development of groupthink.

The second revision needs to be in the role of the leadership of the decision-making group. In the space shuttle Challenger incident, the leadership of the group varied from a shared type of leadership to a very clear leader in the situation. This may indicate that the leadership role needs to be clearly defined and a style that demands open disclosure of information, points of opposition, complaints, and dissension. We propose the leadership style is a crucial variable that moderates the relationship between the group characteristics and the development of the symptoms. Janis (1983) is a primary form of evidence to support the inclusion of leadership style in the enhanced model. His account of why the *same* group succumbed to groupthink in one decision (Bay of Pigs) and not in another (Cuban Missile Crisis) supports the depiction of leadership style as a moderator variable. In these decisions, the only condition that changed was the leadership style of the President. In other words, the element that seemed to distinguish why groupthink occurred in the Bay of Pigs decision and not in the Cuban Missile Crisis situation is the president's change in his behavior.

These two variables, time and leadership style, are proposed as moderators of the impact of the group characteristics on groupthink symptoms. This relationship is portrayed graphically in Fig. 1. In effect, we propose that the groupthink symptoms result from the group characteristics, as proposed by Janis, but only in the presence of the moderator variables of time and certain leadership styles.

Time, as an important element in the model, is relatively straightforward. When a decision must be made within a very short time frame, pressure on members to agree, to avoid time-consuming arguments and reports from outside experts, and to self-censor themselves may increase. These pressures inevitably cause group members to seek agreement. In Janis's original model, time was included indirectly as a function of the antecedent condition, group cohesion. Janis (1983) argued that time pressures can adversely affect decision quality in two ways. First, it affects the decision makers' mental efficiency and judgment, interfering with their ability to concentrate on complicated discussions, to absorb new information, and to use imagination to anticipate the future consequences of alternative courses of action. Second, time pressure is a source of stress that will have the effect of inducing a policy-making group to become more cohesive and more likely to engage in groupthink.

Leadership style is shown to be a moderator because of the importance it plays in either promoting or avoiding the development of the symptoms of the groupthink. The leader, even though she or he may not promote a preferred solution, may allow or even assist the group seeking agreement by not forcing the group to critically appraise all alternative courses of action. The focus of this leadership variable is on the degree to which the leader allows or promotes discussion and evaluation of alternatives. It is not a matter of simply not making known a preferred solution; the issue is one of stimulation of critical thinking among the group.

Impact on Prescriptions for Prevention

The revised model suggests that more specific prescriptions for prevention of groupthink can be made. First, group members need to be aware of the impact that a short decision time frame has on decision processes. When a decision must be made quickly, there will be more pressure to agree, i.e., discouragement of dissent, self-censorship, avoidance of expert opinion, and assumptions about unanimity. The type of leadership suggested here is not one that sits back and simply does not make known her or his preferred solution. This type of leader must be one that requires all members to speak up with concerns, questions, and new information. The leader must know what some of these concerns are and which members are likely to have serious doubts so that the people with concerns can be called upon to voice them. This type of group leadership does not simply assign the role of devil's advocate and step out of the way. This leader actually plays the role or makes sure that others do. A leader with the required style to avoid groupthink is not a laissez faire leader or non-involved participative leader. This leader is active in directing the activities of the group but does not make known a preferred solution. The group still must develop and evaluate alternative courses of action, but under the direct influence of a strong, demanding leader who forces critical appraisal of all alternatives.

Finally, a combination of the two variables suggests that the leader needs to help members to avoid the problems created by the time element. For example, the leader may be able to alter an externally imposed time frame for the decision by negotiating an extension or even paying late fees, if necessary. If an extension is not possible, the leader may need to help the group eliminate the effects of time on the decision processes. This can be done by forcing attention to issues rather than time, encouraging dissension and confrontation, and scheduling special sessions to hear reports from outside experts that challenge prevailing views within the group.

Janis presents, in both editions of his book, several recommendations for preventing the occurrence of groupthink. These recommendations focus on the inclusion of outside experts in the decision-making process, all members taking the role of devil's advocate and critically appraising all alternative courses of action, and the leader not expressing a preferred solution. The revised groupthink framework suggests several new prescriptions that may be helpful in preventing further decision fiascoes similar to the decision to launch the space shuttle Challenger.

REFERENCES

Time. Fixing NASA. June 9, 1986.
Janis, I. L. (1983) *Victims of groupthink*. Boston: Houghton Mifflin.
Janis, I. L. (1983) *Groupthink* (2nd ed., revised). Boston: Houghton Mifflin.
Report of the Presidential Commission on the Space Shuttle Accident. Washington, D.C.: July 1986.

What messages are behind today's cults?

Cults are coming. Are they crazy or bearing critical messages?

By Philip Zimbardo, PhD

Philip G. Zimbardo, PhD, is professor of psychology at Stanford University and a former APA president. He has interviewed and worked closely with survivors of Peoples Temple and their family members, as well as former members of the Unification Church, Scientology, Synanon, Churches of Christ and other cults.

How do we make sense of the mass suicide of 21 female and 18 male members of the Heaven's Gate extra-terrestrial "cult" on March 23? Typical explanations of all such strange, unexpected behavior involve a "rush to the dispositional," locating the problem in defective personalities of the actors. Those whose behavior violates our expectations about what is normal and appropriate are dismissed as kooks, weirdos, gullible, stupid, evil or masochistic deviants.

Similar characterizations were evident in the media and public's reaction to other mass suicides in The Order of the Solar Temple in Europe and Canada, murder-suicide deaths ordered by Rev. Jim Jones of his Peoples Temple members, as well as of the recent flaming deaths of David Koresh's Branch Davidians and the gassing of Japanese citizens by followers of the Aum Shinrikyo group. And there will be more of the same in the coming years as cults proliferate in the United States and world wide in anticipation of the millennium.

Avoiding the stereotypes

Such pseudo-explanations are really moralistic judgments; framed with the wisdom of hindsight, they miss the mark. They start at the wrong end of the inquiry. Instead, our search for meaning should begin at the beginning: "What was so appealing about this group that so many people were recruited/seduced into joining it voluntarily?" We want to know also, "What needs was this group fulfilling that were not being met by 'traditional society?'"

Such alternative framings shift the analytical focus from condemning the actors, mindlessly blaming the victims, defining them as differ-

---

Any stereotyped collective personality analysis of the Heaven's Gate members proves inadequate when tallied against the resumes of individual members.

---

ent from us, to searching for a common ground in the forces that shape all human behavior. By acknowledging our own vulnerability to the operation of the powerful, often subtle situational forces that controlled their actions, we can begin to find

45. What Messages Are behind Today's Cults?

ways to prevent or combat that power from exerting its similar, sometimes sinister, influence on us and our kin.

Any stereotyped collective personality analysis of the Heaven's Gate members proves inadequate when tallied against the resumes of individual members. They represented a wide range of demographic backgrounds, ages, talents, interests and careers prior to committing themselves to a new ideology embodied in the totally regimented, obedient lifestyle that would end with an eternal transformation. Comparable individual diversity has been evident among the members of many different cult groups I've studied over the past several decades. What is common are the recruiting promises, influence agendas and group's coercive influence power that compromise the personal exercise of free will and critical thinking. On the basis of my investigations and the psychological research of colleagues, we can argue the following propositions, some of which will be elaborated:

- No one ever joins a "cult." People join interesting groups that promise to fulfill their pressing needs. They become "cults" when they are seen as deceptive, defective, dangerous, or as opposing basic values of their society.
- Cults represent each society's "default values," filling in its missing functions. The cult epidemic is diagnostic of where and how society is failing its citizens.
- If you don't stand for something, you'll fall for anything. As basic human values are being strained, distorted and lost in our rapidly evolving culture, illusions and promissory notes are too readily believed and bought—without reality validation or credit checks.
- Whatever any member of a cult has done, you and I could be recruited or seduced into doing—under the right or wrong conditions. The majority of "normal, average, intelligent" individuals can be led to engage in immoral, illegal, irrational, aggressive and self destructive actions that are contrary to their values or personality—when manipulated situational conditions exert their power over individual dispositions.
- Cult methods of recruiting, indoctrinating and influencing their members are not exotic forms of mind control, but only more intensely applied mundane tactics of social influence practiced daily by all compliance professionals and societal agents of influence.

The appeal

What is the appeal of cults? Imagine being part of a group in which you will find instant friendship, a caring family, respect for your contributions, an identity, safety, security, simplicity, and an organized daily agenda. You will learn new skills, have a respected position, gain personal insight, improve your personality and intelligence. There is no crime or violence and your healthy lifestyle means there is no illness.

Much cult recruitment is done by family, friends, neighbors, co-workers, teachers and highly trained professional recruiters.

Your leader may promise not only to heal any sickness and foretell the future, but give you the gift of immortality, if you are a true believer. In addition, your group's ideology represents a unique spiritual/religious agenda (in other cults it is political, social or personal enhancement) that if followed, will enhance the Human Condition somewhere in the world or cosmos.

Who would fall for such appeals? Most of us, if they were made by someone we trusted, in a setting that was familiar, and especially if we had unfulfilled needs.

Much cult recruitment is done by family, friends, neighbors, co-workers, teachers and highly trained professional recruiters. They recruit not on the streets or airports, but in contexts that are "home bases" for the potential recruit; at schools, in the home, coffee houses, on the job, at sports events, lectures, churches, or drop-in dinners and free personal assessment workshops. The Heaven's Gate group made us aware that recruiting is now also active over the Internet and across the World Wide Web.

In a 1980 study where we (C. Hartley and I) surveyed and interviewed more than 1,000 randomly selected high school students in the greater San Francisco Bay Area, 54 percent reported they had at least one active recruiting attempt by someone they identified with a cult, and 40 percent said they had experienced three to five such contacts. And that was long before electronic cult recruiting could be a new allure for a generation of youngsters growing up as web surfers.

What makes any of us especially vulnerable to cult appeals? Someone is in a transitional phase in life: moved to a new city or country, lost a job, dropped out of school, parents divorced, romantic relationship broken, gave up traditional religion as personally irrelevant. Add to the recipe, all those who find their work tedious and trivial, education abstractly meaningless, social life absent or inconsistent, family remote or dysfunctional, friends too busy to find time for you and trust in government eroded.

Cults promise to fulfill most of those personal individual's needs and also to compensate for a litany of societal failures: to make their slice of the world safe, healthy, caring, predictable and controllable. They will eliminate the increasing feelings of isolation and alienation being created by mobility, technology, competition, meritocracy, incivility, and dehumanized living and working conditions in society.

In general, cult leaders offer simple solutions to the increasingly complex world problems we all face daily. They offer the simple path to happiness, to success, to salvation by following their simple rules, simple group regimentation and simple total lifestyle. Ultimately, each new member contributes to the power of the leader by trading his or her freedom for the illusion of security and reflected glory that group membership holds out.

> **Our society is in a curious transitional phase; as science and technology make remarkable advances, antiscientific values and beliefs in the paranormal and occult abound, family values are stridently promoted in Congress and pulpits, yet divorce is rising along with spouse and child abuse...**

It seems like a "win-win" trade for those whose freedom is without power to make a difference in their lives. This may be especially so for the shy among us. Shyness among adults is now escalating to epidemic proportions, according to recent research by Dr. B. Carducci in Indiana and my research team in California. More than 50 percent of college-aged adults report being chronically shy (lacking social skills, low self-esteem, awkward in many social encounters). As with the rise in cult membership, a public health model is essential for understanding how societal pathology is implicated in contributing to the rise in shyness among adults and children in America.

A society in transition

Our society is in a curious transitional phase; as science and technology make remarkable advances, antiscientific values and beliefs in the paranormal and occult abound, family values are stridently promoted in Congress and pulpits, yet divorce is rising along with spouse and child abuse, fear of nuclear annihilation in superpower wars is replaced by fears of crime in our streets and drugs in our schools, and the economic gap grows exponentially between the rich and powerful and our legions of poor and powerless.

Such change and confusion create intellectual chaos that makes it difficult for many citizens to believe in anything, to trust anyone, to stand for anything substantial.

On such shifting sands of time and resolve, the cult leader stands firm with simple directions for what to think and feel, and how to act. "Follow me, I know the path to sanity, security and salvation," proclaims Marshall Applewhite, with other cult leaders chanting the same lyric in that celestial chorus. And many will follow.

What makes cults dangerous? It depends in part on the kind of cult since they come in many sizes, purposes and disguises. Some cults are in the business of power and money. They need members to give money, work for free, beg and recruit new members. They won't go the deathly route of the Heaven's Gaters; their danger lies in deception, mindless devotion, and failure to deliver on the recruiting promises.

Danger also comes in the form of insisting on contributions of exorbitant amounts of money (tithing, singing over life insurance, social security or property, and fees for personal testing and training).

Add exhausting labor as another danger (spending all one's waking time begging for money, recruiting new members, or doing menial service for little or no remuneration). Most cult groups demand that members sever ties with former family and friends which creates total dependence on the group for self identity, recognition, social reinforcement. Unquestioning obedience to the leader and following arbitrary rules and regulations eliminates independent, critical thinking, and the exercise of free will. Such cerebral straightjacketing is a terrible danger that can lead in turn to the ultimate twin dangers of committing suicide upon command or destroying the cult's enemies.

> **A remarkable thing about cult mind control is that it's so ordinary in the tactics and strategies of social influence employed.**

Potential for the worst abuse is found in "total situations" where the group is physically and socially isolated from the outside community. The accompanying total milieu and informational control permits idiosyncratic and paranoid thinking to flourish and be shared without limits. The madness of any leader then becomes normalized as members embrace it, and the folly of one becomes folie à deux, and finally, with three or more adherents, it becomes a constitutionally protected belief system that is an ideology defended to the death.

A remarkable thing about cult mind control is that it's so ordinary in the tactics and strategies of social influence employed. They are variants of well-known social psychological principles of compliance, conformity, persuasion, dissonance, reactance, framing, emotional manipulation, and others that are used on all of us daily to entice us: to buy, to try, to donate, to vote, to join, to change, to believe, to love, to hate the enemy.

Cult mind control is not different in kind from these everyday varieties, but in its greater intensity, persistence, duration, and scope. One difference is in its greater efforts to block quitting the group, by imposing high exit costs, replete with induced phobias of harm, failure, and personal isolation.

What's the solution?

Heaven's Gate mass suicides have made cults front page news. While their number and ritually methodical formula are unusual, cults are not. They exist as part of the frayed edges of our society and have vital messages for us to reflect upon if we want to prevent such tragedies or our children and neighbors from joining such destructive groups that are on the near horizon.

The solution? Simple. All we have to do is to create an alternative, "perfect cult." We need to work together to find ways to make our society actually deliver on many of those cult promises, to co-opt their appeal, without their deception, distortion and potential for destruction.

No man or woman is an island unto itself, nor a space traveller without an earthly control center. Finding that center, spreading that continent of connections, enriching that core of common humanity should be our first priority as we learn and share a vital lesson from the tragedy of Heaven's Gate.

The heavy burden of black conformity

BILL MAXWELL

COLUMNIST

Four weeks ago, I spoke to a group in the Tampa Bay area about the need for blacks and whites to cooperate for the good of future generations of young people. A prominent black civil rights activist stormed from the room after I said that blacks must stop seeing racism in the ordinary "comings and goings" of human relations and that "some things are the inescapable hazards of living in a pluralistic society."

A week later, I was showing social service professionals how to write effective letters and guest columns to the editor and how to arrange meetings with the editorial board of their local newspaper when a black man interrupted. He demanded, inappropriately for the topic at hand, that I explain why the *St. Petersburg Times*, the newspaper for which I work, has not employed more black executives and has not appointed a black to the board of directors.

After I said that the paper is slowly changing for the better, that blacks cannot force themselves into executive jobs or onto the board, he stormed out, but not before suggesting that I am an Uncle Tom.

A week ago, as I told a group interested in crime prevention that young blacks—especially males—must learn the practical virtues of citizenship, Perkins T. Shelton, former St. Petersburg NAACP president and one of the self-anointed seers of black esprit, marched out of the auditorium.

Although these acts of rudeness and ugly manners were not directly related, they show that monolithism—the compulsion for sameness and oneness—thrives in black society despite loud cries to the contrary. Certainly, all black Americans are free to speak their minds. But woe unto the errant fool who bucks prevailing thought, who dares to think *un-black*, as it were. Blacks wanting to enjoy an unmolested life must conform to the tenets of the unwritten manifesto of the Soul Patrol, the group to which the three men who walked out on my speeches belong.

What is the Soul Patrol? What are its tenets? And, of course, how do the patrol and its manifesto affect black society in general? The Soul Patrol is not an organized body. Rather, it consists of loosely connected opinion leaders—elected and appointed officials, preachers, journalists, gangsta rappers, business owners, teachers, school administrators and others—who wield considerable influence, who possess the "right" attitude and use coded rhetoric.

These mind cops, practicing the ancient art of saving face for their ethnic group, are said to *think black*. They include the likes of O.J. Simpson attorney Johnny Cochran, U.S. Rep. Maxine Waters, former NAACP Executive Director Benjamin Chavis, Nation of Islam leader Louis Farrakhan. The list does not include the likes of O.J. prosecutor Christopher Darden, Harvard intellectual Henry Louis Gates Jr., English professor Shelby Steele, retired Gen. Colin Powell.

In the broadest sense, the manifesto of the Soul Patrol is the centuries-old prohibition against saying or writing anything negative about fellow blacks in the presence of whites or for their consideration. Its rationale, framed by the instinct of self-preservation, is that negative observations by blacks about other blacks only aid and abet the enemy by justifying racism and other forms of malevolence and by validating ugly stereotypes.

True brethren of color, therefore, do not air the race's dirty linen in public, a stricture that has created the pseudonegritude—false consciousness of and false pride in the cultural and physical aspects of our African heritage—that diminishes the quality of black life. Negritude itself, genuine consciousness and pride, is desirable, undergirding the positive aspects of African-American society.

Genuine negritude realistically assesses our heritage, actively makes our own personal behavior a shining example of the positive and publicly rejects self-immolation. The pseudonegritude of the Soul Patrol's manifesto, however, has produced a pernicious and dangerous cult of silence that embraces unwholesome sacred cows, unsavory personalities, self-defeating behavior and rationalizes various forms of criminality.

So, when I said that young black males often are their own worst enemies, that they should not be permitted to terrorize their neighborhoods, that they must learn to be good citizens, the protectors of negritude saw me as a traitor.

Outsiders would think that because blacks do not discuss their intrarace problems in public, we surely must discuss these problems behind closed doors. The truth is that, because we often are too busy heaping blame on others, we rarely discuss among ourselves the root causes of our own self-destructiveness.

And we see the ugly results of this silence everywhere: in the squalid conditions of our neighborhoods; in the high number of our young men behind bars; in the high incidence of teen pregnancy; in the excessive school dropout rates; in the alarming suspension and expulsion trends; in the crime statistics; in the number of unemployable blacks.

Is the silence of saving face a sensible trade-off for such personal, spiritual and societal carnage? I think not. The real enemies of African-Americans are not the self-critics who speak out publicly, but the blindly loyal soul brothers and sisters who storm out of auditoriums, who bite their tongues even as black life implodes.

Group Processes in the Resolution of International Conflicts

Experiences From the Israeli–Palestinian Case

Herbert C. Kelman
Harvard University

For over 20 years, politically influential Israelis and Palestinians have met in private, unofficial, academically based, problem-solving workshops designed to enable the parties to explore each other's perspective, generate joint ideas for mutually satisfactory solutions to their conflict, and transfer insights and ideas derived from their interaction into the policy process. Most of the work takes place in small groups, but the focus is on promoting change in the larger system. This article discusses 5 ways in which the workshop group serves as a vehicle for change at the macrolevel. It does so by functioning as a microcosm of the larger system, as a laboratory for producing inputs into the larger system, as a setting for direct interaction, as a coalition across conflict lines, and as a nucleus for a new relationship.

The Israeli–Palestinian conflict has long been cited as a typical case of a protracted, intractable conflict. The origins of the conflict go back to the birth of modern political Zionism at the end of the 19th century. Violence first erupted in the 1920s, and, in various forms and with varying degrees of intensity, it has pervaded the relationship between the two peoples since that time. The psychological core of the conflict has been its perception by the two sides as a zero-sum conflict around national identity and national existence, which has led over the years to mutual denial of the other's identity and systematic efforts to delegitimize the other (Kelman, 1978, 1987). Under the circumstances, the parties had been reluctant for a long time to go to the negotiation table and, indeed, to offer each other the assurances and enticements that would make negotiations safe and promising in their eyes.

Nevertheless, in response to a strong initiative from the U.S. administration, Israelis and Palestinians finally entered into a process of direct negotiations, starting with the Madrid Conference in the fall of 1991. The mere fact that the parties were negotiating represented a significant departure in the history of the conflict, but the official talks themselves, which continued in Washington, DC, for nearly two years, did not develop their own momentum and seemed to arrive at an impasse (cf. Kelman, 1992a). In the meantime, however, secret talks between representatives of Israel's Labor Party-led government (elected in June 1992) and the Palestine Liberation Organization, held in Oslo in 1993, produced a dramatic agreement that was signed by the parties on the White House lawn in September 1993. The Oslo accord took the form of an exchange of letters of mutual recognition between the official representatives of the two peoples, followed by a Declaration of Principles (DOP) that stipulated the establishment of a Palestinian authority in Gaza and Jericho as the first step in Palestinian self-rule. Despite the shortcomings of the DOP and despite the fact that the most difficult political issues were left to be resolved in the final-status negotiations, which were scheduled to begin in May 1996, the Oslo accord represents a fundamental breakthrough in the Israeli–Palestinian conflict. That breakthrough derives, in my view, from the mutual recognition of the other's nationhood and each side's commitment to negotiate and make peace with the body that symbolizes and legitimates that nationhood.

It would be foolhardy to insist that the peace process set into motion by the Oslo accords is irreversible. At this

---

Editor's note. Michael G. Wessells served as action editor for this article.

Author's note. This article is based on an address delivered on August 13, 1995, at the 103rd Annual Convention of the American Psychological Association in New York, on receipt of the 1995 Distinguished Group Psychologist Award from Division 49 (Group Psychology and Group Psychotherapy). The award citation read, "Involved in study, research, publication and action, he exemplifies the very best in social science. As a group psychologist, he has studied and practiced conflict resolution in real life terms, and has expanded the reach and influence of group therapeutic understanding. In making a singular contribution to Middle East peace, he models the most creative blends of academics and practice."

The action research program on which this article is based is carried out in collaboration with Nadim Rouhana of Boston College under the auspices of the Program on International Conflict Analysis and Resolution (PICAR) at the Harvard Center for International Affairs. It is supported by grants from the Nathan Cummings Foundation, the Charles R. Bronfman Foundation, the Carnegie Corporation, and the U.S. Information Agency. PICAR (Herbert C. Kelman, Director; Donna Hicks, Deputy Director) is supported by a grant from the William and Flora Hewlett Foundation.

Correspondence concerning this article should be addressed to Herbert C. Kelman, Department of Psychology, William James Hall, Harvard University, Cambridge, MA 02138. Electronic mail may be sent via Internet to hck@wjh.harvard.edu.

writing (October 1996), the indications are that, under the current Likud-led government in Israel, the process will be slowed down but neither reversed nor entirely halted. On the other hand, slowing down the process can seriously undermine the achievement of a final peace agreement. As we have already seen, it may provoke acts of violence and counterviolence, creating an atmosphere unconducive to negotiations, and it may create new facts on the ground—such as the expansion of Israeli settlements in the West Bank—leaving no room for an agreement on the basis of territorial compromise. Although I remain optimistic about the ultimate success of the Israeli–Palestinian peace process, I am less prepared now than three years ago to predict that a peace agreement will be signed by the end of the century. But even if the current phase of the peace process were to fail, the Oslo accord has fundamentally changed the character of the conflict. What is irreversible is the fact that the unthinkable has not only been thought, but it has been acted on—the fact that the two parties have recognized each other's national identity and have, in their negotiations and interactions, acknowledged each other's legitimacy. In this sense, the Oslo accord is a breakthrough that is at least as significant as Anwar Sadat's trip to Jerusalem, which led to the Egyptian–Israeli peace agreement.

What are the forces that led to this breakthrough? On a long-term basis, the Six-Day War of 1967 created a new geopolitical and strategic situation in the Middle East, which led to the gradually evolving recognition on all sides that a historic compromise of the Palestine problem in the form of some version of a two-state solution would best serve their national interests (cf. Kelman, 1988). The powerful political obstacles to such a solution were finally overcome by short-term strategic and micropolitical considerations that can be traced to the Gulf War and the end of the Cold War. The combination of these long-term and short-term developments made negotiations necessary from the point of view of both Israeli and Palestinian interests. But a significant factor contributing to the breakthrough was the conclusion, on both sides, that negotiations were not only necessary but also possible—that they could yield an acceptable agreement without jeopardizing their national existence. This sense of possibility evolved out of interactions between the two sides that produced the individuals, the ideas, and the political atmosphere required for productive negotiations.

A variety of unofficial contacts between the two sides played a significant role in creating this sense of possibility and the climate conducive to negotiations. It is in this context that the third-party efforts in which my colleagues and I have been engaged since the early 1970s contributed to the evolving peace process (Kelman, 1995). Our work illustrates the potential contributions of social psychology and the scholar–practitioner model (Kelman 1992b) to the interdisciplinary, multifaceted task of analyzing and resolving protracted international and ethnic conflicts.

This article focuses on the ways in which the microprocess of the small-group meetings that my colleagues and I organize can serve as a vehicle for change at the macrolevel. To set the stage for this discussion, the article briefly (a) places our work in the context of the emerging field of conflict resolution, (b) describes our particular approach to conflict resolution at the international level, and (c) discusses our efforts to contribute to the Israeli–Palestinian peace process.

The Conflict Resolution Field

In the past two decades or so, the world has witnessed the development and proliferation of a variety of new approaches to conflict resolution, which together constitute a new field of theory and practice (see Kelman, 1993b). The precise boundaries of this emerging field are difficult to draw, and practitioners differ in their view of what should be included and what should be excluded.

Practitioners of conflict resolution work at different levels—ranging from the interpersonal to the international. They operate in different domains, such as the court system, public policy, labor–management relations, interethnic relations, or international diplomacy. They derive their ideas from a variety of sources, such as law, psychotherapy, management theories, group dynamics, peace research, decision theory, the study of conflict resolution in traditional societies, and theoretical models from the entire range of social science disciplines. Despite the diversity in level, domain, and intellectual origins that characterizes the work in this field, there are certain common insights and approaches to practice that run through all of its manifestations. Thus, with different degrees of emphasis, they all call for a nonadversarial framework for conflict resolution, an analytic approach, a problem-solving orientation, direct participation by the parties in conflict in jointly shaping a solution, and facilitation by a third party trained in the process of conflict resolution.

Interaction among scholar–practitioners working at different levels and in different domains is instructive and enriching and contributes significantly to the refinement of theory and technique. At the same time, it is important to keep in mind that the application of general principles requires sensitivity to the unique features of the context in which they are applied. Thus, in my own work over the years on international and intercommunal conflict, I have called attention to the need for knowledge about and experience with the particular features and issues of conflict at these levels and to the danger of direct transfer of experiences from the interpersonal and interorganizational levels to the international arena.

Interactive Problem Solving

The unofficial third-party approach to international and ethnic conflict resolution that my colleagues and I have been developing and applying derives from the pioneering efforts of Burton (1969, 1979, 1984). I have used the term *interactive problem solving* to describe the approach, which finds its fullest expression in problem-solving workshops (Kelman, 1972, 1979, 1986, 1991, 1992b, 1996; Kelman & Cohen, 1986). Within this framework, I have done some work on the Cyprus conflict, and, through the work of my students, associates, and colleagues, I have maintained an active interest in a number of other protracted identity group conflicts around the world, such as the conflicts in Northern Ireland, Sri Lanka, Rwanda–Burundi, the former Yugoslavia, and the former Soviet Union. The primary regional focus of my action research program, however, has been on the Middle East. In particular, since the early 1970s, my colleagues and I have conducted an intensive program of problem-solving workshops and related activities on the Israeli–Palestinian conflict.

Problem-solving workshops are intensive meetings between politically involved but entirely unofficial representatives of conflicting parties—for example, Israelis and Palestinians or Greek and Turkish Cypriots (see Kelman, 1993a). Workshop participants are often politically influential members of their communities. Thus, in our Israeli–Palestinian work, participants have included parliamentarians; leading figures in political parties or movements; former military officers or government officials; journalists or editors specializing in the Middle East; and academic scholars who are major analysts of the conflict for their societies and some of whom have served in advisory, official, or diplomatic positions.[1] The workshops take place under academic auspices and are facilitated by a panel of social scientists who are knowledgeable about international conflict, group process, and the Middle East region.

The discussions are completely private and confidential. There is no audience, no publicity, and no record, and one of the central ground rules specifies that statements made in the course of a workshop cannot be cited with attribution outside of the workshop setting. These and other features of the workshop are designed to enable and encourage workshop participants to engage in a type of communication that is usually not available to parties involved in an intense conflict relationship. The third party creates an atmosphere, establishes norms, and makes occasional interventions, all conducive to free and open discussion, in which the parties address each other rather than third parties or their own constituencies and in which they listen to each other in order to understand their differing perspectives. They are encouraged to deal with the conflict analytically rather than polemically—to explore the ways in which their interaction helps to exacerbate and perpetuate the conflict, rather than to assign blame to the other side while justifying their own. This analytic discussion helps the parties penetrate each other's perspective and understand each other's concerns, needs, fears, priorities, and constraints.

Once both sets of concerns are on the table and have been understood and acknowledged, the parties are encouraged to engage in a process of joint problem solving. They are asked to work together in developing new ideas for resolving the conflict in ways that would satisfy the fundamental needs and allay the existential fears of both parties. They are then asked to explore the political and psychological constraints that stand in the way of such integrative, win–win solutions and that, in fact, have prevented the parties from moving to (or staying at) the negotiating table. Again, they are asked to engage in a process of joint problem solving, designed to generate ideas for "getting from here to there." A central feature of this process is the identification of steps of mutual reassurance—in the form of acknowledgments, symbolic gestures, or confidence-building measures—that would help reduce the parties' fears of engaging in negotiations in which the outcome is uncertain and risky. Problem-solving workshops also contribute to mutual reassurance by helping the parties develop—again, through collaborative effort—a nonthreatening, deescalatory language and a shared vision of a desirable future.

Workshops have a dual purpose. First, they are designed to produce changes in the workshop participants themselves—changes in the form of more differentiated images of the enemy (see Kelman, 1987), a better understanding of the other's perspective and of their own priorities, greater insight into the dynamics of the conflict, and new ideas for resolving the conflict and for overcoming the barriers to a negotiated solution. These changes at the level of individual participants are a vehicle for promoting change at the policy level. Thus, the second purpose of workshops is to maximize the likelihood that the new insights, ideas, and proposals developed in the course of the interaction are fed back into the political debate and the decision-making process in each community. One of the central tasks of the third party is to structure the workshop in such a way that new insights and ideas are likely both to be generated and to be transferred effectively to the policy process.

The composition of the workshop is crucial in this context: Great care must be taken to select participants who, on the one hand, have the interest and capacity to engage in the kind of learning process that workshops provide and, on the other hand, have the positions and credibility in their own communities that enable them to influence the thinking of political leaders, political constituencies, or the general public. It should be noted that the third party's role, although essential to the success of problem-solving workshops, is strictly a facilitative role. The critical work of generating ideas and infusing them into the political process must be done by the participants themselves. A basic assumption of our approach is that solutions emerging out of the interaction between the conflicting parties are most likely to be responsive to their needs and to engender their commitment.[2]

---

[1] For a description of the recruitment process, see Kelman (1992b) and Rouhana and Kelman (1994).

[2] For a more detailed discussion of the workshop ground rules, the nature of the interaction between participants, and the role of the third party, see Kelman (1979), Kelman (1992b), and Rouhana and Kelman (1994).

Contributions to the Israeli-Palestinian Peace Process

Most of the Israeli-Palestinian work that my colleagues and I carried out over the years took place during the prenegotiation phase of the conflict. The primary purpose was to help create a political atmosphere that would encourage the parties to move to the negotiating table. Moreover, until 1990, the workshops that we organized were all one-time events. Although some Israelis and Palestinians, as individuals, participated in several such events, each workshop was self-contained. Because of financial, logistical, and political constraints, we were not able to bring the same group of participants together for more than one occasion.

In 1990, however, we took a major step forward in our work by organizing, for the first time, a continuing workshop (see Rouhana & Kelman, 1994). A group of highly influential Israelis and Palestinians committed themselves initially to a series of three workshop meetings over the course of a year. The first meeting took place in November 1990 and, at the end of the third meeting (in August 1991), the participants decided to continue the process.

In the meantime, external events instigated a second major new development in our work. With the convening of the Madrid Conference in the fall of 1991 and the opening of an official Israeli-Palestinian peace process, our own work moved from the prenegotiation to the negotiation phase of the conflict. We had no doubt—and the participants in the continuing workshop agreed—that there was still a great need for maintaining an unofficial process alongside of the official one. However, with the onset of official negotiations, the purpose and focus of our work had to change (Rouhana & Kelman, 1994). When negotiations are in progress, workshops can contribute to overcoming obstacles to staying at the table and negotiating productively, to creating a momentum for the negotiations, to addressing long-term issues that are not yet on the negotiating table, and to beginning the process of peace-building that must accompany and follow the process of peacemaking.

As Nadim Rouhana and I began to formulate, along with the Israeli and Palestinian participants, the functions of the continuing workshop in the new phase of the peace process, we confronted another new development, which created both opportunities and complications. Our unofficial process was steadily moving closer to the official process. When the official negotiating teams were established, four of the six Palestinian members of the continuing workshop were appointed to key positions on them. With the Labor Party's victory in the Israeli elections in 1992, several of our Israeli participants gained increasing access to the top decision makers. (In fact, eventually, one was appointed to the cabinet and another to a major diplomatic post.) These developments clearly enhanced the political relevance of the continuing workshop, but the overlap between the official and unofficial processes also created some ambiguities and role conflicts.

The meetings of the continuing workshop after the start of the official negotiations focused on the obstacles confronting the peace process at the negotiating table and on the ground but also addressed the question of the functions and composition of the continuing workshop in the new political environment. Altogether, this continuing workshop met over a three-year period. Its final session took place in August 1993, ending just a day or so before the news of the Israeli-Palestinian breakthrough that was achieved in Oslo began to emerge.

In the wake of the Oslo accord, signed in September 1993, there has been general recognition of the role that unofficial efforts have played, directly or indirectly, in laying the groundwork for the Israeli-Palestinian breakthrough. In this context, various observers—within and outside of the Middle East—have acknowledged the contributions of the activities in which my colleagues and I have been engaged over the years. In my own assessment, there are three ways in which our work, along with that of many others, has contributed (Kelman, 1995).

1. Workshops have helped to develop cadres prepared to carry out productive negotiations. Over the years, dozens of Israelis and dozens of Palestinians, many of them political influentials or preinfluentials, have participated in our workshops and related activities, including the continuing workshop in the early 1990s. Many of these individuals were involved in the discussions and negotiations that led up to the Oslo accord. Many have continued to be involved in the peace process, and some have served in the Israeli cabinet, Knesset, and foreign ministry and in leading positions in the various Palestinian political agencies.

2. The sharing of information and the formulation of new ideas in the course of our workshops have provided important substantive inputs into the negotiations. Through the public and private communications of workshop participants—and to some degree also through the communications of members of the third party—some of the insights and ideas on which productive negotiations could be built were injected into the two political cultures. These included shared assumptions, mutual sensitivities, and new conceptions of the process and outcome of negotiations, all of which were developed in the course of workshop interactions.

3. Workshops have fostered a political atmosphere that has made the parties open to a new relationship. Our workshops, along with various other Israeli-Palestinian meetings and projects, have done so by encouraging the development of more differentiated images of the enemy, of a deescalatory language and a new political discourse that is attentive to the other party's concerns and constraints, of a working trust that is based on the conviction that both parties have a genuine interest in a peaceful solution, and of a sense of possibility regarding the ultimate achievement of a mutually satisfactory outcome.

The Oslo agreement, of course, represented only the beginning of what has already been and will almost certainly continue to be a long and difficult process, confronting obstacles and periodic setbacks. Therefore, unofficial efforts alongside the official negotiations continue to be needed. Accordingly, when we decided to close the continuing workshop in the late fall of 1993, we immediately initiated a new project, which built on the experience and achievements of the preceding work. This new project has taken the form of a joint working group on Israeli–Palestinian relations, which held its first meeting in May 1994. The initial emphasis of the group has been on systematic exploration of the difficult political issues—including Israeli settlements, Palestinian refugees, Jerusalem, and the precise nature of Palestinian self-determination—that have been deferred to the final-status negotiations. For the first time in our work, we hope to produce and disseminate one or more joint concept papers, which will frame these issues in terms of the future relationship between the two societies that is envisaged as the long-term outcome of the final agreement.

The Role of Group Processes in Conflict Resolution

Having presented a brief description of our microlevel approach and its contribution to conflict resolution at the macrolevel, I now want to highlight the role that interaction within the small group plays in the larger process.

Most of our work takes place in the context of small groups, composed of three to six representatives of the two sides and two to four third-party facilitators. The focus of all of our efforts is on promoting change in the larger system, but direct interaction in the small-group setting can produce important inputs into the political thinking, the political debate, and the decision-making processes within the two societies and into the formal negotiations between them. Thus, changes at the individual level resulting from interaction in the small group become vehicles for change at the system level.

In the following sections, I discuss five ways in which the workshop group serves as a vehicle for change in the larger system. It does so by functioning as a microcosm of the larger system, as a laboratory for producing inputs into the larger system, as a setting for direct interaction, as a coalition across conflict lines, and as a nucleus for a new relationship. These five functions of the group are not meant to represent different theories or even different dimensions of group process. They are merely different ways of looking at the role of group processes in our intervention model. By looking at the group process from these different angles, I hope to provide a fuller and more nuanced picture of how our microprocess contributes to change at the macrolevel.

The Group as a Microcosm

The group assembled for a workshop can be viewed as a microcosm of the larger system. It is a microcosm not in the sense of a small-scale *model* that reproduces all of the forces of the larger system but in the sense of an *arena* in which the forces of the larger system may manifest themselves. We make no attempt to reproduce the larger system in our workshops. In fact, we try to create an environment that differs significantly from the one in which the conflicting parties normally interact—an environment governed by a different set of norms, in which participants are both free and obligated to speak openly, listen attentively, and treat each other as equals. Nor do we try to represent the entire political spectrum in our workshops. We look for participants who are part of the mainstream in their communities and close to the political center but who are interested in exploring the possibilities of a negotiated, mutually satisfactory solution to the conflict.

The group is a microcosm of the larger system because, despite their relative moderation, the participants share the fundamental concerns, fears, memories, and aspirations of their respective communities. As they interact with each other around the issues in conflict, they reflect their own community's perspectives, priorities, and limits of what is negotiable, not only in what they say but also in how they say it and how they act toward each other. As a result, some of the dynamics of the larger conflict are acted out in the interactions within the workshop group. Participants' interactions in the group context often reflect the nature of the relationship between their communities—their mutual distrust, their special sensitivities and vulnerabilities, their differences in power and minority–majority status—and demonstrate the self-perpetuating character of interactions among conflicting societies.

The advantage of the workshop is that it creates an atmosphere, a set of norms, and a working trust among the participants that enable them to observe and analyze these conflict dynamics at or very near the moment they occur. Such analyses are facilitated by third-party interventions in the form of process observations, which suggest possible ways in which interactions between the parties ''here and now'' may reflect the dynamics of the conflict between their communities (Kelman, 1979). The insights that such observations can generate are comparable to the ''corrective emotional experiences'' that play an important role in individual and, particularly, group psychotherapy (Alexander & French, 1946, pp. 66–68; Frank & Ascher, 1951), although our interventions are always at the intergroup rather than the interpersonal level. That is, interactions between workshop participants are relevant to our purposes only insofar as they can tell us something about the dynamics of the interaction between their communities.

In summary, the character of the workshop group as a microcosm of the larger system makes it a valuable learning experience: It provides opportunities for the participants to gain important insights into the dynamics of the conflict. I turn next to the role of the group in transmitting what is learned into the larger system.

The Group as a Laboratory

The workshop group can also be conceived as a laboratory for producing inputs into the larger system. The metaphor of the laboratory is particularly appropriate because it captures the two roles that workshops play in the macroprocess. A workshop is a specially constructed space in which the parties can engage in a process of exploration, observation, and analysis and in which they can create new products to be fed into the political debate and decision making in the two societies.

Providing a space for exploring issues in the conflict, mutual concerns, and ideas for conflict resolution is one of the key contributions of problem-solving workshops. The opportunity for joint informal exploration—playing with ideas, trying out different scenarios, obtaining a sense of the range of possible actions and of the limits for each party, and discovering potential trade-offs—enhances the productivity of negotiations and the quality of the outcome. Such opportunities, however, are not readily available in official negotiations, in which the participants operate in representative roles, are instructed and closely monitored by their governments, are concerned about the reactions of various constituencies and third parties, and are in the business of producing binding agreements. Problem-solving workshops, by virtue of their nonbinding character, are ideally suited to fill this gap in the larger diplomatic process. The setting, the atmosphere, the ground rules, the governing norms, the agenda, and the interventions of the third party all help to make the workshop group a unique laboratory for the process of open, noncommittal exploration that does not often occur elsewhere in the system, neither in the official negotiations nor in the spontaneous interactions between the conflicting parties.

The process of exploration and joint thinking yields new products, which can be exported into the political process within and between the two communities. This is the second sense in which the laboratory metaphor captures the function of workshops. Indeed the group constitutes a workshop in the literal sense of that term: It is a specially constructed space for shaping products that are then brought back into the two communities. The sharing of perspectives, the conflict analysis, and the joint thinking encouraged in workshops enable the participants to come up with a variety of products in the form of new information, new insights, and new ideas that can advance the negotiation process: differentiated images of the other, which suggest that there is someone to talk to on the other side and something to talk about; understanding of the needs, fears, priorities, and constraints on the other side and, indeed, on one's own side; insight into the escalatory and self-perpetuating dynamics of the conflict relationship; awareness of change and the readiness for change on the other side; ideas for mutual reassurance and other ways of improving the atmosphere for negotiation; ideas for the overall shape of a mutually satisfactory solution; and ideas for redefining the conflict and reframing issues so as to make them more amenable to resolution. These products must then be exported into the political arena. It is essential, therefore, that the individuals selected as workshop participants have not only an interest in mutual exploration and learning, and skills for generating ideas and creative problem solving, but also the capacity and opportunity to utilize what they learn and to inject the workshop products into their respective communities in ways that make a political difference.

In sum, I have described the workshop group as a special space—a laboratory—in which a significant part of the work of peacemaking can be carried out. The unique contribution of the workshop to this larger process is that it provides a carefully designed environment in which constructive social interaction between the parties can take place. Let me, therefore, turn to the third image of the workshop: the group as a setting for direct interaction.

The Group as a Setting for Direct Interaction

Although international conflict and conflict resolution are societal and intersocietal processes, which cannot be reduced to the level of individual behavior, there are certain processes central to conflict resolution—such as empathy or taking the perspective of the other (which is at the heart of social interaction), learning and insight, and creative problem solving—that, of necessity, take place at the level of individuals and interactions between individuals. These psychological processes are by no means the whole of conflict resolution, but they must occur somewhere in the system if there is to be movement toward a mutually satisfactory and stable peace. Problem-solving workshops provide a setting for these processes to occur by bringing together representatives of the conflicting parties for direct interaction under conditions of confidentiality and equality and under an alternative set of norms in contrast to the norms that usually govern interactions between conflicting parties.

The context, norms, ground rules, agenda, procedures, and third-party interventions in workshops are all designed to encourage (and permit) a special kind of interaction, marked by an emphasis on addressing each other (rather than one's constituencies, third parties, or the record) and on listening to each other, an analytical focus, adherence to a "no-fault" principle, and a problem-solving orientation. This kind of interaction allows the parties to explore each other's concerns, penetrate each other's perspective, and take cognizance of each other's constraints (Kelman, 1992b). As a result, they are able to offer each other the reassurances needed for productive negotiation and mutual accommodation and to come up with solutions responsive to both sides' needs and fears.

The nature of the interaction fostered in problem-solving workshops has some continuities with a therapeutic model (Kelman, 1991). Workshop features that reflect such a model are the analytical character of the discourse, the use of here-and-now experiences as a basis for learning about the dynamics of the conflict, and the encouragement of mutual acknowledgments that have both a reassuring and a healing effect. Unlike therapy groups, however, workshops focus not on individuals and their interpersonal relations but on how their interaction may illuminate the dynamics of the conflict between their communities.

An underlying assumption of the workshop process is that products of social interaction have an emergent quality (Kelman, 1992b). In the course of direct interaction, the parties are able to observe firsthand their differing reactions to the same events and the different perspectives these reflect, the differences between the way they perceive themselves and the way the other perceives them, and the impact that their statements and actions have on each other. Out of these observations, they can jointly shape new insights and ideas that could not have been predicted from what they initially brought to the interaction. Certain kinds of solutions to the conflict can emerge only from the confrontation of assumptions, concerns, and identities during face-to-face communication.

The emergence of ideas for solution to the conflict out of the interaction between the parties (in contrast, e.g., to ideas proposed by third parties) has several advantages. Such ideas are more likely to be responsive to the fundamental needs and fears of both parties; the parties are more likely to feel committed to the solutions they produce themselves; and the process of producing these ideas in itself contributes to building a new relationship between the parties, initially between the pronegotiation elements on the two sides and ultimately between the two societies as wholes. Let me turn then to the function of the workshop group in building relationships of both kinds.

The Group as a Coalition Across Conflict Lines

The workshop group can be conceived as a coalition across conflict lines—as part of a process of building a coalition between those elements on each side that are interested in a negotiated solution (Kelman, 1993a). This does not mean that workshop participants are all committed doves. Often, they are individuals who, out of pragmatic considerations, have concluded that a negotiated agreement is in the best interest of their own community. Workshops, then, can be seen as attempts to strengthen the hands of the pronegotiation elements on each side in their political struggle within their own communities and to increase the likelihood that the pronegotiation elements on the two sides will support and reinforce each other in pursuing their common interest in a negotiated solution.

Because the coalition formed by a workshop group (and by the entire array of joint efforts by the pronegotiation forces on the two sides) cuts across a very basic conflict line, it is almost by definition an uneasy coalition. It must function in the face of the powerful bonds that coalition members have to the very groups that the coalition tries to transcend. The coalition may well be perceived as threatening the national community that is so important to the identity, the long-term interests, and the political effectiveness of each coalition partner. As a result, the coalition work is complicated by participants' concern about their self-images as loyal members of their group; by their concern about their credibility at home and, hence, their long-term political effectiveness; by significant divergences in the perspectives of the two sets of coalition partners; and by the fact that even committed proponents of negotiation share the memories, concerns, fears, and sensitivities of their identity group.

Participants' bonds to their national communities create inevitable barriers to coalition work, which require systematic attention if problem-solving workshops are to achieve their goals. Thus, mutual distrust is an endemic condition that complicates coalition work. Even among individuals who have worked together for some time and have achieved a considerable level of working trust, old fears and suspicions that have deep historical roots are easily rearoused by events on the ground or by words and actions of a participant on the other side. Coalition work, therefore, requires a continuing process of mutual testing and reestablishment of working trust. A second impediment to coalition work is alienating language—the use of words or a manner of speaking that the other side finds irritating, patronizing, insulting, threatening, or otherwise oblivious to its sensitivities. One of the valuable outcomes of workshops is growing sensitivity to the meaning of particular words to the other side. Nevertheless, alienating language does crop up, both because participants speak from the perspectives and out of the experiences of their own communities and because the pragmatic terms in which peace is justified to one's domestic audiences (and perhaps to one's self) may appear dehumanizing or delegitimizing to the other side. Examples are the Israeli emphasis on the Palestinian "demographic threat" and the Palestinian emphasis on Israel's superior power as reasons for seeking a compromise. Finally, fluctuations in the political and psychological climate may affect one or the other party, creating a lack of synchronism in the readiness for coalition work between the two sides.

The uneasy quality of a coalition across conflict lines is an inevitable reality, insofar as coalition members are bona fide representatives of their national groups—as they must be if the coalition is to achieve its goal of promoting a negotiated agreement. This reality creates barriers to coalition work, and it is part of the task of the third party to help overcome them. But it is not only difficult to overcome these barriers, it may in fact be counterproductive to overcome them entirely. It is important for the coalition to remain uneasy in order to enhance the value of what participants learn in the course of workshops and of what they can achieve upon reentry into their home communities.

Experimental research by Rothbart and associates (Rothbart & John, 1985; Rothbart & Lewis, 1988) suggests that direct contact between members of conflicting groups may have a paradoxical effect on intergroup stereotypes. If it becomes apparent, in the course of direct interaction with representatives of the other group, that they do not fit one's stereotype of the group, there is a tendency to differentiate these particular individuals from their group: to perceive them as nonmembers. Since they are excluded from the category, the stereotype about the category itself can remain intact. This process of differentiating and excluding individual members of the other group from their category could well take place in workshops in which a high degree of trust develops between the parties. Therefore, it is essential for the participants to reconfirm their belongingness to their national categories—thus keeping the coalition uneasy—if they are to demonstrate the possibility of peace not just between exceptional individuals from the two sides but between the two enemy camps.

An even more important reason why a coalition across conflict lines must, of necessity, remain uneasy relates to what is often called the *reentry problem* (see, e.g., Kelman, 1972; Walton, 1970). If a workshop group

became overly cohesive, it would undermine the whole purpose of the enterprise: to have an impact on the political decisions within the two communities. Workshop participants who become closely identified with their counterparts on the other side may become alienated from their own co-nationals, lose credibility, and hence forfeit their political effectiveness and their ability to promote a new consensus within their own communities. One of the challenges for problem-solving workshops, therefore, is to create an atmosphere in which participants can begin to humanize and trust each other and to develop an effective collaborative relationship, without losing sight of their separate group identities and the conflict between their communities. (Kelman, 1992b, p. 82)

The Group as a Nucleus for a New Relationship

Our work is based on the proposition that in conflicts such as that between Palestinians and Israelis—conflicts about national identity and national existence between two peoples destined to live together in the same small space—conflict resolution must aim toward the ultimate establishment of a new cooperative and mutually enhancing relationship and must involve a process that paves the way to such a relationship. Nothing less will work in the long run, and, even in the short run, only a process embodying the principle of reciprocity that is at the center of a new relationship is likely to succeed. Perhaps the greatest strength of problem-solving workshops is their potential contribution to transforming the relationship between the conflicting parties.

Interaction in the workshop group both promotes and models a new relationship between the parties. It is based on the principles of equality and reciprocity. The participants are encouraged to penetrate each other's perspective and to gain an understanding of the other's needs, fears, and constraints. They try to shape solutions that are responsive to the fundamental concerns of both sides. They search for ways of providing mutual reassurance. Such ideas often emerge from acknowledgments that participants make to each other in the course of their interaction: acknowledgments of the other's humanity, national identity, view of history, authentic links to the land, legitimate grievances, and commitment to peace.

Out of these interactions, participants develop increasing degrees of empathy, of sensitivity and responsiveness to the other's concerns, and of working trust, which are essential ingredients of the new relationship to which conflict resolution efforts aspire. The working trust and responsiveness both develop out of the collaborative work in which the group is engaged and, in turn, help to enhance the effectiveness of that work. Thus, workshop participants can transmit to their respective communities not only ideas toward transformation of the relationship between the communities but also the results of their own experience: They can testify that a cooperative, mutually enhancing relationship is possible and can point to some of the conditions that promote such a relationship.

The joint working group on Israeli–Palestinian relations, which my colleague Nadim Rouhana and I are currently cochairing, is explicitly based on the conception of the group as the nucleus of a new relationship between the two societies. The main purpose of the working group is to focus on the peace-building processes that must follow successful peacemaking and to explore the nature of the long-term relationship envisaged in the aftermath of the final political agreement. At this point, as I mentioned earlier, we are addressing the difficult political issues—settlements, refugees, Jerusalem, Palestinian self-determination—that have been deferred to the final-status negotiations, in the light of the future relationship between the societies. That is, we try to assess different options for resolving these issues from the point of view of their congruence with a long-term relationship that is based on peaceful coexistence, cooperation, and mutual benefit.

Furthermore, we see the working group itself as a model and perhaps even as the seed of an institutional mechanism that a new relationship calls for. In our view, a mutually beneficial relationship between two units that are as closely linked and as interdependent as the Israeli and Palestinian communities requires the development of a civil society across the political borders. A useful institutional mechanism for such a civil society would be an unofficial joint forum for exploring issues in the relationship between the two communities within a problem-solving framework. It is not entirely unrealistic to hope that our current working group may evolve into or at least serve as a model for such an institution. This scenario thus provides an illustration of the way in which a group like our Israeli–Palestinian working group can serve not only as a means for promoting a new relationship between the parties but also as a model and manifestation of that new relationship.

REFERENCES

Alexander, F., & French, T. M. (1946). *Psychoanalytic therapy*. New York: Ronald Press.

Burton, J. W. (1969). *Conflict and communication: The use of controlled communication in international relations*. London: Macmillan.

Burton, J. W. (1979). *Deviance, terrorism and war: The process of solving unsolved social and political problems*. New York: St. Martin's Press.

Burton, J. W. (1984). *Global conflict: The domestic sources of international crisis*. Brighton, England: Wheatsheaf.

Frank, J. D., & Ascher, E. (1951). Corrective emotional experiences in group therapy. *American Journal of Psychiatry, 108*, 126–131.

Kelman, H. C. (1972). The problem-solving workshop in conflict resolution. In R. L. Merritt (Ed.), *Communication in international politics* (pp. 168–204). Urbana: University of Illinois Press.

Kelman, H. C. (1978). Israelis and Palestinians: Psychological prerequisites for mutual acceptance. *International Security, 3,* 162–186.

Kelman, H. C. (1979). An interactional approach to conflict resolution and its application to Israeli–Palestinian relations. *International Interactions, 6,* 99–122.

Kelman, H. C. (1986). Interactive problem solving: A social–psychological approach to conflict resolution. In W. Klassen (Ed.), *Dialogue toward interfaith understanding* (pp. 293–314). Tantur/Jerusalem: Ecumenical Institute for Theological Research.

Kelman, H. C. (1987). The political psychology of the Israeli–Palestinian conflict: How can we overcome the barriers to a negotiated solution? *Political Psychology, 8,* 347–363.

Kelman, H. C. (1988, Spring). The Palestinianization of the Arab–Israeli conflict. *The Jerusalem Quarterly, 46,* 3–15.

Kelman, H. C. (1991). Interactive problem solving: The uses and limits of a therapeutic model for the resolution of international conflicts. In V. D. Volkan, J. V. Montville, & D. A. Julius (Eds.), *The psychodynamics of international relationships, Volume II: Unofficial diplomacy at work* (pp. 145–160). Lexington, MA: Lexington Books.

Kelman, H. C. (1992a). Acknowledging the other's nationhood: How to create a momentum for the Israeli–Palestinian negotiations. *Journal of Palestine Studies, 22*(1), 18–38.

Kelman, H. C. (1992b). Informal mediation by the scholar/practitioner. In J. Bercovitch & J. Z. Rubin (Eds.), *Mediation in international relations: Multiple approaches to conflict management* (pp. 64–96). New York: St. Martin's Press.

Kelman, H. C. (1993a). Coalitions across conflict lines: The interplay of conflicts within and between the Israeli and Palestinian communities. In S. Worchel & J. Simpson (Eds.), *Conflict between people and groups* (pp. 236–258). Chicago: Nelson-Hall.

Kelman, H. C. (1993b). Foreword. In D. J. D. Sandole & H. van der Merwe (Eds.), *Conflict resolution theory and practice: Integration and application* (pp. ix–xii). Manchester, England: Manchester University Press.

Kelman, H. C. (1995). Contributions of an unofficial conflict resolution effort to the Israeli–Palestinian breakthrough. *Negotiation Journal, 11,* 19–27.

Kelman, H. C. (1996). Negotiation as interactive problem solving. *International Negotiation, 1,* 99–123.

Kelman, H. C., & Cohen, S. P. (1986). Resolution of international conflict: An interactional approach. In S. Worchel & W. G. Austin (Eds.), *Psychology of intergroup relations* (2nd ed., pp. 323–342). Chicago: Nelson Hall.

Rothbart, M., & John, O. P. (1985). Social categorization and behavioral episodes: A cognitive analysis of the effects of intergroup contact. *Journal of Social Issues, 41*(3), 81–104.

Rothbart, M., & Lewis, S. (1988). Inferring category attributes from exemplar attributes: Geometric shapes and social categories. *Journal of Personality and Social Psychology, 55,* 861–872.

Rouhana, N. N., & Kelman, H. C. (1994). Promoting joint thinking in international conflicts: An Israeli–Palestinian continuing workshop. *Journal of Social Issues, 50*(1), 157–178.

Walton, R. E. (1970). A problem-solving workshop on border conflicts in Eastern Africa. *Journal of Applied Behavioral Science, 6,* 453–489.

Index

Abney, George, 110
accidents, risk theory and, 210–213
African Americans. *See* blacks
Agape love, 129, 130, 131
Agassiz, Louis, 17
AIDS, volunteerism and, 188–191
alternative medicine, representativeness heuristic and, 43–44
Amway Corporation, reciprocation and, 106–107
Angst, Jules, 17, 18, 19
anti-Semitism, 142
anxiety, love and, 128
anxious-ambivalent relationships, 131
apes, self-awareness of, 10, 12–16
Aron, Arthur, 126, 127
Asian Americans, stereotypes about academic gifts of, 150–151
astrology, representativeness heuristic and, 44
athletic teams: emotions of fans, 36–37; names of, as racist, 140–144
attachment, damage during brain development and, 166
attachment theory, 131
attraction, biological factors involved in physical beauty and, 118–122
attractiveness, ability of people to detect lies and, 73
autobiographical memory, 167–168
automatic evaluations, unconscious mind and, 56
avoidant relationships, 131
Azande, 43

Banaji, Mahzarin, 56–57
bandwagon consensus, pseudosciences and, 85
Bargh, John, 56, 57
beauty, biology of physical, 118–122
birth order, 17–19
blacks: education and, 20–26; health of, and racism, 145; performance of, and racial stereotypes, 148, 149; problems associated with conformity of, 214–215
Blaser, Martin, 40–41
body language, physical attractiveness and, 120, 121–122
Boisjoly, Roger, 205, 206
brain: abnormalities of, and criminal behavior, 161–170; gut feelings and, 88–89
brain stem, 164
brainwashing, 100
Breggin, Peter, 154–160
Bremner, J. Douglas, 166, 169
Bruce, Leo, 110
BUGs, use of reciprocation by Amway Corporation and, 106–107
Bundy, Ted, 161–162, 163
Buss, David, 123, 124
bystanders, pluralistic ignorance and, 197–201

Cant, John, 13, 15–16
career paths, cultural stereotypes and, for women, 146–147
Carter, Jimmy, 106
cars, aggression in driving and, 171–172
causal judgements, representativeness heuristic and, 42–43

Chaiken, Shelly, 56
Challenger explosion: groupthink and, 204–209; risk theory and, 210–213
child abuse: false memories and, 47–50; influence of, and brain abnormalities on criminal behavior, 161–170
chimpanzees, 13, 14, 15, 186–187
Chinese "Doctrine of Signatures," 43, 85–86
Cialdini, Robert, 36, 37
cities, ranking of helpfulness of, 192–196
clambering hypothesis, 13, 15–16
cognitive science, 126
Cohen, Sheldon, 116, 117
Comer, James, 24
commitments, 128
commonplaces, pseudosciences and, 85–86
community marriage policies, 133
confessions: false, 108–111; elicited by interrogation, 108–111
conflict resolution, problem-solving workshops and, 216–224
conformity: problems associated with black, 214–215; strategies of, 93–95
conjunction fallacy, representativeness heuristic and, 42
consensus heuristic, pseudosciences and, 85
corpus callosum, 167
cortex, 164
cortisol, 166
creativity, solitude and, 114–115
criminal behavior, brain abnormalities and, 161–170
Csikszentmihalyi, Mihaly, 32
cults, 92–101
culture: job paths for women and, 146–147; television and, 180–181

Daly, Martin, 156–157, 159, 160
Damasio, Antonio, 88–89
Darley, John, 198–199
Darwin, Charles, 17
Darwinism, social aggression and, 154–160
de Waal, Frans, 16, 186
decision making: groupthink and, 204–209; intuition and, 88–89
Dederich, Charles, 109
DePaulo, Bella, 69–70, 71
depression, lying and, 71
DeSteno, David, 124, 125
Devine, Patricia, 137, 138–139
diencephalon, 164
Dietz, Park Elliot, 163
dissociative identity disorder, 167–168
dissonance theory, 97–98
"doctrine of signatures," 43, 85–86
driving, aggression and, 171–172

Ellison, Ralph, 23, 25
emotional infidelity, sex differences in perception of, and evolutionary psychology, 123–125
Ernst, Cecile, 17, 18, 19
Eron, Leonard, 177, 178, 179, 181–182
Eros love, 129, 130, 131
evolutionary psychology: aggression and, 154–160; sex differences in perception of infidelity and, 123–125

expectancy confirmation, motivational approaches to, 64–68
explanation process, 51–54
extraversion, happiness and, 31

"fake positive" lies, 70
false memories, 47–50
"false negative" lies, 70
false-belief test, self-awareness and, 10
fans, emotions of, of sports teams, 36–37
Fazio, Russell, 136
Fehr, Beverly, 128–129
Fiske, Susan, 137
flow concept, happiness at work and, 32–33
Fogel, Alan, 10
Fox, Robin, 103
Franklin, Joseph Paul, 161–162
free samples, reciprocation and, 106–107
Freedman, Jonathan, 182
Freud, Sigmund, 126
friendships: health and, 116–117; love and, 128–129
frontal lobes, 164

Gallup, Gordon, 13
gender roles, "social dominance" theory in career paths for women and, 147
Genovese, Catherine, 197–198
George, Carol, 166
Gerbner, George, 180–181
Glaser, Ronald, 116
goddess-within commonplace, pseudoscience and, 86
Goodwin, Frederick, 154–160
gorillas, 13, 14, 15
Gottman, John, 132
Gould, Stephen Jay, 8
Gouldner, Alvin, 102
granfalloons, pseudosciences and, 84
graphology, representativeness heuristic and, 44–45
Greenwald, Anthony, 56–57
groupthink, *Challenger* explosion and, 204–209
guns, violence and, 173–176
gut feelings, 88–89

Hahnemann, Samuel, 43
handwriting analysis, representativenssss heuristic and, 44–45
happiness, 27–35
Hare Krishna Society, reciprocation and, 104–105
Hau people, of Paupau New Guinea, 44
Hauser, Marc D., 10
health: racism and, 145; social ties and, 116–117
Healthy Families America, 169
heart disease, racism and, 145
Hendrick, Susan, 129, 130, 131
heuristics, 41; representativeness, and pseudoscience, 40–46, 85–86; selling pseudoscience and, 85–86
hierarchy-attenuating roles, 147
hierarchy-enhancing roles, 147
high blood pressure, racism and, 145
hippocampus, 166–167
Hirt, Edward, 36
HIV, volunteerism and, 188–191
homeopathy, 43

Hrdy, Sarah Blaffer, 18
Huesmann, L. Rowell, 177, 178, 179
Hyman, Ira, 48
hypertension, racism and, 145

imagination inflation, 48–49
immune system, social ties and, 116–117
impression formation, 65–66
infidelity, sex differences in perception of, and evolutionary psychology, 123–125
Ingram, Paul, 108
innuendo, pseudosciences and, 86
"insufficiency of suppression," 164
interaction facilitation, self-presentation and, 66–67
interactive problem solving, conflict resolution and, 216–224
intuition, 88–89
Israel, group processes in resolution of conflict of, with Palestinians, 216–224
"I've heard that one before" phenomenon, 73

Janis, Irving, 204–209
jealousy, sex differences in, and evolutionary psychology, 123–125
job paths, cultural stereotypes and, for women, 146–147
Johnson, Lyndon, 105–106
Jones, Jim, 92–101, 107
Jonestown, analysis of, 92–101, 107

Kahneman, Daniel, 41
Keating, Charles H., 106
Kellermann, Arthur, 174–175
Kiecolt-Glaser, Janice, 116
Koko, 13, 14
Kramer, Peter, 158

language patterns, lying and, 71
Larsen, Reed, 114–115
Latané, Bibb, 198–199
"law of similars," 43
Leakey, Richard, 102–103
Leman, Kevin, 18
Lewis, Dorothy Owen, 161–162, 163, 164, 165–168, 169–170
lie detector tests, 71
lies, 69–71; ability of people to detect, 71, 72–75
limbic system, 164
"log-rolling," 105–106
lost-in-the-mall scenario, 48

Main, Mary, 166
mammals, self-awareness and, 9–10
mania love, 139, 140, 141
MAOIs (monoamine-oxide inhibitors), 155
mark test, self-awareness and, 13
marketing, reciprocation and, 106–107
Markman, Howard, 132
marmots, 186
marriage: education, 132–133; happiness and, 31–32
"marriage mentors," 133
Marshall, Barry, 40–41
Mayr, Ernst, 19
McDonald, Allan J., 206
McNally, Richard, 166
McNeilly, Maya, 145
media, violence in, and children, 177–179
medical beliefs, representativeness heuristic and, 40–41, 43–44, 45–46

memory: autobiographical, 167–168; false, 47–50
message length heuristic, pseudosciences and, 85
Miller, Sherod, 133
mindguarding, 206–207
mirror, self-recognition test, of self-awareness, 9–10, 13, 16
"misinformation effect," 47–48
money, happiness and, 29–31
morality, chimpanzees and, 186–187
Morton Thiokol (MTI), 205–206, 207, 211–213
myelin, 167

NASA (National Aeronautics and Space Administration), *Challenger* explosion and, 204–209, 210–213
National Committee to Prevent Child Abuse, 169
Native Americans, athletic team names and, 140–144
natural commonplace, pseudosciences and, 86
negritude, 215
Nemeroff, Carol, 44
neurological rage, 165
neurotransmitters, 155
New Haven, Connecticut, 24
New York City, New York, 192, 193, 194, 195, 196
Nisbett, Richard, 45
Noller, Patricia, 131
"normal accidents," 211
noticeability, of events, 51–52
Nunez, Mark, 110

Ofshe, Richard, 108–111
Olympic marmots, 186–187
optimism, happiness and, 31
Oslo accord, 216–217, 219–220
Olson, David H., 133
orangutans, 12, 13, 15–16
organic rage, 165

Page, Bradley, 110
Palestinians, group processes in resolution of conflict of, with Israel, 216–224
panhandling, persuasion and, 78–79
Parker, Dante, 110
Parrott, Leslie, 133
passionate love, 127
Pedersen, Darhl, 114, 115
People's Temple, 92
peptic ulcers, representativeness heuristic and, 40–41, 46
perceptual cues, 41
perjury, 109
Perrow, Charles, 211
Perry, Bruce, 166
personal control, happiness and, 31
persuasion: propaganda and, 78–80; selling pseudoscience and, 81–87
Peterson, Steven, 19
phantoms, pseudosciences and, 82–83
physical beauty, biological factors of, 118–122
Pincus, Jonathan, 162–163, 164–165, 167–168, 169
Pinker, Steven, 11
pluralistic ignorance, 197–201
politics, reciprocation and, 105–106
polygraph tests, 71
Porges, Stephen, 9

post-traumatic stress disorder (PTSD), 167, 169
Povinelli, Daniel, 12–16
Pratto, Felicia, 146, 147
prejudice, 136–137, 138–139
PREP (Prevention and Relationship Enhancement Program), 132–133
Prepare, marriage education and, 133
pre-persuasion, pseudosciences and, 85
primates, self-awareness of, 10, 12–16
priming: evaluations of unconscious mind and, 56; prejudice and, 136
problem formulation, 53–54
problem resolution, 54
problem-based explanation, 53
problem-solving workshops, conflict resolution and, 216–224
projective tests, representativeness heuristic and, 45
propaganda, persuasion and, 78–80
prototype approach, to love, 128
prototypes, representativeness heuristic and, 41–42
Proxmire, William, 126
pseudonegritude, 215
pseudoscience: persuasion and, 81–87; representativeness heuristic and, 40–46
psychoanalysis, representativeness heuristic and, 45
psychopharmacology, 155

race: education of blacks and, 20–26; happiness and, 29
racism: in athletic team names, 140–144; health of blacks and, 145
Raine, Adrian, 168
rap music, violence and, 182–183
rationalization trap, pseudosciences and, 83
"rebirthing," 43–44
reciprocation, 102–107
Regan, Dennis, 103–104
relationship skills, marriage education and, 132–133
relationships, happiness and, 31–32
religion: cults and, 92–101; happiness and, 33
representativeness heuristic, pseudoscience and, 40–46, 85–86
reptiles, 9
risk homeostasis, 212
risk theory, accidents and, 210–213
rituals, suicide and, 92–101
road rage, 171–172
Rochester, New York, 193, 194, 195–196
Rorschach test, representativeness heuristic and, 45
Ross, Leo, 45
Rozin, Paul, 44
Ryan, Leo, 92–93

Salovey, Peter, 124, 125
Sawyer, Thomas F., 109, 110
satisfaction, explanation process and, 54
Saxe, Leonard, 69, 70
scarcity heuristic, pseudosciences and, 85
Schacter, Stanley, 127
science commonplaces, pseudosciences and, 86
scorpion flies, 118, 119
secure relationships, 131
self-awareness, 8–11, 12–16
self-censorship, 206
self-esteem, happiness and, 31

self-generated persuasion, pseudosciences and, 84
self-justification, strategies involving, 93–95
self-presentation, interaction facilitation and, 66–67
self-recognition, self-awareness and, 9–10, 12–16
serotonin, aggression and, 154–160
sex differences: in ability to detect lies, 72–73; in happiness, 29; in perception of infidelity, 123–125; in telling lies, 70
sexual abuse, false memories of, 47–50
sexual dimorphism, 157
sexual infidelity, sex differences in perception of, and evolutionary psychology, 123–125
Shaver, Philip, 131
Shawcross, Arthur, 161, 163, 164
situational inferences, from behavior, 60, 62, 63
Six Years With God (Mills), 97
"social dominance" theory, gender roles and, 147
social inferences, making, from behavior, 60–63
social ties, health and, 116–117
solitude, importance of, 114–115
Soul Patrol, 214–215
source credibility, pseudosciences and, 83–84
Specher, Susan, 127, 128
Spencer, Steven, 137
sports teams: emotions of fans of, 36–37; names of, as racist, 140–144

"stereotype threat," performance of women and ethnic minorities and, 148–149
stereotypes: of academic gifts of Asian Americans, 150–151; job paths for women and cultural, 146–147; performance of women and ethnic minorities and, 148–149
Streicher, Julius, 142, 144
stress-response system, brain damage and, 166–167
subjective well-being (SWB), 27–35
subliminal tapes, 85, 86
Suedfeld, Peter, 114
suicide: guns and, 175; ritualistic, 92–101
Sullivan, Louis, 154
Sulloway, Frank, 17, 18, 19
Swensen, Clifford, 129
symmetry, physical attractiveness and, 118–122
Synanon, 108, 109
Szasz, Thomas, 155, 160

tamarins, 10
Teicher, Martin, 166
television, effect of violence on, 180–183
testosterone, levels of, and performance of fan's sports teams, 36–37
Three Mile Island (TMI) nuclear power plant, 211
Tiger, Lionel, 103
Tooby, John, 19
traffic, aggression and, 171–172
trait inferences, from behavior, 60–62, 63
Treisman, Philip Uri, 24
Tucker, Raymond, 129

Tversky, Amos, 41

ulcers, representativeness heuristic and, 40–41, 46
uncertainty, bystander, 197–201
unconscious mind, 56–57; prejudice and, 136

Vaughan, Diane, 210–212
video games, violence and, 182–183
violence: biology of, 154–160; guns and, 173–176; television and, 177–179, 180–183
volunteerism: basic research on, 189; HIV and, 188–191; recruitment of, 189–190; retention of, 190; stages of, 189

Watson, John B., 126
weight-to-hip ratio (WHR), physical attractiveness and, 120, 121–122
Williams, Redford, B., 116
Wilson, David, 167–168
Wilson, Margo, 156–157, 159, 160
Wisconsin Card Sorting Test, 164–165
"wise" schooling, 23–26
women, cultural stereotypes and career paths for, 146–147
woodchucks, 186
word-fluency test, 165
work, happiness and, 32–33
workshops, conflict resolution and problem-solving, 216–224

Yudofsky, Stuart, 165, 169

"zonal theory" of graphology, 45

Credits/Acknowledgments

Cover design by Charles Vitelli

1. The Self
Facing overview—© 1997 by Cleo Freelance Photography.
2. Social Cognition
Facing overview—© 1997 by Cleo Freelance Photography.
3. Social Perception
Facing overview—© 1997 by Cleo Freelance Photography.
4. Attitudes
Facing overview—© 1997 by Cleo Freelance Photography.
5. Social Influence
Facing overview—© 1997 by Cleo Freelance Photography.

6. Social Relationships
Facing overview—© 1997 by Cleo Freelance Photography.
7. Prejudice, Discrimination, and Stereotyping
Facing overview—© 1997 by Cleo Freelance Photography.
8. Aggression
Facing overview—© 1997 by PhotoDisc, Inc.
9. Helping
Facing overview—© 1997 by Cleo Freelance Photography.
10. Group Processes
Facing overview—© 1997 by Cleo Freelance Photography.

*PHOTOCOPY THIS PAGE!!!**

ANNUAL EDITIONS ARTICLE REVIEW FORM

■ NAME: _____ DATE: _____

■ TITLE AND NUMBER OF ARTICLE: _____

■ BRIEFLY STATE THE MAIN IDEA OF THIS ARTICLE: _____
_____

■ LIST THREE IMPORTANT FACTS THAT THE AUTHOR USES TO SUPPORT THE MAIN IDEA:
_____
_____
_____
_____

■ WHAT INFORMATION OR IDEAS DISCUSSED IN THIS ARTICLE ARE ALSO DISCUSSED IN YOUR TEXTBOOK OR OTHER READINGS THAT YOU HAVE DONE? LIST THE TEXTBOOK CHAPTERS AND PAGE NUMBERS:
_____
_____
_____
_____
_____

■ LIST ANY EXAMPLES OF BIAS OR FAULTY REASONING THAT YOU FOUND IN THE ARTICLE:
_____
_____
_____
_____

■ LIST ANY NEW TERMS/CONCEPTS THAT WERE DISCUSSED IN THE ARTICLE, AND WRITE A SHORT DEFINITION:
_____
_____
_____
_____

*Your instructor may require you to use this ANNUAL EDITIONS Article Review Form in any number of ways: for articles that are assigned, for extra credit, as a tool to assist in developing assigned papers, or simply for your own reference. Even if it is not required, we encourage you to photocopy and use this page; you will find that reflecting on the articles will greatly enhance the information from your text.

We Want Your Advice

ANNUAL EDITIONS revisions depend on two major opinion sources: one is our Advisory Board, listed in the front of this volume, which works with us in scanning the thousands of articles published in the public press each year; the other is you—the person actually using the book. Please help us and the users of the next edition by completing the prepaid article rating form on this page and returning it to us. Thank you for your help!

ANNUAL EDITIONS: SOCIAL PSYCHOLOGY 98/99
Article Rating Form

Here is an opportunity for you to have direct input into the next revision of this volume. We would like you to rate each of the 47 articles listed below, using the following scale:

1. Excellent: should definitely be retained
2. Above average: should probably be retained
3. Below average: should probably be deleted
4. Poor: should definitely be deleted

Your ratings will play a vital part in the next revision. So please mail this prepaid form to us just as soon as you complete it.
Thanks for your help!

Rating	Article	Rating	Article
	1. Evolutionary Necessity or Glorious Accident? Biologists Ponder the Self		24. Infidelity and the Science of Cheating
	2. The Tarzan Syndrome		25. The Lessons of Love
	3. First Born, Later Born		26. Rescuing Marriages before They Begin
	4. Race and the Schooling of Black Americans		27. Prejudice Is a Habit That Can Be Broken
	5. Who Is Happy?		28. Breaking the Prejudice Habit
	6. Team Spirit Spills Over into Real Life for Fans		29. Crimes against Humanity
	7. Like Goes with Like: The Role of Representativeness in Erroneous and Pseudoscientific Beliefs		30. Study: Racism Is Health Risk to Black Americans
	8. Creating False Memories		31. Societal Values Dictate Job Paths for Women
	9. The Process of Explanation		32. Minorities' Performance Is Hampered by Stereotypes
	10. Influences from the Mind's Inner Layers		33. Who Is a Whiz Kid?
	11. Inferential Hopscotch: How People Draw Social Inferences from Behavior		34. The Biology of Violence
	12. Motivational Approaches to Expectancy Confirmation		35. Damaged
	13. The Truth about Lying: Has Lying Gotten a Bad Rap?		36. Car Wars: Taming Drivers' Aggression
	14. Spotting Lies: Can Humans Learn to Do Better?		37. Gunslinging in America
	15. Mindless Propaganda, Thoughtful Persuasion		38. Televised Violence and Kids: A Public Health Problem?
	16. How to Sell a Pseudoscience		39. Menace to Society
	17. In Work on Intuition, Gut Feelings Are Tracked to Source: The Brain		40. The Roots of Good and Evil
	18. Making Sense of the Nonsensical: An Analysis of Jonestown		41. Volunteerism and Society's Response to the HIV Epidemic
	19. Reciprocation: The Old Give and Take . . . and Take		42. Cities with Heart
	20. Suspect Confessions		43. Cause of Death: Uncertain(ty)
	21. Solitude Provides an Emotional Tune-Up		44. Group Decision Fiascoes Continue: Space Shuttle *Challenger* and a Revised Groupthink Framework
	22. Social Ties Reduce Risk of a Cold		45. What Messages Are behind Today's Cults?
	23. The Biology of Beauty		46. The Heavy Burden of Black Conformity
			47. Group Processes in the Resolution of International Conflicts: Experiences from the Israeli-Palestinian Case

(Continued on next page)

ABOUT YOU

Name _____ Date _____

Are you a teacher? ❏ Or a student? ❏

Your school name _____

Department _____

Address _____

City _____ State _____ Zip _____

School telephone # _____

YOUR COMMENTS ARE IMPORTANT TO US !

Please fill in the following information:

For which course did you use this book? _____

Did you use a text with this *ANNUAL EDITION*? ❏ yes ❏ no

What was the title of the text? _____

What are your general reactions to the *Annual Editions* concept?

Have you read any particular articles recently that you think should be included in the next edition?

Are there any articles you feel should be replaced in the next edition? Why?

Are there any World Wide Web sites you feel should be included in the next edition? Please annotate.

May we contact you for editorial input?

May we quote your comments?

ANNUAL EDITIONS: SOCIAL PSYCHOLOGY 98/99

BUSINESS REPLY MAIL
First Class   Permit No. 84   Guilford, CT

Postage will be paid by addressee

Dushkin/McGraw·Hill
Sluice Dock
Guilford, CT 06437

No Postage
Necessary
if Mailed
in the
United States